Thought Experiments i
Philosophy, Science, an

Routledge Studies in the Philosophy of Science

Thought Experiments in Philosophy, Science, and the Arts

Edited by Mélanie Frappier,
Letitia Meynell, and James Robert Brown

Routledge
Taylor & Francis Group
NEW YORK   LONDON

First published 2013
by Routledge
711 Third Avenue, New York, NY 10017

Simultaneously published in the UK
by Routledge
2 Park Square, Milton Park, Abingdon, Oxfordshire OX14 4RN

First issued in paperback 2014

*Routledge is an imprint of the Taylor and Francis Group,
an informa business*

Library of Congress Cataloging-in-Publication Data
 Thought experiments in philosophy, science, and the arts / edited by Mélanie Frappier, Letitia Meynell, and James Robert Brown.
   p. cm. — (Routledge studies in the philosophy of science ; 11)
   Includes bibliographical references and index.
 1.   Thought experiments. 2.   Philosophy—Research. 3.   Science—Research. 4.   Arts—Research.   I. Frappier, Mélanie.   II. Meynell, Letitia.   III. Brown, James Robert.
   BD265.T465 2012
   128'.3—dc23
   2011052746

ISBN 978-0-415-88544-7 (hbk)

ISBN 978-1-138-92183-2 (pbk)

ISBN 978-0-203-11327-1 (ebk)

Typeset in Sabon
by IBT Global.

Pour Christian, Thomas, Simon, Nicole et Maurice—MF

Contents

Acknowledgements

This volume was born out of the workshop "Science without Data: The Role of Thought Experiments in Empirical Investigations" held at Dalhousie University in June 2010. Much of its success is due to students like Megan Dean and Eve Roberts, who volunteered their time and skills. We are grateful to all the contributors for their participation in the workshop and their hard work in producing such very fine papers for inclusion in this volume. Samantha Copeland was superb in organizing everything and pulling the disparate pieces together. We also owe much to Kai Miller's sharp editorial and bibliographical skills and to the diligence of Shoshana Deutsh, Michael Doan, Micah Anshan and Thomas Dodge. Our thanks finally go to Adam Auch who created a thorough and useful index in record time.

The workshop, the public events associated with it, and the preparation of this volume were made possible by the Aid to Research Workshops and Conferences in Canada programme of the Social Sciences and Human Research Council (SSHRC), and the financial support of the SSHRC Strategic Knowledge Cluster Situating Science. We also gratefully acknowledge the financial support we received from the Faculty of Arts and Social Sciences, the Faculty of Graduate Studies, the Department of Philosophy, the President's Office, and the Office of the Vice President (Academic) of Dalhousie University. Our thanks finally go to the University of King's College for its continuous financial assistance to this project.

We also owe much to our family members, whose patience and support made it all possible.

Figures

Contributors

Richard T. W. Arthur, Department of Philosophy, McMaster University

James Robert Brown, Department of Philosophy, University of Toronto

Marco Buzzoni, Department of Philosophy and Human Sciences, University of Macerata

Sanjay Chandrasekharan, Homi Bhabha Centre for Science Education, Tata Institute of Fundamental Research

David Davies, Department of Philosophy, McGill University

W. Ford Doolittle, Department of Biochemistry and Molecular Biology, Dalhousie University

Yiftach J. H. Fehige, Institute for the History and Philosophy of Science and Technology, University of Toronto

Mélanie Frappier, History of Science and Technology Programme, The University of King's College

James W. McAllister, Institute of Philosophy, University of Leiden

Geordie McComb, Department of Philosophy, University of Toronto

Letitia Meynell, Department of Philosophy, Dalhousie University

Nenad Miščević, Faculty of Philosophy, University of Maribor and Central European University, Budapest.

Nancy J. Nersessian, School of Interactive Computing and School of Public Policy, Georgia Institute of Technology

John D. Norton, Department of History and Philosophy of Science and Center for Philosophy of Science, University of Pittsburgh

Julian Reiss, Faculty of Philosophy, Erasmus University Rotterdam

Mark Shumelda, Department of Philosophy, University of Toronto

Roy Sorensen, Department of Philosophy, Washington University in St. Louis

Vrishali Subramanian, School of Public Policy, Georgia Institute of Technology

Harald Wiltsche, Department of Philosophy, University of Graz, and Department of Philosophy, University of Toronto

Introduction

James Robert Brown, Letitia Meynell,
and Mélanie Frappier

Except for their being performed in the mind, thought experiments are tantalizingly similar to real experiments. How similar is open to debate. In both cases we set things up, we see what happens, and then we derive some conclusion. When we say "see what happens" we recognize that this might be taken quite literally. One may think that there must be something akin to observations that gives thought experiments their experimental character, but even this is controversial. Indeed, there is no consensus on the epistemic power of thought experiments, their logical character, the nature of their content, or the proper domains of their application. As the first contributions to this volume suggest, this divergence of opinions may very well arise from a need to make precise the roles that imagination, idealization, visualization, and embodiment play in our assessment of the epistemological value of thought experiments. However, as the subsequent papers make clear, although we may have to rethink the relationship between thought experiments and reality, it is undeniable that the former have been central to the history of intellectual life.

The history of physics, for instance, is replete with thought experiments: Newton's bucket, Galileo's falling bodies, Einstein's elevator, and Schrödinger's cat are but a few. Even literature can lay claim to thought experiments with one of the great novelists in the English language describing her work as "simply a set of experiments in life" (George Eliot, quoted in Gaetens 2009, 80). Philosophers have relied heavily on thought experiments to support some of their most important claims. Indeed, because there can be little hope of carrying out real philosophical experiments, thought experiments have been used extensively in the development of philosophical ideas.

Consider the question of personal identity. John Locke famously told the story of a prince whose mind migrated into a cobbler's body (Locke [1700] 1975, 340). Locke took this narrative to be perfectly clear and coherent and concluded from his thought experiment that it is the mind or psychological properties that determine who a person really is, not the body. A philosophical question about personal identity, it seemed, had been settled by a simple thought experiment.

Of course, the matter was not actually settled at all. Others, such as Bernard Williams (1970), have offered very different thought experiments that seem to justify the claim that personal identity consists in identity of body; that is, you are the person you are in virtue of having the same body over time. This seems a very reasonable conclusion to draw if we consider familiar tragic events such as a horrific accident in which the body, though mangled, remains intact, while the psychological and mental properties are radically changed. A person might lose all of her memories, yet when we see the person we naturally think she is the same person we knew in earlier, happier times. The only conclusion it would seem that we can draw from such an example is that the person is the person that she is in virtue of having the same body. In yet another clever thought experiment, Derek Parfit presented a scenario in which a person split like an amoeba. We start with one person and we end up with two. Now, if there is one generally uncontroversial claim in this discussion it is that personal identity is inviolable: A person is unique; no one is two people. So how are we to conceptualize this splitting outcome? The initial person is bodily and psychologically continuous with two people, but cannot be identical to both. Parfit takes the view that the relevant concept is not identity but rather survival. The initial person has survived in the form of two distinct people, but is not identical to either. Parfit then makes further use of the concept of survival by applying it to ourselves over long periods. We should, he thinks, no longer consider ourselves in old age as being identical to the child with whom we are continuous; the child to some degree has survived, and that is all (1971).

This sequence of thought experiments, from Locke to Williams to Parfit, has played a crucial role in thinking about personal identity. And it would be a mistake to think of it as a merely metaphysical issue, given its ethical consequences. After all, if Parfit is right, it seems doubtful that anyone should be rewarded or punished for actions done very long ago, since they are not identical with that person, but have merely survived from an earlier stage. For our purposes, the moral we draw is that it is hard to do philosophy without the benefit of thought experiments. They are part of our tool kit and, just as philosophers analyse our other tools of reasoning, we need to understand them better.

Physics would likewise be impoverished without the benefit of thought experiments. One of the most famous is by Galileo (Galilei [1638] 2000), who argued that all objects fall at the same rate, regardless of their weight. He began by considering Aristotle's view that heavy objects fall faster than light ones (H>L). He imagined a heavy cannonball attached to a light musket ball dropped from a tower. This composite object (H+L) is heavier than the cannonball alone, so it should fall faster (H+L > H). However, because it is a composite object, the lighter musket ball will act as a drag and slow down the heavier cannonball, which means that the composite object will fall slower than the cannonball alone (H+L < H). Now we have a contradiction; the composite object will fall both faster and slower than the heavy object alone, which is absurd. The usual reading of this thought experiment is that it not only signifies the end of Aristotle's theory; it is also the answer to how fast these objects fall—obviously they all fall at the same rate.

Does this mean that we can learn about nature just by thinking? Is science without empirical data possible? It is not easy to reply to the Scholastics who denied Galileo's conclusion on the ground that it was not compatible with their experience of falling objects. In everyday life, heavier objects usually do fall faster than light ones. *Why* should we trust this thought experiment? *How* can experiments performed only in the mind teach us anything about reality? *What* exactly do they teach us?

Although thought experimenting is presumably as old as abstract thought itself, in recent years there has been a flurry of activities devoted to figuring out how thought experiments actually work. There is considerable diversity of opinion. One account (Norton 1991, 2004) claims that thought experiments are in fact arguments, though they may be disguised. Thus if we wish to assess a thought experiment we need to clearly articulate the premises and assess their truth and the validity or strength of the argument. Another account (Nersessian 1993, 2007; Miščević 1992, 2007) claims that thought experiments are in fact mental models. We construct a model in our minds and then we simply read off the relevant conclusions. Yet another account focuses on conceptual structures (Kuhn [1964] 1977; Gendler 2000). Thought experiments, on this view, tell us about our conceptual structure or paradigm (and hence they indirectly tell us about the world) by revealing aspects hitherto unrecognized and perhaps leading us to a new conceptual structure. Finally, though this by no means exhausts the possibilities, there is the view that we have something like *a priori* knowledge of nature (Koyré 1968; Brown [1991] 2010). In the Galileo case for instance, we arrive at the result without the benefit of new empirical evidence and without deriving the result from things we already know. This would seem to be a serious violation of the traditional empiricist outlook, but few are willing to join its champions and embrace some sort of rationalist epistemology. We mention these as a handful of options for consideration. New views and refinements of existing views are being proposed constantly. In this volume, for example, Marco Buzzoni defends a Kantian account of thought experiments, while Yiftach Fehige and Harald Wiltsche insist on the necessity of a phenomenological approach for a proper understanding of the epistemology of thought experiments.

Along with the growing interest in thought experiments there is increasing scepticism about their value. Daniel Dennett has used the expression "intuition pump" in a derogatory way to describe the process of coming to conclusions based on thought experiments. He's done this in a number of publications over several years (e.g., Hoffstadter and Dennett 1981; Dennett 1984, 1991, 1995), but the message is always the same: Thought experiments can be fun and even sometimes instructive, but they are not a reliable source of information about anything; indeed, they are often highly misleading. We should, he claims, always resort to the empirical study of the mind and of nature more generally, rather than any sort of conceptual analysis. Empirical science is where the real surprises lie, and a reliance on thought experiments is really a reliance on nothing more than our prejudices.

Stephen Stich ([1988] 1998) in recent years has been highly influential in promoting experimental philosophy. He aims to solve philosophical problems empirically, rather than through conceptual analysis. Paul Thagard (2010) holds much the same view. Both wish to see much more attention paid to the results of recent cognitive science and the neurosciences rather than the results of traditional philosophical techniques.

There is no question that much of their work is interesting and important and it would be foolish to dismiss it out of hand. Some of the consequences are also potentially of social importance. For instance, Stich and Buckwalter (2011) claim that men and women frequently have different intuitions about important philosophical examples; that is, they do not find the same thought experiments equally plausible. They believe that this is at least part of the explanation for the relative lack of women in philosophy. Everyone's philosophical education involves going through classic thought experiments where one is presumed to have the same intuitions as the community at large and the instructor in particular—otherwise, one is judged to be simply not cut out for philosophy. Often, Stich finds, women disagree with the standard understanding of some of these classic examples, which leaves them feeling discouraged and their professors judging that they have a "tin ear" for philosophy. Stich claims they should have no such negative feelings, but instead we should all conclude that our different intuitions are simply systematically unreliable and we should abandon thought experiments as a tool and intuition as a source of knowledge.

This systematic failure of thought experiments to decide anything in philosophy would be damning were it not for the failure of other reasoning methods to decide philosophical matters decisively. The focus on *philosophical* thought experiments that we find in their criticisms may have prevented Buckwalter and Stich, Dennett, and Thagard from fully appreciating the factors that militate against doing away with thought experiments by obscuring the successes of thought experiments in other domains, particularly in the sciences. While it may be historically dubious that any thought experiment has ever led on its own to the abandonment or adoption of a theory by a scientific community, it is uncontroversial that they have played a prominent role in the development and justification of scientific theories. That philosophical analyses of thought experiments have tended to focus on the sciences may therefore be driven, at least in part, by the fact that it is in the sciences that thought experiments enjoy their least controversial epistemic successes. Insight into the ways in which thought experiments work in the sciences is thus a useful first step in understanding their epistemic power more generally.

As the first three papers of this collection make clear, any deep understanding of the nature and role of thought experiments will demand a closer look at the very aspects that render them epistemologically fraught to many scientists and philosophers of science—namely, imagination, idealization, and visualization. James McAllister opens the volume with "Thought Experiment and the Exercise of Imagination in Science." Because of their reliance on imagination, McAllister notes, thought experiments have been repeatedly accused of offering either an arbitrary description of the world or one that is relatively impoverished compared with what the world might actually be. This in turn implies that the extent to which scientists trust thought experiments depends on whether or not they accept imagination as a tool adequate to apprehend reality. Through examples from the history of science, McAllister shows that while many scientists and natural philosophers have embraced imagination as a legitimate route to reality, many have also been highly sceptical of any device pretending to go beyond empirical observations. Surprisingly, among them we find Galileo and Mach, who are usually characterized as proponents of thought experiments in science. As McAllister explains, this claim is in need of an important qualification: Galileo and Mach both appealed only to thought experiments that do not significantly go beyond the observable domain. This insight suggests that scholars need both to review the history of thought experiments in science and to develop a more nuanced analysis of the fundamental assumptions underlying the use of thought experiments as an epistemologically reliable tool for understanding reality.

The tensions between imagination and scientific realism are further explored by Roy Sorensen in "Veridical Idealizations." Sorensen notes that scientific realism, the doctrine that our scientific theories aim to be literally true, appears to be contradicted by the central role of idealizations in science. This is a special problem for thought experiments since idealization is such a common part of them. To overcome this apparent paradox, Sorensen introduces the idea of "veridical idealization": The detractors of thought experiments are right to argue that explanations based on asserted falsehood and prejudices are malignant, but "*supposed falsehoods* are benign." What emerges, according to Sorensen, is a unified theory of idealization that is liberal, topic-neutral, in accord with standard logic, and properly accountable to scientific realism.

In "What Do We See in a Thought Experiment?" James Robert Brown considers the character of visualization in thought experiments, interrogating the degree to which these visual imaginings are—or should be—realistic. Should the visualizations that are prompted by thought experiments depict what we really would see if we could view the imagined circumstances? Looking at a paradox from special relativity, Brown notes that the "actual appearance" of rapidly moving objects is one of rotation, not contraction (as is widely, but mistakenly, believed). Yet such a mistaken mental image turns out to be much better for solving the physical paradox than a more realistic depiction would be. Brown draws from this a conclusion which mirrors and effectively extends his past Platonist and realist critiques of empiricism: Just as experimental appearances may sometimes obscure the true facts of the matter, so visualized appearances can also mislead. In thought experiments—as with real experiments—the Platonist is "ever ready to abandon appearances in favour of a supposed reality."

The important question of the relation of thought experiments to empirical content is further investigated in the papers presented by Marco Buzzoni and Yiftach Fehige and Harald Wiltsche. These two papers address how thought experiments confront the world, either through their relation to real experiments or the role of experience in determining their content. Though we are prone to forget it, we are not disembodied, pure thinking machines. We come with bodies and minds that may be structured in important ways. This is important to keep in mind when thought experimenting. In "The Body, Thought Experiments, and Phenomenology," Fehige and Wiltsche address the role of embodiment in the performance of thought experiments. They build on David Gooding's idea that thinking and doing are interdependent, so that the activity of thought experimentation is parasitic on the embodied experiences that accompany real experimentation. But Fehige and Wiltsche go well beyond Gooding's naturalistic account, preferring instead a phenomenological approach that stresses the importance of the embodied, experiential first person perspective.

In a similar vein, Buzzoni brings another powerful—yet mostly overlooked—philosophical programme to bear on the issue. "Thought Experiments from a Kantian Point of View" begins with the observation that a successful account of thought experiments must reveal what they share with real experiments that justifies treating them as experiments at all, without reducing one to the other, a move that would render the distinction vacuous. Buzzoni employs a Kantian epistemology to explain that, while real experiments share their conceptual content with thought experiments, because they are physically realized they are importantly distinct. He concludes that "all [real experiments] may also be thought of as realisations of [thought experiments]; and conversely, all empirical [thought experiments] must be conceivable as preparing and anticipating real ones."

The relationship between thought experiments and real ones is further interrogated by Richard T. W. Arthur in "Can Thought Experiments Be Resolved by Experiment? The Case of Aristotle's Wheel." In this paper we are invited to imagine two concentric circles fixed together (say, a wheel and its hub) and rolling out equal lines on the surfaces with which they each make contact. After several rotations, the two circles must have travelled different distances, yet, being fixed together, they have clearly travelled the same distance. Historically, the answers given to this paradox have varied widely, often involving convoluted views of the infinite. Arthur wonders if the paradox generated by this thought experiment can be resolved by a real experiment. The answer to this question, he explains, is complex and depends on what we take the problem posed in the thought experiment to be. We can only answer it once we decide what assumptions we are making and which idealizations we will allow.

As John Norton shows in "Chasing the Light: Einstein's Most Famous Thought Experiment," identifying a thought experiment's central question and its main assumptions is a task that not only requires a careful analysis of the epistemological issues at play, but a subtle understanding of the historical debate in which it appears. In his paper, Norton re-evaluates Einstein's light-chasing thought experiment, which is standardly taken to upend aether theories of electrodynamics. Norton takes issue with this, claiming instead that it is really a thought experiment aimed at so-called emission theories of light. He offers here a major re-evaluation of the historical record, as well as an important new way of understanding a classic thought experiment.

These historical examples inevitably raise questions about the role of thought experiments in current physics. As new data from CERN raise the tantalizing possibility that neutrinos may be able to travel faster than light, detractors of thought experiments may be swift to point out that even the most convincing thought experiments cannot establish scientific claims. But, as Mark Shumelda explains in "At the Limits of Possibility: Thought Experiments in Quantum Gravity," establishing scientific claims may not be the main epistemic role of thought experiments. Through a careful analysis of Eppley and Hannah's thought experiment in support of the quantization of the gravitational field (Eppley and Hannah 1977), Shumelda concludes that thought experiments can be used to impose logical constraints on future scientific theories.

While there are many novel aspects to the aforementioned papers, in one respect they all exemplify mainstream thought on thought experiments: They mostly focus on examples from physics and the history of science. The final six papers in the volume each address other disciplines and genres that have arguably been underinvestigated in the thought experiment literature to date. By addressing other areas in the sciences and arts our authors do not merely show the importance of thought experiments in these neglected areas; they identify aspects and functions of thought experiment that are not so easily seen in the context of physics.

Take, for example, the biological sciences. In "Craig Venter's New Life: The Realization of Some Thought Experiments in Biological Ontology," Ford Doolittle returns to a theme raised by Arthur and Buzzoni—the relation of thought experiments to real experiments. Doolittle suggests that recent results in biology bring to the fore fundamental questions about biological ontology that had previously been the stuff of thought experiment alone. In Venter's experiments a completely synthetic bacterial genome based on the known DNA sequence of one bacterial species replaced the resident natural genome in the cell of another species, founding a new lineage that traces its genetic parentage to nonbiological systems. This makes real several ontological exercises in systematic biology having to do with the nature of species and of life itself. If taken fully to heart, says Doolittle, the thought experiments implied in Venter's accomplishment require us to rethink the meaning of "lineage" in systematics. Just as Kuhn argued that thought experiments can correct conceptual confusions, so it seems Venter's newly created life form can help us recognize contradictions in the practice and theory of biological classification. Still, Doolittle argues, the real experiments cannot actually decide these basic conceptual issues and these problems remain fundamentally in the domain of thought experiments.

In "Genealogical Thought Experiments in Economics," Julian Reiss continues to investigate the conceptual work that can be done with thought experiments. Drawing on two different narratives concerning the origins of money, Reiss argues that these thought experiments not only establish specific concepts of money but point to the role that money plays in society, thus justifying it as an institution. This particular mode of thought experiment, moving from fictional origin stories to normative judgement, constitutes a distinct type, which Reiss dubs "genealogical thought experiments." Thus we find in the social sciences a new type of thought experiment that plays both an explanatory and normative role.

The normative and justificatory function of thought experiments is perhaps less surprising when we look to their role in establishing political theory. Nenad Miščević's "Political Thought Experiments from Plato to Rawls" discusses the long history of thought experiments in political theory from Plato's *Republic* to Rawls' *Theory of Justice*. While Reiss identifies a distinctive type of thought experiment in socio-political theorizing, Miščević emphasizes the similarities between thought experiments in physics and those in politics, which he links to the tradition of utopian and dystopian literature.

This relation between thought experiments and the narrative arts is further explored by Geordie McComb and David Davies. In "Thought Experiment, Definition, and Literary Fiction," McComb takes on the issue of the relationship between thought experiments and literary fictions. Are novels, for instance, a kind of thought experiment? In some ways they appear to be, but these appearances may only be superficial. McComb takes the view that thought experiments, being a cluster concept, come in degrees. Particular novels are more or less similar to thought experiments, but there is no general truth about the thought experimental character of literary fiction.

David Davies considers whether film can effectively function as a philosophical medium in "Can Philosophical Thought Experiments Be 'Screened'?" Part of the puzzle that Davies confronts is to identify what we are doing when we "do philosophy." Davies assumes a broadly analytic approach, which understands philosophy as focusing on argument, conceptual clarification, and various kinds of hypothetical reasoning. The central role of thought experiments in analytic philosophy suggests that film and other narrative arts may indeed offer ways of doing philosophy. However, as Davies shows, the character of these distinctively aesthetic objects raises several objections and complicates the explication of the cognitive function of cinematic and literary thought experiments.

We conclude with a challenge to the project of the volume itself. Sanjay Chandrasekharan, Nancy Nersessian, and Vrishali Subramanian's provocatively titled "Computational Modeling: Is This the End of Thought Experiments in Science?" Here they discuss the relation between traditional thought experimenting and more recent work on computational modelling, arguing that the latter will largely replace the former. The complexity of the natural systems that scientists and engineers are modelling today is such that the relationship between their different elements can only be captured through the new computational visualization tools that are being developed in computer science.

Philosophy has long been seen as giving rise to the particular sciences after the foundations have been set. Perhaps the new powerful computer modelling tools described by Chandrasekharan, Nersessian, and Subramanian are yet another example where a philosophical project will found a new distinctive discipline. Some of us thought experimenters, however, are not quite ready to be put out to pasture. Indeed, as the papers in this volume prove, the functions of thought experiments are sufficiently varied and complex and their characteristic features are so intimately entwined with other cognitive tools, such as idealization, visualization, and imagination, that even as their roles in the sciences, philosophy, and the arts change, we anticipate that they will be an important part of intellectual life for a long time to come.

Research in thought experiments, as we have repeatedly mentioned, is relatively new. So far the main focus has been largely on the famous examples from physics and philosophy. But the circle will grow. We hope that all readers enjoy the contributions to this volume and that some will be moved to make contributions of their own to this field.

REFERENCES

Brown, James Robert. [1991] 2010. *Laboratory of the Mind: Thought Experiments in the Natural Sciences*. 2nd edition. London: Routledge.

Dennett, Daniel C. 1984. *Elbow Room: The Varieties of Free Will Worth Wanting*. Cambridge, MA: MIT Press.

———. 1991. *Consciousness Explained*. Toronto: Little, Brown and Company.

———. 1995. "Intuition Pumps." In *The Third Culture: Beyond the Scientific Revolution*, edited by J. Brockman, 181–197. New York: Simon & Schuster.

Eppley, Kenneth, and Eric Hannah. 1977. "The Necessity of Quantizing the Gravitational Field." *Foundations of Physics* 7: 51–68.

Gaetens, Moira. 2009. "The Art and Philosophy of George Eliot." *Philosophy and Literature* 33 (1): 73–90.

Galilei, Galileo. [1638] 2000. *Two New Sciences*. Translated by Stillman Drake. Toronto: Wall and Emerson.

Gendler, Tamar Szabó. 2000. *Thought Experiment: On the Powers and Limits of Imaginary Cases*. New York: Garland Press (now Routledge).

Hofstadter, Douglas, and Daniel C. Dennett. 1981. *The Mind's I: Fantasies and Reflections on Self and Soul*. New York: Bantam Books.

Koyré, Alexandre. 1968. *Metaphysics and Measurement*. London: Chapman and Hall.

Kuhn, Thomas S. 1964 [1977]. "A Function for Thought Experiments." In *Mélanges Alexandre Koyré, Vol. II, L'aventure de l'Esprit*, edited by I. Bernard Cohen and René Taton, 307–334. Paris: Hermann. Reprinted in Kuhn, Thomas S. 1977. *The Essential Tension*, 240–265. Chicago: University of Chicago Press.

Locke, John.[1700] 1975. *An Essay Concerning Human Understanding*. Edited by Peter H. Nidditch. Oxford: Clarendon Press.

Miščević, Nenad. 1992. "Mental Models and Thought Experiments." *International Studies in the Philosophy of Science* 6: 215–226.

———. 2007. "Modelling Intuitions and Thought Experiments." *Croatian Journal of Philosophy* VII: 181–214.

Nersessian, Nancy. 1993. "In the Theoretician's Laboratory: Thought Experimenting as Mental Modeling." *Proceedings of the Philosophy of Science Association* 2: 291–301.

———. 2007. "Thought Experiments as Mental Modelling: Empiricism without Logic." *Croatian Journal of Philosophy* VII: 125–161.

Norton, John D. 1991. "Thought Experiments in Einstein's Work." In *Thought Experiments in Science and Philosophy*, edited by T. Horowitz and G. Massey, 129–148. Lanham, MD: Rowman & Littlefield.

———. 2004. "Why Thought Experiments Do Not Transcend Empiricism." In *Contemporary Debates in the Philosophy of Science*, edited by C. Hitchcock, 44–66. Oxford: Blackwell.

Parfit, Derek. 1971. "Personal Identity." *The Philosophical Review* 80 (1): 3–27.

Stich, Stephen. [1988] 1998. "Reflective Equilibrium, Analytic Epistemology and the Problem of Cognitive Diversity." *Synthese* 74 (3): 391–413. Reprinted with minor changes in *Rethinking Intuition*, edited by Michael DePaul and William Ramsey, 95–112. Lanham, MD: Rowman & Littlefield.

Stich, Stephen, and Wesley Buckwalter. 2011. "Gender and the Philosophy Club." *The Philosophers' Magazine* 52: 60–65.

Thagard, Paul. 2010. *The Brain and the Meaning of Life*. Princeton, NJ: Princeton University Press.

Williams, Bernard. 1970. "The Self and the Future." *The Philosophical Review* 79 (2): 161–180.

1 Thought Experiment and the Exercise of Imagination in Science

James W. McAllister

1. INTRODUCTION

This chapter is motivated by the belief that further progress in our understanding of thought experiment in science depends on placing the device into a wider discussion of the appeal to imagination in scientific practice. Up to now, scientists and philosophers of science have mainly discussed thought experiment separately from other forms of imaginative thinking. In what follows, I treat thought experiment as an instance of the application of imagination to construct representations of the world.

I use the term "imagination" to denote a mental capacity for conceiving entities, states of affairs, events, and phenomena that have not previously been observed. In a generic sense, imagination plays a role whenever someone originates novel output of any kind, such as when a scientist poses a novel question, designs a novel instrument or experiment, or even simply utters a novel claim. Imagination plays a role in a more specific sense, however, when it is harnessed to construct representations of the world. Scientists use imagination in this sense when they conceive possible features of the world that they have not previously encountered empirically. Imagination is involved whenever scientists posit unobserved, unobservable, or nonactual states of affairs, such as in conjectures, counterfactual reasoning, predictions, models, and idealizations, as well as in thought experiments. This chapter is concerned with the role of imagination in scientific representations of the world in this more specific sense. (On conceptions of imagination, see Sparshott 1990; Thomas 1997, 1999; for historical background, see Kearney 1988.)

Some writers, including some writers on thought experiment, construe the term "imagination" differently, as denoting a capacity for constructing, experiencing, and manipulating mental imagery. In one respect, my use of "imagination" is broader than that, since conceiving unobserved possibilities does not necessarily involve mental imagery: It is possible to imagine an entity without producing a visualization of it. In another respect, my use of the term is narrower, as I focus on conceiving states of affairs not previously observed.

In the next section, I review four commonly held perspectives on imagination in science, and show how they have influenced the attitudes of scientists and philosophers towards thought experiment. In the course of this review, I will identify two objections faced by appeals to imagination in constructing representations of the world: the arbitrariness objection, which alleges that the outcome of an act of imagination is arbitrary, and the poverty objection, which avers that our imagination is insufficiently creative to apprehend reality. I then identify two styles of theorizing, which I call the constructive and determinative styles (Section 3). Theorists in the constructive style believe that these objections are surmountable and are thus no bar to the use of imagination, whereas theorists in the determinative style see these objections as a sufficient reason to reject imagination. I illustrate scientists' attitudes to imagination and their responses to these objections by means of two case studies in the history of physical science: seventeenth-century natural philosophy (Section 4) and nineteenth-century theories of heat and electromagnetism (Section 5). Throughout, I draw conclusions about the domain in which thought experiment carries evidential significance.

2. FOUR PERSPECTIVES ON IMAGINATION IN SCIENCE

Scientists and thinkers on science adopt a variety of perspectives on the proper role of imagination in scientific practice. We may distinguish the following four.

Perspective 1 holds imagination to be an important component of scientific work. Progress in science consists largely in apprehending new features of the world: This is achieved sometimes by observation and sometimes by other means. Imagination is just such an extension or complement of observation: It is the faculty that we use to apprehend the world when observation breaks down (Holton 1978, 1996, 78–102; McMullin 1996). In Isaac Newton's hypothesis that the moon is analogous to a falling apple and Charles Darwin's depiction of life as the outcome of natural selection, these scientists apprehended features of the world for the first time by means of imagination.

Imagination plays an especially important role where features of the world are not merely as yet unobserved, but unobservable in principle or in practice. Such features include past events, structures too small to be detected, and theoretical entities. John Tyndall (1870) emphasized the role of imagination in extending scientific reasoning beyond the visible, arguing that various explanatory atomic and molecular hypotheses, Darwin's theory of pangenesis, and the Kant-Laplace hypothesis on the origin of the solar system could not be entertained without imagination. Similarly, J. H. van 't Hoff ([1878] 1967) defended his practice of imagining three-dimensional molecular structures on the grounds that there was no other way of investigating molecules.

Proponents of hypothetico-deductivism tend to perspective 1. They hold that scientists originate theories by inventive leaps, not guided or constrained by experience. Scientists subsequently deduce the observational implications of their theories and compare them with empirical data. For a hypothetico-deductivist, therefore, the apprehension of unobserved possibilities by means of imagination is an essential step in discovering what is or is not the case. Even Karl R. Popper, who took a logicist line on most issues, granted a prominent role to imagination in the context of discovery (Medawar 1967, 129–155). By contrast, proponents of inductive methods tend to allow imagination a smaller role. They are traditionally less interested in explanatory hypotheses than in empirical laws, and believe that such laws can be built up by observation: The inductive principle that unobserved cases resemble observed cases obviates the need to exercise imagination.

Perspective 1 also supports the use of imagination in the form of thought experiment. The thought experiment by which Albert Einstein addressed the question "How would a light wave appear to an observer following it at the speed of light?" is a typical exercise of imagination (Norton, Chapter 7 of this volume). Platonists explicitly regard thought experiment as a tool for apprehending features of the world by means other than empirical data (Brown 2010).

Perspective 2 is less optimistic. Whereas perspective 1 values the creativeness of imagination, this feature appears from perspective 2 as a source of deception. The fact that an act of imagination is able to apprehend a certain state of affairs does not indicate that the state of affairs is possible, let alone actual. Most people are capable of imagining physical and conceptual impossibilities, such as rocks floating in water and the staircases of M. C. Escher (Gendler and Hawthorne 2002). Thus, imagination is akin to make-believe, pretence, and illusion, and its use in science must be avoided.

The reason imagination does not produce trustworthy representations of the real world, from perspective 2, is that it is insufficiently constrained by reality. The outcomes of acts of imagination are arbitrary. An entity or state of affairs conceived by an act of imagination is just one among many that could be imagined: None of these has any more claim to reality than any other. Since objectivity depends largely on uniqueness, this shows that imagination cannot claim to be objective. Objectivity in science is obtained by the unveiling of facts, according to perspective 2, and not by acts of imaginative creation (Daston 1998).

The fact that it is impossible or difficult to rule out that the outcome of an act of imagination is arbitrary constitutes what I call the "arbitrariness objection." Scientists who mistrust imagination frequently cite the arbitrariness objection against those who would use imagination to construct representations of the world, as we shall see below. The arbitrariness objection is especially effective against attempts to use imagination to apprehend unobservable entities, such as micromechanisms underlying appearances. Hypotheses about unobservable entities are in most cases greatly underdetermined by empirical evidence. This means that there is no effective method to check the arbitrariness of acts of imagination about unobservable entities.

The debate between scientific realism and forms of instrumentalism, empiricism, and positivism is conducted partly in terms of perspectives 1 and 2. Scientific realists hold that claims about unobservable entities are as legitimate and meaningful as similar claims about observables. Representations of the observable domain are constructed by observation, of course, but this tool fails for the unobservable domain. Realists are thus compelled to acknowledge imagination as an extension of observation, as a tool to form representations of unobservable entities. Realists therefore tend to regard imagination as a constructive but reliable guide to the unobservable world.

Instrumentalists, by contrast, decline to accept claims involving nonobservational terms as anything more than empirically adequate, and thus do not need imagination as a supplement to observation. Many arguments for instrumentalism are based on the premise that hypotheses incorporating theoretical terms are underdetermined by empirical data. An example is the "pessimistic induction" (Laudan 1981), which suggests that many empirically successful theories of the past were mistaken in the unobservable entities that they posited. Such arguments embody the belief that the results of acts of imagination are arbitrary, and thus that imagination does not reliably identify unobservable components of the world.

Perspective 2 fosters skepticism about the evidential value of thought experiment too. Because of their reliance on imagination, thought experiments run the risk of yielding conclusions that have no bearing on reality. In several areas in physics, for example, we can devise apparently plausible thought experiments that support mutually incompatible claims (Norton 2004, 45–49). Since there is no experience available to guide thought experiments about brain transplants, similarly, any conclusions drawn from them about personal identity must be counted arbitrary (Wilkes 1993, 15–21).

It sounds superficially as though Ernst Mach was an exception to this account: He is noted both as one of the pioneers of the use of thought experiments in physics and as an instrumentalist—or, more precisely, as a sensationalist, who held that all knowledge is reducible to judgments about sensations. This seeming tension is resolved by pointing out that, in fact, Mach regarded thought experiment merely as a device for releasing "instinctive knowledge" accumulated by experience: He did not consider that it provided nonobservational access to reality (Sorensen 1992, 51–63). Whereas it seems odd to reach this conclusion about the scientist credited with coining the term *Gedankenexperiment*, a Machian thought experiment is a degenerate case of the technique, since it serves to access and reinforce, rather than go beyond, the deliverances of observation.

Perspective 3, like perspective 2, mistrusts imagination. Whereas perspective 2 accuses imagination of being insufficiently constrained by reality, however, perspective 3 charges it with the contrary shortcoming: of failing to transcend the familiar. Imagination is less creative than some assume, as it is difficult to imagine something wholly novel and unprecedented.

Imagination all too often consists of reproducing the familiar in different combinations: In statistical thermodynamics, for example, atoms of a gas are imagined as miniature billiard balls. An act of imagination is always the product of particular intellectual circumstances, and it bears the mark of those circumstances.

This limitation is reflected in theories of imagination that describe the faculty as consisting of the conceptual integration of pre-existing elements of thought (Fauconnier and Turner 2002). Whereas the transfer of conceptual resources between domains is useful in theory formation, and especially in analogical reasoning, it consists of a creativity of a limited kind (Bohm 1998, 41–61). In empirical discoveries, by contrast, scientists are repeatedly confronted with phenomena that cannot be comprehended in terms of the familiar. Far from outstripping the range of empirical experience, as perspective 1 suggests, imagination is broadened by empirical input: Scientists learn after having made discoveries how limited their imaginative powers have been. Perspective 3 is voiced by J. B. S. Haldane ([1927] 1940, 263): "My own suspicion is that the universe is not only queerer than we suppose, but queerer than we *can* suppose."

In this light, the relation between imagination and objectivity takes a new form. Far from failing the standards of objectivity through being unconstrained, imagination falls short of the ideal of objectivity by omitting to emancipate itself from its origins, by not attaining the status of the universal and impersonal good that objectivity is supposed to be.

The fact that it is impossible or difficult to rule out that our imagination is insufficiently creative to apprehend reality constitutes what I call the "poverty objection." As we shall see, this objection, like the arbitrariness objection, is commonly adduced against proposals to rely on imagination to construct scientific representations of the world.

The skepticism of perspective 3 extends to thought experiment too. Daniel C. Dennett (1984, 12) criticizes many thought experiments for being merely intuition pumps, or devices to make explicit one's pre-existing intuitions. David L. Hull (1997, 431) argues that, for this reason, thought experiments are conservative devices that tend to inhibit innovation in science. Whereas physicists in the early years of the development of quantum mechanics proposed many thought experiments, these tended to play a conservative role: Their proposers often intended them to demonstrate the error of quantum theory or at least to reveal conceptual tensions in it. The stimulus for formulating quantum theory was provided by experimental findings, which confronted physicists with the need for concepts that imagination resisted (Wheaton 1983; Miller 1984).

The divergence of perspectives 1, 2, and 3 manifests itself in views of the relation between science and art. Perspective 1, according to which scientists make discoveries by dint of imaginative creation, encourages the view that science resembles art. Perspective 2, by portraying imagination as incapable of yielding objective representations of the world, embodies mistrust of imagination and thereby distances science from art. The accusation by artists that science deadens or stifles imagination may be seen partly as a counterpart of and response to the scientists' mistrust of imagination. Romantic writers, for whom imagination was a key concept, advanced this accusation especially strongly (Abrams 1953; Rousseau 2003). Perspective 3, somewhat surprisingly, opens a way in which science may inspire art. If imagination is extended by perceptual encounter with novel objects, then empirical discoveries in science may stimulate imagination in the arts. This occurred in the seventeenth century, for example, when discoveries made with the telescope and the microscope fed literary imagination (Nicolson 1956).

Perspective 4, lastly, reinstates a positive view of imagination. From perspective 4, imagination is not a tool that scientists are free to use or avoid: On the contrary, it is ineliminably involved in the construction of any scientific representation. Constructing almost any representation of the world involves two activities: observation and rule following. Because both visual stimuli and rules are ambiguous, however, they must be interpreted. This process of interpretation depends on imagination.

The ambiguity of visual stimuli is well documented. In order to make sense of a visual stimulus, the observer must select one interpretation from several possibilities (Hoffman 1998). Imagination is required in this act, since imagination is the faculty of apprehending possible states of affairs that have not yet been observed. A version of this realization has been incorporated into philosophy of science under the label "theory-ladenness of observation" (Hanson 1958). From perspective 4, imagination is not a possible extension of observation, but a constitutive part of it.

In constructing representations of the world, rules of at least two kinds play a part. First, there are rules internal to a representation, determining in what relation parts or aspects of the representation should stand to one another. These rules fix, for example, the requirements that a representation must satisfy if it is to be consistent and continuous. Second, there are rules linking the representation to the world, determining how the representation is to be related to empirical data. In a dynamical model of a system in physics, for example, rules of the first kind tell us how to manipulate the model to predict the future evolution of the physical system, whereas rules of the second kind tell us how to determine whether the model is accurate. The ability to follow rules is thus essential for constructing and using representations.

According to Saul A. Kripke's elaboration of Ludwig Wittgenstein's remarks about rule following, the totality of my experience up to now is insufficient to determine which act counts as following a given rule (Wittgenstein 1958; Kripke 1982). For example, any number can be regarded as the correct continuation of a given number series. The agent must judge in each particular circumstance which act may be regarded as conforming to the rule. This judgment necessarily goes beyond what has been experienced up to now. Hence, rule following requires imagination, since imagination is the faculty for apprehending structures that have not been experienced.

Without imagination, thus, we would not be able either to construct representations from observation or to follow the rules implicit in representations. In sum, any representation of the world depends on imagination. From perspective 4, too, the relation between imagination and objectivity takes another form. Imagination is no longer an external factor that can promote or threaten objectivity, but a factor that partly constitutes objectivity.

Perspective 4 suggests that thought experiment is not merely an extension of observation as a means to construct representations of the world, but rather is partly constitutive of the activity of representing the world. Writers on thought experiment come close to endorsing this position when they analyze thought experiment as a form of mental modeling that is inescapably involved in reasoning about the world (Nersessian 1999; Miščević 2007).

3. CONSTRUCTIVE AND DETERMINATIVE STYLES OF THEORIZING

In this section, I distinguish between two styles of theorizing in the physical sciences, which I call the "constructive" and the "determinative" styles. Proponents of these two styles attribute different roles and value to imagination. The constructive style of theorizing embodies perspective 1, discussed in the previous section. The determinative style, by contrast, often embodies perspectives 2 and 3.

The constructive style of theorizing consists in attempting to account for phenomena by positing an unobservable domain that underlies and causes appearances. In most cases, this domain consists of causal mechanisms, and their unobservability is usually attributed to their being very small or being occult. Because it posits an unobservable domain, the constructive style of theorizing is compelled to appeal to imagination: No other faculty offers access to this domain. Proponents of this style regard imagination as an extension of observation: By virtue of this, they feel justified in regarding the unobservable realm as on a par with the observable.

The determinative style of theorizing, by contrast, rejects the idea of an unobservable domain underlying appearances. Instead, this style consists in positing abstract mathematical structures that determine phenomena uniquely. These mathematical structures may take the form of phenomenological laws or of symmetry and consistency principles, and they may be discovered empirically or deduced from higher-level premises. Because the determinative style of theorizing does not posit an unobservable domain of reality, it has no need of imagination to apprehend it.

Many proponents of the determinative style of theorizing do not just avoid use of imagination, but mistrust it as a tool to construct representations of the world. The reasons for this mistrust often center on the arbitrariness and poverty objections. First, many proponents of the determinative style of theorizing argue that the outcomes of acts of imagination are arbitrary: The hypotheses about causal mechanisms put forward in the constructive style invariably go beyond observational evidence. Because of this, appeals to imagination are not relevant to establishing the mathematical structures governing phenomena. Imagination plays no part, for example, in establishing by experiment a phenomenological law describing a phenomenon. Second, they argue, there is no guarantee that imagination is sufficiently rich to grasp a reality underlying appearances.

Of course, even those who theorize in the determinative style may be regarded as exercising imagination in the generic sense noted in Section 1 to create new ideas. For example, it may require imagination in the generic sense to originate a new mathematical formula. However, proponents of the determinative style do not accept imagination as a means of constructing representations of an unseen domain of reality.

The difference between these styles of theorizing circumscribes the domain in which thought experiment carries evidential significance. We should expect scientists working in the constructive style to ascribe evidential significance to thought experiments, as exercises of the imagination able to clarify the structure of the world. Thought experiments will be absent from theorizing in the determinative style, by contrast, as scientists working in this style will feel no reason to use them and will often furthermore mistrust them.

4. IMAGINATION IN SEVENTEENTH-CENTURY NATURAL PHILOSOPHY

In this section and the next, I use historical case studies to investigate the contrasting attitudes towards imagination and thought experiment in the constructive and determinative styles of theorizing. My first case study is set in seventeenth-century natural philosophy. Mechanism in the seventeenth century sought to account for appearances by positing imperceptible corpuscles in motion. Because the properties and motions of corpuscles could not be apprehended by observation, adherents of mechanism were unable to present conclusive empirical evidence for their views. They thus turned to imagination.

Imagination played two roles in mechanism. First, it provided global support for the doctrine by allowing natural philosophers to apprehend the domain of corpuscles. Second, it provided support for individual mechanistic explanations of observable phenomena by allowing the apprehension of proposed mechanisms. Most forms of mechanism adopted a distinction between primary and secondary qualities of objects. The primary qualities of an object were its intrinsic properties, such as its size, shape, mass, and motion. The secondary qualities of objects, by contrast, were the power to produce in us ideas of colors, sounds, odors, tastes, and the like. The causes of these ideas were the primary qualities of corpuscles. Thus, imagination was required both in order to apprehend the primary qualities of corpuscles, and in order thereby to account for the secondary qualities of macroscopic objects (Meinel 1988; Wilson 2002).

The work of René Descartes exemplifies the appeal to imagination in mechanicism. In his *Regulae ad directionem ingenii* of 1628, Descartes acknowledged imagination as one of four faculties used in cognition, alongside understanding, sense, and memory. In Descartes's philosophy, imagination played a role in all cognition, including the perception of observable objects. Imagination also had a specific role in the cognition of unseen objects, however: Acting as an intermediary between direct observation and pure reasoning, it allowed the apprehension of unseen entities, including imperceptible corpuscles. (On imagination in Descartes, see Park, Daston, and Galison 1984, 311–326; Sepper 1996, 211–238; Schouls 2000.)

Descartes appealed to imagination to gain cognitive access to the unobservable domain that he had postulated. In various treatises, such as *La Dioptrique*, *Les Météores*, and *L'Homme*, Descartes asked his readers to imagine a series of mechanisms capable of producing all observable physical and physiological phenomena. Descartes's most sustained use of imagination as a tool to construct representations of this world came, however, in the posthumously published *Le Monde*. There he introduced the following thought experiment:

> Allow your thought to wander beyond this world to view another, wholly new, world, which I call forth in imaginary spaces before it. [. . .] Let us suppose that God creates anew so much matter all around us that, in whatever direction our imagination may extend, it no longer perceives any place that is empty. [. . .] Let us add further that this matter may be divided into as many parts and shapes as we can imagine, and that each of its parts can take on as many motions as we can conceive. (Descartes [1664] 1998, 21–23; for further discussion, see Ariew 2005)

This is not a "new world" at all, of course, but the chaotic initial state of the actual world, which will be brought by the laws of nature to produce all observable phenomena of matter and light.

Descartes was aware of both objections to imagination described above. He implicitly acknowledged the arbitrariness objection in the *Principia philosophiae* by saying that God could have produced the phenomena that we perceive in innumerably different ways: The causes postulated by Descartes to explain some effects might thus not correspond to those that God chose (Ariew 2005, 137–138). Descartes responded to the arbitrariness objection by assuming that God had embedded necessary relations in the world, which allowed us certain knowledge of physical reality (Osler 1994). On this basis, he argued that the knowledge of the domain of corpuscles gained by imagination was no less trustworthy than knowledge of the observable world yielded by observation.

Similarly, Descartes acknowledged the poverty objection: He noted in his *Meditationes de prima philosophia* of 1642 that he was unable distinctly to imagine a chiliagon (a thousand-sided polygon) despite being able to demonstrate certain properties of it by means of the intellect (Cottingham, Stoothoff, and Murdoch 1985, 50). Descartes responded to the poverty objection by arguing that the mechanisms underlying the world of appearances are so basic that we can be certain our imagination can apprehend them. In *Le Monde*, he continued:

> Pause again [. . .] to consider this chaos, and note that it contains nothing which you do not know so perfectly that you could not even pretend to be ignorant of it. For the qualities that I have placed in it are only such as you could imagine. And as far as the matter from which I have composed it is concerned, there is nothing simpler or more easily grasped in inanimate creatures. The idea of that matter is such a part of all the ideas that our imagination can form that you must necessarily conceive of it, or you can never imagine anything at all. (Descartes [1664] 1998, 23–24)

Galileo Galilei did not share Descartes's interest in explaining appearances by appeal to unobservable mechanisms. For Galileo, to explain natural phenomena meant essentially to establish a mathematical model of them. In such a model, true conclusions were derived from true and evident principles. The conclusions could then be regarded as true without empirical confirmation, although some confirmation might be helpful in practical cases. Physical truth was thus reduced to mathematical truth, and physical necessity to mathematical necessity (Clavelin [1968] 1974; Wisan 1978).

In consequence, Galileo had little use for imagination, for three reasons. First, a domain of unobservable mechanisms—which would require imagination as a means of access—played little or no role in his natural philosophy. Galileo seldom speculated about causal mechanisms underlying phenomena: His attempted explanation of the tides by appeal to the motions of the earth was atypical (Galilei [1632] 1953, 416–465; for an alternative interpretation, see Ducheyne 2006). Mostly, he allowed the mathematical structures to stand on their own. For example, he did not accompany his statement of the law of free fall in the *Discorsi* by discussion of the cause of the fall of bodies:

> The present does not seem to me to be an opportune time to enter into the investigation of the cause of the acceleration of natural motion, concerning which various philosophers have produced various opinions [. . .]. Such fantasies, and others like them, would have to be examined and resolved, with little gain. (Galilei [1638] 1974, 158–159)

Second, Galileo's primary aim was to enunciate mathematical laws describing phenomena. Imagination had no role in this activity, since, as Galileo believed, mathematical laws could be discerned directly in the phenomena. Third, Galileo cited the poverty objection, believing imagination to be too limited to apprehend natural causes. In his discussion of comets in *Il Saggiatore*, for example, Galileo argued that imagination was a poor source of causal explanations in natural philosophy because nature invents far more causes than the human mind can conceive:

> I could illustrate with many more examples Nature's bounty in producing her effects, as she employs means we could never think of without our senses and our experiences to teach them to us—and sometimes even these are insufficient to remedy our lack of understanding. So I should not be condemned for being unable to determine precisely the way in which comets are produced, especially in view of the fact that I never boasted that I could do this, knowing that they may originate in some manner that is far beyond our power of imagination. (Galilei [1623] 1957, 258)

For these reasons, Galileo rejected appeals to imagination in natural philosophy (Park, Daston, and Galison 1984, 302–310).

This reconstruction may strike some as odd, since Galileo is celebrated for his thought experiments (McAllister 2005). Galileo's thought experiments, however, did not strictly speaking involve imaginary cases. For Galileo, thought experiments were not ways of apprehending as yet unobserved features of the world, but rather demonstrations of features of the world that were already known: They did not extend observation, as imagination is supposed to do, but confirmed it. Like Machian thought experiments, Galilean thought experiments turn out to be a degenerate case of the technique.

These considerations suggest that a contrast usually drawn between Descartes and Galileo should be reversed. On the usual view, Descartes was a rationalist who shunned imagination for logic and method. Nineteenth-century romantic writers, who saw reason and imagination to some extent as opposed, took Descartes as an enemy of imagination, for example. Galileo, instead, is often portrayed as an imaginative thinker and writer, who devised ingenious arguments and employed artful rhetoric. On my view, by contrast, the roles are inverted. Descartes relied on imagination as a tool for investigating the world, as he was forced to do by his positing a domain of invisible mechanisms; Galileo rejected imagination, holding that mathematical laws that are apparent to the expert eye determine phenomena.

5. IMAGINATION IN NINETEENTH-CENTURY PHYSICS

The contrast between constructive and determinative styles is visible also in theorizing about physics in the nineteenth century. Some schools felt that theorizing should draw on imagination, whereas others mistrusted imagination and believed that theorizing should shun it.

A molecular-mechanical school, led by Pierre-Simon Laplace and Siméon-Denis Poisson, dominated French physics for a period in the early nineteenth century. This school sought to account for all physical phenomena in terms of forces postulated to act between molecules, by analogy with Newtonian gravitation. The method of this school was hypothetico-deductive. To account for a phenomenon, the physicist first hypothesized a configuration of molecules and the laws governing the forces that acted between them. The molecules might be particles of ponderable matter or of imponderable matter, such as particles of caloric fluid, and they might exert attractive or repulsive forces. Second, the physicist deduced the observational implications of the hypothesis and compared these with empirical data.

For example, Laplace explained capillarity by hypothesizing molecules that exerted short-range attractive forces, and showing that this hypothesis accounted for observational data. Poisson and others accounted for elasticity on the hypothesis that elastic bodies were composed of molecules exerting forces on one another that depended on displacement.

The molecular-mechanical school used the constructive style of theorizing. Like the Cartesian approach, it relied on imagination to apprehend configurations of molecules and the forces that they exerted: Such hypotheses could not be derived from empirical data, since the postulated microstructures were not accessible to observation. This approach had the advantage of providing a possible causal explanation of phenomena.

The molecular-mechanical school also tended to attribute evidential significance to thought experiments. Its thought experiments delved into the domain of mechanisms underlying the appearances to draw conclusions about what was the case. The two best-known thought experiments of the molecular-mechanical school, Laplace's demon thought experiment in mechanics and Poisson's spot thought experiment in optics, enrolled imagination to extend observation (Schlesinger 1996, 470–473; Sorensen 1992, 191).

Not all French physicists joined the molecular-mechanical school, however. Another group, led by Joseph Fourier, criticized it on two grounds. First, they noted that the molecular-mechanical approach required hypotheses to be formulated in terms of dynamics, regardless of the domain of physics under study. The critics found this requirement inflexible, and also that it seemed to presuppose that dynamics is the fundamental branch of physics to which all other areas could be reduced. This criticism is a form of the poverty objection, since it takes issue with imagination for being capable only of acting on familiar terms.

Second, they criticized the molecular-mechanical school for aiming at the discovery of causes that were not accessible to observation. They argued that many different hypotheses about the causes of phenomena were conceivable, none of which could be established with any certainty. This criticism is a form of the arbitrariness objection, since it takes issue with the fact that imagination, by going beyond what is observable, in many cases yields conceptions that lack objectivity and for which there is no compelling empirical motivation. By contrast, the observed regularities of phenomena and the empirical laws derived from observation and experiment were independent of all hypotheses about causes and formed the proper basis of theorizing. These empirical laws were neutral as between any causal hypotheses that could be devised.

This group of physicists formed an analytical-positivist school, inspired by Joseph Louis Lagrange's earlier project to reduce mechanics to mathematics. The method of this school was to establish regularities of phenomena by observation and experiment, to formulate empirical laws that described these regularities, and finally to formulate general theories from which these laws followed. The approach did not include positing hypotheses about the hidden causes of appearances. In short, this group used the determinative style of theorizing.

In his 1816 essay, "Précis historique de la propagation de la chaleur," Fourier emphasized that a general theory of heat propagation was independent of hypotheses about the propagation mechanism:

> The fundamental equations are demonstrated in the most clear and most rigorous manner without it being necessary to examine if the propagation is carried out by way of radiation in the interior of the solids, whether or not it consists in the emission of a special matter that the molecules interchange with each other, or if it results, like sound, from vibrations of an elastic medium. It is always preferable to restrict oneself to the enunciation of the general fact indicated by observation, which is no other than the preceding principle. One shows thus that the mathematical theory of heat is independent of all physical hypotheses; and in effect the laws to which the propagation is subject are admitted by all physicists in spite of the extreme diversity of their sentiments on the nature and the mode of its action. (Quoted from Herivel 1975, 225)

Fourier brought this approach to completion in his treatise, *Théorie analytique de la chaleur*. He stated his credo on the opening page: "Primary causes are unknown to us; but are subject to simple and constant laws, which may be discovered by observation, the study of them being the object of natural philosophy" (Fourier [1822] 1955, 1). Fourier's theory of heat was based on laws of heat conduction derived from observation and experiment. Fourier took these laws as the axioms of his theory of heat, just as he believed Newton's laws constituted the axioms of Newtonian dynamics.

André-Marie Ampère, while differing from the analytical-positivist school in some respects, followed a similar path in formulating his theory of electrodynamics. He prefaced his treatise with an account of how a general theory is built up from empirical laws, which he called *formules* ("formulae"):

> The principal advantage of the formulae which are thus immediately inferred from some general facts, given by a number of observations

sufficient to make their certainty incontestable, is that they remain independent both of the hypotheses used by their authors in the search for these formulae and of the hypotheses that may be substituted subsequently. [. . .] The same holds for the formula by which I have represented electrodynamic action. Whatever the physical cause to which one wishes to attribute the phenomena produced by this action, the formula that I have obtained will always remain the expression of the facts. If one succeeds in deducing it from one of the considerations by which one has explained many other phenomena, such as attractions according to the inverse square of the distance, attractions that become insensible at any appreciable distance from the particles between which they are exerted, vibrations of a fluid that pervades space, etc., one will have proceeded a step further in that domain of physics; but that research [. . .] will change nothing of the results of my work, since in order to accord with the facts, it will always be necessary for the adopted hypothesis to accord with the formula that represents them so completely. (Ampère [1824] 1958, 3–5)

Partly on the strength of these considerations, the analytical-positivist school in French physics largely succeeded the molecular-mechanical school during the first half of the nineteenth century (Herivel 1966, 121–124; Fox 1974; on similar developments in German physics, see Caneva 1978).

The analytical-positivist school, in mistrusting imagination, also withheld evidential significance from thought experiments. Fourier, Ampère, and like-minded physicists simply had no use for thought experiments: There was for them no concealed domain of causes that could be usefully probed by means of thought experiment.

The program of positing, by means of imagination, hidden mechanisms underlying phenomena, which waned in France with the decline of the molecular-mechanical school, continued in Britain. William Thomson (later named Lord Kelvin) expressed the goal most forcefully:

My object is to show how to make a mechanical model which shall fulfil the conditions required in the physical phenomena that we are considering, whatever they may be. At the time when we are considering the phenomenon of elasticity in solids, I want to show a model of that. At another time, when we have vibrations of light to consider, I want to show a model of the action exhibited in that phenomenon. [. . .] It seems to me that the test of "Do we or not understand a particular subject in physics?" is, "Can we make a mechanical model of it?" (Thomson [1884] 1987, 111)

In this program, theorizing in electromagnetism involved devising arrangements of rods, wheels, weights, and springs that would replicate the behavior of molecules and the electromagnetic ether. For example, in 1862 James Clerk Maxwell developed a model of the ether involving wheels and vortices that accounted for several aspects of the propagation of light and its behavior in magnetic fields. Similarly, Thomson devoted much effort to elucidating the microscopic structure that the ether would have to possess in order to be both elastic enough to transmit light waves and yet not so viscous as to resist the motion of solid bodies.

Thomson's and Maxwell's approach differs from the molecular-mechanical approach of Laplace and his followers in some important ways. First, Maxwell's "method of physical analogy" consists in beginning with the phenomena and supplying a physical content by analogy with a better-understood domain of physics. Second, the hypotheses entertained by Thomson and Maxwell are more varied than those of the molecular-mechanical school, which confined themselves to configurations of molecules and force laws. Nonetheless, the approach of Thomson and Maxwell was clearly a successor of the molecular-mechanical school and shared its reliance on imagination (Kargon 1969).

Pierre Duhem, looking back some decades later on these developments, discussed the role of imagination in them (Duhem [1914] 1991, 55–104; Tiles 1988). He contrasted the theorizing of French and German physicists, which he identified with the mathematical style of Fourier and Ampère, with that of English physicists, which he identified with the model-based style of Thomson and Maxwell. According to Duhem, French and German physicists gave the following characterization of a physical theory:

> The mind contemplates a whole group of laws; for this group it substitutes a very small number of extremely general judgments, referring to some very abstract ideas; it chooses these primary properties and formulates these fundamental hypotheses in such a way that all the laws belonging to the group studied can be derived by deduction that is very lengthy perhaps, but very sure. This system of hypotheses and deducible consequences, a work of abstraction, generalization and deduction, constitutes a physical theory in our definition. (Duhem [1914] 1991, 55)

No appeal to imagination was required in this deductive structure. By contrast, English physicists had a different notion of theory:

> Theory is for him [the English physicist] neither an explanation nor a rational classification of physical laws, but a model of these laws, a model not built for the satisfying of reason but for the pleasure of the imagination. [. . .] Thus, in English theories we find those disparities, those inconsistencies, those contradictions which we are driven to judge severely because we seek a rational system where the author has sought to give us only a work of imagination. (Duhem [1914] 1991, 81)

Not all the models and other products of imagination put forward by Thomson and Maxwell can be described as thought experiments. It is clear, however, that, in order to gain evidential significance, thought experiments require conceptual assumptions that—like those of Thomson and Maxwell—portray imagination as a reliable and informative technique for apprehending the world.

6. CONCLUSIONS

I have attempted to demonstrate in this chapter that thought experiment constitutes one manifestation of a larger repertoire of devices and approaches to the natural world that some scientists adopt and others reject. Thought experiment relies on the exercise of imagination to construct representations of the world, and consequently presupposes the validity of imagination as a means to apprehend reality. One style of theorizing, which I have dubbed "constructive," views imagination as an unproblematic extension of observation: In this style, thought experiment takes its place as a legitimate cognitive tool. Another style of theorizing, which I have dubbed "determinative," is more sensitive to the arbitrariness and poverty objections. On the strength of these objections, this style of theorizing mistrusts the use of imagination in science and thereby also declines to attribute evidential significance to thought experiment.

This work has two main consequences for our notion of thought experiment: one broad and one specific. The broad consequence is to add a further element to the survey of the domains in which thought experiment carries evidential significance. In earlier work, I argued that thought experiment acquires evidential significance only on particular metaphysical assumptions. These include the thesis that science aims at uncovering "phenomena," universal and stable modes in which the world is articulated, and the thesis that phenomena are revealed imperfectly in actual occurrences. Only on these assumptions does it make sense to bypass experience of actual occurrences and perform thought experiments (McAllister 1996, 2004). In the present chapter, I have argued that there is a further factor that helps determine where thought experiment carries evidential significance: the degree to which scientists regard imagination as a legitimate tool to apprehend reality.

The specific consequence is to call into question the centrality of thought experiment in the work of two thinkers who have so far been regarded as archetypal exponents of the method: Galileo and Mach. Each of these thinkers had strong grounds for doubting that imagination was a legitimate tool for apprehending reality. In different ways, both Galileo and Mach were generally skeptical of the use of hypotheses that went beyond observational evidence. Whereas it is undeniable that both Galileo and Mach left us with lines of reasoning that are called thought experiments, we should acknowledge that the thought experiments of both thinkers share an odd feature: In not going beyond the observable domain, they represent a degenerate case. Galileo appears to have designed his thought experiments not to go beyond observation in any way, but rather to provide additional confirmation of results obtained by mathematical modeling, sometimes to the point of making observation unnecessary. Mach seems to have regarded his use of thought experiments as a device to unlock empirical knowledge that had been laid down in intuition. Whereas I have not attempted in this chapter a systematic re-examination of the thought experiments proposed by Galileo and Mach, I suggest that the material I have presented offers an initial indication that something is amiss in the standard view of thought experiments in the work of these two historical figures.

ACKNOWLEDGEMENTS

I presented some portions of this chapter at the workshop "Science without Data? The Role of Thought Experiments in Empirical Investigations," Dalhousie University, June 2010. I thank James Robert Brown, Mélanie Frappier, and Letitia Meynell for organizing the workshop and for inviting me to contribute to the present volume.

REFERENCES

Abrams, M. H. 1953. *The Mirror and the Lamp: Romantic Theory and the Critical Tradition.* New York: Oxford University Press.

Ampère, André-Marie. [1824] 1958. *Théorie mathématique des phénomènes électro-dynamiques uniquement déduite de l'expérience.* Paris: Blanchard.

Ariew, Roger. 2005. "Descartes's Fable and Scientific Methodology." *Archives Internationales d'Histoire des Sciences* 55: 127–138.

Bohm, David. 1998. *On Creativity,* edited by Lee Nichol. London: Routledge.

Brown, James Robert. 2010. *The Laboratory of the Mind: Thought Experiments in the Natural Sciences.* 2nd edition. London: Routledge.

Caneva, Kenneth L. 1978. "From Galvanism to Electrodynamics: The Transformation of German Physics and Its Social Context." *Historical Studies in the Physical Sciences* 9: 63–159.

Clavelin, Maurice. [1968] 1974. *The Natural Philosophy of Galileo: Essay on the Origins and Formation of Classical Mechanics.* Translated by A. J. Pomerans. Cambridge, MA: MIT Press.

Cottingham, John, Robert Stoothoff, and Dugald Murdoch, eds. 1985. *The Philosophical Writings of Descartes.* Vol. 2. Cambridge: Cambridge University Press.

Daston, Lorraine J. 1998. "Fear and Loathing of the Imagination in Science." *Daedalus* 127 (1): 73–85.

Dennett, Daniel C. 1984. *Elbow Room: The Varieties of Free Will Worth Wanting.* Cambridge, MA: MIT Press.

Descartes, René. [1664] 1998. *Treatise on Light.* In *The World and Other Writings,* edited by Stephen Gaukroger, 3–75. Cambridge: Cambridge University Press.

Ducheyne, Steffen. 2006. "Galileo's Interventionist Notion of 'Cause'." *Journal of the History of Ideas* 67: 443–464.

Duhem, Pierre. [1914] 1991. *The Aim and Structure of Physical Theory.* 2nd edition. Translated by Philip P. Wiener. Princeton, NJ: Princeton University Press.

Fauconnier, Gilles, and Mark Turner. 2002. *The Way We Think: Conceptual Blending and the Mind's Hidden Complexities*. New York: Basic Books.

Fourier, Joseph. [1822] 1955. *The Analytical Theory of Heat*. Translated by Alexander Freeman. New York: Dover.

Fox, Robert. 1974. "The Rise and Fall of Laplacian Physics." *Historical Studies in the Physical Sciences* 4: 89–136.

Galilei, Galileo. [1623] 1957. *The Assayer*. In *Discoveries and Opinions of Galileo*, edited by Stillman Drake, 229–280. Garden City, NY: Doubleday.

———. [1632] 1953. *Dialogue Concerning the Two Chief World Systems—Ptolemaic and Copernican*. Translated by Stillman Drake. Berkeley: University of California Press.

———. [1638] 1974. *Two New Sciences*. Translated by Stillman Drake. Madison: University of Wisconsin Press.

Gendler, Tamar Szabó, and John Hawthorne, eds. 2002. *Conceivability and Possibility*. Oxford: Clarendon Press.

Haldane, J. B. S. [1927] 1940. *Possible Worlds*. London: Evergreen Books.

Hanson, Norwood Russell. 1958. *Patterns of Discovery: An Inquiry into the Conceptual Foundations of Science*. Cambridge: Cambridge University Press.

Herivel, John. 1966. "Aspects of French Theoretical Physics in the Nineteenth Century." *British Journal for the History of Science* 3: 109–132.

———. 1975. *Joseph Fourier: The Man and the Physicist*. Oxford: Clarendon Press.

Hoff, J. H. van 't. [1878] 1967. *Imagination in Science*. Translated by Georg F. Springer. Berlin: Springer.

Hoffman, Donald D. 1998. *Visual Intelligence: How We Create What We See*. New York: Norton.

Holton, Gerald. 1978. *The Scientific Imagination: Case Studies*. Cambridge: Cambridge University Press.

———. 1996. *Einstein, History, and Other Passions*. Reading, MA: Addison-Wesley.

Hull, David L. 1997. "That Just Don't Sound Right: A Plea for Real Examples." In *The Cosmos of Science: Essays of Exploration*, edited by John Earman and John D. Norton, 428–457. Pittsburgh, PA: University of Pittsburgh Press.

Kargon, Robert. 1969. "Model and Analogy in Victorian Science: Maxwell's Critique of the French Physicists." *Journal of the History of Ideas* 30: 423–436.

Kearney, Richard. 1988. *The Wake of Imagination: Ideas of Creativity in Western Culture*. London: Hutchinson.

Kripke, Saul A. 1982. *Wittgenstein on Rules and Private Language: An Elementary Exposition*. Cambridge, MA: Harvard University Press.

Laudan, Larry. 1981. "A Confutation of Convergent Realism." *Philosophy of Science* 48: 19–49.

McAllister, James W. 1996. "The Evidential Significance of Thought Experiment in Science." *Studies in History and Philosophy of Science* 27: 233–250.

———. 2004. "Thought Experiments and the Belief in Phenomena." *Philosophy of Science* 71: 1164–1175.

———. 2005. "The Virtual Laboratory: Thought Experiments in Seventeenth-Century Mechanics." In *Collection, Laboratory, Theater: Scenes of Knowledge in the 17th Century*, edited by Helmar Schramm, Ludger Schwarte, and Jan Lazardzig, 35–56. New York: De Gruyter.

McMullin, Ernan. 1996. "Enlarging Imagination." *Tijdschrift voor Filosofie* 58: 227–260.

Medawar, Peter B. 1967. *The Art of the Soluble*. London: Methuen.

Meinel, Christoph. 1988. "Early Seventeenth-Century Atomism: Theory, Epistemology, and the Insufficiency of Experiment." *Isis* 79: 68–103.

Miller, Arthur I. 1984. *Imagery in Scientific Thought: Creating 20th-Century Physics*. Boston: Birkhäuser.

Miščević, Nenad. 2007. "Modelling Intuitions and Thought Experiments." *Croatian Journal of Philosophy* 7: 181–214.

Nersessian, Nancy J. 1999. "Model-Based Reasoning in Conceptual Change." In *Model-Based Reasoning in Scientific Discovery*, edited by Lorenzo Magnani, Nancy J. Nersessian, and Paul Thagard, 5–22. New York: Kluwer.

Nicolson, Marjorie Hope. 1956. *Science and Imagination*. Ithaca, NY: Cornell University Press.

Norton, John D. 2004. "Why Thought Experiments Do Not Transcend Empiricism." In *Contemporary Debates in Philosophy of Science*, edited by Christopher Hitchcock, 44–66. Oxford: Blackwell.

Osler, Margaret J. 1994. *Divine Will and the Mechanical Philosophy: Gassendi and Descartes on Contingency and Necessity in the Created World*. Cambridge: Cambridge University Press.

Park, Katharine, Lorraine J. Daston, and Peter L. Galison. 1984. "Bacon, Galileo, and Descartes on Imagination and Analogy." *Isis* 75: 287–326.

Rousseau, George S. 2003. "Science, Culture, and the Imagination: Enlightenment Configurations." In *The Cambridge History of Science*. Vol. 4, *Eighteenth-Century Science*, edited by Roy Porter, 762–799. Cambridge: Cambridge University Press.

Schlesinger, George N. 1996. "The Power of Thought Experiments." *Foundations of Physics* 26: 467–482.

Schouls, Peter A. 2000. *Descartes and the Possibility of Science*. Ithaca, NY: Cornell University Press.

Sepper, Dennis L. 1996. *Descartes's Imagination: Proportion, Images, and the Activity of Thinking*. Berkeley: University of California Press.

Sorensen, Roy A. 1992. *Thought Experiments*. New York: Oxford University Press.

Sparshott, Francis. 1990. "Imagination: The Very Idea." *Journal of Aesthetics and Art Criticism* 48: 1–8.

Thomas, Nigel J. T. 1997. "Imagery and the Coherence of Imagination: A Critique of White." *Journal of Philosophical Research* 22: 95–127.

———. 1999. "Are Theories of Imagery Theories of Imagination? An Active Perception Approach to Conscious Mental Content." *Cognitive Science* 23: 207–245.

Thomson, William. [1884] 1987. "Notes of Lectures on Molecular Dynamics and the Wave Theory of Light." In *Kelvin's Baltimore Lectures and Modern Theoretical Physics: Historical and Philosophical Perspectives*, edited by Robert Kargon and Peter Achinstein, 7–263. Cambridge, MA: MIT Press.

Tiles, J. E. 1988. "Iconic Thought and the Scientific Imagination." *Transactions of the Charles S. Peirce Society* 24: 161–178.

Tyndall, John. 1870. *Essays on the Use and Limit of the Imagination in Science*. London: Longmans, Green and Co.

Wheaton, Bruce R. 1983. *The Tiger and the Shark: Empirical Roots of Wave–Particle Dualism*. Cambridge: Cambridge University Press.

Wilkes, Kathleen V. 1993. *Real People: Personal Identity without Thought Experiments*. Oxford: Clarendon Press.

Wilson, Catherine. 2002. "Corpuscular Effluvia: Between Imagination and Experiment." In *Wissensideale und Wissenskulturen in der frühen Neuzeit*, edited by Wolfgang Detel and Claus Zittel, 161–184. Berlin: Akademie Verlag.

Wisan, Winifred L. 1978. "Galileo's Scientific Method: A Reexamination." In *New Perspectives on Galileo*, edited by Robert E. Butts and Joseph C. Pitt, 1–57. Dordrecht: D. Reidel.

Wittgenstein, Ludwig. 1958. *Philosophical Investigations*. 2nd edition. Translated by G. E. M. Anscombe. Oxford: Blackwell.

2 Veridical Idealizations

Roy Sorensen

> "I don't believe in hypothetical situations, Mr. Donaghy. That's like lying to your brain".
>
> —Kenneth Parcell (*30 Rock*, The "Oprah" Episode)

Is idealization a counterexample to scientific realism? The realist says scientists aim at a true description of reality. Many realists go on to say we are justified in believing in the existence of the laws and entities postulated by scientists because that provides the best explanation of the accuracy of their predictions. W. V. O. Quine ([1948] 1980) frames this as commitment rather than entitlement; ontological honesty compels us to accept any entity that is indispensable to our best theory. If that means accepting the existence of sets or other abstract entities, then so be it. Thus, Quine, a former nominalist, soldiers on from scientific realism to mathematical realism.

Idealization appears to break up this forced march from science to metaphysics. Scientists wittingly employ false assumptions to explain and predict. Falsification is counterproductive in the pursuit of truth. So scientific realism appears to imply that idealization would be worse than ineffective. Yet scientists *do* idealize.

The instrumentalist says the scientist merely aims at the prediction and control of phenomena. For instance, Milton Friedman denies that the falsehood of assumptions is relevant, explaining that "theory is to be judged by its predictive power for the class of phenomena which it is intended to explain" (1953, 8). Even false predictions are tolerable—as long as they occur outside the intended range of the theory. Given that scientists are indifferent to the truth and often believe idealizations will promote prediction and control, the instrumentalist predicts that the scientists will idealize.

Consequently, idealization looks like a crucial experiment for philosophy of science. The instrumentalist predicts that scientists idealize. The realist predicts they do not. Since scientists idealize, the instrumentalist prevails.

The instrumentalist deserves extra credit if his prediction is correct. For his prediction is bold. It reveals at least one false premise in the syllogism: Explanation implies understanding. Understanding implies truth. Therefore, idealization is never explanatory.

Catherine Elgin (2004) specifically rejects the second premise. She feels no need to substitute *truths* that could serve as the objects of understanding.

She analyzes idealizations *directly* as felicitous falsehoods. Elgin struggles to reconcile her liberality with the practice of debunking "explanations" by exposing the falsehood of their premises. There is a graveyard of explanations founded on phlogiston, coronium, and ether. They were pronounced dead because their existence implications were false. Falsehood is also the diagnosis for the zombie explanations propounded by pseudo-scientists.

Perhaps Catherine Elgin would find the following compromise congenial. Concede to the debunkers that understanding is factive when the explanation indispensably relies on *asserted* premises. But deny that understanding always relies solely on *asserted* premises. An explanation that relies merely on supposition is not jeopardized by falsehood. Consider *reductio ad absurdum* explanations in mathematics. Euclid explained why there is no largest prime number by assuming there is a largest prime number. Or consider W. K. Clifford's (1901, 100) conditional proof explanation of why there is a size limit for organisms. He supposes that there are cubical organisms that absorb nutrients through their surfaces. Since the ratio of the organism's volume to surface area grows at geometric rate, the organism must use more and more surfaces to maintain its mass. After all the sides are used, the organism must stop growing.

Since suppositions clearly contribute to understanding within mathematics while false assertions at most yield instructive misunderstandings, we acquire an "off the shelf" account of why *asserted* falsehoods are explanatorily malignant but *supposed* falsehoods are benign.

Historically, scientific realists have employed an expanding circle of increasingly flexible propositional attitudes. Aristotle demanded *knowledge*. Fallibilists thought this insistence on strict demonstration was excessive; they relaxed the requirement to rational belief. Probabilists took the further step of diluting attitude into *degrees of belief* and explicating rationality with probability theory. Karl Popper made the case for falsifiable guesses in *Conjectures and Refutation* (1963)

Supposition is the next step in this march toward detachment. Previous steps were often coupled with repression of the old attitudes. The probabilists cast Aristotle's insistence on knowledge as dogmatic. Popper casts the probabilists as confusing physics with metaphysics. Since I am modeling my realism on the proofs in logic textbooks, I am compelled to include assertion alongside supposition. No suppositional proof is possible without this attitudinal pluralism. At the very least, the conclusion must be asserted. And much of the interest of conditional proof depends on the prospect of an eventual *modus ponens* or *modus tollens* (purely assertoric argument forms).

The major aim of my model is defensive. I wish to disarm the threat posed by idealization. However, I also wish to add a minor positive argument in favor of scientific realism: It is the only view that accommodates the small but significant amount of functional lying that does occur in science. Instrumentalists oversolve the problem of idealization by precluding all lying in science.

I finish this essay with examples of veridical idealizations. They show that idealization does not reveal any scientific role for deliberately false *assertions*. The concept of veridical idealization serves as memorable damper on the analogy between idealization and lying.

1. NATURE OF SUPPOSITION

Scientific realism is compatible with classical logic. Classical logic has inference patterns in which a premise is temporarily assumed for the sake of argument:

Conditional Proof	*Reductio ad Absurdum*
1. Suppose P.	1. Suppose P.
2. From P derive Q.	2. From P derive some contradiction.
3. Conclude that if P then Q.	3. Conclude not-P.

In contrast to an assertoric proof, only the conclusion is asserted in a suppositional proof.

Proofs commonly incorporate a mixture of asserted premises and suppositional premises. Logicians segregate each suppositional branch by indentation (or brackets). The indented statements are inactivated; they cannot license unindented steps in the derivation.

Thanks to the salience of indentation, a student in the back of the lecture hall can spot a suppositional section of a proof even if he is too far away to discern the fine print. The ensuing detachment from the truth can be understood even if the student's autism makes him incapable of make-believe (Stanley 2001). Supposition requires no departure from literality. An autistic student who is baffled by idioms, proverbs, and metaphors may be fluent in the idealizations of Euclid, Archimedes, and Isaac Newton. Indeed, many autistic students excel in mathematics, physics, and engineering (Baron-Cohen et al. 2007). It is also striking that their empathic peers are often poor at supposition. Pragmatic proficiency pollutes suppositional reasoning with conversational implicatures only appropriate to *testimony*.

Effective supposition draws on systematicity rather than empathy. The empathic are self-conscious about their inferential promiscuity. They compensate by adopting the perspective of the rigidly literal thinker (the dual of the autistic strategy of "hacking into" the social world by adopting strategies such as behavioral mirroring, memorizing social scripts, and applying maxims of politeness).

Although the rules for conditional proof fluently elucidate supposition within a mathematical context, the rules are too permissive for counterfactuals (Lewis 1973, 31–36). In a mathematical conditional proof, we may add any previously asserted premise to the reasoning under the scope of the supposition. This would be disastrous for a counterfactual that has a demonstrably false antecedent. If the negation of this antecedent has been derived at a previous stage, it can mix with a supposition of the antecedent. The ensuing contradiction trivializes the suppositional reasoning.

Counterfactuals force restrictions on many classic inference rules: strengthening the antecedent, contraposition, and transitivity become problematic. These classic rules work well for material conditionals and, indeed, for any *constantly* strict conditional. But *variably* strict conditionals create subtle problems that ignite diagnostic controversies. These complications prevent logic textbooks from constituting a perfectly general, operational account of the nature of supposition. The textbooks also fail to address the psychological and pragmatic aspects of suppositions.

2. SUPPOSITION CONTRASTED WITH BELIEF

The propositional *attitudes* underlying the speech acts of assertion and supposition have divergent characters. Belief is involuntary. With no more control than a compass needle that points north, belief points toward truth.

The needle of supposition is neutral. The freedom with which we suppose makes us slavishly suggestible at a superficial level. You cannot resist my command "Suppose there is a largest prime number". The only defiance you can muster is a refusal to invest inferential energy. Even this passive resistance requires techniques of self-distraction that are apt to be swamped by automatic mental processes. Natural selection has favored parents who actively deduce threats to their naïve offspring—even though they often find this preoccupation distressing (and eventually annoying to their maturing children).

Perhaps delusion is more a matter of runaway supposition than runaway belief. The delusion is a "given" that requires no evidence to initiate and cannot be disconfirmed by evidence—yet it is capable of incorporating new evidence (thanks to reasoning that involves a mixture of assertion and supposition). Suppositions are incorrigible—except for the failures of expression known as "slips of the tongue". Tellingly, the deluded will acquiesce when they have *misarticulated* their delusion.

The involuntariness of beliefs explains why beliefs do not vary with context. You cannot believe there is a largest prime number for one purpose and believe there is no largest prime for another purpose.

Belief is also sensitive to peer disagreement. News that we disagree over a calculation demonstrates that at least one of us mishandled the evidence. If we believe that there is no difference in our reliability, then we both lose belief in our respective conclusions. David Christensen (2007) argues that philosophers should have a parallel loss of confidence in their philosophical opinions (because there is almost always a peer who disagrees). However, when philosophers are merely varying in what they *suppose,* they ought to be undeterred by diversity.

Supposition is permissive. Belief is not (White 2005). When neighboring logic students discover that they have made different suppositions in a proof, the news has the same significance as the discovery that they walked different paths from the same dormitory to reach the classroom. The variation does not entail any error. There is only pressure to make the same supposition when the reasoners are engaged in a joint project that demands coordination. The strategies for eliciting this convergence contrast with the strategies for eliciting agreement. For instance, I can appeal to the consequences of the supposition to justify making it: "There is extra credit for those who use conditional proof" or "The instructor will think you lazy if you resort to *reductio ad absurdum*". But I cannot persuade you to *believe* there is a largest prime number with "Your mother will be pleased if you believe there is a largest prime". Nor is belief responsive to the inducement of collateral truth: "If you adopt the false belief that productive researchers go to Heaven, then you work diligently and discover many new truths". Belief has the same myopia as natural selection, never having the foresight to take one step back to take two steps forward.

Supposition is an arena for style, taste, and panache. For there is genuine choice. Supposition is to belief as cooking is to digestion.

Beliefs are grandiose, aspiring to an ideal of agglomeration (enshrined in Jaakko Hintikka's (1962) "doxastic logic" as the principle that belief collects over conjunction: From [Bp & Bq] infer B[p & q]). Beliefs *ought* to fit together in a coherent whole. This synoptic ambition is in tension with the requirement that belief be sensitive to the risk of error. Since small chances of error commonly add up to a big chance of error, a conjunction of beliefs does not entail that there is a belief in that conjunction. Thus the author of a book has grounds to apologize in the preface for the errors that are bound to be in the text (Makinson 1965).

No such humility is in order for the author of a conditional proof. Suppositions are noncommittal, so no risk is taken. This is a different type of safety than offered by stipulated truth. Confidence is not an issue for the supposer because he is not taking a stand on the supposition's truth-value. When the geographers at the 1884 International Meridian Conference stipulated that the prime meridian for longitude and timekeeping passes through the center of the transit instrument at the Greenwich Observatory in the United Kingdom, they believed what they stipulated. Had they merely supposed the proposition, no belief would ensue. A successful stipulation yields truth by convention. A successful supposition yields truth by proof— the truth of the conclusion, not the supposition. Supposition is altruistic. Stipulation is narcissistic.

Suppositions agglomerate in the sense that supposing P and then making the subordinate supposition Q in the same is equivalent to supposing P and Q. However, suppositions do not agglomerate when made independently. If I suppose P to deduce R and then suppose not-P to deduce S, then I have not thereby supposed P & not-P.

These points about agglomeration show that supposition cannot be reduced to belief in conditionals—contrary to Peter Langland-Hassan

(2011). Beliefs in conditionals fail to agglomerate because of the standard concern about accumulated uncertainties. Suppositions agglomerate unreservedly with their subordinate suppositions and *sharply* resist agglomeration with their independent suppositions. (And the resistance is *not* based on a gradual accumulation of risk.)

We attribute belief only when we wish to attribute potential reasoning. This means a capacity for conditional proof and *reductio ad absurdum*. The reasoner wishes to make valid inferences. So we need to picture the reasoner as being able to pose a suppositional question: "Suppose the premises are true; does the conclusion follow?" The attribution of belief and supposition comes as an inseparable package. Given this unbreakable bond, there is no parsimonious advantage in scrimping with only belief.

As Donald Davidson (1975) notes when dwelling on our difficulties at avoiding oversophistication of animal beliefs, *content* tends to be holistic; attributing a little content pressures attribution of ancillary content. A related holism extends to propositional *attitudes*; attributing one attitude pressures the attribution of ancillary attitudes. The attitudes work *together*, like fingers on a hand. Idealization relaxes the fist of science, exposing the opposable thumb of supposition.

I may suppose a hypothesis for one purpose and suppose its negation for another purpose—perhaps just to demonstrate the consequence is independent of the hypothesis. In a conditional proof, you assume as many premises as you please and conjoin them at your discretion. There is no need to be thrifty because the result does not depend on the truth of the suppositions. The only pressure to economize comes from the three surviving Gricean maxims that apply to supposition: Only suppose what is germane (Relevance), only as much as needed to support the conclusion (Quantity), and in an orderly way (Manner). The only maxim orphaned by supposition is the maxim of quality (say only what is true).

The aim of supposition is success, not truth (although there is an indirect concern for the truth of its *conclusion*). The attitude of supposition is under the reasoner's control. Although unfettered by truth, supposition is still corrigible. There can be a slip in which one fails to suppose what one intended to suppose. The physicist Murray Gell-Mann (1994, 263) credits a discovery about strange particle decay to a slip of the tongue. He was explaining why his earlier hypothesis failed. Gell-Mann intended to say, "Suppose I = 5/2", but instead he said, "Suppose I = 1". This should have been a nonstarter because the only admissible values for baryons were assumed to be integral values of a half such as 1/2, 3/2, 5/2, and so on. But having blurted out "I = 1" Gell-Mann recognized its correctness.

David Hume correctly denied that there is an ethics of belief. Belief is involuntary. One cannot choose what to believe.

There is an ethics of supposition. One can choose to make a denigrating supposition. The nineteenth-century opponent of natural selection, Fleming Jenkins, imagines a white sailor shipwrecked on an island of blacks. Strength of numbers will prevent this island's race from turning white—or even yellow. Jenkins' supposition can be criticized as an action. Racist beliefs, in contrast, are merely *symptomatic* of immorality.

Richard Feynman was once picketed by feminists for a hypothetical example involving a female motorist who challenges a police officer's definition of "speed".

> "Why did it have to be a woman driver?" they said. "You are implying that all women are bad drivers."
>
> "But the woman makes the cop look bad," I said. "Why aren't you concerned about the cop?"
>
> "That's what you expect from cops!" one of the protesters said. "They're all pigs!"
>
> "But you *should* be concerned," I said. "I forgot to say in the story that the cop was a woman!" (Feynman 1988, 75)

The content of a supposition can be supplemented at will. The content of belief is fixed by the evidence.

Unlike fantasy, a supposition is intended to coerce a belief. Suppositions support assertions, never the reverse, for suppositions need no evidential support. A supposition cannot be criticized for being false, improbable, or unprovable.

Nor can suppositions be criticized for being jointly inconsistent. A mathematician can give one conditional proof based on the supposition that the solution is an even number and another conditional proof based on the supposition that the solution is an odd number. The arguments are co-propoundable. Suppositional proofs are pluralistic. When a Bayesian wants to demonstrate how updating generates consensus, he will arbitrarily stipulate a variety of initial probabilities just to illustrate how divergent prior probabilities must converge on the same posterior probability.

New evidence that an assertion is true always provides further reason to assert it. New evidence that a supposition is true does not always provide further reason to suppose it. Indeed, news of the truth of Fermat's theorem provided decisive reason for some mathematicians to abandon their attempt to disprove the theorem by *reductio ad absurdum arguments*.

Our interest in suppositional proof is explained by our *general* interest in conditionals and impossibility theorems. Suppositional proof is topic-neutral. If we model idealization as a premise of a purely assertoric proof, then the idealization will take on the air of a lie or fiction or metaphor or something even less well understood. Happily, idealization is an instance of something logicians understand well: the supposition that initiates conditional proof and *reductio ad absurdum*.

The versatility of suppositional proof explains why idealizations take such heterogeneous forms. Michael Weisberg is too pessimistic when he says that the disparate motives for idealizations splinter them in such a way

> that some classic, epistemic questions about idealizations will not have unitary answers. We cannot expect a single answer to questions such

as: What exactly constitutes idealization? Is idealization compatible with realism? Are idealization and abstraction distinct? Should theorists work to eliminate idealizations as science progresses? Are there rules governing the rational use of idealization, or should a theorist's intuition alone guide the process? (2007, 639)

The distinction between supposition and assertion allows us to be lumpers rather than splitters, answering all the questions Weisberg abandons.

Here are my answers: Idealization is constituted by suppositions that are pitched toward our strengths (pattern recognition, cheater detection, belief-desire psychology) and away from our weaknesses (meager working memory, bias, wishful thinking). Idealizers seek tractability, memorability, and transmissibility (rather like myth makers). Since logicians supply validity conditions for conditional proof and *reductio ad absurdum*, there are rules governing the rational use of idealization. In addition to explaining how idealizations get quarantined from assertoric reasoning, the rules generate surprising predictions—such as the existence of sub-idealizations corresponding to subordinate suppositions. Suppositions are topic-neutral so there is no restriction to abstractions. Since suppositional reasoning is perfectly satisfactory even by mathematical standards, there is no general need to eliminate idealization. For instance, mathematicians have no reductive program against suppositional proof. However, not all proofs are explanatory. For instance, computers tend to be addicted to *reductio ad absurdum* because it plays to their strength—brute force. Their rambling *reductios* do not generate the orgasmic "Aha!" of understanding. So human beings prefer direct proofs—which have a stronger tendency to satisfy Gricean maxims of relevance and manner. But as with all proofs, explanation is a supererogatory service.

An idealization that succeeds as proof may fail as explanation. This distinction accounts for our ambivalence toward "minimal idealizations". These strip down the causal story to just its most potent causal factors. Minimal idealizations tend to be misleading as explanations because of the implicature that all of the factors are represented. The misled economist concludes that all people are selfish because the rational pursuit of self-interest explains the bulk of social science effects.

3. MISCONCEIVING IDEALIZATION AS ATTENUATED ASSERTION

Weisberg defines idealization as "the intentional introduction of distortion into scientific theories" (2007, 639). Just as the falsehood of a lie is no accident, the falsehood of an idealization is deliberate. The falsehood is not a mistake or a side effect. Weisberg says all of this as a *proponent* of scientific realism.

In *How the Laws of Physics Lie*, Nancy Cartwright (1983) characterizes the idealizations as falsehoods that help make laws applicable. She takes this much as common ground with realists.

Historically, Cartwright's claim of common ground is all too correct. Realists comply with the assumption that idealization involves assertion—albeit of some attenuated sort.

Ernan McMullin (1985) treats idealizations as, in effect, *temporary* assertions of falsehoods. After Galileo simplifies a situation to untangle various causal influences, he successively reintroduces complexities, returning to a more and more realistic situation. For instance, to attain a more accurate description of the cannonball's descent the scientist can begin with its rate of descent in a vacuum and then consider its rates in thicker and thicker media. The lies get closer and closer to the truth.

McMullin's analysis appeals to the ideal of verisimilitude. At first blush, this ideal is directly relevant because assertions aim at truth. It is self-defeating to say, "p is false but I assert that p". However, it is also self-defeating to say, "p is merely close to the truth but I assert p". So the hitch is that assertion is perfectionist; mere proximity to the truth is not close enough.

Converting to Karl Popper's *Conjectures and Refutations* (1963) will not provide relief. Guessing is also perfectionist because it also aims at truth. It is self-defeating to say, "'All prime numbers are odd' is merely close to the truth but I guess that all prime numbers are odd".

Verisimilitude does permit us to rank some false *assertions* over other false *assertions*. The smaller the deviation from the truth, the easier a correction that will yield full truth. Smaller deviations from the truth tend to generate less severe consequences than larger deviations. (Thus a lie that is closer to truth is preferred over a lie that is far from the truth.) Verisimilitude is especially instructive when there is a feedback mechanism that allows us to "home in".

However, this rationale for verisimilitude does not directly extend to suppositions. A false supposition is not an error. For suppositions do not aim at truth. There is no self-defeat in a mathematician saying, "'There is no largest prime' is true but I hereby suppose that there is a largest prime".

A supposition with low verisimilitude (or none at all in the case of a *reductio ad absurdum*) can support a conclusion with high verisimilitude. For some purposes (such as preparing for a potential *modus ponens* inference), one might prefer suppositions that have a high degree of verisimilitude. But this would not yield a general account of suppositional proof.

Instrumentalists are unimpressed by the fact that realists can rummage through the history of science and find many instances of "Galilean idealization". Instrumentalists correctly object to McMullin that often there is no "homing in" on the truth. For instance, in population biology, theories are confirmed by the fact that the leading models converge on their predictions for purely hypothetical data.

> Then, if these models, despite their different assumptions, lead to similar results, we have what we can call a robust theorem that is relatively free of the details of the model. Hence, our truth is the intersection of independent lies. (Levins 1966, 20)

As a champion of robustness analysis, Michael Weisberg (2006) should readily agree that conditional proof can yield results that do not owe their interest merely as potential premises of an assertoric proof. A theory can be confirmed or disconfirmed by virtue of which conditionals it entails. Conditional proof has epistemic autonomy.

Theoreticians can be just as minimal. Ernst Ising modeled atoms and molecules as points along a line that could be in one of two states. He wanted a simple method of studying the ferromagnetic properties of metals. Ising's strategy was to ignore all but the most predicatively potent factors. Since the goal is simplicity rather than fidelity, it would be counterproductive to add factors in the pursuit of verisimilitude.

Idealizers commonly introduce falsehoods that they have no plans to "correct". With a disturbing resemblance to speculative philosophers, physicists assert hypotheticals whose antecedents are impossible. (Newton's first law says that an undisturbed object will continue in its state of motion or rest, yet the law of universal gravitation precludes undisturbed objects). Or consider the resilience of Archimedes' law of the lever: "Magnitudes are in equilibrium at distances reciprocally proportional to their weights". Einstein's speed limit on causal processes rules out perfectly rigid objects. But Archimedes' laws linger after this impossibility proof.

Some idealizations improve empirical adequacy beyond what any realistic interpretation affords. Scientists persist in appealing to centrifugal force and the Coriolis force when their fictive status is common knowledge.

In addition to providing a permanent home for forces that do not exist, physicists deliberately cultivate diversity in their idealizations. When an experimenter proves a result, he tries to replicate it with very different experimental apparatus. This variety shows that result is not an artifact of one approach. Levins (1966) describes three evolutionary models that all imply that "in an uncertain environment species will evolve broad niches and tend toward polymorphism".

But physicists go beyond the pursuit of variety and on to mutually inconsistent models—which are then simultaneously applied (Morrison 2000). The liquid drop model of the atomic nucleus is based on the analogy with a (charged) fluid drop. The shell model derives the nucleus' properties from those of the constituent protons and neutrons. The underlying strategy cannot be that the point of departure is close to the truth.

Levins goes further, audaciously *preferring* that the sources apply conflicting sub-methodologies:

> The multiplicity of models is imposed by the contradictory demands of a complex, heterogeneous nature and a mind that can only cope with a few variables at time: by the contradictory desiderata of generality, realism, and precision: by the need to understand and also to control: even by the opposing esthetic standards which emphasize the stark simplicity and power of a general theorem as against the richness and the

diversity of living nature. These conflicts are irreconcilable. Therefore, the alternative approaches even of contending schools are part of larger mixed strategy. But the conflict is about method, not nature, for the individual models which, while they are essential for understanding reality, should not be confused with that reality itself. (1966, 26)

Levins' case for multiple modeling is reminiscent of rationales for devil's advocacy. But instead of assigning the advocate a conclusion to defend, we assign a methodology.

Competing theoretical desiderata (generality, accuracy, simplicity, specificity, and so on) impose pressure on the scientist. It is impossible to satisfy this constituency. Any particular model will be forced to make trade-offs. And there is often no uniquely best trade-off. So these desiderata are best satisfied by having many models making different trade-offs.

4. THE LYING METAPHOR

Scientists do lie in their role as scientists (not just when engaged in professional misconduct). In 1856, the British Surveyor General of India, Andrew Waugh calculated that Mount Everest had a height of exactly 29,000 feet. But to avoid the impression that this was just a round estimate, Waugh publically announced the height as 29,002 feet. Social psychologists routinely lie to experimental subjects (Hertwig and Ortmann 2008, 64–67). Compilers of mathematical tables insert a few slight errors "as a trap for would-be plagiarists" (L. J. Comrie, quoted by Bowden 1953, 4). Historians of medicine use false names and confound circumstances to protect the privacy of patients (Mukherjee 2010, xiv). These genuine lies *support* scientific realism and *refute* instrumentalism. For these functional lies should be impossible if scientists never make assertions in their role as scientists. Actors cannot lie on stage because they cannot assert. Scientists can lie (while conforming to their role as scientists) and so are making assertions.

The title of Nancy Cartwright's *How the Laws of Physics Lie* (1983) intimates that the lies go to the heart of science. If we neglect the distinction between asserting and supposing, the lying metaphor will look alarmingly apt. Idealization will resemble a noble lie—a foundational falsehood told for the sake of a higher end.

We have seen how Ernan McMullin excuses idealization as a temporary false assertion that will be subsequently ameliorated by falsehoods that are closer and closer to the truth. Another excuse for a lie is that it was a *forced* assertion. Consider the cartographer's slogan "All maps lie". There is too much going on to be accurately represented. So the cartographer is forced to offer a distorted picture. Similarly, an idealizer is forced to radically simplify. Like the cartographer, he should compensate by offering a diversified portfolio of idealizations. Fredrich Nietzsche pictures all scientists as in the cartographer's dilemma and defends their lies as the price of insight.

In *Scientific Perspectivism* (2006), Ronald Giere interprets idealizers as making *relativized* assertions. Instead of asserting p they assert from the vantage point of a model. Models are like obligatory lenses (or the bacteriologist's staining of specimens—or color vision itself). One can never gaze at reality directly. Absolute assertion is a myth. Thus Giere avoids Nietzsche's literal attribution of lying while agreeing with Nietzsche's claim that interests and convention color scientific descriptions.

Giere has oversolved the problem. Cartographers protect their copyright by including trap streets and slight magnitude errors. These are literal lies that are not washed away by relativization to a perspective. These are among the asserted features of the map.

Perspectivalists overlook the fact that suppositions are discharged to support straight assertions. The conclusion of a conditional proof or *reductio ad absurdum* is not made from the perspective of the supposition. It is a flat-out assertion.

Michael Strevens regards idealizations as *indirect* assertions—hyperbole in which the truth is conveyed by falsehood. To idealize away X (gravity, friction, air resistance, electrical influences) is to indirectly deny that X is significant for the purpose at hand. Idealizations are like pointers about tactfulness; they tell us what ought to be ignored. We can ignore small inaccuracies (because they will not accumulate). We can ignore random errors (because they cancel out). And we can ignore some biases (because the direction of the bias is *against* the conclusion).

However, Strevens overlooks the distinction between what a modeler assumes and what his model actually entails. Consider one of Strevens' own illustrations, in which he notes that

> in explaining the appearance of a rainbow, it is assumed that raindrops are perfect spheres. . . . In fact, local forces will tend to deform the drops slightly. By assuming zero deformation, the model asserts that deformations within the normal range make no difference to the existence of rainbows. (Strevens 2008, 322)

The modeler may be assuming that zero deformation makes no difference but his model implies that a perfect sphere would trap the light in an internal reflection. Some deformation is essential to allow light to exit the drop.

Too much smoothing maroons us on a frictionless plane. We need a little grit to proceed. For instance, game theory inadvertently exaggerates the difficulties of coordination problems by idealizing away the little deviations from perfect symmetry that help create salient options. In cosmology, a little asymmetry between matter and antimatter is needed to answer "Why is there *now* something rather than nothing?"

A direct reading of "assuming zero deformations" and other idealizations is needed to explain how they can backfire. If the idealizers were indirectly asserting that the size of the deformation is insignificant, then an overidealization objection would be based on misinterpretations of the indirect speech act (as when pragmatically impaired individuals overlook sarcasm and earnestly object, "The opposite is true!").

Finally, there are theories that treat idealizations as *pretend* assertions (Toon 2010). An idealization is akin to a story. In David Lewis' account of fiction, the storyteller must pretend to meet the requirements of testimony:

> The author purports to be telling the truth about matters he has somehow come to know about, though how he has found about them is left unsaid. That is why there is a pragmatic paradox akin to contradiction in a third person narrative that ends ' . . . and so none were left to tell the tale'. (1983, 266)

The narrator feigns compliance with Grice's maxim of quality.

Kendall Walton (1990) emphasizes the epistemic role of props. If any stump counts as a bear, then the discovery of a new stump constitutes the discovery of a new bear. Thus empirical discoveries can be incorporated into a game of make-believe. Scientists do resemble children when manipulating scale models.

However, supposition differs from pretend assertion in that the supposer does not pretend to meet the epistemological obligations of assertion. Suppose that the strong force were 2% stronger. Then there would be no stable hydrogen and therefore no stars and therefore none of the chemical diversity essential to life. It would be self-defeating for the physicist to feign knowledge that this supposition is true.

A second difference is that supposition is a component of a suppositional proof. A pretend assertion does not figure in this argument form.

The epistemology of supposition is forward looking. The supposer must be ready to answer "What will this prove?" The epistemology of assertion is backward looking. The asserter must be able to cite the basis for his claim (in readiness for the challenge "How do you know?").

5. THE MYTH OF FALSEHOOD

The popularity of "Idealizations must be false" is partly manifested by how often the lying metaphor is echoed. The principle figures centrally in attempts to define idealization and to differentiate idealization from other phenomena.

There is some variation in whether the falsehood is conceived as known, actual, or merely asserted. Martin R. Jones writes, "My starting point, then, is the suggestion that we should take idealization to require the assertion of a falsehood, and take abstraction to involve the omission of a truth" (2005, 175). Notice how Jones' distinction between idealization and abstraction mirrors the distinction between lying and misleading (in which relevant truth is omitted). The misleader deflects his conversational wrongdoing from a violation of maxim quality ("Say what is true") to a violation of manner ("Say what is relevant").

Andreas Hüttemann wields *known falsehood* as the criterion to distinguish idealizations from hypotheses: "A hypothesis may turn out to be wrong: an idealization is known to be wrong (if it concerns theoretical assumptions)" (2002, 178). What about cases in which the physicist is agnostic about the truth-value of his assumption? Hüttemann categorizes these cases as neither idealization nor hypotheses. Consider textbook authors discussing the assumption of a quadratic potential:

> [It] is not made out of strong conviction in its general validity, but on grounds of analytical necessity. It leads to a simple theory—the harmonic approximation—from which precise quantitative results can be extracted. (Ashcroft and Mermin 1976, 422)

Hüttemann dutifully applies his falsehood requirement: "The above-mentioned procedure is—strictly speaking—not an idealization because it is not *known* to be false. It is, however, not a clear case of a hypothesis either, since it is not invoked because it is assumed to be true" (Hüttemann 2002, 183; emphasis in the text).

The belief that idealizations must be false (or known to be false or believed to be false or asserted to be false) is related to the myth that the antecedents of subjunctive conditionals ("counterfactuals") must be false. Specialists on counterfactuals reject this. For instance, under David Lewis' possible worlds analysis of counterfactuals, a counterfactual is true if its consequent is true in the nearest possible world in which the antecedent is true. Since modal proximity is measured in terms of similarity, and anything is perfectly similar to itself, a counterfactual with a true antecedent is true if its consequent is true (Lewis 1973, 36–38).

Absence of representation as truth differs from representation of an absence of truth. The idealizer has not switched from asserting truths to asserting falsehoods. He has switched from asserting to supposing.

One heuristic for relevance is actuality. This encourages fallacious assimilation of suppositions to digressions. Since scientists are anxious to emphasize actuality (especially when drawing contrasts with religion, metaphysics, and morality), suppositions can seem out of place in scientific discourse. Scientists tend to assume that the only point of asserting a conditional is in the hope of performing a future *modus ponens* or *modus tollens*. Thus they infer that a conditional with an antecedent which is known to be false must be useless as an instrument of inquiry (even if it has merit as entertainment or consolation). So when scientists realize that they themselves assert many such conditionals in the laboratory, they experience the counterexamples as anomalies.

The anomaly is resolved by two epistemological truisms. First, people are modest enough to realize that some of their self-attributions of knowledge are fallible and so they may later employ a conditional that they currently regard as having an antecedent that they know to be false. Second, conditionals can be used to replicate the reasoning of people who do not know as much as the replicator—those ignorant of the fact that p will act on conditionals that have not-p as an antecedent. So even if conditionals were only useful as inference tickets, many of them would continue to be serviceable despite some people knowing that the antecedent is false and so could not figure in a sound *modus ponens* interest.

6. VACUOUS CONDITIONALS

As a matter of fact, conditionals can be instructive even when the falsehood of their antecedents is common knowledge:

Humphry Davy: If Michael Faraday is awake, then he is in the laboratory.
Mrs. Davy: If that is true, Faraday is diligent.

After they learn that Faraday is asleep, Humphry Davy's conditional continues to be informative for the reason Mrs. Davy extracts with her embedded conditional.

Employment opportunities for vacuous conditionals expand when they migrate from deductive to inductive arguments. Take the appeal to verisimilitude:

If P then Q.
P is close to the truth.
Therefore, Q is close to the truth.

Although the premises do not entail the conclusion, the argument has inductive strength. Consider this instance:

If the earth is a sphere, then its surface area is 4π times the square of the earth's radius.
"The earth is a sphere" is close to the truth.
Therefore, "The surface area of the earth is 4π times the square of its radius" is close to the truth.

Little differences rarely make a significant difference. So the premises make the conclusion probable.

Knowing what can be safely ignored is sometimes a purely empirical matter. But often these parameters for a thought experiment can themselves be illuminated by thought experiment.

Consider the question of when small objects can be safely substituted for large ones. At height n the surface of a cube is $6 \times n^2$ but its volume balloons to n^3. So the rate at which size matters increases with the number of relevant dimensions. Since shadows only involve the side facing the light source, a small cube may safely substitute for a big cube. But *heating* an object involves its entire mass. Architects can safely shadow model a cubical building with a miniature cube but thermal modeling will be much more distortive.

Standards also matter. For some purposes, we will need more accuracy and so need to accommodate the fact that the earth's spin makes it bulge in the middle. But we can deal with this with another round of idealization: Suppose that the earth is an oblate sphere . . .

7. VERIDICAL SUPPOSITIONS

A supposition can be true even if the speaker regards it as absurd. When asked whether zero is odd or even, some people treat the question as an invitation to fantasy. They hear the question as a subjunctive conditional: "If zero were odd or even, which would it be?"—akin to "If women were numbers, would they be odd or even?" Good-natured conversationalists whimsically extrapolate from principles such as "Odd and even numbers alternate" and answer "Zero would be even". They are surprised that mathematicians endorse their recreational reasoning as a sound argument.

Suppositions are sometimes guided by processes that are more reliable than their supposers realize. As illustrated by blind sight and subliminal perception, common sense and introspection underestimate the accuracy of perceptions made under poor conditions. A precipitous decline in reliability is exaggerated into complete unreliability. Presentations of words can be so fleeting (when displayed by a tachistoscope) that there is no conscious awareness of perception. Yet when forced to conjecture on how a word is to be completed, the subject's "wild guesses" are fairly accurate (substantially less accurate than in full exposures but still far better than chance). Although people are usually overconfident, they are underconfident about their peripheral vision, their ability to recognize people from behind, and their acuity in low illumination.

Idealizations always take place against a suite of background beliefs that hedge commitment to the assumption. Relative to these pessimistic but contingent concessions, the idealization should be false. When these inhibiting background beliefs are mistaken, the idealizations can be surprisingly accurate.

8. IDEALS AND THE PEAK SHIFT EFFECT

Some of these background beliefs are general. After physicists discovered that stimuli were continuous, they characterized normal perception as systematically misleading because the senses lump phenomena into categories. For instance, it is impossible to paint a realistic looking rainbow without grouping the colors in bands. Consequently, the physicists apologized for this distortion in their illustrations of rainbows. They believed the categories were conventional and that anthropologists would discover cultural variation in color perception.

After Berlin and Kay (1969) presented surprising evidence that the categories were culturally universal, psychologists reconsidered what is really entailed by the physical continuity of the light spectrum. Many began to regard the pictures of the rainbows as accurate.

The physicists were influenced by the idea that colors are secondary qualities. The perceiver makes a contribution to color reality—not a distortion. The ideal becomes real.

Consider speech perception. According to the motor theory, we perceive spoken words by identifying the vocal tract gestures that originate them. When you listen to me talk, you empathically match what you heard with how you would try to produce my sounds. Your matching repertoire comes in discrete categories. Therefore, you reconstruct the sounds as discrete even if they are continuous. For instance, since you can only articulate *ba*'s and *pa*'s, you hear only *ba*'s and *pa*'s, but nothing in between (despite the sounds varying along the voicing continuum). So you exaggerate the similarities within a category and exaggerate the differences between categories.

When you listen to sounds as speech, you figure out how you would have produced those sounds. Since you pick from discrete options, the precise menu sharpens rough vocalizations. The ideal shapes what is heard.

Metaphysicians have postulated many types of ideals that would make idealization reliable. Plato buttressed our suppositions with a realm of forms. James Brown (1991) modernizes this infrastructure to accommodate thought experiments in physics. Brian Ellis (2009) contends that idealizations work because nature is organized into a hierarchy of natural kinds. They distill essences.

Many idealizers have doubts about such ideals and so curb their expectations. If their doubts turn out to be ill-founded, then the doubters will be pleasantly surprised by how frequently their idealizations are veridical.

There are general grounds for the power of ideals. Train an animal to distinguish between a positive and a negative stimulus. Interestingly, an extreme (and unprecedented and even unrealistic) version of the positive stimulus will then elicit a stronger response than the positive stimulus itself! This shift in maximal responding is called "peak shift" by learning theorists. This robust result from learning theory suggests that some idealizations may exploit the peak shift effect.

Consider Plato's fascination with the forms. No one sees a perfect cube so how could the Greeks come to value the perfect cube over (ir)regular cubes? Answer: Peak shift to a physically impossible cube. Our spatial vocabulary itself might be a tool chest for peak shift effects.

Psychologists have used the peak shift effect to explain the effectiveness of caricatures (Rhodes 1997). Mild distortions of a photograph improve the judged fidelity of the photograph and are more effective for recognition of the person from the photograph. Stronger distortions undermine the fidelity but do not undermine the improvement in recognition. The effects can be measured quantitatively because of improvements in morphing software. The peak shift may explain why we recognize patterns more easily from idealizations than from realistic descriptions.

9. BACKGROUND BELIEFS ABOUT DEPICTION

A physicist's beliefs about how pictures are composed will influence whether he regards them as distortions. This background will interact with the physicist's foreground beliefs about the phenomena in question.

In 1537, Walter Ryff published *Geometrical Gunnery*. His front piece depicts a town under artillery fire (Dijksterhuis 1961, 271). The trajectories of the cannonballs are indistinguishable from ellipses.

But turn the page. The reader discovers that Ryff regards the illustration as a simplification. He is a neo-Aristotelian. Ryff believes that the actual path is tripartite: During the first stage of flight, the ball travels straight because of the impetus of the exploding gunpowder. The second stage of flight is circular because the ebbing, forced motion competes with the natural motion of the ball. Third, after the impetus is exhausted, the ball travels wholly naturally—straight down toward the center of the earth.

Ryff regards the elliptical paths of the artist's cannonballs as aesthetic concessions. The eye prefers a gentle curve to a sharp angle. Accordingly, the artist rounds out the trajectory.

The fact that Ryff's elliptical idealization is correct does not, in itself, disarm the threat posed by idealization. Given that Ryff aims to describe the true path of projectiles, we are still left wondering why he illustrates with a path that he *believes* to be a false path.

The veridical nature of the idealization helps by shifting the question to a more tractable one: Given that Ryff aims to describe the true path of projectiles, why does he illustrate with a *supposed* path. The question gets easier by transcending distractions: Why do *describers* ever resort to *supposing*?

At an operational level, the answer can be found in the well-established practice of conditional proof and *reductio ad absurdum*. Their relevance can be amplified by noting that idealization occurs in logic and mathematics. At an etiological level, David Barnett (2010) gives a rational reconstruction of how the practice of supposition would grow out of a language community that initially lacked the practice.

10. SUB-IDEALIZATIONS

Suppositional proofs may contain embedded suppositions (so we should expect sub-idealizations).

After Johannes Kepler became convinced that the orbits of the planets are not circular, he concluded that the planets are not under the total control of the sun. Each planet has a degree of self-locomotion—and so must have a soul. On the basis of some preliminary curve fitting and perhaps under the influence of creation myths in which eggs figure so prominently, Kepler conjectured that each planet's orbit has the shape of an egg.

The egg is difficult to describe mathematically because of its asymmetry; it is tapered at one end. Ellipses are tapered symmetrically at both ends. Kepler knew that Archimedes had already worked out the areas of ellipse sectors. So Kepler used an ellipse to approximate the egg. Eventually Kepler realized that if he put the sun at one focus of the ellipse, the data fit. So although the ellipse was not a veridical idealization of its target (the egg), it was a veridical idealization of its target's target (the orbit of Mars).

Sometimes a match with the target's target is not regarded as a *fortunate* hit. When we estimate the size of errors, our aim is to model the mismodeling, not the phenomenon itself. If the model of the model of F gives us correct values for F, then we have *mis*modeled the model of F. A veridical idealization would yield a model of F that matched the errors we observed.

Our second-order efforts at modeling modeling can themselves be the subject of modeling. Thus there can be an open-ended hierarchy of idealizations without a collapse into first-order modeling.

11. VERIDICAL APPROXIMATIONS

What makes an idealization an idealization is its intent, not its effect. Approximations may fortuitously yield exactly correct outputs for some inputs.

In mathematical contexts, veridical idealizations are *necessarily* correct. Consider a student who knows that the area of a rectangle is the product of its length and width. When he confronts a parallelogram, he is not sure how to calculate its area. It is plausible that the parallelogram's area will increase if one side is made longer. He expects any such addition is small. So the student treats each parallelogram as if it were a rectangle, unsure of how much error will be introduced by the departure from 90-degree angles. Later he learns that all of his calculations are exactly correct.

Students accustomed to handheld calculators often think translation of fractions into decimal notation involves a loss of information. When confined to decimal notation, they regard $1/3 = .333 \ldots$ as only approximately true. When they multiply the right-hand side by three, they think that the product, $.999 \ldots$, does not quite equal 1 (which is true for any *finite* iteration of 9's). But in fact, 1 = .999 . . . is exactly true (if it were untrue, there would be a real number between the two numbers).

12. UNDERSTANDING WITHOUT BELIEF

To understand the behavior of pendulums, Galileo eventually was led to experiments with inclined planes that liberated the pendulum bob from its tether. These experiments down U-shaped ramps led to experiments with ramps that were more and more obtuse. To reduce friction and air resistance, Galileo constructed progressively artificial laboratory situations.

Eventually Galileo was driven to thought experiments. In the final case, the ramp is laid out flat, along a frictionless, infinite plane within a vacuum. This thought experiment suggested that the ball would move forever in a straight line. Galileo accepted the eternality but regarded the straight path as misleading (as "a bug rather than a feature" in engineering jargon). In the *Dialogues*, Galileo reasons that if an object moved perpetually in a straight line, it would leave the universe. In view of this absurdity, Galileo continued to subscribe to the Greek doctrine that the circle is the natural form of motion. This conservatism prevented him from discovering Newton's first law of motion. Galileo did not believe the conclusion of his idealization.

Thought experimenters frequently do *modus tollens* when they should have done *modus ponens*. They conduct a sound conditional proof but then incorporate this into a *"reductio ad absurdum"* by treating the consequent as an absurdity. (The absurdity of a literal *reductio* is a contradiction, so the loose talk of a *reductio ad absurdum* is hyperbole—an emphatic *modus tollens*.)

One of Aristotle's reasons for rejecting the vacuum is that bodies of different weight would fall with equal velocity. This thought experiment gave Aristotle knowledge of the conditional produced by the subordinate proof.

Siméon Poisson in 1818 correctly deduced that if light were composed of waves, then interference should produce a white spot at the center of a "shadow" of a perfectly round object cast by a point source. This conditional proof was scientific progress because it advanced understanding of the consequences of the wave theory. Poisson naturally assumed that the progress went further—that he had set up an easy *modus tollens* that would furthermore refute the wave theory. Thus he was shocked when Dominique Arago executed the experiment and the absurd white spot materialized.

Understanding suffices for some scientific progress. Therefore, some thought experiments succeed even when they fail to provide knowledge (or even belief). Consequently, there is sometimes a point to conducting a thought experiment even if you know your audience will never believe you. Perhaps this explains why thought experimenters persist with audiences that are skeptical about their value.

13. SUPPOSITION AND LYING

Anti-realists concede that idealizations are not really lies. They trace the difference to an absence of an intent to deceive.

This is the wrong explanation. Some suppositions are intended to deceive. In push polling, one asks the respondent a "what if" question that insinuates the truth of the antecedent. Propagandists insincerely propound suppositional proofs. When Vice President Cheney defended torture with ticking time bomb thought experiments, he was criticized for conveying the impression that the idealized circumstances were representative. Some scientists also conduct idealizations that they know to be misleading or fallacious. In *Against Method*, Paul Feyerabend (1975) argued that Galileo's idealizations were propaganda.

Pictures cannot be lies because they are not discursive. Suppositions are discursive but are not the right kind of discourse. All lies are *assertions*. No supposition is an assertion. And all idealizations are suppositions.

ACKNOWLEDGEMENTS

Earlier versions of this paper were presented at the "Science Without Data" Workshop, Halifax, June 18, 2010, University of Wyoming, September 2, 2010, University of Missouri, October 1, 2010, Philosophy Students' Association at the University of Geneva, December 10, 2010, and at the Pacific American Philosophical Association, April 20, 2011, with Anjan Chakravartty and Ulrich Meyer as commentators. I thank them and audience members for their helpful comments and suggestions.

REFERENCES

Ashcroft, N. W., and N. David Mermin. 1976. *Solid State Physics*. Philadelphia: HRW International Editions.

Barnett, David. 2010. "Zif Would Have Been If: A Suppositional View of Counterfactuals." *Noûs* 44: 269–304.

Baron-Cohen, Simon, Sally Wheelwright, Amy Burtenshaw, and Esther Hobson. 2007. "Mathematical Talent Is Linked to Autism." *Human Nature* 18 (2): 125–131.

Berlin, Brent, and Paul Kay. 1969. *Basic Color Terms: Their Universality and Evolution*. Berkeley: University of California Press.

Bowden, B. V. 1953. "A Brief History of Computation." In *Faster Than Thought*, edited by B. V. Bowden. London: Pitman Publishing.

Brown, James R. 1991. *The Laboratory of the Mind*. London: Routledge.

Cartwright, Nancy. 1983. *How the Laws of Physics Lie*. Oxford: Oxford University Press.

Christensen, David. 2007. "Epistemology of Disagreement: The Good News." *Philosophical Review* 116 (2): 187–217.

Clifford, W. K. 1901. *Lectures and Essays* vol. 1, edited by Leslie Stephen and Frederick Pollock, London: MacMillan.

Davidson, Donald. 1975. "Thought and Talk." In *Mind and Language*, edited by S. Guttenplan, 7–23. Oxford: Oxford University Press.

Dijksterhuis, E. J. 1961. *The Mechanization of the World Picture*. Translated by C. Dikshoorn. New York: Oxford University Press.

Elgin, Catherine Z. 2004. "True Enough." *Philosophical Issues* 14: 113–131.

Ellis, Brian. 2009. *The Metaphysics of Scientific Realism*. Durham, UK: Acumen.

Feyerabend, Paul. 1975. *Against Method*. London: Verso.

Feynman, Richard. 1988. *What Do You Care What Other People Think?* New York: W. W. Norton.

Friedman, Milton. 1953. "The Methodology of Positive Economics." In *Essays in Positive Economics*. Chicago: University of Chicago Press.

Gell-Mann, Murray. 1994. *The Quark and the Jaguar*. New York: W. H. Freeman and Company.

Giere, Ronald. 2006. *Scientific Perspectivism*. Chicago: University of Chicago Press.

Hertwig, Ralph, and Andreas Ortmann. 2008. "Deception in Experiments: Revisiting the Arguments in Its Defense." *Ethics and Behavior* 18 (1): 59–92.

Hintikka, Jaakko. 1962. *Knowledge and Belief*. Ithaca, N.Y.: Cornell University Press.

Hüttemann, Andreas. 2002. "Idealizations in Physics." In *Symbol and Physical Knowledge: On the Conceptual Structure of Physics,* edited by Massimo Ferrari and Ion-Olimpiu Stamatescu, 177–192. Berlin: Springer-Verlag.

Jones, Martin R. 2005. "Idealization and Abstraction." *Poznan Studies in the Philosophy of the Sciences and the Humanities* 86 (1): 173–218.

Langland-Hassan, Peter. 2011. "Pretense, Imagination, and Belief: The Single Attitude Theory." *Philosophical Studies*.

Levins, Richard. 1966. "The Strategy of Model Building in Population Biology." In *Conceptual Issues in Evolutionary Biology*, edited by Elliott Sober, 18–27. Cambridge, MA: MIT Press.

Lewis, David. 1973. *Counterfactuals*. Cambridge, MA: Harvard University Press.

———. 1983. "Truth in Fiction." In *Philosophical Papers,* Vol. 1, 261–275. New York: Oxford University Press.

Makinson, D. C. 1965. "The Paradox of the Preface." *Analysis* 25: 205–207.

McMullin, Ernan. 1985. "Galilean Idealization." *Studies in the History and Philosophy of Science* 16: 247–273.

Morrison, Margaret. 2000. *Unifying Scientific Theories*. Cambridge: Cambridge University Press.

Mukherjee, Siddhartha. 2010. *The Emperor of All Maladies: A Biography of Cancer*. New York: Scribner.

Popper, Karl. 1963. *Conjectures and Refutations: The Growth of Scientific Knowledge*. London: Routledge.

Quine, W.V. [1948] 1980. "On What There Is." Reprinted in *From a Logical Point of View*. Cambridge: Harvard University Press.

Rhodes, Gillian. 1997. *Superportraits: Caricatures and Recognition*. London: Routledge.

Stanley, Jason. 2001. "Hermeneutic Fictionalism." In *Figurative Language*, special issue of *Midwest Studies in Philosophy* 25 (1), edited by Peter French and Howard Wettstein, 36–71.

Strevens, Michael. 2008. *Depth: An Account of Scientific Explanation*. Cambridge, MA: Harvard University Press.

Toon, Adam. 2010. "Models as Make-Believe." In *Beyond Mimesis and Convention* (Boston Studies in the Philosophy of Science 262), edited by Roman Frigg and Matthew Hunter, 71–96. Dordrecht: Springer.

Walton, Kendall. 1990. *Mimesis as Make-Believe*. Cambridge, MA: Harvard University Press.

Weisberg, Michael. 2006. "Robustness Analysis." *Philosophy of Science* 73: 730–742.

———. 2007. "Three Kinds of Idealization." *Journal of Philosophy* 104 (12): 639–659.

White, Roger. 2005. "Epistemic Permissiveness." *Philosophical Perspectives* 19 (1): 445–459.

3 What Do We See in a Thought Experiment?

James Robert Brown

What do we see in a thought experiment? The question is disarmingly simple but quickly becomes perplexing when we try to give an answer. The analogous question for real experiments is easy: We see objects and processes such as streaks in a cloud chamber, the height of a column of mercury, the changing colour in a chemical reaction, and so on. Even acknowledging the theory-ladeness of observation, the objects of perception in a real experiment are unproblematic. We might be tempted to say the same about thought experiments, given that they are so similar to real experiments. In both we set things up, let them run, then we see what happens, and we finish by drawing a few morals. The only difference it would seem is that a thought experiment is done in the imagination.

In *De rerum natura*, Lucretius attempts to show that space is infinite. If there is a boundary to the universe, we can toss a spear at it. If the spear flies through, then it isn't a boundary after all. And if the spear bounces back, then there must be something beyond the supposed edge of space, a cosmic brick wall that is itself in space, that stopped the spear. Either way, there is no edge of the universe; space is infinite. In typical fashion we visualize some situation; we carry out an operation; we see what happens. Though we use empirical concepts, we often can't carry out an actual empirical test. Imagination is a substitute. However, the example also illustrates the fallibility of a thought experiment. In this case we've learned how to conceptualize space so that it is both finite and unbounded.

This is a typical thought experiment. Would it not be right then to simply say we see the same sorts of things we see in real experiments, except that they are in the imagination instead? The answer is no; at least it is no in one important respect. I will try to show why, and then say what it is that we actually do see in a thought experiment. An example from special relativity will be used to make the case.[1] Let's turn to that now.

Einstein was perhaps the greatest thought experimenter ever. Only Galileo is his equal. Special and general relativity are both peppered with thought experiments, some of which are central to the creation of new principles and laws, while others play a more pedagogical role. To begin, let's review some of the basics of special relativity, starting from the two main postulates.

> *Postulate 1*: Laws of nature are the same in every inertial frame.
> *Postulate 2*: The speed of light is constant; it has the same value, *c*, in every frame.

There is no need to comment on these postulates, since special relativity is widely known. It is, however, worth recalling that the postulate of relativity stems from Galileo's thought experiment that asks us to imagine we're in a ship that could be either in port or moving at sea in very calm waters. We cannot see out to tell which. Inside birds are flying around in all directions, fish swim with ease in all directions, and so on. From this we conclude that there is no difference between rest and motion; only constancy of motion matters. The second principle, concerning the constancy of light speed, stemmed from repeated and well-confirmed observations and is also an ingredient in Maxwell's electrodynamics.

We do, however, need a definition of "simultaneity," a concept that turns out to be hugely important in special relativity.

> Distant events e_1 and e_2 in inertial frame F are *simultaneous* if and only if light flashes from the two events meet at a spatial midpoint in F.

This definition, which was proposed by Einstein, seems intuitively correct and natural, given the second postulate that says in effect that light travels at a constant speed *c*. The big surprise comes when we try to mix this concept of simultaneity with the first postulate that in effect says all inertial frames are equivalent.

Suppose we have two frames, associated with the train and the track, respectively; the train is moving at velocity *v* in the track frame. Let e_1 and e_2 be separated events (light flashes). The observer in the track frame is midway between e_1 and e_2, and receives signals from each event at the same

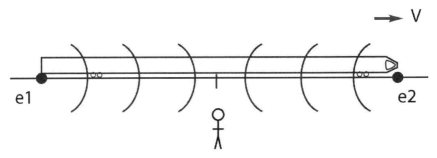

Figure 3.1   Events e_1 and e_2 are simultaneous in the track frame.

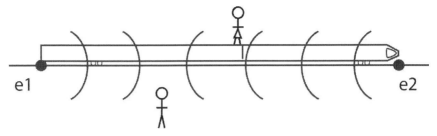

Figure 3.2 Event e_2 is earlier than e_1 in the train frame.

time. Therefore, given the definition, events e_1 and e_2 are simultaneous *in the track frame.*

However, some time passes while the light signals come to the midpoint and during that time the train has moved forward, into the light from e_2. An observer midway on the train frame receives the signal from e_2 before e_1. So the event e_2 is earlier than e_1 *in the train frame.* We now draw a momentous conclusion: *The simultaneity of distant events is relative to a frame.* That is, two events might be simultaneous in one frame but not simultaneous in another. This is the first of many profound discoveries in special relativity. From the postulates and definition, and a bit of algebra, we can derive other remarkable consequences, such as the length contraction and time dilation formulae. (See any text on special relativity for details.)

So far this is standard stuff, the basic facts and the normal presentation of them in special relativity. Einstein developed it this way (Einstein [1905] 1923) and most expositors follow him. The use of thought experiments to bring out the details of special relativity is typical.

The mathematics of special relativity is rather simple; high school algebra will do. The hard part is coming to understand the new concepts of space and time and how they interact with one another. When teaching special relativity, conceptual puzzles are often given to help develop a novice's intuitions. One of the nicest of these is the car-garage example, which is based on the length contraction of moving objects.

A moving object, according to special relativity, will contract in the direction of its motion. Suppose an object, say, a metre stick, which has length L_0 when at rest in an inertial frame, is moving at velocity v. Then its length in the rest frame is

$$L_v = L_0 \sqrt{1 - v^2 / c^2}$$

This is the standard formula for length contraction, commonly known as the Lorentz contraction formula. As one can readily see from the formula, the faster an object moves in a given frame, the shorter it is in that frame, and in the limit of reaching the velocity of light, it contracts to zero length. Those encountering relativity for the first time should be warned. An object

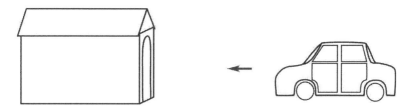

Figure 3.3   The car and the garage in relative motion with velocity *v*.

does not have a length, *simpliciter*. It has a length in a given frame and that length will vary from frame to frame, depending on the relative velocity. The metre stick, or any other object, exists in all frames, so has all velocities and all lengths between its maximum, known as the rest length, and arbitrarily short lengths when moving very close to (but never quite reaching) the speed of light.

Once length contraction is digested, we can move to the car-garage puzzle (Figure 3.3). It is posed as a conceptual paradox: Can a moving car fit inside a garage or not? Both answers, yes and no, seem correct. Resolving the paradox leads to considerable insight into special relativity—hence its pedagogical value.

Let's suppose that the car and the garage both have the same rest length of, say, six metres. The car is moving toward the garage at a very high

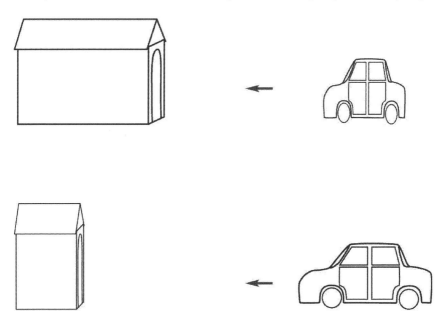

Figure 3.4   *Top:* In the garage frame the car is contracted, so it will fit inside the garage. *Bottom:* In the car frame the garage is contracted, so the car will not fit inside.

velocity v. From the garage frame's point of view, the car will be Lorentz contracted in the direction of motion, because of its velocity, so it will be much shorter than six metres and thus will easily fit inside the six metre garage (Figure 3.4, *top*). This reasoning is quite correct. So far, so good.

But remember the equality of all inertial frames. That means the car can be considered the rest frame and the garage is moving at velocity v toward it. From the car frame point of view, the garage, which has a rest length of six metres, will be Lorentz contracted, due to its motion, so it will be shorter than six metres in the car frame (Figure 3.4, *bottom*). Consequently, the garage will be too short for the car to fit inside, even for an instant. That reasoning is correct, too. But now we have a paradox: The car will fit inside and the car will not fit inside the garage. Special relativity seems to lead to an outright contradiction.

Notice how easily and elegantly we arrived at this paradoxical conclusion by means of a simple thought experiment (or, if you like, a pair of thought experiments). We did not have to know the actual relative velocity v, nor did we have to calculate the actual contraction of either the car or garage. We can easily visualize how the whole business goes and arrive at the paradoxical conclusion. This has all the hallmarks of a typical thought experiment.

The problem we now face is how to resolve the paradox. What went wrong with the reasoning? As a matter of fact, nothing is wrong with the reasoning in either case. In the garage frame, the car really does fit inside the garage (if only for an instant), and in the car frame the car really does not fit inside the garage. But at this stage we're left dangling and want to know why, since it certainly seems paradoxical.

The answer lies in the relativity of simultaneity, mentioned at the outset. In the garage frame, the rear bumper of the car is inside the garage before the front bumper has burst through the back wall of the garage. This means that the car is wholly in the garage for some brief time. However, in the car frame, due to the relativity of simultaneity, the front bumper of the car breaks through the back wall of the garage before the rear bumper is inside the garage. In short, according to the car frame, the car is never wholly inside. The two frames (car and garage) disagree on the order of events. That is key to understanding and resolving the paradox. Bizarre, yes, but not a contradiction.

From a pedagogical point of view the car-garage paradox and its resolution reinforce the crucial lesson of the relativity of simultaneity, whose consequences are enormous. Events that are simultaneous in one frame need not be simultaneous in another. The thought experiment does not itself resolve the paradox, but it very nicely sets it up for resolution.[2]

In describing the car-garage example, I noted how easy it was to carry out as a thought experiment; no tricky computations were needed; it was simple, qualitative, pictorial reasoning. Yet there is something wrong with saying this. There is a problem, but it is not with special relativity or with the setting up of the thought experiment, nor is it with the analysis

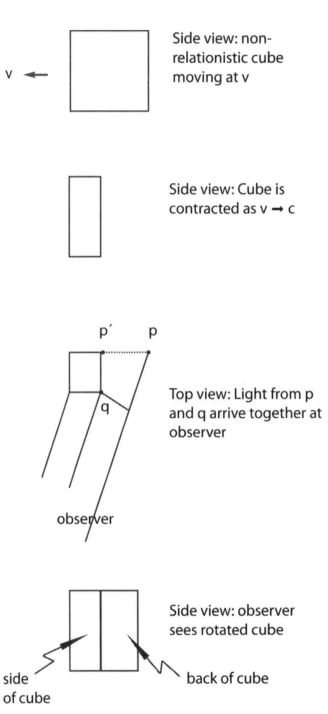

Side view: non-relationistic cube moving at v

Side view: Cube is contracted as v → c

Top view: Light from p and q arrive together at observer

Side view: observer sees rotated cube

Figure 3.5   The appearance of rotation of rapidly moving objects.

and solution of the paradox. The problem is with thinking it is a case of simple, qualitative, pictorial reasoning. There is a rather serious complicating feature.

Rapidly moving objects are indeed Lorentz contracted. But they do not *look* contracted, rather they look quite different. Normally we try to visualize things realistically in a thought experiment. We imagine Einstein chasing a light beam or Galileo dropping musket and cannon balls from the Leaning Tower of Pisa. But this way of proceeding would not work here. The visual appearance of a rapidly moving object in special relativity is not contracted. It looks quite different; it appears to be rotated, with the degree of rotation depending on the relative velocity. This was only discovered in the late 1950s and is still not widely known, even among physicists. Roger Penrose (1958) discovered that a moving sphere would still look spherical, not contracted, and James Terrell (1959) extended the result to all moving objects regardless of shape. (Weisskopf 1960 is a good exposition.)

This means that in the garage frame, the car, of course, will be Lorentz contracted, but it would not look that way. Instead, it would look rotated (Figure 3.6). Now we have a new problem on our hands.

In the thought experiment earlier, we could tell what was happening by a kind of visual inspection. In our imagination we could observe the contracted car or the contracted garage and we reasoned from these simple images. But with rotation, our intuition would be confused. We would not see the paradox the way we should and we would have no hope of realizing how to solve it. The rotated car looks like it will crash sideways into the garage, as if it had hit an icy patch on the road and started to slide sideways. Instead of fitting nicely inside the garage, it looks as if the rapidly moving car will smash the garage to bits by hitting it sideways.

What is going on? For the first half century in the life of special relativity the appearance of rotation was not even known. In the second half century it was ignored. Somehow we managed to get it right, in spite of this problem. What's going on?

Interestingly, in the history of thought experiments, there are important examples that have played on deliberate ignorance. Galilean relativity (mentioned earlier) stems from Galileo's ship. We are inside a ship watching birds fly around, fish swimming in a tank, and so on. We suppress the

Figure 3.6   In the garage frame the rapidly moving car looks rotated.

information that we are either at rest in a port or moving at sea in a completely smooth ocean on the grounds that we cannot look outside. Could we tell the difference, anyway? No. The birds fly around inside the cabin just the same in either case. Everything looks the same whether we're moving or not. Galileo concludes that the only thing that matters is what we would now call inertial motion. Rest and uniform motion in a straight line are equivalent as far as physics is concerned. In the thought experiment we made ourselves ignorant of being at rest or in motion and now we discover that it does not matter, anyway; they are physically equivalent. Similarly, in Einstein's elevator we are ignorant of whether we are at rest in a gravitational field or accelerating in empty space. We see that the behaviour of light will be the same either way and so we conclude that there is some sort of equivalence between gravity and accelerating motion. Again, our self-imposed ignorance turns out to be irrelevant. Or to put it in even stronger terms: We were not ignorant after all, since there is no difference to be ignorant about.

Self-imposed ignorance is something to keep in mind. We can ignore some things in a thought experiment, such as the colour of a falling object. Stipulating ignorance may be another matter. The car-garage example seems to present a serious challenge to a popular thesis. The identity or continuity thesis, as it is sometimes called, is the claim that thought experiments are real experiments, or at least continuous with them. This is a much stronger claim than saying that they are similar, which is unquestionably true. Roy Sorensen, for instance, claims that "A *thought experiment* is an experiment that purports to achieve its aim without benefit of execution" (1992, 205). The appearance of rotation in a real experiment would be unavoidable. The fact that we "see" something different in a thought experiment, namely, a contracted but not rotated car, shows that this particular thought experiment is not the same thing as a real experiment, executed or not. John Norton takes a very different view from Sorensen. He says thought experiments are filled with "irrelevant particulars." I will briefly discuss his view below.

It's tempting to say we see the god's-eye view. This metaphor is often associated with the idea of *the one true description of reality*. Such an idea is often dismissed out of hand, but as a card carrying realist I have no particular problem with it (as long as we ignore its religious overtones). However, we are concerned with thought experiments here, so we must focus on the "view" part of the god's-eye view and take it rather seriously. Two related metaphors come to mind: *the view from nowhere* and *the view from everywhere*. Both of these are used frequently in place of the god's-eye view and, though metaphoric, convey the same idea: the uniquely true and objective description of reality. Let's consider each in turn, taking them rather literally, that is, taking them to be a view situated somewhere in space.

The view from nowhere would treat the car-garage problem as one-dimensional. After all, this is all that really matters to the physics of the situation; nothing is happening in other dimensions. In particular, there would be no observer standing off to the side in the one-dimensional account. So, the Lorentz contraction of the car (or the garage) would not be seen. It would simply be computed by the observer situated in the one dimension. Rotation does not arise, since it requires a second dimension. We get the right answer in this case (i.e., in the garage frame, the car fits inside the garage and in the car frame the car does not fit inside), but it cannot be called a thought experiment. Some might be tempted to call it such, but I think this would violate the reasonable requirement that a thought experiment be in some important sense visualized; otherwise it is merely hypothetical. In the one-dimensional case, we cannot stand aside and see what is happening. If we locate ourselves in the one dimension, we just see the car as a point. Crucially, the one-dimensional case differs from the standard thought experiment, where Lorentz contraction is actually observed. Doing things this one-dimensional way is a departure from the standard way of presenting the car-garage paradox. The standard way is much superior, since it makes the paradox clear to anyone without needing to do a calculation. John Wheeler famously declared "Wheeler's First Moral Principle: Never make a calculation until you know the answer" (Taylor and Wheeler 1992, 20). Thought experiments often make this injunction easy to obey, but the view from nowhere interpretation would undermine any hope.

Next, let us try understanding the god's-eye view as the view from everywhere. This would treat the problem as two-dimensional. Of course, the view from everywhere means all perspectives in all dimensions, but only two of these dimensions actually matter to the problem. This time rotation would be observed. But this is exactly what we don't want. Since we rightly ignore or deny rotation in the car-garage paradox, the view from everywhere cannot be the right version of the god's-eye view either.

What about a top view? Again we would observe rotation, but this time the rear of the car would rise and the car would move toward the garage, as if running on its front wheels. Once again, our intuitions would be hopelessly confused.

We seem to have reached an impasse. We want something like a god's-eye view, but when we try to put flesh on the bones, it comes to naught. What we need is something like this: There is a true description of what is going on, but rotation is not part of that description. Though we do rightly ignore rotation in the thought experiment, we are still not in a position to say why. A distinction might help.

We normally distinguish theories from observations. But observation is not well understood. Of course, it is theory-laden, but that only begins to touch on the complexities. There is an intuitive distinction between the observable and the theoretical. It was the basis of a great deal of positivist philosophy of science. Streaks in cloud chambers are observable while electrons are not. Yet physicists regularly talk about observing electrons. On the other hand, they claim that quarks cannot be seen, because they cannot be separated within a proton; any attempt to do so would require so much energy that the process would create new particles and the quarks would still be hidden inside.

These issues are a long way from being settled. But a distinction has been introduced which is growing in popularity and which sheds a lot of light on several related issues. It is the distinction between *data* and *phenomena*. The former are more or less raw sightings, while phenomena are idealizations of some sort that are constructed out of data. We talk about making observations within a thought experiment, so it should come as no surprise that issues concerning the nature of observation will be relevant.

The distinction between data and phenomena is easily understood in Figure 3.7. Phenomena, in the form of an artist's drawing on the right, are constructed or abstracted out of data, the bubble chamber photo on the left, often with help of a theory. Bogen and Woodward (1988) have developed this idea considerably as have James McAllister (1996, 2004) and others. On this account, it is phenomena, not data, that theories explain and that are used to test those theories. No theory could hope to explain the chicken scratches on the left.

Perhaps we could take thought experiments to be phenomena.[3] That is, the objects of perception in a thought experiment are visual as in a real experiment, but typically they are streamlined, cleaned up, and idealized as are phenomena. In the car-garage example, if performed in reality, we would see rotation, since it's part of the data. But in the thought experiment,

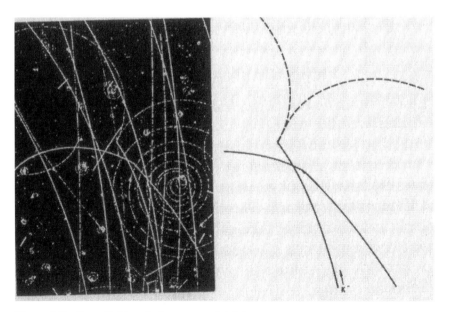

Figure 3.7 Data (*left*) and phenomena (*right*).

we see only contraction, which is the phenomenon. This is quite different from the previous ways we articulated a god's-eye view. But it may be a candidate: God sees phenomena, not data. Phenomena involve idealization of some sort, so let us turn briefly to that. The type of idealization may turn out to be key.

There are several ways in which idealization might take place. One of these is sometimes called *Aristotelian*. Such an idealization ignores some features, but will not ignore causal features that are truly at work. If Aristotle himself were discussing falling bodies, he would ignore, for instance, the colour of the body, but he would not ignore the resistance of the air. Colour plays no role in how a body falls, but air does. A second type of idealization is called *Galilean*. Here, one goes much further than Aristotle would and actually falsifies nature. Thus, if Galileo himself were considering the motion of bodies, he would posit a vacuum, a frictionless plane, and so on. Real bodies do not move in a vacuum and they incur friction when sliding on a plane. Aristotle ignores, but Galileo distorts. The difference, no doubt obvious, is very important. Aristotle could not allow himself to think about a body falling in a vacuum, since, according to him, a vacuum is impossible. Ignoring colour is harmless, but ignoring the atmosphere would be fatal. The difference is relative to the background theory at issue. Galileo's physics does not require an atmosphere, but Aristotle's does. In a vacuum an object would not know how to move. A rock or a flame would not be able to detect its location, its natural place, and which way to move to get to it. To ignore the atmosphere, according to Aristotle, would be to fall into incoherence.

Ernan McMullin has made much of this distinction (McMullin 1985) and upholds it for both real experiments and what he calls "subjunctive reasoning," by which he means to include thought experiments. Galileo's falling bodies thought experiment fits this pattern nicely. It not only ignores the colour of the bodies, as an Aristotelian version would do, but it ignores air resistance as well.

We can see Aristotelian and Galilean idealizations at work in various famous thought experiments—for instance, in the following Aristotelian examples:

- The trolley car—ignore the age, gender, and the clothes of each person involved
- Searle's Chinese Room—ignore the occupation and politics of the person in the room
- Falling bodies—ignore the colour of the cannon and musket balls

Instances of Galilean idealizations would include the following:

- Falling bodies—ignore air friction
- Galileo's ship—ignore the rocking motion when at sea
- Newton's bucket—ignore the material universe

- Einstein's elevator—ignore the magnitude of acceleration or the gravitational field that would need to be so large as to kill any human observer

What about the car-garage example? Does it involve idealizations in the Aristotelian, Galilean, or any other interesting sense?

In typical Aristotelian fashion we ignore the car's colour. And along with typical Galilean idealizations, we make assumptions in the car-garage example that are outright distortions; that is, they are as physically unrealistic as the assumption of a vacuum was for Galileo. A car moving at a velocity approaching the speed of light relative to a garage is, for instance, highly fanciful. The rubber tire, for instance, would melt. Could we actually discern whether it is at any time wholly within the garage, or is it going much too fast for our actual measuring instruments to tell? These problems seem, in principle, no different than ignoring air resistance. We simply stipulate what we want in the way of premises and hope we are not begging the question. So far the car-garage example fits the Galilean mould.

However, the example differs in one important respect from the Galilean idealization framework. It does not merely falsify reality the way Galileo would; it falsifies appearances as well. That is, it falsifies appearances in the thought experiment. The Lorentz contraction of the car is treated as objectively real, but rotation is not. In this we seem to have a different type of idealization on our hands, one that applies only within thought experiments. I will call it *Platonic* idealization, in keeping with the practice of naming it after a famous representative or source of inspiration.

We start a thought experiment by making it as close to a real experiment as we can. Often we idealize within a thought experiment in the Aristotelian way. Thus, in the car-garage example, we ignore the colour of the car. We do not deny that it is coloured; we simply ignore it. If someone insists on knowing the colour of the car, we could stipulate anything we want, knowing that it would have no effect on the result. For instance, we could say it is a red car driven by Uncle Bob, who is returning from the store with a fresh lemon for Aunt Mable's tea. These extraneous facts would have no impact on the outcome.

When we ignore the appearance of rotation, we are doing something much more significant than ignoring colour. This is more like Galileo stipulating that there is no friction on the inclined plane or no air resistance that impedes a falling object. We are stipulating that in the thought experiment the car does not rotate; it only Lorentz contracts. We are not falsifying nature as Galileo does by stipulating no air friction. After all, in reality there is no rotation. We are falsifying the thought experiment by stipulating no rotation. It's as if we said, "Visualize a situation in which a car is Lorentz contracted but is not rotated." It is certainly possible to do this, but it conflicts with the laws of physics. After all, we see Lorentz contraction thanks to the photons emitted from the side of the car, but rotation would then be visible, too, since photons are coming from the back of the car as well.

Platonic idealization conflicts with the common view that thought experiments are imaginary versions of real experiments and are similar to them. The problem, of course, is solved by abandoning the claim that they must be similar in this respect. The problem is serious and the solution is drastic, since we normally see with light. We are being asked to imagine seeing something but seeing it without light, or to see with light that does not obey the actual laws of light. It is one thing to eliminate air friction on a cannon ball by having it move in a vacuum—in imagination or in reality. It is quite another to eliminate air friction on a bird by having it fly in a vacuum. Can we imagine a bird flying in empty air? We can certainly imagine it moving along with its wings flapping. But is this a legitimate idealization, since the air is physically necessary for the bird to fly? Probably not. Is the car-garage case similarly problematic?

If we reflect on this a moment, its bizarreness will become obvious. Galilean idealization says, yes, there is air friction in reality, but ignore it; assume the object is moving in a vacuum. We are then asked: Now, how do things look? Platonic idealization says, yes, the car will look rotated, but ignore it; assume that it does not rotate. Again, we are asked: Now, how does it look? This borders on paradox, but it is not a contradiction. It does not succumb to the bird-flying-in-a-vacuum problem, since seeing Lorentz contraction in a thought experiment does not depend on light the way a bird depends on the air to fly.

This should not be confused with exaggerations, which are commonplace in thought experiments. Einstein imagined running so fast he caught up with a light beam. This, of course, is biologically absurd, but there is no conflict with the thought experiment situation in thinking it. To imagine seeing Lorentz contraction without the appearance of rotation is a contradiction or very close to it. We see with light. It is the finite speed of light that leads to the Lorentz contraction and to the appearance of rotation. It is not easily denied, the way biological facts are easily denied in a physics thought experiment. And yet we do it.

John Norton's account of thought experiments involves idealization of a sort. He claims, "Thought experiments are arguments which: (i) posit hypothetical or counterfactual states of affairs, and (ii) invoke particulars irrelevant to the generality of the conclusion" (1991, 129). I disagree with Norton about thought experiments being arguments, but will not pursue that point here.[4] I will focus on the "irrelevant particulars" clause. Norton elaborates:

> This condition gives thought experiments their thought-like character. For if they did not posit such states of affairs they would not be thought experiments; they would be the description of a real experiment or state of affairs. Thus we cannot base a thought experiment on the supposition that projectiles on the earth's surface have roughly

parabolic trajectories; for they really do have roughly parabolic trajectories and, so far, we have only given an accurate description of the
way things really are. But we could begin a thought experiment by
supposing *counterfactually* that projectiles followed trajectories which
are the arcs of circles. Or we could incorporate parabolic trajectories in
a thought experiment if in addition we suppose *counterfactually* that
lightweight projectiles are not impeded by air resistance or if we consider a *hypothetical* projectile of some specified size, shape and composition. (1991, 130)

What is important in Norton's example is what he leaves out. He rightly
notes our freedom in specifying the trajectory of a projectile (parabola,
arc of a circle, and so on). Analogously, we could stipulate that the car is
moving directly forward on all four wheels toward the garage or that it is
almost upright on its rear wheels. What Norton does not capture in this
passage is that we might discover something new about the car. We stipulate its motion but then discover that it looks rotated. In Norton's account
of "irrelevant particulars" there is no room for such surprises. Implicit in
his account is that what we see is what we stipulate, neither more nor less.

Much of what Norton says about irrelevant particulars is surely right,
just as Aristotle is right about the irrelevance of the car's colour. He is also
right, in effect joining Galileo, in saying we are free to posit a vacuum for
things to move in. What is needed in his account is some consideration for
the appearance of rotation, which is indeed an irrelevant particular, but
one that cannot be stipulated away with the wave of a hand at the outset.
Rotation comes as a surprise, not part of the initial stipulation, and needs
some reasoned analysis to be eliminated.

As I earlier mentioned, the car-garage example is somewhat messy,
since it was discovered and solved long before the visual appearance of
rotation was discovered. But this should not get in the way of a proper
understanding. Now that we know about the appearance of rotation in
rapidly moving objects, we must take it into account in relevant thought
experiments. And the right way to take it into account is to stipulate that
it does not occur. This is Platonic idealization. Then we visualize in the
right way, that is, the way that correctly solves the problem. We see a
contracted car (in the garage frame) and a contracted garage (in the car
frame). This is how the thought experiment gives rise to the initial paradox and points toward the solution.

Empiricists would say that appearances give us reality, or that appearances are all the reality we can hope for. Scientific realists reject this
and say that appearances are often misleading, even though they can and
usually do provide evidence of reality. Thought experimenters might say
appearances give us reality, but it is the appearances within a thought
experiment that do this. A Platonist about thought experiments, that is,
someone who champions Platonic idealization would deny this and claim

instead that some thought experimental appearances can be misleading and should be rejected. Roughly, a Platonist thought experimenter stands to other thought experimenters as a scientific realist stands to empiricists, ever ready to abandon appearances in favour of a supposed reality, even in a thought experiment.

ACKNOWLEDGEMENTS

I am grateful for all the oral comments by participants at the conference and especially to Mélanie Frappier for extensive written comments on an earlier draft of this paper. I also thank SSHRC for its financial support.

NOTES

1. I mentioned this example briefly in the second edition of Brown ([1991] 2011), but it needs a fuller discussion, which I will try to provide here.
2. Another paradox, known as the pole-barn paradox has the same form. A man with a long pole runs into a barn. Will the pole fit inside the barn or not? The resolution is the same as the car-garage example. Taylor and Wheeler (1992) present the details.
3. I suggested this in Brown ([1991] 2011), but did not think to link it to cases such as the car-garage example.
4. My objections can be found in various places, including Brown ([1991] 2011).

REFERENCES

Bogen, J., and J. Woodward. 1988. "To Save the Phenomena." *Philosophical Review*, 97: 303–52.
Brown, James Robert. [1991] 2011. *The Laboratory of the Mind*. 2nd Edition. London and New York: Routledge.
Einstein, A. [1905] 1923. "On the Electrodynamics of Moving Bodies." In *The Principle of Relativity*, by H. Lorentz, A. Einstein, H. Weyl, and H. Minkowski, 35–65. New York: Dover.
McAllister, James. 1996. "The Evidential Significance of Thought Experiments in Science." *Studies in History and Philosophy of Science* 27 (2): 233–250.
———. 2004. "Thought Experiments and the Belief in Phenomena." *Philosophy of Science* 71 (5): 1164–1175.
McMullin, E. 1985. "Galilean Idealization." *Studies in History and Philosophy of Science* XVI: 247–273.
Norton, J. 1991. "Thought Experiments in Einstein's Work." In *Thought Experiments in Science and Philosophy*, edited by T. Horowitz and G. Massey. Savage, MD: Rowman and Littlefield.
Penrose, R. 1958. "The Apparent Shape of a Relativistically Moving Sphere." *Proceedings of the Cambridge Philosophical Society* 55: 137.
Sorensen, R. 1992. *Thought Experiments*. Oxford and New York: Oxford University Press.

Taylor, E. F., and J. A. Wheeler. 1992. *Spacetime Physics*. 2nd edition. New York: Freeman.

Terrell, J. 1959. "Invisibility of the Lorentz Contraction." *Physical Review* 116: 1041–1045.

Weisskopf, V. 1960. "The Visual Appearance of Rapidly Moving Objects." *Physics Today* 13: 24–27.

4 The Body, Thought Experiments, and Phenomenology

Yiftach J. H. Fehige and Harald Wiltsche

Our explorative contribution to the ongoing discussion of thought experiments might already surprise by its very title, and this is for at least two reasons. First, isn't the topic of thought experiments exclusively part of the domain of analytic philosophy? Second, isn't the point of thought experimentation to leave the body behind while withdrawing into the laboratory of the mind? We are inclined to answer negatively to both questions.

While endorsing the majority view that skepticism about thought experiments is not well justified, in what follows we attempt to show that there is a kind of "bodiliness" missing from current accounts of thought experiments. That is, we will suggest a phenomenological addition to the literature. First we will contextualize our claim that the importance of the body in thought experiments has been widely underestimated. Then we will discuss David Gooding's work, which contains the only explicit recognition of the importance of the body to understanding thought experiments. Finally, we will introduce a phenomenological perspective on the body, which will give us the opportunity to sketch the power and promise of a phenomenological approach to thought experiments.[1]

1. THE MISSING BODY FROM 1811 TO 2011

The practice of thought experiments is probably as old as the human mind. Thought experiments have been recorded since the times of ancient Greek philosophy (see Ierodiakonou 2005). They became a subject matter of philosophical reflection in the eighteenth century, beginning with Kant (see Kühne 2005, 95–105) and not with Ernst Mach as it is still commonly believed. From the beginning, thought experiments have been widely perceived as an instance of bodiless cognition.

Kant refers to philosophical thought experiments as "experiments of pure reason" (see Kant 1998, 112 [BXXI]). Kant's experiments of pure reason test transcendental principles by demonstrating "that experience would assume a fundamentally different form if the tested [transcendental] principle were false" (see Kalin 1972, 322–323). These tests require a drastic disconnect from the kind of experience that originates from embodied existence. Hans Christian Ørsted, who actually introduced the technical term "thought experiment" in its Danish version *Tanke-experiment* (see Ørsted [1811] 1920, 172), refers to Kant's *Metaphysical Foundations of Natural Science* as a treasure trove of scientific thought experiments. According to Ørsted, thought experiments in science "set our mind itself in creative activity in order to develop lively and vigorous knowledge" (Ørsted [1811] 1998, 295). There is no mentioning that the creativity under consideration is embodied.

In this respect the situation did not change when many decades after Kant and Ørsted, in the 1990s, the debate between James R. Brown and John D. Norton arose (see Brown 2011; Norton 1996). The former introduced a Platonic account of thought experiments. The latter countered with the claim that thought experiments are epistemologically dispensable, arguing that they are no more than arguments. But both share the view that our bodies do not matter much in thought experiments. Brown highlights an intellectual perception with the mind's eye. The body has nothing of significance to contribute here. The same is true for Norton, who accounts for thought experiments in terms of abstract propositional reasoning.

Currently, almost nobody shares Brown's Platonism, and only a few sympathize with Norton's idea that we can eliminate thought experimentation for the performance of propositional lines of reasoning. Among the many who disagree with Brown and Norton, Gooding has probably been the only author to draw explicit attention to the significance of embodiment for thought experimentation. The biggest challenge in substantiating this claim is to spell out what exactly "embodiment" means. The idea of embodied cognition has been understood in many different ways. Thus, some of what follows will be dedicated to differentiating between embodiment à la Gooding, and the bodiliness involved in thought experiments offered by a phenomenological approach.

We think Gooding is right when he claims that the body matters in thought experiments. Yet we are reluctant to accept the kind of naturalism that informs his views. The main reason for our reluctance is not only the many philosophical problems pertaining to naturalism (see, e.g., Sklar 2010). We are gesturing towards a phenomenological approach to the body, and we do this for at least three reasons. *First,* the opinion repeatedly expressed in the literature has been that one of the central methods in phenomenology, namely the *eidetic reduction,* is an instance of thought experimenting (see Froese and Gallagher 2010; Lotz 2007, 9; Mohanty 1991; Myers 1986, 109). *Second,* when analytic philosophy and phenomenology come into contact, especially in the area of the mind-body problem, thought experimenting seems to be an ideal means to encourage more constructive interaction between the two schools. That is, while thought experiments are frequently used as a tool of analytic philosophers, the method of phenomenology seems to make available a more direct familiarity with the mind (as we will show below), and this is something from which analytic philosophy could profit. *Third*, the bodily component of thought experimentation suffers from a complete lack of philosophical attention. The development of a phenomenological approach to this component of thought experimenting would be a useful and viable task, because it was phenomenology that reappropriated the body as a subject matter of philosophy (see, e.g., Hammer 1974, 81; Welton 1999). The German philosopher Hermann Schmitz developed a *system of philosophy* out of a phenomenology of the body (see Schmitz 1964–1980). His central claim is that all we are is body, and it is the body that holds the key to understanding ourselves and everything else there is. Since, so far, Schmitz' comprehensive philosophy of the body is rather underrepresented in the Anglophone debate, we are going to include some of his work in the following discussion of the *bodily component of thought experimenting* in order to demonstrate the feasibility of a phenomenological approach to thought experiments. First, however, we will discuss Gooding's case for a philosophy of science that is guided by the principle of what he calls "hands over heads." This principle is central in Gooding's theory of the bodily dimension of thought experiments. The principal aim of the next section is to have a look at this theory in order to motivate our search for a phenomenological approach to thought experiments.

2. "HANDS OVER HEADS": GOODING ON THOUGHT EXPERIMENTS

Despite his pursuit of "naturalistic approaches to science" (Gooding 1992, 51), Gooding has argued that "thought experiments are useful, powerful, elegant and important" (Gooding 1993, 280). To rationalists like Alexandre Koyré or Brown, he has conceded "the importance of thought experiments in generating new science" (Gooding 1992, 69). Yet while they are indeed "conducted entirely within the world of representations," Gooding believes that thought experiments wrongly suggest "that representations are self sufficient" (Gooding 1990, 203). In general, Gooding argues, to play "down the empirical and material aspect of scientific thinking in favor of the march of ideas and arguments" (Gooding 1990, 203) is "just bad philosophy." It is bad philosophy because it follows the principle of "heads over hands." This principle, claims Gooding, has already misled the study of science for too long. We need to do better. We need to get the body into the picture. Hands come first, then the head. This is also true for the scientific practice of thought experimentation.

According to Gooding, the crucial question about thought experiments asks how "scientists go from the actual to the possible, on to the impossible, and return to an actual world *altered* by that journey" (Gooding 1990, 204). Like Mach (1897 [1905]), Sorensen (1992), and Buzzoni (2008),[2] Gooding has defended what we call *experimentalism* in response to that question. What this means becomes clear when he says, for example, "Thought experiments are conducted in mental laboratories but they do not thereby cease to be experiments" (Gooding 1993, 281). This is experimentalism in a nutshell and one way to account for the apparent cognitive efficacy of thought experiments. The basic idea of experimentalism is simple: If we take real-world experiments to be of cognitive value due to their experimental character, then we have sufficient reason to do the same with respect to thought experiments, since the difference between the two is less than often thought.

Mach has argued for experimentalism by drawing attention to the fact that real-world experiments and thought experiments alike employ the methodological principle of *variation* (see Kujundzic 1998). Roy A. Sorensen has argued for experimentalism in terms of *logical regimens* that are common to both thought experiments and real-world experiments in relating an imagined scenario to a target theory. Marco Buzzoni follows Kant's notion of experiment and argues that the experimental character is a matter of *putting a question to nature*. He thereby puts thought experiments and real-world experiments into a (non-Hegelian) *dialectical* relationship: "Granted that no thought experiment can be a whole experiment, it is also the case that without thought experiments there could be no experiments" (Buzzoni 2008, 96).

In Gooding's case there is no (non-Hegelian) dialectical, but a much weaker relationship between real-world experiments and thought experiments. Gooding is closer to Mach and Sorensen in this respect. But he is closer to Buzzoni in that he emphasizes the relationship between thinking and doing. The relation between thought experiments and real-world experiments is a function of "the interdependence of thinking and doing" (Gooding 1990, 204). The experimental character is defined in terms of testing the "practicability of doing something in just the way required by the theories in the world as represented by theory. In other words, theory is criticized through the practices that link it to those aspects of the world that it purports to be about" (Gooding 1993, 280). Gooding's version of experimentalism clearly articulates his basic conviction that doing, and in this sense the body, matters for cognition. We are encouraged to consider visual perception. An "example of the importance of doing to seeing is Sidney Bradford. Blind from infancy, his sight was restored by corneal grafts after fifty years. At first Bradford could see only those objects he had already explored by touch" (Gooding 1992, 45). Examples like this reassure Gooding that a careful analysis of the bodily component of cognition enables philosophers of science to see most effectively that the "assumption about the priority of head over hands" (Gooding 1992, 47) is a myth. What matters in each experiment, argues Gooding, is a relation between actual and possible worlds, and it is the *body* that connects the two realms. But the importance of the body can come into view only if philosophers of science realize that textbook experiments substantially involve "editing out much of what went into achieving the results" (Gooding 1992, 46). We have to bring into focus the locality and situatedness of experimental science, Gooding claims. Then we will come to realize that every experiment operates at the intersection of the two worlds of the actual and the possible, and that it is the body that makes possible real-world experiments and thought experiments alike.

Gooding's approach to thought experiments might come as a surprise if one is inclined to believe that it is especially the *detachment from the body* that allows for thought experimentation. Gooding is aware of this. Hinting at Quinean language-centrism, Gooding states that thought experimenting is a "sort of experimentation that becomes possible when semantic ascent is largely complete" (Gooding 1990, 203). Yet at the same time, he argues that embodiment makes the semantic ascent (and thus thought experiments) possible in the first place. Bodies do this in the following two ways.

First, for those encountering a thought experiment, mental participation in the world of the thought experiment is only possible by the thought experiment's narrative, because it initiates a process of constructing less familiar features through familiar ones, and this process is a function of embodiment. By means of seeing, feeling, or interacting with objects in the world of the thought experiment, *unfamiliar* features can manifest in a plausible manner: "I contend that T[hought]-experimenters must have learned enough about a world of one kind (through vision, touch and hearing) to access other, less familiar worlds. The very possibility of participating depends on familiarity with ordinary perceptual experience of any kind. T[hought]-experimenters must be *at home in their bodies*" (Gooding 1993, 285).

Second, for those developing a thought experiment, there must be a direct appeal to ordinary properties of objects. Otherwise the resulting thought experiment's narrative will not establish an intelligible, sensory framework for understanding the procedures and phenomena that make up the experiment in question. We are only *familiar* with these properties because of our embodiment. No embodiment, no experiment of any kind. This is to say that every experiment reflects a creative play between the familiar and the unfamiliar. This crucial aspect in the development of thought experiments comes to light when we remove those layers of the experiment-narratives that we find in textbooks. They conceal four important features of observation and experiment: (1) the *non-linearity* of observation and experiment; (2) the importance of *human agency* in the manipulation and transformation of real and imaginary objects; (3) the *interaction* of concepts, precepts, and objects; and (4) the creativity due to *uncertainty* (Gooding 1992, 47). Concealment of these features of experimental practice in experiment-narratives is an effect of various types of narrative reconstruction (Gooding 1992, 50). Each type involves (i) different *activities*, (ii) different kinds of *narration*, and (iii) the achievement of different *ends*. To illustrate the basic idea, let us look at an example of the type of narrative reconstruction that

Gooding calls *cognitive reconstruction*: Temporal ordering is imposed by the scientist on his or her perceptions in order to make sense of them in relation to the uniform forward time progression of an external physical reality. What happens during cognitive reconstruction in this case is that the scientist assimilates the nonlinear time of conscious experience with the linear time progression of an external physical reality. Such processes of cognitive reconstruction and other types of narrative reconstruction by scientists are well documented in their notebooks, sketches, and letters, Gooding declares. They involve activities like the construction of a perceived object, the creation of interaction patterns with other entities than these objects, and a good amount of reasoning to relate observation and theory. Narrative reconstruction aims to represent and communicate the observed while implementing it into an argument in favor of or against the relevant pieces of theory.

3. "GROUNDING" GOODING'S EXPERIMENTALISM

Experimentalists need to ground the experimental character that unites real-world experiments and thought experiments; otherwise, it remains unclear where the epistemic power of experiments comes from. Mach (1897 [1905]) and Sorensen (1992) ground their experimentalist accounts with a kind of evolutionary theory, which only in Sorensen's case is clearly of a Darwinian kind. Buzzoni (2008), on the other hand, appeals to a certain tradition of understanding the Kantian *a priori,* and tells us a story about the indispensable role that the transcendental nature of the mind plays in conjunction with operationalized ways of obtaining experience in experimentation outside of the mind. To play on Gooding's metaphor, Buzzoni argues for "head *and* hands" in contrast to Mach's and Sorensen's "*head* over hands." Gooding commits himself to "*hands* over head."

What grounds this priority of hands over head is a reference to human agency and some related empirical and material considerations. If we understand human agency, then we understand experimentation, be it in the head or in the real world. Understanding human agency in turn is a function of understanding procedures. Procedures are "sequences of acts or operations whose inferential structure we do not yet know. The term procedural connotes know-how" (Gooding 1992, 53). What is basic is skill, not conceptual knowledge or the intentionality of acts—"rationales for actions often emerge as understanding develops or as an account unfolds" (Gooding 1992, 53). In mapping experimental processes in real time, he therefore "represents human agency directly, by a line, against which an active verb is presented" (Gooding 1992, 60). This is to separate the material things that are subject to this agency from related choices and decisions, as well as from related conceptual changes. Experimentation is mainly a function of embodiment, because human agency is bodily. Gooding's body is the *necessary condition* for intervening with the world, and it instantiates a relatively *autonomous parameter* in the process of experimental practice. The body is the source of agency, which in turn enables the scientist to move from one event or object to the next. This is the same agency that makes possible the scientific production of potentially novel events and objects, which helps to drive scientific research.

While Gooding's consideration certainly makes a noteworthy case for "hands over heads," we are wondering if the body is well perceived in his account of thought experiments. From a phenomenological perspective a number of serious problems can be raised.

4. "GROUNDING" PHENOMENOLOGY—THE *EPOCHÉ*

From a phenomenological point of view, some of Gooding's claims, especially with respect to the role of the body, may sound familiar. Phenomenologists ranging from classical thinkers such as Edmund Husserl, Maurice Merleau-Ponty, Jean-Paul Sartre, or Aaron Gurwitsch, to contemporary scholars like Samuel Todes, Maxine Sheets-Johnstone, or Hermann Schmitz have emphasized that the body is a necessary condition for the possibility of any encounter with the natural world. Yet the body of phenomenology is not identical with the one Gooding has in mind. In order to show this, we need first to say something about the general scope of phenomenological philosophy. Only then will it become clear where we see the potential in the phenomenological elucidation of the body to shed some additional light on the philosophical understanding of the bodily component of thought experiments.

As phenomenology is concerned with the reflective analysis of phenomena, it seeks to analyze the "how" of the different modes of experience and not their "what," that is, their actual content. With regard to this task, phenomenology, as it was developed by Husserl, draws upon Franz Brentano and the notion of intentionality. Unlike in Gooding, intentionality comes first in terms of philosophical method because it is taken to be the crucial characteristic of consciousness. To say that consciousness is intentional is to recognize that there is an essential correlation between an act of consciousness (the noetic aspect such as perceiving, knowing, imagining, etc.) and an object *as* it is meant and intended (the noematic aspect, i.e., the object *as* perceived, the object *as* known, the object *as* imagined, etc.). Phenomenology, then, deals with the systematic analysis of various noetic-noematic correlation-structures.

In spelling out the intentional correlations between subject and world, phenomenology pursues a traditional epistemological goal: Phenomenologists seek to identify those conditions that make our thought and experience of natural objects possible. Yet as Husserl has stressed in detail, this kind of reflective analysis is impossible without certain methodological precautions (e.g., Husserl 1983, Ch. 4). Husserl's reasoning goes as follows: Usually, when we are directed towards the world within the *natural attitude*,[3] we implicitly accept a number of unquestioned presuppositions. Most fundamentally, we implicitly presuppose that there exists a world which consists of a multitude of objects and that these objects can be investigated by means of empirical methods. This fundamental presupposition is constitutive for any empirical investigation, be it scientific or extra-scientific in nature. However, if the validity of our empirical claims depends on this fundamental presupposition, it also follows that we cannot rely on the findings of our empirical investigations when asking for the conditions that make our thought and experience of natural objects possible. According to Husserl, the basic failure of naturalistic philosophy is that it assumes empirical knowledge is possible in order to explain the possibility of empirical knowledge. Husserl sought to avoid this vicious circularity by introducing the method of the phenomenological *epoché* (see Moran 2008).

To perform the phenomenological *epoché* is to abstain from all those presuppositions which we usually take for granted and which in sum make up the natural attitude. However, it is important to note that in performing the *epoché* we do not actively doubt any of these presuppositions. The *epoché* is merely methodological in nature; it is primarily designed to identify the conditions of the possibility of natural thought and experience without falling prey to vicious circularities. Yet by embracing this methodological tool, phenomenologists also commit themselves to an approach which is both reflective and descriptive. The aim of phenomenological analysis is not to construct theories in order to answer epistemological questions. In performing the *epoché,* phenomenologists strive for a presuppositionless description of phenomena and for the reflective exposure of those structures which are necessary for our different forms of natural encounters with the world.

With these methodological considerations in mind, we are now in a position to contrast Gooding's views about the body with those of phenomenology.

5. ON THE PHENOMENOLOGICAL BODY

As we have seen, Gooding advances the body within a naturalistic framework. This is to say that whatever role the body might be playing in thought experiments, any characterization of this role will be empirical in nature. From a naturalistic perspective in which the totality of reality is equivalent to the physical realm, the human body is just another (albeit highly complex) spatiotemporal object. Now, the point of phenomenology certainly is not to say that this view is altogether mistaken. It would be quite peculiar to deny that the human body is *also* a physical thing which can be investigated by empirical means. And it would be just as dogmatic to deny that empirical findings about the interactions between embodied actors and the world are in principle futile if a philosophical elucidation of thought experiments is at stake. However, what phenomenologists are eager to emphasize is that there are aspects of the human body which cannot, in principle, be addressed by empirical means. It is especially the constitutive role that the body plays in our natural encounters with the world which seem to fall outside the naturalistic picture. Yet it is exactly this constitutive role which, on a phenomenological view, is of utmost importance for our understanding of the relations between subject and the world.

One way to show that the body plays such a constitutive role is to take a closer phenomenological look at how we perceive spatiotemporal objects. These objects are, as Husserl and others have emphasized on numerous occasions, always and necessarily given perspectively. This is to say that spatiotemporal objects can never be given adequately; that is, a particular intention towards a spatiotemporal object can never specify every aspect of the object in question. At any point in time, a spatiotemporal object has, for instance, a back side which is momentarily hidden due to the subject's vantage point. This fact, however, has severe implications for the way the phenomenon of perception is to be understood: That spatiotemporal objects are always given perspectively also means that every perspectival appearance of an object not only presupposes something which appears, but also someone for whom the perspectival appearance appears (Zahavi 1994, 65). Or in other words, since spatiotemporal objects always appear from a certain distance and from a certain angle, their givenness presupposes a "zero-point of orientation" (e.g., Husserl 1989, 166) from which the perception and interaction with spatiotemporal objects occur. This "zero-point" is, according to phenomenology, the human body, which serves as the irreducible center of spatial orientation. It is only due to its embodiment in space that the subject is able to perceive its natural surroundings from a first-person perspective.

Yet being the "zero-point of orientation" is by no means the only constitutive function the body plays in the course of our natural perception. The constitution of perceptual reality is also dependent on the experience of bodily movements or, to use Husserl's original term, on *kinaesthetic experience*. With regard to this aspect, a possible argument goes as follows:[4] As we have seen, intentions towards spatiotemporal objects always have "excess content" over what is actually given in perceptual experience. This is to say that we are usually intentionally directed towards spatiotemporal objects *in their unity*, even though only perspectival appearances of these objects are actually given. However, this discrepancy between what is perceptually given and what is picked out by the intention raises the question of how the meaning-content of "spatiotemporal objects in their unity" is constituted. How are we able to be intentionally directed towards, say, a table, if a series of perspectival profiles is all that is actually given? How do we know that changing appearances are appearances *of one and the same thing?*

The answer, from a phenomenological viewpoint, is to say that every act towards a spatiotemporal object is related to a manifold of potential acts which would complete what is left indeterminate about the object as it is intended in a given act. Yet the unity between these potential acts is dependent on a specific "I can" (e.g., Husserl 1968, 391), that is, on non-thematic knowledge about the potentiality of bodily movement. According to Husserl, any actual perception refers to a manifold of "perceptions that we *could* have, if we *actively directed* the course of perception otherwise: if, for example, we turned our eyes that way instead of this, or if we were to step forward or to one side, and so forth" (Husserl 1960, 44). Thus, the body is not only the fixed center in relation to which perspectively given objects and primordial space unfolds itself; it is also the medium by means of which the intentional directedness towards spatiotemporal objects becomes possible.

As we have seen so far, phenomenology regards the *body as a necessary condition of the possibility of the perception and interaction with the natural world*. The body is not merely a vehicle which allows a disembodied subject to navigate through its physical surroundings. Since the intentional directedness towards spatiotemporal objects and even our most basic concept of primordial space always presupposes bodily situatedness, the idea of a disembodied subject turns out to be highly questionable, and thus Gooding's dissociation of the body in the sense of one physical object among others from the lived body in his reconstruction of the bodily dimension of thought experimentation becomes problematic. Phenomenologically construed, the body and the subject are inextricably intertwined. Gooding's body is a problematic abstraction and runs the risk of underestimating the bodily character of the hands in his notion of "hands over heads."

However, the just mentioned difference is by no means the only discrepancy between Gooding's view of the body and a phenomenological account. The methodological considerations of the previous section help to bring out another important point: If it is true that embodiment is the condition of the possibility of natural thought and experience, it also follows that the phenomenological notion of the body cannot be equivalent to the natural notion of physical bodies or things. Since the constitution of the latter presupposes the former, we have to distinguish sharply between lived bodies (in German: *Leiber*) and physical bodies or things (in German: *Körper*). The former is phenomenologically described after the *epoché*; the latter is described with respect to the various scientific or extra-scientific natural attitudes. As we saw earlier, phenomenologists do not deny that the lived body can be treated as a physical thing amongst others. The possibility to do so, however, depends on a basic acquaintance with the very concepts of natural "thinghood" and natural (i.e., primordial) space, which in turn presupposes the constitutional capacities of an embodied subject. Or as Dan Zahavi has put it: "My original and immediate relation to my body is not an experience of the body as an object. Quite to the contrary, we are here dealing with a self-objectivation [sic], which just like every other perceptual experience is dependent upon and made possible by the unthematized co-functioning body-experience" (Zahavi 1994, 69). Thus, from a phenomenological perspective, Gooding's body has to be supplemented by a deeper, further-reaching conception of the lived body.

In order to indicate the sense in which the phenomenological alternative to Gooding's exclusive focus on the physical body could affect the interpretation of thought experiments, a concrete example might help. Let us therefore turn to Newton's well-known "bucket experiment."

6. NEWTON'S BUCKET

"Newton's bucket" can be found in Newton's *Principia* (Newton [1729] 2002, 741–742). It "is one of the most celebrated and notorious examples in the history of thought experiments" (Brown 2011, 7). One of the reasons it is so fascinating (and ideal for the present discussion) is the ease with which it employs very familiar objects and procedures in order to "show the existence of absolute space" (Brown 2011, 7). Absolute space is something quite exotic from the perspective of familiar objects and procedures.

The thought experiment goes as follows. First, you imagine yourself filling a bucket halfway with water and suspending it from some fixed point with a rope. You twist the rope more and more by rotating the bucket. There are now three distinct stages to observe. In the first, after the rope has taken all the twisting that it can take, but before you have let go of the bucket, there is no relative motion between the water and the bucket. The level of the water is flat. In the second stage, you release the bucket and notice that there is now relative motion between the water and the bucket as the bucket spins while the water remains stationary, still flat in the bucket. In the third stage, there is once again no relative motion between the water and the bucket because both are spinning at equal velocities, but this time the level of the water is concave as it has crept up the side of the bucket. This is all very familiar, yet we are now presented with something that is not: It seems we must posit the existence of something to explain the difference between the first and the third stages. In each, there is no relative motion between the bucket and the water, but there *is* a difference in the curvature of the water level. Since everything else has been abstracted away, there is nothing else in relation to which the bucket could be spinning, save absolute space. You can come to the same conclusion by considering another situation in which two rocks are attached by a rope. Far away from gravity and any point of reference, you notice that there is tension in the cord. Again, you seem forced to admit the existence of something in relation to which the system must be rotating, since the only way to explain this tension in the absence of a detectable relative motion is revolution. In each case the imagined rotation drives you to accept the idea that absolute space is the only explanation for this phenomenon established in the "laboratory of the mind."

According to Hans Reichenbach, "only by passing through a state of absolutism in the theory of space . . . we have been led to the deeper insights we have today" (Reichenbach 1958, 212). To uphold a "hands over heads" approach to account for thought experiments as important as Newton's bucket experiment, one needs to show that thought experiments in general and Newton's bucket experiment in particular have a life of their own in the following sense. If a thought experiment is employed in the context of two contradictory theories (T_1 and T_2), where a version of the thought experiment, call it V_1, supports T_1, and a modified version of the thought experiment, call it V_2, supports T_2, we may say that the thought experiment has a life of its own if and only if the evidential force of V_1 remains partly intact despite a conscious acceptance of T_2 in light of V_2, and this evidential force cannot simply be reduced to a theoretical mistake that is accessible only from T_2. From the perspective of Gooding's account, this is certainly the case when comparing Ernst Mach's version of the bucket thought experiment, V_2 (see, for a further discussion, Kühne 2005, 191–202), with Newton's original version of it, V_1, the former being employed in favor of a relativistic conception of physical space (T_2). Hence Gooding's approach succeeds in this respect. Newton's original version of the bucket thought experiment retains evidential force despite a conscious acceptance of relativistic physics, and this is a function of the familiarity of the involved objects and procedures as well as the generally accepted method of idealization in physics, which allowed Newton to work with an empty universe. Without going into further details of a comparison between Newton's and Mach's versions of the bucket thought experiment, our point is to highlight how a phenomenological approach to thought experimenting can complement the emerging picture of the relative autonomy of the "laboratory of the mind" in at least two important respects. First, we will suggest an account of the origin of absolute space from the perspective of a phenomenology of the body. Then we will suggest several ways to characterize the quality of thought experiments concerning space from a phenomenological perspective, which are not meant to be exclusive, of course, but which can serve to complement other perspectives.

7. ON ABSOLUTE SPACE

We will now turn to the first point: how the notion of absolute space may be introduced in a thought experiment from a phenomenological perspective. In 1921 the British physicist Alfred A. Robb expressed how strongly repelled he was by the "idea that events could be simultaneous to one person and not simultaneous to another; which was one of Einstein's chief contentions. . . . If two physicists *A* and *B* agree to discuss a physical experiment, their agreement implies that they admit, in some sense, a common world in which the experiment is supposed to take place" (Robb 1921, v–vi). Given

Gooding's characterization of experiments as being located at the intersection of the actual and the possible, Robb's claim that every conceivable experiment presupposes the idea of a "common world" certainly makes sense. Phenomenologists would say that the very foundation of this "common world" is the domain of what we would like to call the *possibilities of the lived body*. In a phenomenological view, these possibilities are not only irreducible to metaphysical, logical, epistemological, and nomological possibilities, they are also crucial for the philosophical understanding of any thought experiment in physics generally, and those about space in particular. This is because, phenomenologically construed, the domain of the possibilities of the lived body is inextricably linked with the notion of primordial space on which all other (scientific and extra-scientific) conceptions of space are founded.

As we have just seen, phenomenology argues for a priority of the lived body, which implies a priority of primordial space. This is of utmost importance for the interpretation of thought experiments about space. To support such an assertion, we must make the following claim plausible: The possibility and quality of any thought experiment on space is (among other things) a function of (1) there being a space that is both prior and irreducible to scientific (i.e., mathematical and physical) conceptions of space, and (2) there being ways to account for the relationship between this space and other kinds of space. In order to establish (1) and (2), we want to supplement the methodological repertoire introduced above with some fundamental insights that can be found in Schmitz' phenomenology of the body.

8. THE SPACE OF VASTNESS AND THE ABSOLUTE LOCALITY OF THE LIVED BODY

While Schmitz' work is almost entirely ignored, especially in the English-speaking world, we believe that his phenomenology of the body could lend considerable support to a philosophy of science that follows the principle of "hands over heads." Yet we cannot do more here than to focus on one aspect of (thought) experiments on space, namely on its relation to the lived body and to primordial space. In addition, we can only glimpse into Schmitz' extensive work on space (Schmitz 1964–1980, Vol. III, Part 1), not to mention its relationship to his overall philosophical system that is based on his comprehensive phenomenology of the body.[5]

According to Schmitz, by putting "head over hands," philosophy since Plato has committed a grave error. The *discovery of the mind* brought about the *masking of the lived body* (Schmitz 1964–1980, Vol. II, Part 1, 441). This has caused a number of problems, including the reality of space. Only phenomenology is able to correct the unfortunate development of the last 2,500 years, argues Schmitz. Very generally, space is most accurately described as a *vastness* (in German: *Weite*) that can be given purely or shaped to a certain form. Vastness is an *Ur-phenomenon* that cannot be fully explicated in the form of a definition (Schmitz 1984–1980, Vol. III, Part 1, 7–10). Yet it articulates itself in every kind of lived-bodily experience. This is because the lived body must be defined by a position that is absolute. Otherwise we are not able to accommodate experiences like those documented in reports of *phantom limbs* (Schmitz 1964–1980, Vol. II, Part 1, 5–24). The space that corresponds to the lived body is therefore the *space of vastness, which is unmeasurable* (see Schmitz 1964–1980, Vol. III, Part 1, 203–208). The place of the lived body is absolute in retraction from vastness. In a nutshell, bodiliness is defined in terms of absolute location. But lived bodiliness, which gives meaning to a human life and everything there is, is a function of the relationship between vastness and narrowness (in German: *Enge*). Vastness and narrowness are the primordial poles of bodily existence (see Schmitz 1964–1980, Vol. II, Part 1, 163, 213).

An example might help to illustrate the dynamics involved in any lived body as it originates from the simultaneous and counteracting tendencies towards vastness and narrowness. Let us assume that the tendency towards vastness and narrowness is in equilibrium in the bodies of two persons who engage in sexual intercourse. Schmitz describes the increasing arousal that eventually culminates in orgasms in terms of the dynamics emerging from the simultaneous and counteracting tendencies towards vastness and narrowness. He identifies three stages of "voluptuousness" (in German: *Wollust*) (see Schmitz 1964–1980, Vol. II, Part 1, 220–223). What happens at the first stage is also exemplified when we experience a breeze on a very hot summer day. The lived body begins to dissipate into small islands, something that is not possible while the lived body is still in the grip of the tendency to narrowness. At the second stage the two tendencies towards vastness and narrowness begin to counteract rhythmically. What happens at this stage can be also experienced while having a swim, for example. Intermittently, the tendency towards narrowness can be dominant, although the tendency towards vastness predominates overall. At a third stage the competition between the two forces can be so strong that the two tendencies disconnect. That is what we experience in an orgasm. At this point the space of vastness comes to the fore in pure form (see Schmitz 1964–1980, Vol. III, Part 1, 167–169).

Given Schmitz' phenomenology of the space of vastness, we would like to suggest the following: If there is anything that can be taken as a lived-bodily possibility to account for (thought) experiments on absolute space, then probably it is the space of vastness as it is primarily articulated in all bodily life insofar as bodiliness is defined in terms of absolute locality. Familiar objects of relative locality in a physical space as well as the procedures involving them are secondary in terms of conditions of possibility. This is the point we would like to make against Gooding. Focusing on relative locality misses the domain of the possibilities of the lived body. It does not even get the body in its absolute locality in focus, not to mention the space of vastness that defines the lived body. A (thought) experiment on absolute space is, we suggest, the better the more it authentically preserves the phenomenon of the space of vastness as given in bodiliness. In this respect, Newton's bucket experiment is arguably a good one. But this is certainly not enough for a (thought) experiment on absolute space to be deemed successful on the whole as far as phenomenological criteria are concerned. In addition, given the unity of vastness and the fact that it underlies all kinds of space (see Schmitz 1964–1980, Vol. III, Part 1, 193–203), the quality of a thought experiment on space depends on the way it respects the relationships between different ways of forming vastness, that is, different kinds of space. We have not said much yet about these relationships but much of the work of Schmitz is dedicated to analyzing them. Most basic is the question, "What relates the different kinds of space?" According to Schmitz, it is *directedness* that matters for a phenomenological classification of different kinds of space and a phenomenological characterization of their relationship. The central idea is as follows.

9. FROM ABSOLUTE SPACE TO THE SPACE OF PHYSICS

We start with the space of vastness, which is the most basic kind of space. From here we develop the other kinds of space in terms of directedness by which the two counteracting tendencies towards vastness and narrowness are related (see Schmitz 1964–1980, Vol. II, Part 1, 98, 163, 213). When experiencing climate, for example, we experience the *space of vastness*, and can express this space as a subject in utterances like "*It* is humid." Sometimes we can experience this space also when perceiving a sound, like that of a screeching circular saw (Schmitz 1964–1980, Vol. III, Part 1, 47–54). But when *direction* begins to mediate the retraction of the lived body from vastness (Schmitz 1964–1980, Vol. III, Part 1, 54–71), then vastness takes on a different form and gives rise to a different kind of space. The direction can be of one of four types. We call it the *space of lived-bodily directedness* with respect to the first three types, and the *space of location* with respect to the last one.

Breathing in and out is an example of the first type. A second type is exemplified when handling tools. Here we touch upon the bodily dimension on which Gooding has placed a special emphasis in his reflection on the bodily component of thought experiments. As we have argued in the previous sections, phenomenologically speaking, Gooding is mistaken when locating this bodily dimension outside of the *space of lived-bodily directedness*. Gooding's mistake is a result of the fact that the second type of directedness is such that its origin is not noticeable to the lived body *directly*. It requires mediation through an interaction between body and extra-bodily objects. Yet it is still the *space of lived-bodily directedness* that is involved here—not the physical space in which the physical body has a well-defined location in terms of relative position. A third type of directedness relates to the overlap between the lived body and the physical body and has rudimentary geometrical characteristics, resulting from an interplay of right/left, up/down, following the position of the physical body. It is still the *space of lived-bodily directedness* that is involved here.

Finally, a fourth type of directedness and thus space culminates in a cluster of space-conceptions which is very different from the previous three: Take, for instance, the geographical north-south or Euclidean space. In these examples, vastness has lost its relation to the lived body and takes on the space of what we call the *space of location*. This is to say that, unlike in the previous three cases, this conception of space does not place the lived body at the "zero point of orientation." As Husserl has shown in his last major publication, the *Crisis* (Husserl 1970), the theoretical accomplishment of a scientific space-conception which does not imply any reference to the lived body was constitutive for the development of modern science. However, according to Husserl, it is also crucial to keep in mind that such a conception of space is an *idealization* which in principle cannot be experienced by any embodied subject. Or, to put it differently, just as we can think about geometrical objects like ideal circles, embodied subjects can think about conceptions of space which are detached from any reference to the lived body. Yet, for embodied subjects, neither ideal circles nor bodiless spaces can be directly given *without the mediation of a particular theory*. From the phenomenological perspective one could say, therefore, that naturalistic programs with respect to space in philosophy of science have gained plausibility only because the *space of lived-bodily directedness* and the *space of location* were theoretically misunderstood. The above-described directedness is either described along the lines of the *space of location*, or it is presupposed that the *space of location* is prior to the *space of lived-bodily directedness*. In each case a naturalistic program can gain plausibility, implying that the bodily component of (thought) experiments about space must be explained exclusively in terms of standards of familiarity with objects and proper procedures in the space of location. The situation changes if we employ the sketched phenomenology of space to characterize the bodily component of thought experimenting with which Gooding is justly concerned.

10. ON HOW TO RELATE DIFFERENT TYPES OF SPACE

As we have seen in the preceding sections, phenomenologists argue that a particular conception of space is the condition of the possibility of the givenness of physical things. Whenever we interact with our natural surroundings, a basic acquaintance with certain characteristics of spatiality is always already presupposed. On a phenomenological view, however, the most fundamental conception of primordial space is not formal as it is, for instance, in Kant. In analyzing the "How" of the givenness of physical things, essential characteristics of spatiality can be intuitively described. Furthermore, it is possible to show how these essential characteristics are related to bodily phenomena like kinaesthetic movements. To put it in a nutshell: From a phenomenological perspective, the notions of subjectivity, embodiment, and primordial space are not only inextricably related; they are also equally fundamental if we are to ask for the necessary conditions of our natural world-involvement. In Schmitz, as we have seen, this is the case because subjectivity is a function of bodiliness which in turn is a function of counteracting tendencies towards vastness and narrowness. Yet if all this is true, two problematic aspects of Newton's thought experiment can be pointed out. This is one way to illustrate how it is possible to assess the quality of a thought experiment from a phenomenological point of view.

First, if space is properly described as a necessary condition of the possibility of the givenness of natural objects, how can some of these objects—namely, water, a bucket, and a rope—stand in a *causal* relationship with something that is the necessary condition of the very givenness of these objects? Phenomenologically construed, the assumption that a causal relation of this kind exists is a conflation of two different levels of analysis; it is a conflation of phenomena which are to be analyzed within the natural attitude and phenomena whose proper analysis requires the methodologically motivated abandonment of all those presuppositions which are usually constitutive for natural interactions with the world.

Second, and more importantly—however we judge the theoretical merits of Newton's bucket both from a systematic and a historical point of view—Newton's conception of absolute space certainly is a result of the fourth type of directedness and thus belongs to the above-mentioned cluster of idealized space-conceptions which are characterized by their detachment from the lived body. Now, the genuinely phenomenological point of a critique of Newton's bucket experiment is that it does not pay appropriate attention to the kind of relationship this thought experiment establishes between the lived body space—which, as we have argued, is the condition of the possibility of the givenness of familiar objects like water, buckets, and ropes—and scientific space which, as we have also tried to show, transcends the sphere of that which can be subject to an experience of the lived body. The apparent persuasiveness of Newton's thought experiment stems from the ease with which it seems to make the acceptance of absolute space inevitable due to the familiarity of objects and procedures. This is also the point of Gooding's approach. However, a closer phenomenological analysis shows that we are also led to this conclusion because Newton's thought experiment seems to involve two conceptions of space which are *categorically* distinct: While the imagination of familiar objects like water, buckets, and ropes clearly presupposes a basic acquaintance with lived body space, Newton's absolute space is a theoretical conception which in principle transcends the first-person perspective of embodied subjects. On this view, then, the error of Newton's thought experiment is to import a theoretical artifact into an arrangement of worldly objects without paying attention to the noetic differences between particular conceptions of scientific and extra-scientific space.

11. CONCLUSION

Of course, much more remains to be said about Newton's thought experiment, in particular, and a phenomenological approach to thought experiments in general. Our critical discussion of Newton's bucket could turn out to be shortsighted in the light of claims that this thought experiment has nothing to do with absolute space (see Laymon 1978). At this time we are confident that these claims do not affect our analysis negatively. Moreover, it might be that more steadfastly "processual" phenomenological approaches in the spirit of Sheets-Johnstone reach deeper than our phenomenological discussion. But "deeper" does not mean "more true," and it is very unlikely that it will invalidate our criticisms of Gooding's naturalistic view on the bodily component of thought experiments. It is also likely that we have missed in our explorations the way in which the social realm influences the lived body. In fact this is indeed a problem as far as Schmitz' phenomenology is concerned. But soft spots like this can only encourage further discussion on the importance of the body in thought experiments, and thereby include the work of Gail Weiss, Judith Butler, and others to get hold of the social dimension of the lived body.

We hope some basic tenets of a possible phenomenological contribution to the ongoing debate have become clear. From a phenomenological perspective, our natural interactions with the world are mediated by various natural attitudes which in turn consist of a number of typically unquestioned presuppositions. While some of these presuppositions are highly contingent, some others qualify as necessary conditions of the possibility of our natural world-involvement. Certain general characteristics of embodiment and spatiality belong, as we have tried to indicate, to the latter group. Since phenomenologists are predominantly concerned with the analysis of implicit presuppositions of this kind, phenomenological methodology could be, we believe, of considerable importance for the philosophical understanding of thought experiments. While more detailed analyses will be necessary in order to justify this general claim, our aim in this paper has been to show that the phenomenological elucidation of the relations between the lived body and primordial space can lend additional, non-naturalistic support to contemporary "hands over heads" approaches. We agree with Gooding that the principle of "head over hands" is misleading. Yet as we have shown, Gooding's "hands" are part of the lived body. A naturalistic account of "hands over heads" must therefore fall short.

ACKNOWLEDGEMENTS

This contribution is fully collaborative. It was funded in part by the Austrian Science Fund (project number: J3114). Many thanks to Jim Brown, Mélanie Frappier, Letitia Meynell, and Mike Stuart for helpful feedback to an earlier draft of this paper.

NOTES

1. It should be noted right from the outset that, in a similar sense in which there is not just *one* analytic movement, but rather a number of individuals working in roughly the same philosophical spirit, there is not just one unified phenomenological approach. This justifies our talk of a "phenomenological approach," although we are actually considering only the work of Edmund Husserl and Hermann Schmitz. Also, we cannot emphasize enough that we are aware of the significant differences between Husserl and Schmitz as far as phenomenological method is concerned. See Schmitz (1964–1980, Vol. III, Part 1, 1–7). For a short summary of Schmitz' criticisms of Husserl see Schmitz (1980, 15). We believe that Schmitz overplays the differences and don't think that the differences between his and Husserl's phenomenology have any relevance for the way in which we are about to use their respective phenomenological insights into the nature of the body.
2. It probably should be mentioned that there are significant differences between these four experimentalist approaches to thought experiments. See Buzzoni (2008, 74–80). But they are irrelevant for our considerations.
3. According to Husserl, the natural attitude is the attitude within which we stand before we take up a reflective stance towards the "How" of our world-involvement. This is to say that it is only by means of philosophical reflection that we are able to unveil those presuppositions which underlie our scientific and extra-scientific interactions with the world (see, e.g., Husserl 1983, §30).
4. More radical ways to understand the role of kinaesthesis were, for instance, formulated by Maxine Sheets-Johnstone (2000). On her view, the bodily ability to move oneself is the precondition not only for human agency and the acquisition of skills, but also for any intentional contact with our worldly surroundings.
5. Schmitz' work has defined the foundations of the Society for New Phenomenology (SNP), which is preparing an English translation of his *System der Philosophie*. In our view, this is long overdue as it most likely will open up new and original venues for a fruitful reception and critical discussion of his views, which are extensively substantiated in an exceptional manner. This is not to say that we would endorse all of Schmitz' views. On the contrary, we are aware of several significant shortcomings of his philosophy. However, none of them are significant enough to justify an ignorance of his work. For more information about the SNP see "What Is New Phenomenology?" www.gnp-online.de/index.php?id=15&L=1 (accessed October 1, 2011).

REFERENCES

Brown, James R. 2011. *The Laboratory of the Mind: Thought Experiments in the Natural Sciences*. 2nd edition. New York and London: Routledge.

Buzzoni, Marco. 2008. *Thought Experiment in the Natural Sciences. An Opera-tional and Reflexive-Transcendental Conception*. Würzburg: Königshausen & Neumann.

Froese, Tom, and Shaun Gallagher. 2010. "Phenomenology and Artificial Life: Toward a Technological Supplementation of Phenomenological Methodology." *Husserl Studies* 26: 83–106.

Gooding, David C. 1990. *Experimenting and the Making of Meaning*. Dordrecht: Kluwer Academic Publishers.

———. 1992. "The Procedural Turn; or, Why Do Thought Experiments Work?" In *Cognitive Models of Science*, edited by Ronald N. Giere, 45–76. Minneapolis: University of Minnesota Press.

———. 1993. "What is Experimental about Thought Experiments?" *Proceedings of the Philosophy of Science Association* 2: 280–290.

Hammer, Felix. 1974. *Leib und Geschlecht. Philosophische Perspektiven von Nietzsche bis Merlau-Ponty und Phänomenologisch-Systematischer Aufriß*. Bonn: Bouvier.

Husserl, Edmund. 1960. *Cartesian Meditations. An Introduction to Phenomenology*. Translated by Dorion Cairns. The Hague: Martinus Nijhoff.

———. 1968. *Phänomenologische Psychologie. Vorlesungen Sommersemester*. Edited by Walter Biemel. The Hague: Martinus Nijhoff.

———. 1970. *The Crisis of the European Sciences and Transcendental Phenomenology. An Introduction to Phenomenological Philosophy*. Translated by David Carr. Evanston, IL: Northwestern University Press.

———. 1983. *Ideas Pertaining to a Pure Phenomenology and to a Phenomenological Philosophy. First Book. General Introduction to a Pure Phenomenology*. Translated by Fred Kersten. The Hague: Martinus Nijhoff.

———. 1989. *Ideas Pertaining to a Pure Phenomenology and to a Phenomenological Philosophy. Second Book. Studies in the Phenomenology of Constitution*. Translated by Richard Rojcewicz and André Schuwer. Dordrecht: Kluwer.

Ierodiakonou, Katerina. 2005. "Ancient Thought Experiments: A First Approach." *Ancient Philosophy* 25: 125–140.

Kalin, Martin G. 1972. "Kant's Transcendental Arguments as Gedankenexperimente." *Kant-Studien* 63: 315–328.

Kant, Immanuel. 1998. *Critique of Pure Reason*. Translated and edited by Paul Guyer and Allen W. Wood. Cambridge: Cambridge University Press.

Kühne, Ulrich. 2005. *Die Methode des Gedankenexperiments*. Frankfurt am Main: Suhrkamp.

Kujundzic, Nebojsa. 1998. "The Role of Variation in Thought Experiments." *International Studies in the Philosophy of Science* 12: 239–243.

Laymon, Raymond. 1978. "Newton's Bucket." *Journal of the History of Philosophy* 16: 399–413.

Lotz, Christian. 2007. *From Affectivity to Subjectivity: Husserl's Phenomenology Revisited*. Hampshire: Palgrave Macmillan.

Mach, Ernst. 1897 [1905]. "Über Gedankenexperimente." *Zeitschrift für den physikalischen und chemischen Unterricht* 10: 1–5. English edition: 1905. *Knowledge and Error*. Translated by J. McCormack, 134–147. Dordrecht: Reidel.

Mohanty, J. N. 1991. "The Method of Imaginative Variation in Phenomenology." In *Thought Experiments in Science and Philosophy*, edited by Tamara Horowitz and Gerald Massey, 261–272. Lanham, MD: Rowman & Littlefield.

Moran, Dermot. 2008. "Husserl's Transcendental Philosophy and the Critique of Naturalism." *Continental Philosophy Review* 41: 401–425.

Myers, Mason C. 1986. "Analytical Thought Experiments." *Metaphilosophy* 17: 109–118.

Newton, Isaac. [1729] 2002. *The Mathematical Principles of Natural Philosophy.* Reprinted in *On the Shoulders of Giants*, edited by Stephen Hawking, 733–1160. Philadelphia and Leipzig: Running Press.

Norton, John. 1996. "Are Thought Experiments Just What You Thought?" *Canadian Journal of Philosophy* 26: 333–366.

Ørsted, Hans Christian. [1811] 1920. "Første Indledning til den almindelige Naturlaere." Reprinted in *Naturvidenskabelige Skrifter*, Vol. III, 155–190. Kopenhagen: Andr. Fred. Host & Son.

———. [1811] 1998. "First Introduction to General Physics: A Prospectus of Lectures in This Science." In *Selected Scientific Works of Hans Christian Ørsted*, translated and edited by Karen Jelved, Andrews D. Jackson, and Ole Knudsen, 282–309. Princeton, NJ: Princeton University Press.

Reichenbach, Hans. 1958. *The Philosophy of Space and Time.* Translated by Maria Reichenbach and John Freud. New York: Dover.

Robb, Alfred. 1921. *The Absolute Relations of Space and Time.* Cambridge: Cambridge University Press.

Schmitz, Hermann. 1964–1980. *System der Philosophie.* 5 volumes (in 10 parts). Bonn: Bouvier.

———. 1980. *Neue Phänomenologie.* Bonn: Bouvier.

Sheets-Johnstone, Maxine. 2000. *The Primacy of Movement.* Philadelphia: John Benjamins.

Sklar, Lawrence. 2010. "I'd Love to Be a Naturalist—If Only I Knew What Naturalism Was." *Philosophy of Science* 77: 1121–1137.

Sorensen, Roy A. 1992. *Thought Experiments.* Oxford: Oxford University Press.

Welton, Donn, ed. 1999. *The Body. Classic and Contemporary Readings.* Oxford: Blackwell.

Zahavi, Dan. 1994. "Husserl's Phenomenology of the Body." *Études Phénoménologiques* 19: 63–84.

5   Thought Experiments from a Kantian Point of View

Marco Buzzoni

1. INTRODUCTION

It makes intuitive sense to connect real experiments (REs) and thought experiments (TEs) in the natural sciences in a way that might account both for their unity and their distinction. We think of them as united because empirical REs and TEs tell us about the same empirical reality, and it would be hard to deny that their outcomes may either coincide or clash. We think of them as distinct because it would be just as hard to claim that their functions are identical, either by declaring that real execution is superfluous or by reducing TEs to the formulation of questions that can be answered only by REs.

It seems therefore to be a desideratum for any theories of TE that they neither separate REs and TEs so sharply that their connection becomes unintelligible, nor connect them so closely that their difference disappears. However, as we shall see, the main views on TEs prove themselves unable to salvage this intuitive and pre-theoretical understanding of the relation of unity and distinction between REs and TEs in the natural sciences. The main purpose of this paper is to show that this relation can be best explained by taking up some fundamental tenets of Kant's epistemology.

Even though Hans Christian Ørsted introduced the term "thought experiment" (*Tankeexperiment*) with the purpose of clarifying an aspect of mathematics and its relation to physical knowledge in Kant, the Kantian point of view had no impact on the historical development of the concept (Ørsted 1822; Witt-Hansen 1976). Thus, when about two decades ago James Robert Brown said that a Kantian point of view was lacking in the critical literature on TEs (Brown 1991a, 156), his claim was fundamentally correct: There was no Kantian theory of TE, apart from Ørsted's unsuccessful one, when—stimulated by Brown's intriguing observation—I started to develop a theory of TEs that was at once both transcendental and operationalist.

A glance at the history of the philosophy of science is sufficient to find an explanation of this historical fact (without excluding other possible accounts): Since its beginnings at the end of the nineteenth century, philosophy of science consistently rejected the existence of *a priori* knowledge in

Kant's sense. This occurred, either (1) in the empiricist spirit of Mach, neo-positivism, and Popper, or (2) in the conventionalist spirit of Poincaré and Duhem, later carried on by the relativist philosophy of science of the 1960s and by the "sociological turn," which construed the *a priori* as changeable as a function of historically shifting pragmatic interests.[1] The reason for the rejection of the *a priori* was the same in both cases: Kant's *a priori* is based upon the presupposition that Euclid's geometry and Newton's theory are true, but the history of science (the rise of non-Euclidean geometries, Einstein's theories of relativity, quantum theory) has shown this presupposition to be false. Kant's *a priori* is therefore also an error, perhaps an inevitable one (before Riemann, Einstein, and the founders of quantum physics), but nevertheless an error.

These two ways of rejecting Kant's *a priori* in the philosophy of science preside over the two following trends in the current discussion on TEs: the empirical-naturalist (Mach [1883] 1933, [1905] 1926a; Hempel 1965)[2] and the sociological-constructivist (Kuhn [1964] 1977).[3] In contrast with these interpretations of TEs, the rationalists or Platonists, rather than reject the concept of the *a priori,* rethought it according to the modern rationalistic (Koyré 1939) or Platonist tradition (Brown 1991a, 2004). Since Kuhn's *per se* very interesting attempt to overcome the empirical versus analytical opposition is fundamentally flawed—for he failed to find a third consistent point of view and oscillates between these two poles[4]—I shall confine myself to examining briefly the empirical-naturalist and the rationalist-Platonic approaches as regards their ability to save our intuitive, pre-theoretical understanding of the relation of unity and distinction between REs and TEs in the natural sciences.

2. MACH'S AND NORTON'S EMPIRICIST CONCEPTION OF TES

As far as the unity of REs and TEs is concerned, Ernst Mach highlights a fundamental similarity, namely the "method of variation": While in REs it is natural circumstances, in TEs it is representations that are made to vary in order to see the consequences of those variations.[5]

But what about the distinction between TEs and REs? Mach argues that the similarity between REs and TEs depends on the fact that the latter presuppose some experiences; that is, TEs presuppose that some REs have already been performed, at least at the level of common sense. From Mach's radical empiricist perspective, TEs must draw on a previous stock of experiences: The play of the imagination can properly start only when physical experience is sufficiently rich.[6] This stock of experiences explains how TEs can produce new knowledge apparently without resorting to experience, as well as how they can lead us astray. From this point of view, REs are logically and chronologically prior to TEs.

However, it is as clear to Mach as it is to Duhem that experiments would be unintelligible without theory: Experience would be blind if it did not occur against a theoretical background.[7] Thus, Mach proposed what is now known as theory-ladenness. For example, TE, he writes, is

> a necessary *precondition* for physical experiment. Every experimenter and inventor must have the planned arrangement in his head before translating it into fact. . . . Galileo must see the experimental arrangement for investigating free fall well represented in his phantasy before he can realise it. (Mach [1905] 1926a, 187; Engl. transl., 136–137; original italicisation restored)

In this sense, however, TE precedes RE, which cannot be separated from it:

> Deliberate, autonomous extension of experience by physical experiment and systematic observation are thus always guided by thought and cannot be sharply limited and cut off from thought experiment. (Mach [1905] 1926b, 202; Engl. transl., 149)

As to which kind of experiment has primacy over the other, Mach wavers between two theses that taken literally are incompatible—namely, the empiricist subordination of TEs to real ones and the rationalist precedence of the former over the latter. In the absence of the conceptual tools needed to solve this opposition, the two theses form an outright contradiction in Mach's thought.

The most important empiricist notion of TE, namely Norton's, tries to eliminate this contradiction by arguing in favour of the autonomy of TEs, on the basis of their argumentative structure—their starting from certain premises so as to arrive at certain conclusions.

TEs "are arguments which (i) posit hypothetical or counterfactual states of affairs, and (ii) invoke particulars irrelevant to the generality of the conclusion" (Norton 1991, 129). To be more precise, TEs can always be reconstructed as deductive or inductive arguments ("reconstruction thesis") and, more importantly, they must always be evaluated as such:

> The outcome is reliable only insofar as our assumptions are true and the inference valid. . . . [W]hen we evaluate thought experiments as epistemological devices, the point is that we should evaluate them as arguments. A good thought experiment is a good argument; a bad thought experiment is a bad argument. (Norton 1996, 335)

The logical structure of TEs guarantees that they are distinct from REs. However, are they also somehow intrinsically connected with one another? There is an objection, among the many which have been raised against Norton, that is very instructive for our purposes. According to this objection, the translation of a TE into formal terms (*i.e.*, the elimination of pictures and diagrams concomitant with their translation into propositional contents) causes a partial loss of the original meaning or content, to the point that the experiment becomes unintelligible.[8]

Taken literally, the objection is inconclusive since it sets forth no reason *in principle* why this must happen. Therefore, Norton is right in countering this objection by *de facto* reconstructing many paradigmatic TEs as arguments: It is plausible to assume that the same may be done even for experiments that have not yet undergone such a reconstruction (Norton 2004, 50).

However, it is not difficult to find a reason in principle why a TE, stripped of all irrelevant particulars and reduced to a pure argument, would lose all empirical meaning. Even though in a TE this or that particular empirical element may be "irrelevant to the generality of the conclusion" (for example, in Einstein's lift experiment it is irrelevant whether the observer is or is not a physicist), *it is not irrelevant that TEs are generally performed by constructing particular cases, which need concrete elements that are in principle reproducible in specific spatio-temporally individuated situations*. The concrete particularity, the individuality of the examples of empirical TEs, is not irrelevant since these examples are the touchstone for testing the coherence, the explanatory power, and the empirical truth of the hypotheses that underlie the experiments. TEs, stripped of any reference to concrete experimental apparatuses and situations, are confined to a domain of purely theoretical statements and demonstrative connections, thereby losing their connection with REs.[9]

It is perhaps to avoid objections of this kind that Norton, as we have seen, takes the term "argument" to include inductive ones. However, this strategy fails, since Norton by "inductive argument" means an argument that is valid within a formal calculus (Norton 2004, 54–55). This restriction of the meaning of the term "inductive," far from solving the difficulty and enabling us to distinguish between empirical and logical-mathematical TEs, just confirms that difficulty: In this sense, an inductive argument, like a deductive one, may be tested as to its logical validity (suitably understood, for example, as to its capacity of preserving probability), but not as to the correspondence of its conclusions with reality. If, on the other hand, we do not take the expression "inductive argument" in a narrowly logical-formal sense, we clearly must overstep the logical-discursive horizon of argument (as well as the limits of Norton's notion of TE) by referring to the real world and to our ability to identify law-like regularities by actively and methodically intervening in it through experimentation.

3. BROWN'S PLATONISM

According to Brown, even though most scientific knowledge must be explained along the usual empiricist lines, there is in physics some *a priori* knowledge, which is gained through what he calls "platonic TEs":

> A *platonic thought experiment* is a single thought experiment which
> destroys an old or existing theory and simultaneously generates a new
> one; it is *a priori* in that it is not based on new empirical evidence nor
> is it merely logically derived from old data; and it is an advance in
> that the resulting theory is better than the predecessor theory. (Brown
> 1991a, 77)[10]

Setting aside other grounds on which Brown's view may be criticised,[11]
I now wish to point out that his Platonist conception, just like empiricism,
oscillates between an unacceptably radical separation between REs and
TEs and their virtual conflation. Brown holds that REs and TEs are similar because in both there is a passage to a "proposition." However, they
are also different because "a RE carries us from a perception (and some
possible background propositions) to a proposition," while in a TE "the
perception is not sense perception, but rather an intuition, a case of seeing
with the mind's eye" (Brown 2004, 1132).

The problem lies in the fact that sometimes Brown seems to want to
claim that REs too amount to "an intuition, a case of seeing with the
mind's eye," that is, to an intuition of Platonic essences or, more precisely,
of "natural kind properties" (Brown 1991a, 45–46). Moreover, unlike
Plato, Brown does not rule out the fallibility of intellectual intuition, and
therefore also of TEs (including Platonic ones). Brown cites as an example
the Einstein-Podolsky-Rosen TE, which he says we now know to be false
(Brown 1991b, 124–125). In this way, the distinction that Brown tried to
draw between real and thought (even if only "Platonic") experiments fades
away completely.

As a consequence of this virtual conflation of TEs and REs, Brown's position becomes circular. Once it has been recognised as fallible, the Platonic
intuition of essences can be tested only by explicit argumentation at the
proper epistemic level. How can we decide between radically different competing interpretations of a TE, while avoiding the vicious circularity involved
in yet another appeal to the intuition of essences as the testing criterion?

In my opinion, the only way out of this logical circle is ultimately to
accept an operative testing criterion for empirical TEs. Between *a priori*
and empirical knowledge there is an essential difference that hinges on their
corrigibility. In the case of empirical knowledge, the possibility of detecting and correcting errors *depends on the possibility of real interactions
between our body and the surrounding world*, that is, on something that
is accessible to all beings endowed with reason and with a body. If we can
now say that the Einstein-Podolsky-Rosen TE is probably wrong, this is
because we have at our disposal real, intersubjectively reproducible scientific experiments that justify this assertion, not because of improved or
repeated intuitions. If this difference is obscured, any relevant difference
between REs and TEs disappears. In this way, both Brown and the empiricists, because of the paradoxically convergent effects of opposite reasons,

end up unable to articulate the relationship between TEs and REs, either separating them completely, so that they are totally unrelated, or virtually conflating them.

4. OUTLINES OF A KANTIAN THEORY OF
TES IN THE NATURAL SCIENCES

We have seen that the main interpretations of TE cannot do justice to our intuitive, pre-theoretical understanding of the relation of both unity and distinction between REs and TEs. Let us now consider whether it is possible to take up again a Kantian approach to TEs, even though neither a distinction between TEs and REs, nor even the term *Gedankenexperiment*, is to be found in Kant.[12]

As is well known, according to Kant, (1) all "*a priori* knowledge" is independent of all experience (KrV B 3, AA 28; B 117, 269, AA 99–100, 187), (2) the *a priori* is the condition upon which all experience depends (KrV B 269, AA 188), and (3) its distinctive traits are "unconditional necessity" and "true," "strict," or "absolute universality" (cf. KrV B 3–5, AA 28–30; B 64, AA 68).

That Kant attributes some content to the (synthetic) *a priori* is indubitable, since he believed that Newton's physics would provide us with universal and necessary knowledge, needing no further substantial modification. It is referring to this sense of the *a priori* that Josiah Royce, for one, rightly observed that Kant seems to believe that the *a priori* pure forms of intuition (and also the *a priori* forms of the understanding, *i.e.*, the categories) are "determinate, . . . finished, . . . for us absolutely predetermined by our constitution" (Royce 1905, 198).

As I stated above, Kant's tendency to attribute a particular, scientific content to the *a priori* was rightly rejected by the main trends in contemporary philosophy of science and deserves no further attention. The same holds true of Hans Christian Ørsted's conception of TE, which—as has been shown—was meant as a method to build a sort of *a priori* physics.[13]

However, there is in Kant an opposite and in my opinion more fundamental tendency to consider the (synthetic) *a priori* in a purely functional sense. It is in connection with this sense of the *a priori* that Kant develops some of the best-known tenets of his philosophy. He emphasises again and again that the unschematised categories have insufficient meaning to give us the concept of an object. He rightly says that categories not applied to sense content are "merely functions of the understanding for concepts" and "cannot . . . be employed in any manner whatsoever," neither empirical nor transcendental.[14] And it is in connection with this sense of the *a priori* that Kant claims that the "I think" is an empty idea, devoid of content: No manifold is given through the "I," taken as a simple representation.[15] Since the "I think," as the synthetic unity of apperception, must always accompany all perceptions, it cannot be a perception or, as Kant calls it, a "concept" (*Begriff*). This is also the main point of Kant's criticism of the paralogisms of pure reason. Since the "I think" is the supreme condition of the possibility of experience, it cannot have a content of its own and must be conceived as a mere form or function. Finally, it is in this connection that Kant says that the *a priori*, as the condition of experience, is always already in experience, but neither *precedes* nor *follows* experience—that is to say, it does not exist independently of experience.

My interpretation of TEs and their relation to REs relies strictly on this sense of the *a priori*, which is purely *formal* (or rather, *functional*)[16] and is contrasted by Kant with the *material* conditions which are given through sensation. This sense of the *a priori* can provide the grounding for a non-naturalistic theory of TEs that is different from Brown's Platonist conception and that may be called Kantian with some justification, being both transcendental and operational at the same time.[17] I shall now proceed to give a brief outline of this theory of TEs.

Let us start from Kant's well-known definition of "experiment." According to Kant, a (real) experiment is a "question put to nature" (*Frage an die Natur*), where the experimenter is not viewed "in the character of a pupil who listens to everything that the teacher chooses to say, but of an appointed judge who compels the witnesses to answer questions which he has himself formulated" (KrV B XIII, AA III 10). In other terms, the experimental setting is arranged so as to show which of the answers anticipated in the mind by a hypothesis formulated in accordance with the requirements of reason will actually occur.

Among the philosophers who have developed Kant's notion of experiment may be mentioned Ernst Cassirer:

> As to which of the possible relational connections are actually realized in experience, experiment, in its result, gives its answer. But this answer can only be given when the question has previously been clearly stated; and this process of stating the question goes back to conceptions, which analyse immediate intuition according to conceptual standpoints. (Cassirer 1910, 341; Engl. transl., 257)

This notion of experiment as a "question put to nature" suggests a very important feature for a corresponding concept of TE. TEs must share with REs this *theoretical-dialogical* nature. TEs too have a determinate meaning only if they are (implicitly or explicitly) understood as answers to theoretical questions put to nature and its laws. Thought experiments, even concretely realised ones, would remain ambiguous if their underlying theoretical hypotheses were not specified.

At the same time, here we find the most important similarity along with the most important difference between REs and TEs. While both types of experiments ask questions about nature and its laws, only TEs, relying on previously accepted knowledge, anticipate in thought nature's specific answers. This suggests a general definition of TE which one can expect to be compatible with the main conceptions of TE:

> *An empirical TE anticipates, at the theoretical, discursive, or linguistic level, a hypothetical experimental situation so that, on the basis of previous knowledge, we are confident that certain interventions on the experimental apparatus will modify some of its aspects (or "variables") with such a degree of probability that the actual execution of the experiment becomes superfluous.*

Differences between competing views on TEs only arise when one tries to define more precisely the nature and justification of that "previous knowledge" on the basis of which TEs, as long as they are taken as valid, reach their conclusions without appealing to REs. According to Brown, this is *a priori*, Platonic knowledge; for Mach it is exclusively empirical knowledge; for Norton it is empirical knowledge, and logical knowledge only as far as logic ultimately adds no content to empirical knowledge; in Kuhn's conception of TE, this previous knowledge is given by the paradigms and by their theoretical-practical commitments (Kuhn [1964] 1977).

Now, how ought we to interpret this "previous knowledge" from a Kantian point of view, and precisely from the point of view of a functional, non-hypostatised *a priori*?

According to the functional conception of the *a priori, reason cannot, by means of empirical TEs, come to conclusions that are valid independently of experience.* In this sense, my point of view coincides with the previously discussed empiricist positions about TEs. The particular content of any empirical TE must be in principle ultimately reducible to sensation (or rather *to empirical-operational interventions on reality, that is, to experimentation*). Whatever resists this reduction thereby shows itself to be an arbitrarily introduced factor, which is legitimate only if this factor disappears in the final result. Moreover, this operational reducibility—whose details I am unable to discuss in this paper—is fully in agreement with Kant's claim that—unlike in mathematics and philosophy—any doubts or misunderstandings in physics can in principle always be identified and sooner or later eliminated by means of experience:

> In experimental philosophy the delay caused by doubt may indeed be useful; no misunderstanding is, however, possible which cannot easily be removed; and the final means of deciding the dispute, whether found early or late, must in the end be supplied by experience. (KrV B 452–453, AA III 292, lines 27–31)

On the one hand, both REs and TEs are methodical procedures guided by certain hypotheses. At the same time, however, the aim of such hypotheses is to understand, by applying the method of systematic variation, how a certain experimental apparatus varies in response to our specific operational interventions on it. Empirical TEs too can answer theoretical questions using experimental apparatuses, from simple surfaces and spheres to very complex mechanisms. This is why TEs (spanning from Galileo's simple ones about falling bodies to the more complex one involving Schrödinger's unhappy cat) have the same constitutive elements as REs—namely, a theory and a particular, well-specified experimental apparatus. We modify some aspects of the apparatus intentionally, in order to see the effects of these modifications in the light of (1) the hypothesis that has to be tested and (2) assumptions, knowledge, or skills accepted as obvious because they are underpinned by independently confirmed empirical observations.

However, if we wish to remain committed to a Kantian point of view, the empiricist claim of the reducibility in principle of all knowledge contents to experience must be made compatible with the irreducibility of the mind to any real content given by experience. Strictly speaking (and it is here that the functional interpretation of the *a priori* becomes decisive), what is untenable, from a Kantian point of view, is not the fundamental principle common to all empiricist positions, according to which all knowledge must in the end be reduced to sensation, but only the naturalistic claim that empiricism and its fundamental principle may be justified by appealing to experience. From a Kantian-transcendental point of view, the validity claim concerning empiricism and its fundamental principle may be vindicated only from a non-naturalistic point of view, which Kant precisely called both "transcendental" and "*a priori*." In this sense, a Kantian theory of TE sides decidedly with Brown's Platonism and stands in sharp contrast with Mach's, Norton's, and obviously Kuhn's views of TEs.

Both points of view—the empirical-operational reducibility and the transcendental irreducibility of TEs to REs—may be illustrated by briefly referring to Kant's dialectical distinction between knowing and thinking, which is a good starting point in the development of a conception that neither equates nor radically separates, but rather connects REs and TEs, while keeping them distinct.

Thinking as such is only the act of subsuming the synthesis of the manifold to the unity of apperception:

> I can *think* whatever I please, provided only that I do not contradict myself, that is, provided my concept is a possible thought. This suffices for the possibility of the concept, even though I may not be able to answer for there being, in the sum of all possibilities, an object corresponding to it. (KrV B XXVI, fn., AA 17; cf. also KrV B 93–94, AA 85–86)

In order to have *knowing*, thinking must be applied to a given intuition (B 145–146, AA 116). On the one hand, Kant's distinction between thinking and knowing stresses the irreducible independence of thought from experience.

On the other hand, however, Kant's distinction corresponds to that between the transcendental-functional and the empirical-material aspect of scientific knowledge. Kant's distinction both closely connects and distinguishes in principle between the *thinking* transcendental subject (the "I think") and the object that is *known*. In other words, it not only distinguishes, but also connects the transcendental and the empirical points of view.

The unity and distinction between thinking and knowing is the leading idea in Kant's criticism of the ontological argument, which contains a fallacy owing to a confusion between "to exist" and "to be conceived of as existing," that is, between actual existence and existence only in thought ("gedachte[r] Existenz": cf. *Der einzig mögliche Beweisgrund zu einer Demonstration des Daseins Gottes*, AA II 156, line 14).

In this connection, Kant's example of a hundred dollars (or thalers) is very instructive because it is perhaps the best way, both theoretically and intuitively, to understand both the reducibility and the irreducibility of TEs to REs. On the one hand, "the real contains no more than the merely possible. A hundred real thalers do not contain the least coin more than a hundred possible thalers." On the other hand, "My financial position is, however, affected very differently by a hundred real thalers than it is by the mere concept of them (that is, of their possibility). For the object, as it actually exists, is not analytically contained in my concept, but is added to my concept (which is a determination of my state) synthetically" (KrV B 627, AA III 401).

In the light of this distinction, I would say that, from the perspective of the analysis of the intensions of the respective concepts—that is, from the point of view I designate as "positive" (empirical and/or logical-formal)—REs and TEs coincide completely, as do the hundred real dollars and the hundred merely thought ones.[18] In a positive sense, my conception of a hundred dollars remains the same irrespective of whether I own them or not. In the same sense, every (empirical) TE corresponds to a real one that satisfies the same conceptual characteristics, and vice versa. *All REs may also be thought of as realisations of TEs; conversely, all empirical TEs must be conceivable as preparing and anticipating real ones: They must, that is, anticipate a connection between objects which, when thought of as realised, makes the TE coincide completely with the corresponding real one.* As far as their conceptual content is concerned, simply to imagine that the experimental apparatus, counterfactually anticipated in a TE, has really been constructed is sufficient to erase any difference between TEs and REs. However, just this "imagining," this capacity of the mind to assume every real entity as a possible entity, underpins the difference in principle—a properly transcendental difference—between TEs and REs. On a transcendental level, REs and TEs are distinct in principle. This distinction cannot be suppressed, since it is the same distinction between the hypothetical-reflexive domain of the mind (which can always contradict itself) and reality (which can always occur and develop in only one way).

Paraphrasing Kant, (empirical) TEs without REs are empty; REs without TEs are blind. It is crucial to avoid contrasting REs and TEs as if they were completely autonomous and reciprocally independent entities. Their relationship is to be thought of as a connection between elements that, even though they cannot be reduced to one another (there is nothing less reducible than the contrast between what is real and what is merely thought or imagined), cannot be separated without losing all determinate meaning.

As I remarked above, for Kant it is a typical empiricist mistake, due to the empiricists' failure to understand transcendental analysis, to believe that the *a priori precedes* or *follows* experience, to believe, that is, that the *a priori* exists independently of experience. The *a priori*, as the condition of experience, is always already in experience, and all experience is always already synthesis *a priori*. Kant's example of the hundred dollars makes exactly this point: Thought dollars, like TEs, exist only in the sphere of the possible, while real dollars, like REs, occupy a specific place among the interactions between our bodies and the surrounding reality; but *neither thought nor real entities could exist outside their mutual relationship.*

It could be objected that TEs, insofar as they contain idealisations, are impossible to realise. They either contain fictional entities (*e.g.*, frictionless planes) or represent situations which are *per se* impossible to realise. Newton imagines an empty universe except for two spheres: No RE could correspond to this TE.

To be sure, there are many TEs whose requirements of empirical realisability and technical-operational testability seem, at first sight, to be in principle unsatisfiable. The first crucial point, however, is that no hypothesis suggested by an *empirical* TE can ever be *absolutely* unrealisable (for example, because it assumes states of affairs impossible to be realised at the same time and from the same point of view). Empirical TEs are held to be scientifically useful and reliable because it is presupposed that, if they were realised, the sequence of events *that they describe according to causal connections, which we assume to be operative in the real world*, would occur in the way they anticipate, and would lead to the consequences that they predict. This holds in principle, no matter how remote the realisability *de facto* of certain TEs may be.

Most importantly and more generally, the presence of idealisations and counterfactual assumptions in TEs prevents neither their realisation nor the possibility of obtaining from them concrete empirical information which extends our mastery of reality.

It was Weber who first clearly saw the intimate association between the foundation of our knowledge and counterfactual assumptions. The decisive point of Weber's analysis of the famous Marathon battle example is the fact that the understanding of causal connections is not hindered, but indeed made possible, by the use of counterfactual conditionals. In order to understand the causal-probabilistic importance of an event such as the battle of Marathon for the development of Greek culture and Western civilisation, a historian must start by asking (explicitly or implicitly) what would have happened if the Persians had won rather than the Greeks. The historian must answer this question *by abstracting from what really happened and constructing an ideal, or possible, course of events.* As Weber aptly puts it, "In order to penetrate to the real causal interrelationships, *we construct unreal ones*" (Weber [1906] 1982, 287; Engl. transl., 185–186).[19]

Weber's concept of ideal type can be easily extended to the natural sciences, since it exemplifies that characteristic of experiments (both thought and real) that Mach called "method of variation." Not only historians, but also natural scientists, in order to explain an event, must answer the question about what might have happened had certain circumstances been different. However, since the construction of ideal types, as interpreted above, both basically coincides with the construction of TEs and is a necessary tool for the empirical knowledge of reality, the construction of a TE is an essential aspect of all REs; indeed, it is the condition of their possibility.

It is irrelevant whether Galileo's refutation of Aristotle's theory of free fall was a mere TE or whether it was actually performed. In either case, Galileo ignored certain variables, such as the lack of friction with the medium, and all those qualities that, in Galileo's terminology, reside in the "sensitive body," such as colour, smell, taste, and so on. *This serves the purpose both of circumscribing and simplifying the object of investigation (which as a result becomes somewhat idealised), and, especially, of making experiments in principle reproducible in a technical, and not only mental, sense.*

When in a TE we claim that a surface is perfectly smooth or that the arms of a balance are perfectly symmetrical, we imagine an ideal entity which provides a rule, a norm, or a criterion. Without this criterion, we would be unable even to *conceive of* the imperfections and empirical deviations that characterise *real* situations; we would be unable to measure those empirical deviations and to search for their causes; finally, we would be unable to realise technically increasingly symmetrical balance arms and increasingly smooth surfaces: An essential condition for the claim that friction "causes" a moving body to stop is that we can reduce friction, *concretely making* surfaces that increasingly approximate the ideal type of a frictionless surface, and note the corresponding reduction of the effect of friction.[20]

Obviously, this cannot be understood in the sense that there is and there must always *de facto* be a perfect correspondence between REs and TEs, if only because the latter—positively considered, that is, considered as a particular TE thought by a particular thinking person at a particular time and in a particular place—are always also the hypothetical anticipations of REs yet to be realised. However, *all REs may also be thought of as realisations of TEs; and conversely, all empirical TEs must be conceivable as preparing and anticipating real ones: They ought to anticipate a connection between objects which, when thought of as realised, makes the intension of the TE coincide completely with the corresponding real one.*

NOTES

1. Cf. for example Mach ([1883] 1933, 458–459), Poincaré ([1902] 1968, 74–75), Reichenbach (1920), Bridgman (1927), and Popper (1963, Ch. 7). It may be objected that this claim does not take into account the so-called "relativized *a priori*" (cf. *e.g.* Friedman 1999). However, a relativised *a priori* whose changing depends upon the growth of experience and knowledge is by no means Kantian, because it cannot answer, in principle, any *quaestio juris*, *i.e.*, it can neither justify the validity of an inference nor the truth of a knowledge claim. On this point, cf. Buzzoni (2005).
2. Cf., more recently, Norton (1991), Sorensen (1992), and Gooding (1990, 1994). This interpretation was also developed from the viewpoint of John-son-Laird's theory of mental models (*e.g.*, Miščević 1992, 2007; Nersessian 1993; Gendler 2004), and by insisting on the role that intuitions play in thought experiments (*e.g.*, Brendel 2004; Gendler 2007; Fehige 2011).
3. Cf., more recently, McAllister (1996, 2004), Arthur (1999), and Gendler (2000).
4. For the justification of this claim, I must refer the reader to Buzzoni (1986, 2005, 2008, Ch. 2, §6).
5. Cf. Mach ([1905] 1926b, 202–203; Engl. transl., 149).
6. Cf. Mach ([1905] 1926a, 187–188; Engl. transl., 136–137).
7. Mach ([1905] 1926a, 188, fn.; Engl. transl., 146, n. 6).
8. Cf. especially Brown (1997) and Arthur (1999, 219).
9. On this point cf. also Buzzoni (2004, 158–160) and Cohnitz (2006, 111).
10. Cf. also Brown (1997, 2004, 2007, 2011).
11. Cf. *e.g.* Norton (2004), Miščević (2007), Häggqvist (2007), Starikova (2007), Buzzoni (2008, Part I, Ch. 4).
12. However, it should be noted that Kant's concept of "Experimente der reinen Vernunft" are relevant to the notion of TE in philosophy; cf. *e.g.* KrV B XVIII–XXI, fn., AA III 13–14; KrV B 452–453, AA III 292–293. On this point, cf. Buzzoni (2011). Kant's *Kritik der reinen Vernunft* is quoted in the English translation by Kemp Smith (London: Macmillan 1929) following the pagination of the 1787 (B) edition; I have always also indicated the page number of the "Akademieausgabe" (AA).
13. On Ørsted's (and Kant's) mistake, cf. especially Kühne (2005, 97–98, 116, 135). Cf. also Cohnitz (2008, 407–408) and Buzzoni (2011).
14. Cf. respectively KrV B 187, AA 139; KrV B 305, AA III 208. Cf. also KrV B 307–308, AA III 210, lines 31–35.
15. KrV B, §16, AA 110, lines 23–24 ("durch das Ich als einfache Vorstellung ist nichts Mannigfaltiges gegeben").
16. In order to prevent misunderstandings, as far as this aspect of the *a priori* is concerned, from now on I will always use the word "functional," instead of Kant's "formal," which will only be used in its most usual meaning in philosophy of science, as a covering term for logical and mathematical knowledge. Cf. also Note 18.
17. The point of view which I am trying to reconcile with a Kantian perspective is not "operational" in Bridgman's sense, but is, roughly speaking, in Dingler's (cf. Dingler 1928). In some important respects, Dingler's perspective was similar to Peirce's and Dewey's pragmatism. In Germany, this tradition continued with the methodical constructivism of the Erlangen-Konstanz and Marburg schools (cf. *e.g.* Lorenzen 1968; Janich 1969). An "operationalist" point of view, even though usually removed from its original context, has been attached to interventionist theories of causality (cf. *e.g.* Woodward 2003). In Italy, cf. especially Agazzi's operationalism (cf. Agazzi 1969), which

was important for my technical operationalism. The latter takes as its basic assumption and as its methodical starting point concrete human beings pursuing different determinate goals; these agents—through their bodies—find themselves always already in operational or technical interaction with the surrounding world. From this point of view there is an intrinsic connection between theory and experiment, as there is between science and technique; this connection is integral to the properly human—at once theoretical-evaluative and technical-operational—use of our bodies. In comparison with American pragmatism and German constructivism, however, human beings' capacity to *conceptualise and evaluate* reality and human beings' capacity to interact with reality are both primary (cf. Buzzoni 2004, 2007, 2008).

18. While "empirical" is used here in a pragmatic and operational sense (*i.e.*, as relative to what can be acquired by active sensory-bodily experience), "formal" is not meant here in one of Kant's senses (*i.e.*, as synonymous with "functional"), but as relative to a particular logical and/or mathematical content; "positive" is used here as the general term for both "empirical" and "formal," thereby designating all knowledge of *particular* contents (be it knowledge of a table or of a mathematical theorem). The opposite but correlative term for "positive" is "transcendental," in the most general and usual Kantian sense: pertaining to all knowledge which is not so much occupied with objects as with the mode of our knowledge of objects insofar as this mode of knowledge is to be possible *a priori* (cf. Kant KrV B 25, AA 43, lines 17–19).

19. When Weber proposes the counterfactual possibility of a Persian victory at Marathon, his intention is not just to construct a TE that will clarify certain conceptual connections or remove certain ambiguities; rather, he believes that this TE is also *an essential tool for understanding reality, and in particular its causal connections* (cf. also Weber 1904).

20. For more details on this fundamental point, cf. Buzzoni (2008, Ch. 3, §5), where references to the relevant literature can also be found.

REFERENCES

Agazzi, Evandro. 1969. *Temi e problemi di filosofia della fisica*. Milan: Manfredi.

Arthur, Richard. 1999. "On Thought Experiments as *A Priori* Science." *International Studies in the Philosophy of Science* 13: 215–229.

Brendel, Elke. 2004. "Intuition Pumps and the Proper Use of Thought Experiments." *Dialectica* 58: 89–108.

Bridgman, Percy Williams. 1927. *The Logic of Modern Physics*. New York: MacMillan.

Brown, James Robert. 1991a. *The Laboratory of the Mind: Thought Experiments in the Natural Sciences*. London: Routledge.

———. 1991b. "Thought Experiments: A Platonic Account." In *Thought Experiments in Science and Philosophy*, edited by Tamara Horowitz and Gerald J. Massey, 119–128. Savage, MD: Rowman & Littlefield.

———. 1997. "Proofs and Pictures." *The British Journal for the Philosophy of Science* 48: 161–180.

———. 2004. "Peeking into Plato's Heaven." *Philosophy of Science* 71: 1126–1138.

———. 2007. "Thought Experiments in Science, Philosophy, and Mathematics." *Croatian Journal of Philosophy* 7: 3–27.

———. 2011. "Über das Leben im Labor des Geistes." *Deutsche Zeitschrift für Philosophie* 59: 65–73.

Buzzoni, Marco. 1986. *Semantica, ontologia ed ermeneutica della conoscenza scientifica. Saggio su T. S. Kuhn.* Milan: Angeli.

———. 2004. *Esperimento ed esperimento mentale.* Milan: Angeli.

———. 2005. "Kuhn und Wittgenstein: Paradigmen, Sprachspiele und Wissenschaftsgeschichte." In *Zeit und Geschichte/Time and History*, edited by F. Stadler and M. Stöltzner, 38–40. Kirchberg a.W: Ludwig Wittgenstein Gesellschaft.

———. 2007. "Zum Verhältnis zwischen Experiment und Gedankenexperiment in den Naturwissenschaften." *Journal for General Philosophy of Science* 38: 219–237.

———. 2008. *Thought Experiment in the Natural Sciences. An Operational and Reflexive-Transcendental Conception.* Würzburg: Königshausen+Neumann.

———. 2011. "Kant und das Gedankenexperiment. Über eine kantische Theorie der Gedankenexperimente in den Naturwissenschaften und in der Philosophie." *Deutsche Zeitschrift für Philosophie* 59: 93–107.

Cassirer, Ernst. 1910. *Substanzbegriff und Funktionsbegriff. Untersuchungen über die Grundfragen der Erkenntniskritik.* Berlin: Bruno Cassirer. Authorised English edition (quotations are from this edition): 1923. *Substance and Function and Einstein's Theory of Relativity.* Translated by William C. Swabey and Marie Collins Swabey. Chicago and London: The Open Court.

Cohnitz, Daniel. 2006. *Gedankenexperimente in der Philosophie.* Paderborn: Mentis.

———. 2008. "Ørsteds 'Gedankenexperiment': eine Kantianische Fundierung der Infinitesimalrechnung?" *Kant-Studien* 99: 407–433.

Dingler, Hugo. 1928. *Das Experiment. Sein Wesen und seine Geschichte.* Munich: Reinhardt.

Fehige, Yiftach J. H. 2011. "Gedankenexperimente in der Offenbarungstheologie? Eine erste Annäherung." *Deutsche Zeitschrift für Philosophie* 59: 109–129.

Friedman, Michael. 1999. *Logical Positivism Reconsidered.* Cambridge: Cambridge University Press.

Gendler, Tamar Szabó. 2000. *Thought Experiment. On the Power and Limits of Imaginary Cases.* New York and London: Garland.

———. 2004. "Thought Experiments Rethought and Reperceived." *Philosophy of Science* 71: 1152–1163.

———. 2007. "Philosophical Thought Experiments, Intuitions, and Cognitive Equilibrium." *Midwest Studies in Philosophy of Science* 31: 68–89.

Gooding, David. 1990. *Experiment and the Making of Meaning. Human Agency in Scientific Observation and Experiment.* Dordrecht: Kluwer.

———. 1994. "Imaginary Science." *The British Journal for the Philosophy of Science* 45: 1029–1045.

Häggqvist, Sören. 2007. "The A Priori Thesis: A Critical Assessment." *Croatian Journal of Philosophy* 7: 47–61.

Hempel, Carl Gustav. 1965. *Aspects of Scientific Explanation and Other Essays in the Philosophy of Science.* New York: Free Press.

Janich, Peter. 1969. *Die Protophysik der Zeit. Konstruktive Begründung und Geschichte der Zeitmessung.* Mannheim: Bibliographisches Institut (2nd edition 1980, Frankfurt a.M.: Suhrkamp).

Koyré, Alexandre. 1939. *Études galiléennes.* Paris: Hermann.

Kuhn, Thomas S. [1964] 1977. "A Function for Thought Experiments." In *L'aventure de l'Esprit*, Vol. II, edited by I. Bernard Cohen and René Taton, 307–334. Paris: Hermann. Reprinted 1977 in *The Essential Tension: Selected Studies in Scientific Tradition and Change*, 240–265. Chicago: University of Chicago Press.

Kühne, Ulrich. 2005. *Die Methode des Gedankenexperiments*. Frankfurt a.M.: Suhrkamp.

Lorenzen, Paul. 1968. *Methodisches Denken*. Frankfurt a.M.: Suhrkamp.

Mach, Ernst. [1883] 1933. *Die Mechanik in ihrer Entwickelung. Historisch-kritisch dargestellt*. Leipzig: Brockhaus.

———. [1905] 1926a. "Über Gedankenexperimente." In *Erkenntnis und Irrtum*. 5th edition, 183–200. Leipzig: Barth. English edition: 1976. "On Thought Experiments." In *Knowledge and Error*, translated by T. J. McCormack, 134–147. Dordrecht and Boston: Reidel.

———. [1905] 1926b. "Das physische Experiment und dessen Leitmotive." In *Erkenntnis und Irrtum*. 5th edition, 201–219. Leipzig: Barth. English edition: 1976. "Physical Experiment and Its Leading Features." In *Knowledge and Error*, translated by T. J. McCormack, 148–161. Dordrecht and Boston: Reidel.

McAllister, James. 1996. "The Evidential Significance of Thought Experiments in Science." *Studies in History and Philosophy of Science* 27: 233–250.

———. 2004. "Thought Experiments and the Belief in Phenomena." *Philosophy of Science* 71: 1164–1175.

Miščević, Nenad. 1992. "Mental Models and Thought Experiments." *International Studies in the Philosophy of Science* 6: 215–226.

———. 2007. "Modelling Intuitions and Thought Experiments." *Croatian Journal of Philosophy* 7: 181–214.

Nersessian, Nancy. 1993. "In the Theoretician's Laboratory: Thought Experimenting as Mental Modeling." *Philosophy of Science Association* 1: 291–301.

Norton, John D. 1991. "Thought Experiments in Einstein's Work." In *Thought Experiments in Science and Philosophy,* edited by Tamara Horowitz and Gerald J. Massey, 129–148. Savage, MD: Rowman & Littlefield.

———. 1996. "Are Thought Experiments Just What You Thought?" *Canadian Journal of Philosophy* 26: 333–366.

———. 2004. "Why Thought Experiments Do Not Transcend Empiricism." In *Contemporary Debates in Philosophy of Science*, edited by C. Hitchcock, 44–66. Malden, Oxford, and Carlton: Blackwell.

Ørsted, Hans Christian. 1822. "Über Geist und Studium der allgemeinen Naturlehre." *Journal für Chemie und Physik* 36: 458–488.

Poincaré, Henri. [1902] 1968. *La science et l'hypothèse*. Paris: Flammarion.

Popper, Karl R. 1963. *Conjectures and Refutations*. London: Routledge & Kegan Paul.

Reichenbach, Hans. 1920. *Relativitätstheorie und Erkenntnis a priori*. Berlin: Springer.

Royce, Josiah. 1905. "Kant's Doctrine of the Basis of Mathematics." *The Journal of Philosophy, Psychology and Scientific Methods* 2 (8): 197–207.

Sorensen, Roy A. 1992. *Thought Experiments*. Oxford and New York: Oxford University Press.

Starikova, Irina. 2007. "Picture-Proofs and Platonism." *Croatian Journal of Philosophy* 7: 81–92.

Weber, Max. 1904. "Die "Objektivität" sozialwissenschaftlicher und sozialpolitischer Erkenntnis." *Archiv für Sozialwissenschaft und Sozialpolitik* 19, 22–87. Reproduced 1922 in *Gesammelte Aufsätze zur Wissenschaftslehre*. Tübingen: Mohr; 2nd edition: 1951; 5th edition (quotations are from this edition): 1982, 146–214; English edition: 1949. "'Objectivity' in Social Science and Social Policy." In *The Methodology of the Social Sciences*. Translated by E. A. Schils and H. A. Finch, 50–112. Glencoe, IL: The Free Press.

———. 1906. "Kritische Studien auf dem Gebiet der kulturwissenschaftlichen Logik." *Archiv für Sozialwissenschaft und Sozialpolitik* 22: 143–207.

Reproduced 1922 in *Gesammelte Aufsätze zur Wissenschaftslehre*. Tübingen: Mohr; 2nd edition: 1951; 5th edition (quotations are from this edition): 1982, 215–290; English edition: 1949. "Critical Studies in the Logic of the Cultural Sciences." In *The Methodology of the Social Sciences*. Translated by E. A. Schils and H. A Finch, 113–188. Glencoe, IL: The Free Press.

Witt-Hansen, Johannes. 1976. "H. C. Ørsted, Immanuel Kant, and the Thought Experiment." *Danish Yearbook of Philosophy* 13: 48–65.

Woodward, James. 2003. *Making Things Happen. A Theory of Causal Explanation*. Oxford and New York: Oxford University Press.

6 Can Thought Experiments Be Resolved by Experiment?

The Case of Aristotle's Wheel

Richard T. W. Arthur

1. INTRODUCTION

The question I am addressing in this paper is whether thought experiments can be resolved by experiment. But one might ask first: Are thought experiments performable at all? The answer, of course, depends on how you define a thought experiment. According to one prevalent conception, "the key point of difference between ordinary experiments and thought experiments is that ordinary experiments are executed and thereby provide fresh information".[1] On this conception, the fact that a thought experiment cannot be performed is part of what makes it a thought experiment. If the experiment could be executed, then it would just be a design of an experiment, rather than a distinct category of thing.

But I can think of three counterexamples to this conclusion, two of them involving cases that are widely accepted as thought experiments, and the third an intriguing case that has not previously been discussed as an example of a thought experiment.

The first of these is John Bell's thought experiment in which he constructs a case to demonstrate that the local hidden variable approach to quantum theory is in conflict with the predictions of orthodox quantum theory. Eventually experiments were conducted, notably by Alain Aspect and co-workers, which confirmed what had never been in serious doubt.[2]

The second is Galileo Galilei's famous thought experiment concerning the dropping of two balls of different weights attached by a string, in refutation of Aristotle's theory that they would fall at different speeds. Here Koyré, and more recently Jim Brown, have claimed that the conclusion to be drawn follows with such rigour as not to require experimental testing, although of course the results do confirm Galileo's conclusion.[3]

The third is the case I propose to treat here, the so-called *Rota Aristotelica* or "Aristotle's Wheel", which as far as I know has not been discussed in the literature of thought experiments. When I first selected this case I thought it was an interesting and straightforward example of a thought experiment that could in fact be performed. It had functioned, particularly in the hands of Galileo, just as a thought experiment should: It is an imagined scenario, with accompanying diagram, one that leads to paradox, so that it is apparently physically impossible, and it is designed to promote reflection on the principles involved. But it is easily performable, and the result is such as to undermine Galileo's use of it to argue for the composition of matter out of an actual infinity of atoms. What I discovered after further research, however, is that it is still an open question what conclusion should be drawn from the thought experiment. Thus in using this example to try to determine whether some thought experiments are resolvable by experiment, I was led inexorably into questions about what assumptions are constitutive of the experiment, and what idealizations are allowable. I still claim that this is an example of a thought experiment whose correct conclusion can be confirmed by actual experiment, but I conclude that in general the performability of a thought experiment depends on what assumptions are taken to constitute the experiment, and what idealizations are allowable.

In fact, I argue that similar considerations about the difficulty of identifying the constitutive assumptions and allowable idealizations of a thought experiment apply to the case of Galileo's thought experiment with the unequal weights, even though it is agreed that it *can* be performed. I take its conclusion to be that two unequal bodies of the same specific gravity but different weights falling in the same medium will reach the same terminal velocity, as is confirmed experimentally and enshrined in Stokes' Law. Galileo's assumptions here are that the fall is taking place in a medium (less dense than the falling stones) and that in these circumstances a constant terminal velocity (the "natural velocity") will be reached by each of the bodies if they fall for long enough. His argument establishes that, despite their unequal masses, the weights will fall with the same natural velocity. Koyré and Brown interpret the thought experiment as concerning two bodies falling in a vacuum, Galileo's conclusion being that, despite their unequal masses, the weights will fall with the same acceleration, so that they will have the same final velocity after falling for the same time. On the first interpretation considerably more argument is required to establish what would happen in a vacuum, since the existence of a medium and a natural velocity (depending on the specific gravity of the material) are constitutive assumptions of the experiment. On Brown's and Koyré's interpretation, the existence of a vacuum is an idealising assumption, a limiting case of a less and less resisting medium, so that the conclusion follows automatically. On the first interpretation, the case can be put to the experimental test by dropping two heavy balls of the same material in a very viscous fluid, and then dropping two balls of differing specific gravities in the same fluid. In the first case they will fall with the same speeds whether they are attached or not; in the second, they will fall with the same (intermediate) speed only if they are attached. On Brown and Koyré's interpretation, two bodies falling to Earth far above its atmosphere will fall together without separating, whether attached or not, thus providing empirical confirmation of Galileo's experiment, although, of course, pretty good confirmation can be obtained by dropping them from the Leaning Tower of Pisa, since the resistance of the air does not have a very significant drag effect on cannonballs falling through that height.

2. THE *ROTA ARISTOTELICA*

Like many thought experiments, Aristotle's Wheel involves a paradox. The gist of this paradox is very easy to convey. Imagine two concentric wheels, one rigidly fixed inside another. More concretely, imagine a chariot wheel rotating in a rut in an ancient road in such a way that its hub is continuously in contact with the surface of the street, while the wheel itself is continuously in contact with the bottom of the rut. Suppose the hub has a radius r and the wheel has radius R. Then after n rotations of the wheel, the point A initially in contact with the road will have travelled a distance $2\pi R n$ while the point C on the hub will have traced exactly $2\pi r n$. But $R \gg r$. So AB $\gg$ CD!

What is the solution to this paradox? When I investigated by looking for contemporary resolutions, I discovered two quite distinct, indeed incompatible, resolutions. According to David Darling,

> A one-to-one correspondence exists between points on the larger circle and those on the smaller circle. Therefore, the wheel should travel the same distance regardless of whether it is rolled from left to right on the top straight line or on the bottom one. This seems to imply that the two circumferences of the different-sized circles are equal, which is impossible. How can this apparent contradiction be resolved? The key lies in the (false) assumption that a one-to-one correspondence of points means that two curves must have the same length. In fact, the cardinalities of points in a line segment of any length (or even an infinitely long line or an infinitely large n-dimensional Euclidean space) are all the same. (Darling 2004, 24)

I confess that to me this seemed to miss the point of the paradox entirely. It is not being argued that $2\pi R n = 2\pi r n$ because there is a 1–1 correspondence

Figure 6.1 The *Rota Aristotelica*.

between the points on the rims of the two wheels. On the contrary, it is granted that $2\pi Rn \gg 2\pi rn$, but this is paradoxical because the hub or nave of the wheel, being fixed to the wheel, must turn through precisely the same number of revolutions as it does, so that AB must equal CD. This, it would seem, can only happen if either (case 1) with the outer rim the driver, the hub slips against the surface of the road (so that CD > $2\pi rn$), or (case 2) with the hub the driver, the wheel slips against the bottom of the rut (so that AB < $2\pi Rn$), or perhaps both. This is the standpoint taken by the second of the two resolutions I found, which the online Archimedes Project takes as authoritative:

> As for the nave of the wheel, the case is otherwise. It is drawn in a right line by the same force as the wheel; but it only turns round because the wheel does so, and can only turn in the same time with it. Hence it follows, that its circular velocity is less than that of the wheel, in the ratio of the two circumferences; and therefore its circular motion is less than the rectilinear one. Since then it necessarily describes a right line equal to that of the wheel, it can only do it partly by sliding, and partly by revolving, the sliding part being more or less as the nave itself is smaller or larger. (Hutton 1815, 341)

What is interesting about this is that these two responses to the paradox correspond quite well to the main lines of response taken historically. Galileo, for instance, offers a response that is similar to the "Cantorian" one offered by Darling, in that it also appeals to considerations of 1–1 correspondence between an actual infinity of points on each of the hub and wheel, and to how this nevertheless allows for a difference in the lengths of paths travelled. On the other hand, his contemporary Mersenne, like many others, insists that the paradox is resolved by an appeal to slippage by whichever of the two circles is not driving the motion.

Let us begin with Galileo. In his discussion in *Two New Sciences*, Galileo began by considering two concentric hexagons. As the outer hexagon galumphs along the line ABQX . . . S one side at a time, one of its sides or one of its vertices is always in contact with the line. But as the outer wheel rotates through the first sixth of a revolution, the centre of the hub G travels through an arc to C, and with it the inner hub hexagon is also raised up in an arc. Thus whereas the outer hexagon pivots about B, on the line ABQX . . . S, the point I about which the inner one pivots traces an arc above the straight line HIOPYZT before its next side IK comes down to coincide with OP. There is therefore a gap IO in the contact of the perimeter of the inner polygon with the "road" HIOPYZ . . . T. This is, of course, repeated six times per revolution. Thus while the six sides of the outer polygon equal the line ABQX . . . S, the line traced by the inner polygon consists in six sides and five skipped arcs, so that it differs from it only by "the length of one chord of one of these arcs" (Galilei [1638] 1914, 22).

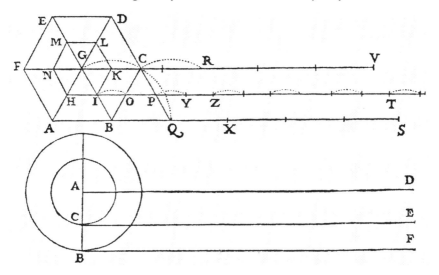

Figure 6.2 Galileo's *Rota* as shown in *Two New Sciences* (Galilei [1638] 1914, 21).

This talk of the smaller circle skipping parts of the line suggests that the same might be occurring when we extrapolate this analysis to infinity, regarding each circle as a polygon with infinitely many sides. Whereas the outer one's sides make continuous contact with the bottom of the rut, the inner one's contact is interrupted by an infinity of gaps, which add to the difference in the lengths of the paths. The vertices of the two circles are equinumerous, but those of the smaller circle do not make continuous contact with the road: It would slide. Galileo has Sagredo suggest something like this:

> SAGR. It seems to me that one may say that just as the center of the circle, by itself, carried along the line AD is constantly in contact with it, although it is only a single point, so the points on the circumference of the smaller circle, carried along by the motion of the larger circle, would slide over some small parts of the line CE. (Galilei [1638] 1914, 23)

But Galileo will have none of it. In the first place, his mouthpiece Salviati argues, there is no reason why one point rather than another should slide, so that, if there is any sliding, each of the infinite number of points of the smaller circle will slide over a finite segment of CE; but this would "make an infinitely long line, while as a matter of fact the line CE is finite" ([1638] 1914, 24). Second, since the two circles are rigidly attached to one another, they change their point of contact equally often, so that no point of the smaller circle can be in contact with CE at more than one point. The solution, then, would appear to be to have the gaps in the smaller circle's passage over the road infinitely small, but still adding to a finite quantity.

In fact, this could be argued to hold generally. If the points are not parts, differences in lengths could simply be the result of different infinite aggregates of infinitely small gaps summing to different finite lengths. Thus it is that Galileo extrapolates this reasoning to solid bodies in general: "Now this which has been said concerning simple lines must be understood to hold also in the case of surfaces and solid bodies, it being assumed that they are made up of an infinite, not a finite, number of atoms" ([1638] 1914, 25). Thus Aristotle's Wheel is used by Galileo as an argument for the composition of matter out of an infinity of point-atoms separated by infinitely small indivisible voids.

So in Galileo's case the paradox of Aristotle's Wheel functions as a thought experiment should. We have an apparently physically possible situation, described diagrammatically, leading to an anomalous result. Analysis reveals that the cause of the anomaly is a false conception of the continuous. If the continuum consists in indivisible points separated by indivisible gaps, then it is impossible for them to compose to a finite length so long as the indivisibles are finite. But if the gaps are infinitely small it is possible for an infinity of them to compose to a finite length, and also possible for there to be a difference in length of two lines containing the same infinite number of points.

How was this solution received? Well, if we look to Galileo's chief advocate in France, Marin Mersenne, the translator and disseminator of his dialogues, the answer would have to be: not very well. To Galileo's solution Mersenne objects in his commentary on Galileo's *Two New Sciences* in 1639 that "if the smaller circle always jumps a point of its line without touching that point, it follows that the line is not continuous, and consequently that it is not a line."[4] Mersenne had actually treated the problem earlier in the preface to his translation of Galileo's *Mechanics* in 1634, where he proposed that the solution is that the smaller circle simply slides, as can be seen by actually performing the experiment: "And when the small circle is moved by the large one, the same part of the small one touches a hundred parts of the large one, as experiment will make apparent to all those who perform it in sufficiently great volume."[5] Mersenne repeats this explanation in terms of sliding in his 1639 commentary (Drabkin 1950, 173). Fermat, apparently, sympathised with Mersenne's point of view, and also held that Galileo had misunderstood the problem.[6]

One thing that is apparent from this comparison of reactions to Aristotle's Wheel is that there is no consensus on precisely what the paradox is. Mersenne gives what I consider to be the correct solution. If there are n revolutions of the wheel with no slippage at the bottom of the rut, then a point on the rim of the hub will have travelled a distance of only $2\pi rn$, but the wheel will have travelled $2\pi Rn$ (which is greater than $2\pi rn$ in proportion to how much greater R is than r). This will only have been possible if the circumference of the hub has been carried slipping and sliding over the road to make up the difference. The proof of this is that if one actually does the experiment, one will observe this slipping and sliding.

But on a second line of interpretation, that misses the point of the paradox, as well as the fruitful lines of inquiry that are engendered by interpreting it properly. Galileo represents this line of interpretation. So do Robert Boyle and others who discuss the *Rota Aristotelica* in the context of the composition of matter, and its rarefaction and condensation. According to this interpretation, the two lines AB and CD are in fact necessarily equal, and the point is to explain how this could be. It is not legitimate to try to resolve a thought experiment, such as this seems to be, by an appeal to merely empirical factors like slipping and sliding. For them the problem is this: Given that the two lines are equal, how can this happen without slipping or sliding?

Interestingly, this is the line taken by Israel Drabkin, in his very scholarly and thorough treatment of the Wheel, when he notes "our problem is how it is possible for the paths to be equal without compensatory slipping in the sense indicated" (Drabkin 1950, 166). Accordingly, he takes a significant advance in the treatment of the paradox to be Roberval's proof that the lines traced by a point on the rim of each circle *are* equal. If the outer wheel is the "driver", then its path will be a *cycloid*; and the path of the point on the rim of the hub will be the curve known as the *curtate cycloid*. Writes Drabkin,

> [F]rom a kinematical viewpoint, we may say that any point on the circumference of the smaller circle has a motion which is the resultant of (1) a simple rotation of the smaller circle (such as would, by itself, cause the point to describe a circle), and (2) a translational motion equal in direction and magnitude to the translational motion of the larger circle. The resultant path of the point is the prolate[7] cycloid [as Roberval first proved]. It is the magnitude of this translational component that makes it possible for the smaller circle, while making only as many revolutions as the larger, to trace a path equal to that traced by the larger. (Drabkin 1950, 163–164)

Once this is established, the problem can be well defined. The condition is no sliding, which Drabkin, like Galileo, interprets to mean that no point on the rim can ever be in contact with a finite part of the road:

> But this, unfortunately, is where the problem *begins*, not where it ends. For though the smaller circle traverses a distance equal to that traversed by the larger, it does not keep pace with the larger by sliding over the tangent, if by 'sliding' we mean that a point on the circumference is at

Figure 6.3   Roberval's cycloids.

any time in contact with a finite segment of the tangent. For the rotary motion of the smaller circle is continuous, as is that of the larger, and consequently the point of tangency is continuously changing. How it is possible for the paths to be equal without compensatory sliding in the sense indicated is the nub of the problem. (1950, 164–165, my emphasis)

Thus according to Drabkin, the "paradox involved belongs with those having to do with continuity and infinite divisibility." He acknowledges the "Cantorian" solution, without committing himself to it. Those trying to resolve the paradox "on the basis of the Cantorian analysis", he writes, "will view the path of the smaller circle (equal to the circumference of the larger) as containing an infinite aggregate of points which may be put in one-to-one correspondence with (and is, in this sense, similar to) the aggregate represented by the points on the circumference of the smaller circle" (1950, 166). Although the path of a point on the circumference of the smaller circle traces a distance equal to the circumference of the larger circle, and this is greater than the circumference of the smaller circle, the two circles are aggregates of the same (infinite) number of points. The paradox therefore arises from confusing the number of points in the two unequal circumferences with their measures. But, Drabkin concedes, not everyone is happy with this resolution.

Certainly this was the case historically, as his analysis reveals. He examines the solutions given by Boyle, Tacquet, and Jean-Jacques d'Ortous de Mairan (Fontenelle 1717)[8] in the century after *Two New Sciences* appeared, all of which reject Galileo's actual infinity of extensionless points, and opt for some kind of infinitesimal sliding. Mairan's is representative. "If at every infinitesimal moment each infinitesimal element of the arc of the smaller circle (in Case I) is in contact with a longer infinitesimal element of the base line, there is, in that sense, a 'sliding'" (Drabkin 1950, 194). Drabkin comments:

MAIRAN'S definition, which is generally accepted, in its essence declares that there is sliding whenever the path traced by a rolling circle in one revolution is not equal to the circumference of the circle. But in my opinion this definition does not, by itself, constitute an answer to the paradox. (1950, 195)

Thus we have a genuine disagreement about what the paradox consists in. On the interpretation I favour, the thought experiment engenders a paradox which can be resolved by thinking the problem through, and whose resolution can be confirmed by doing the actual experiment. On Drabkin's and Galileo's, the problem is conceptual. That is, the paradox is part of a thought experiment, and it *cannot* be resolved by actual experiment without violating one of the conditions of the thought experiment, namely, no sliding. Drabkin is disappointed that Mersenne, having once (like Galileo and Boyle) seen the solution to lie in considerations of rarefaction and condensation, should have reverted to the explanation in terms of sliding.[9] And he expresses surprise that "Mersenne strangely ascribes this explanation ['sliding'] to Aristotle" (1950, 174).

Let us then turn, somewhat belatedly, to the original formulation of the paradox. The author of the *Mechanical Problems*, it is now generally accepted, was not Aristotle, even though it has been traditionally ascribed to him. Most scholars argue that it must nevertheless have been someone of the Peripatetic school, because of the use of the Aristotelian terminology and the framework of mover and moved to describe motion.

Against this consensus, Thomas Winter (2007, iii–ix) has recently offered arguments that the author of *Mechanical Problems* was in fact Archytas of Tarentum (428–347 BCE). Winter argues for an early date based on the weapons and devices discussed,[10] and suggests that Archytas is the only one of twelve ancient writers on mechanics mentioned by Vitruvius that fits the bill. I neither want nor need, for present purposes, to become embroiled in scholarly disputes about authorship. But the content of the *Mechanical Problems* is consistent with what we know of Archytas' approach to mathematics: Diogenes Laertius reports that Archytas' attempt to duplicate the cube by constructing two mean proportionals, reproduced in Book VIII of Euclid's *Elements*, was the first geometrical construction to employ "mechanical motion", that is, lines generated by moving figures.[11] If Archytas was in fact

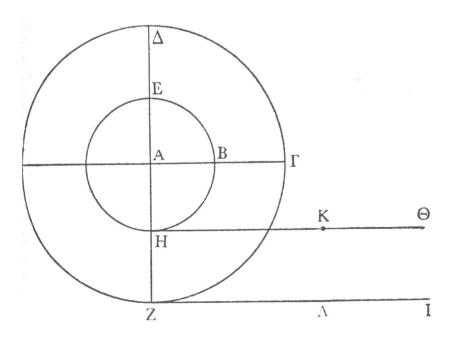

Figure 6.4   The original *Rota Aristotelica* (Aristotle [1936] 1955, 391).

the author of the *Rota,* that would make it one of the oldest thought experiments of which we have any record. In fact, it would be as old as another influential thought experiment attributed to the same Archytas, later made famous by Lucretius: the thought experiment that cast doubt on the finiteness of the extent of the cosmos by asking what would happen if someone standing near the boundary were to throw a javelin through it.[12]

At any rate, our thought experiment is stated as Problem 24 of the *Mechanical Problems,* as follows:

> 24. A difficulty arises as to how it is that a greater circle when it rolls describes a line of the same length as a smaller circle, if the two are concentric. When they are rolled separately, then the lines they describe are in the same ratio as their respective sizes. Again, assuming that the two have the same centre, sometimes the line they describe is the same length as the smaller circle would describe by itself, and sometimes it is the length of the larger circle's path. Yet it is obvious the larger circle rolls out a longer line. (Aristotle [1936] 1955, 387, translation slightly altered)

> As, then, nowhere does the greater [circle] stop and wait for the less in such a way as to remain stationary for a time at the same point (for in both cases both are moving continuously), and as the smaller does not skip any point, it is remarkable that in the one case the greater should travel over a path equal to the smaller, and in the other case the smaller equal to the larger. (Aristotle [1936] 1955, 391)

Here we see the condition of "no skipping" entrenched in the formulation of the problem, thus explaining why some authors have insisted that sliding could not be a solution. In fact, however, it seems that the author of the *Mechanical Problems* takes the view that since the problem, as stated, leads to a paradoxical conclusion, there is something wrong with the premises. Either the path traced out by the centres of each of the wheels is $2\pi Rn$, as it will be if the larger circle drives the motion, or it will be the smaller length, $2\pi rn$, as when the smaller wheel is the driver. The speed of rotation will be the same in the two cases. But these are two different rotations, whose centres are only accidentally the same:

> When, then, the large circle moves the small one attached to it, the smaller one moves exactly as the larger one; when the small one is the mover, the larger one moves according to the other's movement. But when separated, each of them has its own movement. If anyone objects that the two circles trace out unequal paths though they have the same centre, and move at the same speed, his argument is erroneous. It is true that both circles have the same centre, but this fact is only accidental, just as a thing might be both "musical" and "white". For the fact

of each circle having the same centre does not affect in the same way in the two cases. When the small circle produces the movement the centre and origin of movement belongs to the small circle; but when the large circle produces the movement the centre belongs to it. Therefore what produces the movement is not the same in both cases, though in a sense it is. ([1936] 1955, 395)

What leads to the paradox, then, on this interpretation, is the assumption that the case can be considered without identifying which of the circles is the driver. If it is the larger wheel, then since points on the smaller one are forced to make contact with a larger length, it will slide; if the smaller one is the driver, the larger one must be forced to trace out a shorter length than it rotates. Thus the two wheels, when fixed together, cannot trace the same length in *n* revolutions without one of them slipping against the surface, either the wheel in the rut or the hub on the road.

Let me now summarise my conclusions.

1. I contend that Aristotle's Wheel has a good claim to be regarded as a thought experiment, indeed one of the first. It is an imagined scenario, with accompanying diagram, that leads to a paradoxical conclusion, and it has generated much speculation about foundational questions, in this case the composition of matter and the continuum.
2. According to the so-called "Cantorian" interpretation, the paradox results from the fact that if the two unequal concentric circles trace out equal lines, this implies that their circumferences must be equal. But this involves confusing the equality of the number of points on each circumference, which can be put into 1–1 correspondence, with the equality of their measures.

    This, I claim, misses the point completely. No one claimed the wheel and hub were equal because the points on their rims could be put into 1–1 correspondence. The equality of the measures follows from the conditions of the paradox, namely that the wheel and hub, being rigidly attached together, are forced to travel the same distance. If there is no slippage and they trace equal lines, $2\pi rn = 2\pi Rn$, so that $r = R$.
3. This is what led some authors to see the paradox's resolution as entailing that either the circumference of the small circle must become expanded, or that of the large one contracted. Thus if the large one (the wheel) is the driver, the hub must expand while moving! This is, in effect, Galileo's solution.

    But this beggars belief: The hub clearly does not expand until it becomes the same radius as the wheel—if this happened, no chariot would ever get stuck in a rut again! Expansion and contraction are no solution.
4. A more charitable interpretation of Galileo's version of the thought experiment is that the hub skips over infinitely many infinitely small

gaps, which sum to a finite length, namely $2\pi Rn - 2\pi rn$. Mersenne and others regarded this solution as betraying the idea of a continuum. Moreover, one might add, if the gaps are, as Galileo claimed, *"non quante"*, it is difficult to see how they could be greater or smaller. This led to Mairan's proposal that the non-driver wheel would undergo sliding along infinitesimal segments of the line, with the infinitesimals of that wheel in contact with infinitesimals of the line in the ratio of the radii of the two wheels. That solution, of course, breaks the condition that there should be no slippage; it relaxes it to Galileo's claim that there should be no slippage along any *finite* segment of the line.

5. What, then, of Roberval's proof that a point on the circumference of the hub would trace a curtate cycloid of the same length as the cycloid traced by a point on the circumference of the wheel? Roberval effected his proof by combining the tangential component of the point's rotational motion with its translational motion by the parallelogram of motions (itself stated for the very first time in Problem 23 of the *Mechanical Problems*!). But this assumes that, with the outer circle (wheel) the driver, the hub is forced to move with the translational velocity of the wheel. This can only happen if there is continuous slippage between the hub and the road, so this reduces to the same solution as Mairan's.

6. I therefore conclude that the answer to Drabkin's problem of "how it is possible for the paths to be equal without compensatory slipping in the sense indicated" (Drabkin 1950, 166) is that it is only possible if one allows continuous infinitesimal slippage of the kind proposed by Mairan, which Drabkin rejects. If one regards it as a condition of the thought experiment that there should be no sliding at all, the paradox simply indicates that this cannot be done.

Of course, continuous infinitesimal slippage is not physically realistic. It presupposes perfect frictional contact between the driver wheel and its surface, and perfectly frictionless contact between the trailer wheel and its surface. Whatever perfect symmetry there is in the ideal case, one can expect it to be broken in practice, where there will be no perfect evenness of friction between surfaces.

Thus I believe the correct interpretation is that implicit in the analysis of Archytas/Aristotle, spelled out explicitly by Mersenne: There is indeed slippage, and that is the end of the matter. The ruts were deep in ancient roads, and sparks flew off the naves of the chariots! Real experiment resolves Problem 24 of *Mechanical Problems* completely—provided we agree on what the problem is!

It remains to consider what general morals can be drawn from this case. One might be that, before we can agree on the resolution of a thought experiment, we have first to agree on what the thought experiment is! Second, whether the thought experiment is performable as an actual experiment will depend on identifying exactly what it is, of course, but also on which idealizing assumptions are thought to be essential to the thought experiment, and which are thought to be accidental.

To further illustrate these points, let me very briefly consider in closing one of the two cases I mentioned at the beginning of this paper, Galileo's thought experiment concerning the dropping of two balls of different weights attached by a string, in refutation of Aristotle's theory that they would fall at different speeds. (The third, the Bell-Aspect case, I will reserve for another time.)

> Aristotle declares that bodies of different weight, in the same medium, travel [. . .] with speeds which are proportional to their weights . . . and that a stone of twenty pounds moves ten times as rapidly as one of two; but I claim this is false, and that if they fall from a height of fifty or a hundred cubits, they will reach the earth at the same moment. (Galilei [1638] 1914, 65)

James R. Brown asserts that Galileo's thought experiment establishes this conclusion independently of experiment. As is well known, Salviati gets Simplicio to agree that a heavier body H will fall faster than a lighter one L, and that "the more rapid one will be partly retarded by the slower" (Galilei [1638] 1914, 63). But now if the two stones are tied together, H will be retarded by L, so H + L will fall more slowly than H. But H + L is heavier than H, so "the heavier body moves with less speed than the lighter", contrary to the supposition (Galilei [1638] 1914, 63). Says Brown, "We have a straightforward contradiction, the old theory is destroyed. Moreover a new theory is established; the question of which falls faster is obviously resolved by having all objects fall at the same speed" (Brown 1991, 76).

But as I have indicated elsewhere in my own analysis of this thought experiment (Arthur 1999), there are many subtleties here. First, from a modern point of view, two balls falling in a vacuum will undergo uniform acceleration, and if they fall through the same height, they will have the same terminal velocity; but this is an instantaneous velocity, a concept that is only approximated by Galileo's notion of degree of speed, and is not the same as the notion of velocity employed here, which just means how fast a given distance is covered. On the other hand, here the stones are falling in a medium; and in a medium they reach a terminal velocity, their "natural velocity", which is specific to the medium and the specific gravity of the body. This is how Galileo sets up the thought experiment:

> There can be no doubt but that one and the same body moving in a single medium has a fixed velocity which is determined by nature and which cannot be increased except by the addition of momentum [*impeto*] or diminished except by some resistance which retards it. (Galilei [1638] 1914, 63)

What Simplicio says here for Galileo is, in fact, known to be true: Under the right conditions, bodies falling in a medium will eventually attain such a fixed velocity by Stokes' Law. So, under the assumption that the two bodies are falling in a medium, have the same specific gravities, and have reached their "natural velocity", adding one such body to another will make a combined body with the same specific gravity as either of the two separately. This is why Galileo could have such confidence that "even without further experiment, it is possible to prove clearly, by means of a short and conclusive argument, that a heavier body does not move more rapidly than a lighter one, provided both bodies are of the same material, and in short such as those mentioned by Aristotle" (Galilei [1638] 1914, 62).

Thus my reading of what constitutes the thought experiment is very different from Brown's. The two stones' having the same specific gravity is a constitutive assumption, as is the fact that the bodies are falling in a medium. If two bodies with very different specific gravities are dropped in a jar containing very viscous fluid, one of them will fall faster than the other. If they are attached together, they will fall at some intermediate velocity. This shows that Brown's conclusion—that the thought experiment immediately establishes that "all bodies fall equally fast"—is itself too fast. Galileo's conclusion does not follow unless these conditions are fulfilled. If there is no medium, they will not reach a "natural velocity" at all, and we learn nothing about their behaviour in a vacuum directly from this thought experiment. (It takes Galileo many pages of further argumentation to establish what will happen to bodies falling in a vacuum.) But if these conditions of the thought experiment are met, then the thought experiment works perfectly. There is no need to do the experiment, but if it is done, it confirms the analysis.

This example also conforms to the morals I drew from the Wheel. It all depends on what the problem identified by the thought experiment is taken to be, what the constitutive assumptions are, and what idealizing assumptions are allowed. Having established these things, we see that in this case too, what was concluded from the thought experiment can be confirmed by an actual experiment. So a thought experiment cannot be defined as an imaginative or conceptual representation of a phenomenon that cannot be produced in practice: In at least some cases, it can, and in such cases we expect that actual experiments will either confirm resolutions of any paradox raised by the thought experiment, or throw more light on what the constitutive assumptions of the thought experiment are.

NOTES

1. This quotation is from Sorensen (1992, 241). He is merely summarising common knowledge. The point of his discussion, however, is to draw parallels between thought experiments and ordinary ones.

2. Of course, Aspect's actual experiments were not just trivial realisations of Bell's thought experiment. Considerable ingenuity had to be put into constructing an apparatus that would test the abstract scenario Bell had described and into devising further experimental arrangements to rule out extraneous explanations. Nevertheless, I contend, they still described what they were doing as experimentally testing Bell's inequalities, which Bell had derived by a thought experiment alone.

3. See Brown (1991, 77–79, 95–96) and Koyré (1968, 75, 88).

4. "[S]i le moindre cercle saute tousiours un poinct de sa ligne sans le toucher, il s'ensuit qu'elle n'est pas continuë, & partant qu'elle n'est pas ligne." M. Mersenne. *Les Nouvelles Pensees de Galilei mathematicien & ingenieur du duc de Florence* (Paris, 1639, 31); quoted from Drabkin (1950, 175).

5. "Et lors que le petit est meu par le grand, une mesme partie du petit, touche cent parties du grand, comme l'experience fera voir a tous ceux qui la feront en assez grand volume." M. Mersenne, trans. *Les Mechaniques de Galilee mathematicien* (Paris, 1634, 18–19); quoted from Drabkin (1950, 174). Drabkin observes that this was not Mersenne's first attempt on the problem, and that in an earlier attempt he had mentioned how "some have sought an analogy between the action of the concentric circles and the processes of rarefaction and condensation", precisely as Galileo was later to do (Drabkin 1950, 173).

6. Drabkin quotes a letter of August 10, 1638, from Fermat to Mersenne in which Fermat says that he had sent him long before his thoughts on Problem 24 of the "*Méchaniques* d'Aristote" (Drabkin 1950, 188, *my emphasis*). But that manuscript is no longer extant, so we don't know what Fermat's objections were.

7. As a referee has pointed put to me, "the point on the smaller figure should describe a curtate cycloid and not a prolate one. So Drabkin got the wrong name (but the right figure nonetheless). If it was the hub keeping its course, then we would have the point on the wheel describing a prolate cycloid."

8. In his entry "Sur la roue d'Aristote" in the 1715 *Histoire de l'Académie Royale des Sciences,* Fontenelle summarises the report on *Aristotle's Wheel* that Mairan had sent to the Académie.

9. Similarly, Drabkin writes: "The latest commentator on the passage shows a similar superficiality. He writes: 'It is not easy to be sure whether he <the author of the *Mechanica*> has seen the true solution of this problem, viz: in one case <Case II> the circle revolves on H9 while the larger circle both rolls and slips in ZI'" (1950, 167, n. 8).

10. Winter notes that the author "seeks the principle behind gear trains, windlasses, levers, and the slings with which the Greeks threw spears. But our sought author does not know about catapults." He does not explain why Archytas would not have known about catapults, which were invented by Dionysius the Elder of Syracuse in 399.

11. Diogenes Laertius (1925): "83. He was the first to bring mechanics to a system by applying mathematical principles; he also first employed mechanical motion in a geometrical construction, namely, when he tried, by means of a section of a half-cylinder, to find two mean proportionals in order to duplicate the cube" (*Lives*, Book VIII, §83). According to Diogenes Aristotle wrote "On the Philosophy of Archytas, three books" (*Lives*, Book V, §25). Is it not possible that one of these three "books" is a transcription of a *Mechanical Problems* by Archytas?

12. The other problems treated in the *Mechanical Problems* are all eminently practical in nature, and many exploit the same kind of combination of straight and circular motions for their resolution: (6) "Why is it that the

higher the yard-arm, the faster the ship travels with the same sail and the same wind?", (8) "Why are round and circular things easier to move than things of other shapes?", (10) "Why is an empty balance easier to move than a weighted one?", (11) "Why are heavy weights more easily carried on rollers than on carts, though the latter's wheels are larger while the circumference of rollers is small?", (26) "Why is it more difficult to carry long timbers on the shoulders by the end than by the middle, provided that the weight is equal in the two cases?" (Diogenes Laertius 1925).

REFERENCES

Aristotle. [1936] 1955. *Minor Works*, with an English translation by W. S. Hett. Cambridge, MA: Harvard University Press/London: William Heinemann.

Arthur, R. T. W. 1999. "On Thought Experiments as *a Priori* Science." *International Studies in the Philosophy of Science* 13 (3): 215–229.

Brown, James R. 1991. *The Laboratory of the Mind: Thought Experiments in the Natural Sciences*. London: Routledge.

Darling, David J. 2004. *The Universal Book of Mathematics: From Abracadabra to Zeno's Paradoxes*. Hoboken, NJ: Wiley.

Diogenes Laertius. 1925. *Lives of the Eminent Philosophers*. Books V and VIII. Translated by Robert Drew Hicks. http://en.wikisource.org/wiki/Lives_of_the_Eminent_Philosophers/Book_V   http://en.wikisource.org/wiki/Lives_of_the_Eminent_Philosophers/Book_VIII#Archytas (accessed August 23, 2011).

Drabkin, Israel E. 1950. "Aristotle's Wheel: Notes on the History of a Paradox." *Osiris* 9: 162–198.

Fontenelle, Bernard Le Bovier de. 1717. "Sur la roue d'Aristote." In *Histoire de l'Académie Royale des Sciences Année 1715*. Paris: Imprimerie Royale.

Galilei, Galileo. [1638] 1914. *Dialogues Concerning Two New Sciences*. Translation of *Discorsi e dimostrazioni matematiche, intorno à due nuove scienze*, by Henry Crew and Alfonso de Salvio. New York: Macmillan. www.questia.com/PM.qst?a=o&d=88951396 (accessed August 23, 2011).

Hutton, Charles. 1815. *A Philosophical and Mathematical Dictionary*. New edition. Vol. 2. London.

Koyré, Alexandre. 1968. "Galileo's Treatise 'De Motu Gravium': the Use and Abuse of Imaginary Experiment." In *Metaphysics and Measurement: Essays in Scientific Revolution*. London: Chapman and Hall.

Sorensen, Roy A. 1992. *Thought Experiments*. Oxford: Oxford University Press.

Winter, Thomas N. 2007. "The *Mechanical Problems* in the Corpus of Aristotle." DigitalCommons@University of Nebraska–Lincoln. http://digitalcommons.unl.edu/classicsfacpub/68 (accessed August 23, 2011).

7 Chasing the Light
Einstein's Most Famous Thought Experiment

John D. Norton

1. INTRODUCTION

How could we be anything but charmed by the delightful story Einstein tells in his "Autobiographical Notes" of a striking thought he had at the age of sixteen? While recounting the efforts that led to the special theory of relativity, he recalled

> a paradox upon which I had already hit at the age of sixteen: If I pursue a beam of light with the velocity *c* (velocity of light in a vacuum), I should observe such a beam of light as an electromagnetic field at rest though spatially oscillating. There seems to be no such thing, however, neither on the basis of experience nor according to Maxwell's equations. From the very beginning it appeared to me intuitively clear that, judged from the standpoint of such an observer, everything would have to happen according to the same laws as for an observer who, relative to the earth, was at rest. For how should the first observer know or be able to determine, that he is in a state of fast uniform motion?
>
> One sees in this paradox the germ of the special relativity theory is already contained. (Einstein 1951, 52–53 [1979, 48–51])

Einstein is celebrated for devising penetrating thought experiments and here we are offered a thought experiment that contains the germ of his great discovery. Yet the thought experiment is so simple that it could arise in the playful musings of a sixteen year old. It is little wonder that this thought experiment is widely cited and praised.

All this is deceptive. The thought experiment is unlike Einstein's many other thought experiments in two ways. First and foremost, unlike them, it is entirely unclear how this thought experiment works. Upon encountering the thought experiment, most readers likely find the imagery quite vivid and even seductive. But they should be, and typically will be, left with a sense of incomplete understanding. Just why, they should ask, is the frozen light of this thought experiment problematic? The question is unlikely to be pursued. Most readers expect Einstein's thought to be abstruse and a failure of understanding to be the reader's fault. That may often be the case, but in this instance, the opacity is no fault of readers. It is not at all clear how the thought experiment works. As will be recounted in Section 2 below, if we read the thought experiment as securing a fatal defect of the then dominant ether-based theories of electrodynamics, it fails. This is the "physical problem" to be addressed here.

Readers seeking help in understanding this curious failure will find little help in the secondary literature. As I shall explain in Section 3, that literature almost never acknowledges the problem. It may simply paraphrase Einstein's text, perhaps hoping the reader will penetrate the thought experiment in a way the author did not. Or it may discourage a reader from seeking cogent explication by praising Einstein's prescient intuition. We are to admire his ability to see fragments of the relativity theory to come in what Einstein (1956, 10) elsewhere called a "child-like thought experiment," but we lesser minds should not expect to understand how he saw it. And worse, an author may feign understanding and give the thought experiment an explication that connects poorly with Einstein's text. The unfortunate reader now has two problems: to understand Einstein's text and to understand the explication!

Second, there is a "historical problem," as I shall call it, to be laid out in Section 4. The thought experiment was conceived by Einstein in late 1895–early 1896 and involves a confident assertion of what Maxwell's equations permit. Yet the young Einstein was not to learn Maxwell's theory until around 1898. Is Einstein merely describing a thought experiment from 1895–1896? Or is the thought experiment now also intermingled with later analyses?

My solution to both physical and historical problems is to suggest that Einstein's thought experimenting with frozen light persisted well into his researches that lead up to the 1905 special theory of relativity. Versions of the thought experiment were conducted after Einstein had mastered Maxwell's equation. During this time, Einstein gave long and serious consideration to emission theories of light. In them, the speed of a light beam is c, not with respect to the ether, but with respect to the emitter. These emission theories were Einstein's best and perhaps only hope of realizing a principle of relativity in electrodynamics, prior to his recognition that these efforts would require a new theory of space and time. I will propose that Einstein's "Autobiographical Notes" version of the thought experiment recounts powerful reasons for abandoning emission theories, if in abbreviated form. These theories and some of Einstein's discussion of them will be described in Section 5. The rereading of Einstein's thought experiment as providing objections to emission theories will be given in the concluding Section 6. The thought experiment is then seen to succeed in offering reasons as clear and cogent as in any of Einstein's other thought experiments. It has the added benefit of clarifying cryptic remarks Einstein made elsewhere concerning his discarding of emission theories.

In what follows, I will take the above-quoted presentation of the thought experiment from "Autobiographical Notes" as the canonical version of the thought experiment. My purpose here is to explicate this version of the thought experiment. While I will discuss reports of other versions below, this one is both its best-known exposition and, presumably, the one that Einstein drafted most cautiously. It was written for a text that Einstein knew would be his official autobiography.

2. PHYSICAL PROBLEM

The thought experiment calls upon some elementary physics of light waves from Maxwell's electrodynamics. In that theory, space is filled with an all-pervading medium, the ether. Electric and magnetic fields arise as states of that ether. A propagating light wave is a sinusoidal electric and magnetic field whose waveform propagates at c, the speed of light. In these essentials, the theory's account of propagating light differs little from one of waves propagating over water. The ether corresponds to the water, and the electric and magnetic field strengths correspond to the displacement of the water's surface into peaks and troughs.

Einstein's thought is simple. If he were somehow to chase after that propagating waveform at c, he would catch the wave and move with it, much as a surfer catches a water wave. He would find a frozen light wave. But that possibility, Einstein declares, is untenable for three reasons, and in that failure he finds the germ of the special theory of relativity.

What remains unclear is just *how* Einstein's three reasons establish that the frozen waveform is untenable and thereby create difficulties for the nineteenth-century account of light. His target, presumably, is the ether state of rest around which Maxwell's electrodynamics is constructed. Yet an ether theorist can readily defeat each of the three reasons Einstein lists. To see how they are defeated, let us dissect Einstein's text to expose the three reasons and juxtapose an ether theorist's natural response (see Table 7.1).

Once the ease of the ether theorist's response is seen, Einstein's thought experiment becomes more than puzzling. It seems to rest on elementary oversights unworthy of an Einstein. He appears to demand experiences that we do not have simply because we are moving slowly. We do not see frozen light since we are not moving at c. Einstein also seems to have become an inept theorist. He disallows the compatibility of frozen light with Maxwell's theory, when a two-line computation in the theory—given in my endnote—shows that a rapidly moving observer would be surrounded by frozen light. Finally, Einstein's concluding rhetorical question is answered directly by an ether theorist. When you find light frozen, you are moving very fast.

Table 7.1   An Ether Theorist's Response to Einstein

	Einstein wrote:	*The Ether Theorist's Response*
	"I should observe such a beam of light as an electromagnetic field at rest though spatially oscillating. There seems to be no such thing, however, . . ."	
1	" . . . neither on the basis of experience . . ."	We do not experience frozen light since we are not moving at c through the ether. If we were moving that fast through the ether, we would experience frozen light.
2	" . . . nor according to Maxwell's equations."	Not so. A very short calculation[1] shows that Maxwell's equations predict that light becomes frozen for observers moving at c through the ether.
	"From the very beginning it appeared to me intuitively clear that, judged from the standpoint of such an observer, everything would have to happen according to the same laws as for an observer who, relative to the earth, was at rest."	
3	"For how should the first observer know or be able to determine, that he is in a state of fast uniform motion?"	Observers know they are moving rapidly with respect to the ether simply because light has become frozen. Analogously, surfers know they are moving since their position on the wave does not change.

3. COMMENTARIES

We should give Einstein the benefit of the doubt when he writes something that seems trivially and fatally wrong. However, that charity should not extend to a failure to recognize that we face a problem in reconstructing Einstein's intentions. That failure is widespread among commentaries written on Einstein's thought experiment. While I am far from having surveyed all such commentaries,[2] my small explorations have turned up only a tiny fraction of commentaries that admit to a problem.

Perhaps the clearest is Adolf Grünbaum's (1973, 371–375). He rehearses some of the concerns I express above and concludes memorably:[3]

> In view of the presumably flimsy character of the appeal to experience and of the redundancy of (2) with (3) among the reasons given by

Einstein, we are pretty much left with his intuitive confidence in the principle of relativity as the basis for his assumption [light is the fastest signal *in vacuo*]. (1973, 374–375)

Einstein's former collaborator, Banesh Hoffmann (1982, 94–97), lays out the objection to Einstein's second reason. He recapitulates the easy demonstration in a non-relativistic spacetime of the possibility of frozen light, but he finds a prescience in Einstein's psychological reaction to the thought experiment.[4] Olivier Darrigol (1996, 289–290) is less eager to exculpate Einstein. He judges Einstein's reminiscence "either false or misdated" and concludes: "We should therefore regard the widespread belief that Einstein had an inborn trust in the relativity principle as a myth. In fact, he originally believed in Maxwell's electromagnetic ether." Citing Darrigol's analysis, Marc Lange (2002, 201) reviews the difficulties of reading Einstein's thought experiment as a prompt in a list of discussion questions. He asks, provocatively, "Is Einstein's famous argument from 'riding on a beam of light' flawed?" but does not apparently take a stand himself.

These critical reactions are exceptional. Virtually all commentaries fail to acknowledge that something appears to be amiss. The most benign of these, such as Martinez (2009, 213–214), merely report Einstein's remarks without attempting elucidation. The exposition may even be a rather close paraphrase. Whitrow[5] says that

> the beam of light would then appear as a spatially oscillating electromagnetic field at rest. But such a concept was unknown to physics and at variance with Maxwell's theory. (1973, 11)

There is no further explication, so the reader is apparently intended to understand these remarks directly. Fortunately, some reports flag to the reader that there might be a problem. Immediately after quoting Einstein's text, Bergia[6] concedes:

> We deliberately restrain ourselves from touching upon the point of logical internal consistency in this passage (Grunbaum); we rather call attention to the "intuitive" conclusion it leads to: as a spatially oscillatory field at rest "does not make sense," no observer, i.e. no material body, can reach the velocity *c*. (1979, 84)

Other authors are less ready to admit the problem as they struggle to clarify Einstein's remarks. Holton finds Einstein's narrative to have

> its exact parallel in the 1905 paper, in the conceptual leap from a simple experiment (indeed, also a kind of *Gedanken* experiment—the relative motion of conductor and magnet) to the general principle from which the content of relativity theory will derive. (1973, 293)

Here Holton refers to the magnet and conductor thought experiment that initiates Einstein's famous "On the Electrodynamics of Moving Bodies" (Einstein 1905), in which he first presents special relativity. That thought experiment derives from a fact in ether-based electrodynamics. A magnet at rest in the ether is surrounded by a magnetic field. A magnet moving in the ether is surrounded by a magnetic field and an induced electric field, arising through the magnet's motion. One might expect this electric field to be an experimentally detectible sign of the magnet's motion in the ether, for one can detect the electric field from its ability to create a measurable electric current in a conductor in the vicinity of the magnet. Yet, Einstein reported, a curious combination of effects leads to the same current in the conductor no matter whether the magnet is at rest in the ether or moving in it.[7]

The similarity, Holton continues, persists in the details of the two experiments. They are

> physically of precisely the same kind: in one case the question concerns the electric and magnetic fields a moving observer finds to be associated with a light beam; in the other case, it concerns the electric and magnetic fields experienced by a moving conductor; and the solutions in both cases follow from the same transformation equations. (1973, 293)

While there are some similarities here, they do not extend to the point at issue. Einstein's inference in the case of the magnet and conductor thought experiment is clear and unequivocal. Ether theories of electromagnetism are positing a state of rest that is, in this case, mysteriously obscured from detection. Einstein's inference in the case of the chasing a light beam thought experiment is apparently flawed; it is not clear how it creates a problem for ether-based electrodynamics.

In the course of the nineteenth century, ether-drift experiments had sought to measure the slight shift in the speed of light that ought to result from the earth's motion in the ether. It later became a much-celebrated fact that no effect was measured by these experiments. Miller calls on this as a partial explanation of Einstein's remarks:

> At sixteen, Einstein must have known of some, or perhaps all, of the famous ether-drift experiments, thus accounting for the comment: "However there seems to be no such thing . . . on the basis of experience." (1981, 169)

The difficulty with this reading is that Einstein's "no such thing" refers directly to "an electromagnetic field at rest though spatially oscillating" and there is quite some gap to be closed between that and the very slightly slowed or sped up light that eluded the terrestrial ether-drift experiments.

Miller (1981, 169) also repeatedly points to Einstein's wording "intuitively clear" in relation to his early conviction in the principle of relativity.

Other authors go further and emphasize Einstein's prescient intuition in celebratory tones, perhaps intending to forestall a demand for explanation of Einstein's reasoning. Sartori praises Einstein's "inspired intuition":

> The seed of the theory of relativity had evidently been planted when Einstein was only sixteen years old! The idea that light has the same speed in all inertial frames, so difficult for an ordinary mind to grasp, was a quite natural one for Einstein. He was prepared to accept it even without strong experimental evidence. (1996, 53–54)

Yet other authors struggle to make Einstein's discomfort with frozen light credible through ornamenting Einstein's account with picturesque details. Bernstein attempts to clarify Einstein's dismissal of frozen light by remarking:

> It would be like coming across a pond which had a wavy surface but the waves did not move. This would certainly appear "paradoxical." (2006, 62)

While the image of a pond with frozen waves is striking, it is not the one that would match Einstein's construction. One needs to add that Einstein is chasing after the waves. Then it would be trivial that an Einstein chasing the waves on the water's surface would find frozen waves. They would not appear paradoxical. More inventively, Schwartz and McGuiness (1979, 75–76) locate the puzzle in the fact that an Einstein, traveling with light, would be unable to see his reflection in a hand-held mirror included in the illustrations. While that would be true, it is not at all clear from his text that this is just what troubled Einstein in the thought experiment.

Finally, in an apparent eagerness to provide a seamless account, an author may end up misstating the physics. Kaku relates how Einstein found that his aversion to frozen light was vindicated when he later learned Maxwell's theory:

> When Einstein finally learned Maxwell's equations, he could answer the question that was continually on his mind. As he suspected, he found that there were no solutions of Maxwell's equations in which light was frozen in time. But then he discovered more. To his surprise, he found that in Maxwell's theory, light beams always traveled at the same velocity, no matter how fast you moved. (2004, 45)

This is supposedly what Einstein learned as a student at the Zurich Polytechnic, where he completed his studies in 1900, well before the formulation of the special theory of relativity. Yet the results described are precisely what is *not* to be found in the ether-based Maxwell theory Einstein would then have learned. That theory allows light to slow and be frozen in the frame of reference of a sufficiently rapidly moving observer. The results Kaku describes are the ones that obtain in Maxwell's theory only after it is ported to the space and time of Einstein's special theory of relativity.

In sum, even though Einstein's "Autobiographical Notes" account appears to relate a sequence of inferences readers can follow, the celebrated thought experiment is poorly understood. Very few authors admit this directly. Most feign understanding and the positive proposals offered connect poorly with each other and with Einstein's text.

4. HISTORICAL PROBLEM

When a report by Einstein creates this much confusion, we need to proceed carefully. First, we need to be secure in our sources. The canonical text of Einstein's "Autobiographical Notes" contains an oddity. It indicates that he found the paradox at age sixteen. Since he was born on March 14, 1879, that coincides with the year March 1895–March 1896. Another report (cited below) locates the thought experiment in Einstein's school year at Aarau, which lasted from late October 1895 to September 1896. These dates coincide well enough to place the thought experiment in late 1895 to early 1896.

The historical problem this creates is that the "Autobiographical Notes" narrative has an essential role for Maxwell's equations. Yet we know from other reports that Einstein did not learn Maxwell's theory until his university studies around 1898 (see Stachel et al. 1987, 223–235).

We have two other accounts of the thought experiment. Neither mentions Maxwell's equations and both are distinctive in emphasizing the hesitancy of Einstein's conclusion. In a reminiscence of his year at the gymnasium in Aarau, Einstein wrote:

> During this year in Aarau the following question came to me: if one chases a light wave with the speed of light, then one would have before one a time independent wave field. But such a thing appears not to exist! This was the first child-like thought experiment related to the special theory of relativity. Discovery is not a work of logical thought, even if the final product is bound in logical form. (1956, 10)

Einstein admits the thought experiment was "child-like" and his concluding sentence seems to warn us that we should not expect the logic of the thought experiment to be fully evident.

The second account comes from the gestalt psychologist Max Wertheimer, who interviewed Einstein in 1916 as part of Wertheimer's research in psychology. His report of the interview was published posthumously in 1945 in his volume *Productive Thinking*:[8]

The problem began when Einstein was sixteen years old, a pupil in the Gymnasium (Aarau, Kantonschule). . . .

The process started in a way that was not very clear, and is therefore difficult to describe—in a certain state of being puzzled. First came such questions as: What if one were to run after a ray of light? What if one were riding on the beam? If one were to run after a ray of light as it travels, would its velocity thereby be decreased? If one were to run fast enough, would it no longer move at all? . . . [W's ellipses] To young Einstein this seemed strange.

. . . When I asked him whether, during this period, he had already had some idea of the constancy of light velocity, independent of the movement of the reference system, Einstein answered decidedly: "No, it was just curiosity. That the velocity of light could differ depending upon the movement of the observer was somehow characterized by doubt. Later developments increased that doubt." (Wertheimer 1959, 214–215)

Once again, Maxwell's equations have no role and the certainty of the "Autobiographical Notes" account is replaced by mere discomfort, puzzlement, and doubt.

The historical problem is to reconcile these differences in the accounts of the thought experiment. The solution, I propose, is straightforward. Einstein may have first hit upon the idea of chasing light as a sixteen year old. However the thought experiment evolved as his researches evolved. In its earliest form, it was, in major part, the precocious imaginings of an inventive sixteen year old, driven as much by intuition as reason. This early form of the thought experiment is reported by Wertheimer and by Einstein's second report. Einstein's "Autobiographical Notes" account, however, reports a later development of the thought experiment. It is a version undertaken when Einstein had some command of Maxwell's equations and, through the thought experiment, arrives at results more definite than the mere puzzlement and doubt of the sixteen year old.

While this may solve the historical problem, it only deepens the physical problem. For if "Autobiographical Notes" reports a thought experiment undertaken by an older, more knowledgeable and more capable Einstein, how could he get it so wrong? My solution to this deepened physical problem is that Einstein is not aiming the thought experiment against ether theories of electromagnetism, but against a different sort of theory.

5. EMISSION THEORIES AND THEIR PROBLEMS

Some years before Einstein sent his completed special theory of relativity to the journal *Annalen der Physik*, he became convinced that the principle of relativity must hold for electrodynamic processes, even if Maxwell's theory did not allow it. The thought experiment that played a decisive role in forming this conviction was his magnet and conductor thought experiment. That thought experiment showed him that what you could measure in electrodynamics did not distinguish uniform motion from rest in the ether. Yet Maxwell's theory treated the two cases very differently. Somehow, Einstein concluded, Maxwell's theory must be changed so that the resulting theory conforms with the principle of relativity.

We can see most simply the sort of changes needed if we consider light, which is, in Maxwell's theory, just a propagation of waves in the electric and magnetic fields.

In Maxwell's theory, a light wave in a vacuum always propagates at the same speed, c, with respect to the ether. So measuring the speed of a light beam gives observers an easy way to determine their motion in the ether. If they find the light to move at c, the observers are at rest in the ether. If they find the light frozen, they are moving at c in the ether. Since observers can determine their absolute motion, the theory violates the principle of relativity.

The alternative theory that Einstein began to pursue was an "emission theory." In such a theory, the speed of light *in vacuo* is still c. But it is not c with respect to the ether; it is c *with respect to the source* that emits the light. In such a theory, observing the speed of a light beam tells observers nothing about their absolute motion. It only reveals their motion with respect to the source that emitted the light. If they find the beam to propagate at c, the observers are at rest with respect to the emitter. If they find the beam to be frozen, they are fleeing from the source at c. All the intermediate cases are possible too. In general, observers can only ascertain their relative velocity with respect to the source.

A distinctive property of this emission theory is that there is no single velocity of light; the velocity will vary according to the velocity of the emitter.

All this just pertains to one part of electrodynamic theory, the propagation of light. In order to mount a complete emission theory in which the principle of relativity holds, Einstein would need to propagate these sorts of changes throughout the complete theory. One might imagine that such modification would be extremely hard to carry out. It turns out, however, that one can make a lot of progress very quickly. On the basis of numerous clues that Einstein left in later writings, I believe it is possible to discern quite credible candidates for the theories or theory fragments Einstein developed; and these have been reconstructed in some detail in Norton (2004, §§2–3).[9]

These efforts, I believe, would initially have seemed quite promising. That fact presumably encouraged Einstein to persist in his efforts to find a serviceable emission theory. Einstein persisted for years, as he recalled in a 1920 recollection:

> The difficulty to be overcome lay in the constancy of the velocity of light in a vacuum, which I first believed had to be given up. Only after years

of [*jahrelang*] groping did I notice that the difficulty lay in the arbitrariness of basic kinematical concepts. (Einstein [1920] 2002, 280)

Eventually Einstein did give up on an emission theory. There is an indication that the struggle with the emission theory was long and arduous. After he had proposed his special theory of relativity, Einstein was asked repeatedly whether an emission theory was viable. Einstein's correspondence after 1905 and some manuscript sources contain a wealth of objections that reflect serious probing of the possibility of an emission theory and from many perspectives.

These many objections by Einstein are collected and discussed in Norton (2004, §4). For what follows, two of these many objections are important:

- A serviceable emission theory cannot characterize light waves solely by intensity, color, and polarization, but would need to add a velocity property, which light is known not to possess.
- A serviceable emission theory cannot be formulated in terms of differential equations.

The second objection means that the theory cannot look like a local field theory of the type of Maxwell's theory. In such a theory, the laws are expressed by relations that hold at one point in space and time. These differential equations relate the rate of change in space and time of the fields at that point to the field magnitudes at that point. Once one knows these rates of change, one can find how the fields change as one moves to neighboring points, and from this information piece together the disposition of the fields throughout space and time.

If one is unfamiliar with the details of electrodynamic theory, it will be entirely unclear how these two objections pose problems for an emission theory. One might suppose these details will be obvious to an expert. However, even if one knows some electrodynamic theory, the working of the objection remains unclear. Why should the fact that light has only the properties of intensity, color, and polarization be a problem? And how can one show that no emission theory at all can be formulated in terms of differential equations?

6. THE THOUGHT EXPERIMENT AS AN OBJECTION TO EMISSION THEORIES

Einstein's chasing light thought experiment stayed with him after its initial conception, when he was sixteen years old. It remained in his repertoire of important test cases after 1898, when he had learned the details of Maxwell's theory. In this later period, it did not provide a cogent objection to ether-based theories of electrodynamics. Rather, I propose, it provided powerful and devastating objections to the emission theories, whose exploration and rejection figured essentially in Einstein's researches prior to his 1905 special theory of relativity. It is this, I suggest, that merited inclusion of the thought experiment in Einstein's "Autobiographical Notes" and in a form that included invocation of Maxwell's equations.

In the thought experiment, Einstein offered three objections to frozen light. They fail as objections to an ether-based electrodynamics. An emission theory also allows light to slow when an observer chases after it and to freeze if the pursuit is fast enough. If we read Einstein's objections as leveled against an emission theory of light, they succeed, forcefully.

" . . . on the basis of experience . . ."

The first objection is that we do not experience frozen light. That objection has little force against an ether theory since it merely reflects the fact that we are not moving at c in the ether. In an emission theory, light emitted by a body receding from us propagates slower than c. The speed of recession of the source is subtracted from c to find the speed we will measure. In the extreme case, if the source recedes from us at c, we will find the light emitted by the source to be frozen. As this moving source passes through space, it paints a frozen light wave across space. The universe is filled with many luminous bodies. All it takes is for there to be *just one* light source moving at or near c with respect to us for our space to be painted with frozen light. That is a firm prediction of the emission theory. Yet we have never experienced such a thing. An emission theory can only survive, then, if we make the dubious assumption that no fast-moving luminous bodies have passed through our corner of space—not even one. This is the first failure of an emission theory.[10]

" . . . according to Maxwell's equations . . ."

The second objection is that Maxwell's equations forbid frozen light. One might think that Maxwell's equations have no place in an emission theory, for the emission theory replaces them with a new theory. That is not entirely correct. Maxwell's theory remains the crowning triumph of nineteenth-century physics. It enjoyed massive experimental support and the import of those experiments cannot be undone. A new theory of electrodynamics could not dispense with Maxwell's theory entirely. The new theory can only deviate from it in realms in which Maxwell's theory has not been thoroughly tested. The realm in which the theory has been most thoroughly tested is that of electric and magnetic fields that do not change with time, electrostatics and magnetostatics. Whatever else a new theory might change, this part would have to remain unchanged and must be duplicated within the new theory.

This most secure part of Maxwell's theory prohibits frozen waveforms in a vacuum built out of electric and magnetic fields. It only allows combinations of static fields that dilute in space by the familiar inverse square law. Yet an emission theory, Einstein now saw, must allow the static sinusoidal curves of frozen light in every inertial frame of reference. That is, an emission theory must conflict with that part of Maxwell's theory that we can be sure will survive. This is the second failure of an emission theory.

" . . . a state of fast uniform motion . . ."

Finally, Einstein asks how observers finding frozen light can determine that they are in a state of rapid uniform motion. It is a rhetorical question and Einstein leaves it to readers to fill in the details. Those details can only be recovered if we recreate the background presumed by the rhetorical question. In the context of an emission theory, the state of rapid motion mentioned can only mean rapid motion *with respect to the light source*. The theory has been devised so that there is no absolute motion.

Determining this motion with respect to the source, I will now argue, is essential if the emission theory is to function as a serviceable theory, supporting predictions of future states. Einstein's suggestion is, I believe, that we cannot find this velocity from the instantaneous state of the wave and that leads to the failure of the theory as a predictive system.

To see the problem, recall how Maxwell's theory is used to make predictions. We take the electric and magnetic fields in space at one moment. Through Maxwell's equations, this instantaneous state of the fields then fixes their time rates of change. From these time rates of change, we infer the future states of the fields a moment later, and so on for the whole future of the fields.

A similar sort of analysis turns out to fail for an emission theory. Einstein's chasing light thought experiment provides a simple case of the failure. Our initial state is a sinusoidal wave of fields spread through space. From that initial state alone, we cannot tell if the fields belong to a wave propagating past us at high speed, or if they belong to a wave frozen in space that fails to propagate at all. If we cannot distinguish the cases, we cannot predict what will happen next. To know which case is before us, we need also to know whether the wave was produced by a source that is at rest with respect to us; then we have a propagating wave. Or was it, we must ask, produced by a source receding at c from us; then we have a wave frozen in time.

To answer, we need to know our velocity with respect to the source. Einstein reports his presumption that the same laws hold for rapidly moving observers as for those on earth. That means that we cannot resort to any absolute velocity to help decide which case is before us. Our velocity with respect to the source must somehow be recovered from properties of the instantaneous state of the wave.

At this point, Einstein's initially cryptic objection to an emission theory reported elsewhere becomes decisive. The intrinsic properties of light comprise only intensity, color, and polarization, but *not* a velocity property. That is, there is no way to use the instantaneous properties of the fields to determine how they will develop in time. Is the waveform frozen in time? It is propagating rapidly? No local determination of its instantaneous properties can tell us.[11]

Why is that such a troubling outcome? In modern terms, it is a failure of determinism, that is, a failure of the present state of things to determine the future. We know from elsewhere that failures of determinism troubled Einstein greatly. He followed the nineteenth-century tradition of equating causation with determinism. The indeterminism of modern quantum theory was initially regarded as a failure of causation and this dire way of thinking of the failure would have played some part in Einstein's celebrated complaint about quantum theory: that he could not believe that God played dice with the universe. The equation of determinism and causation is expressed rather clearly by Einstein's statement in a 1950 speech that

> the laws of the external world were also taken to be complete, in the following sense: If the state of the objects is completely given at a certain time, then their state at any other time is completely determined by the laws of nature. This is just what we mean when we speak of 'causality.' Such was approximately the framework of the physical thinking a hundred years ago. ([1950] 2005)

Here is the third failure of emission theories. They cannot be formulated in a way that the present state determines the next and all future states. Emission theories contradict causality and cannot be used for prediction. A formulation of an emission theory must be global in the sense that it must keep track of how each wave field was created.

This third failure can be expressed in a more succinct way. Maxwell's theory is specified by differential equations through which the rates of change of the fields are derived from the instantaneous states of the fields. Einstein had now concluded that an emission theory could not be formulated in this way. Here now is an explanation of Einstein's other cryptic objection to emission theories: that they could not be formulated in terms of differential equations.

The third objection of Einstein's thought experiment turns out to be an abbreviated complaint that emission theories will be defective causally, in the nineteenth-century sense of the term, and unable to make predictions of future states from present states. This reading of the thought experiment enables us also to make sense of two of Einstein's otherwise cryptic remarks on emission theories made elsewhere.[12]

We can summarize the reading proposed in a table analogous to the one given in Section 2 (see Table 7.2).

Table 7.2 Einstein's Approach Contrasted to an Emission Theory

Einstein wrote:	*Interpretation in an Emission Theory*
"I should observe such a beam of light as an electromagnetic field at rest though spatially oscillating. There seems to be no such thing, however, . . ."	
1 " . . . neither on the basis of experience . . ."	In an emission theory, we would expect to experience frozen light since any rapidly receding light source paints a frozen waveform across space.
2 " . . . nor according to Maxwell's equations."	An emission theory must agree at least with the electrostatic and magneto-static parts of Maxwell's theory. Those parts prohibit sinusoidal, static fields in empty space.
"From the very beginning it appeared to me intuitively clear that, judged from the standpoint of such an observer, everything would have to happen according to the same laws as for an observer who, relative to the earth, was at rest."	In an emission theory, the observer can-not call upon an absolute velocity to answer the rhetorical question Einstein poses next.
3 "For how should the first observer know or be able to determine, that he is in a state of fast uniform motion?"	Given the instantaneous state of a wave, in an emission theory one needs to know one's state of motion with respect to the emitter to know whether the wave will propagate or not. That velocity is not encoded in the instan-taneous state of the waveform, so an emission theory is indeterministic and cannot be formulated in terms of dif-ferential equations.

NOTES

1. In Maxwell's theory, a propagating plane lightwave of wavelength λ and frequency v can be given by the two sinusoidal fields $\mathbf{E} = \mathbf{E}_0 \sin 2\pi\ (x/\lambda - vt)$ and $\mathbf{H} = \mathbf{H}_0 \sin 2\pi\ (x/\lambda - vt)$, where $\mathbf{E}$ and $\mathbf{H}$ are the electric and magnetic field strengths and x and t are the usual space and time coordinates adapted to the ether frame of rest. If we transform to a frame moving at c in the +x direction of propagation of the wave, the new coordinates X, T adapted to the moving frame are related to the original ether frame coordinates by X = x−ct and T = t. Since $c = \lambda v$, we have $x/\lambda - vt = (x-ct)/\lambda$. Hence in the new frame, the transformed fields are $\mathbf{E} = \mathbf{E}_0 \sin 2\pi\ (x-ct)/\lambda = \mathbf{E}_0 \sin 2\pi X/\lambda$ and

$H = H_0 \sin 2\pi (x-ct)/\lambda = H_0 \sin 2\pi X/\lambda$. These transformed waves are independent of the frame time T. They are frozen. (The field strengths **E** and **H** transform invariantly in Newtonian space and time.)

2. No doubt my survey has missed many writers and I apologize to those I missed. However, my sample was large enough for me to be confident that the population as a whole fails overwhelmingly to admit that reading Einstein's text is problematic.

3. Grünbaum's reasons (2) and (3) mentioned in his text agree fairly well with reasons 2 and 3 of my table.

4. "[I]nnovation in science is often a triumph of intuition over logic." Hoffmann proposes that Einstein could not have considered seriously the classical result that light will be slowed relative to an observer who chases after it, for this admissibility of slowed light would eventually have forced the idea on Einstein of frozen light. Hoffmann suggests: "Having sensed the existence of a profound paradox, he may have experienced a psychological blocking that prevented him from giving serious consideration to sluggish light." While Hoffmann's efforts to elucidate Einstein's remarks are commendable, they are obscure in that the only paradox Hoffmann recovers is a psychological sense of discomfort in Einstein. (Both quotes from Hoffman 1982, 97.)

5. The text is derived from a BBC radio broadcast in 1967 and this portion of it was spoken by Whitrow as part of a dialog.

6. Presumably Adolf Grünbaum is intended in the following quote. Bergia's bibliography (1979, 88) contains a reference to Grunbaum, A., "The special theory of relativity" in *An Introduction to the Theory of Relativity*, edited by W. G. V. Rosser (London: Butterworths, 1964). There is no Grünbaum text in my copy of this volume. Rosser is the entire volume's author, not editor.

7. For elaboration on Einstein's magnet and conductor thought experiment, see Norton (Forthcoming).

8. We can have some confidence in Wertheimer's narrative. It relates Einstein's recollections in 1916, some twenty years after the event. Einstein's own two narratives are written forty and fifty years after the event. Wertheimer also solicited Einstein's appraisal of the chapter in draft and Einstein replied that he found it "on the whole good." See Norton (2004, 77, fn 31) for further details of Einstein and Wertheimer's correspondence and for my suggestion that reading Wertheimer's draft in 1943 may have instigated Einstein's recounting of the thought experiment in his 1946 drafting of "Autobiographical Notes."

9. These efforts proceed from two ideas. First, as Einstein learned from the magnet and conductor thought experiment, one should allow that electric and magnetic field quantities may not transform invariantly under changes of inertial frame. A pure magnetic field may transform into a combination of magnetic and electric fields. Second was an idea later developed by Ritz. Maxwell's theory can be re-expressed in terms of retarded potentials. In this approach electromagnetic quantities at some point in space and time are assembled from all the electromagnetic effects that propagate to that point from other source charges. The rule used in assembling those effects is that they propagate at c in the ether. Ritz's theory sought conformity with the principle of relativity merely by adjusting this rule. Electromagnetic effects are now assumed to propagate at c with respect to the motion of the source charge.

10. I have found only one other author who considers the possibility that this first objection may have been leveled by Einstein against some sort of emission theory of light: Grünbaum (1973, 373).

11. Einstein's demand for this velocity property is not unreasonable. A simple one-dimensional Klein Gordon field ϕ satisfies the field equation $[(\partial/\partial t)^2 - (\partial/\partial x)^2 - m^2]\,\phi = 0$. Its plane wave solutions are $\phi = \exp i\,(\omega t - kx)$, where the frequency ω and wave number k satisfy $m^2 = k^2 - \omega^2$.

Since ω and k are related to the speed of the wave v by $v = \omega/k$, it follows that the speed of the wave is fixed by the wave number according to $v = (1 - m^2/k^2)^{1/2}$. The wave number k provides the velocity property Einstein sought. The special case of a frozen wave arises when the wave number $k = m$. If one finds a wave whose instantaneous state is $k = m$, then it must be frozen. An analogous analysis fails for light since does it not have a non-zero characteristic parameter m.

12. See Norton (2004, §5) for further discussion.

REFERENCES

Bergia, Silvio. 1979. "Einstein and the Birth of Special Relativity." In *Einstein: A Centenary Volume*, edited by A. P. French, 65–89. Cambridge, MA: Harvard University Press.

Bernstein, Jeremy. 2006. *Secrets of the Old One: Einstein, 1905*. Springer/Copernicus Books.

Darrigol, Olivier. 1996. "The Electrodynamic Origins of Relativity Theory." *Historical Studies in the Physical and Biological Sciences* 26: 241–312.

Einstein, Albert. 1905. "Zur Electrodynamik bewegter Körper." *Annalen der Physik* 17: 891–921.

———. [1920] 2002. "Fundamental Ideas and Methods of the Theory of Relativity, Presented in Their Development." Doc. 31 in *The Collected Papers of Albert Einstein. Volume 7: The Berlin Years: Writings, 1918–1921*, edited by Michel Janssen et al. Princeton, NJ: Princeton University Press.

———. [1950] 2005. "Physics, Philosophy, and Scientific Progress." (International Congress of Surgeons, Cleveland, Ohio, 1950). *Physics Today*, June: 46–48.

———. 1951. "Autobiographical Notes." In *Albert Einstein: Philosopher-Scientist*. 2nd edition. Edited by P. A. Schilpp, 2–95. New York: Tudor Publishing. Reprinted with a correction as *Autobiographical Notes*. 1979. La Salle and Chicago: Open Court.

———. 1956. "Autobiographische Skizze." In *Helle Zeit—Dunkle Zeit*, edited by Carl Seelig, 9–18. Zurich: Europa Verlag.

Grünbaum, Adolf. 1973. "Philosophical Foundations of the Special Theory of Relativity, and Their Bearing on Its History." In *Philosophical Problems of Space and Time*. 2nd edition, 341–409. Dordrecht: Reidel.

Hoffmann, Banesh. 1982. "Some Einstein Anomalies." In *Albert Einstein: Historical and Cultural Perspectives*, edited by G. Holton and Y. Elkana, 91–105. Princeton, NJ: Princeton University Press.

Holton, Gerald. 1973. "Einstein, Michelson and the 'Crucial' Experiment." In *Thematic Origins of Scientific Thought: Kepler to Einstein*, 261–352. Cambridge, MA: Harvard University Press.

Kaku, Michio. 2004. *Einstein's Cosmos: How Einstein's Vision Transformed Our Understanding of Space and Time*. New York: W. W. Norton/Atlas Books.

Lange, Marc. 2002. *An Introduction to the Philosophy of Physics: Locality, Fields, Energy, and Mass*. Malden, MA: Blackwell.

Martinez, Alberto. 2009. *Kinematics: The Lost Origins of Einstein's Relativity*. Baltimore: Johns Hopkins University Press.

Miller, Arthur I. 1981. *Albert Einstein's Special Theory of Relativity*. Reading, MA: Addison-Wesley.

Norton, John D. 2004. "Einstein's Investigations of Galilean Covariant Electrodynamics prior to 1905." *Archive for History of Exact Sciences* 59: 45–105.

———. Forthcoming. "Einstein's Special Theory of Relativity and the Problems in the Electrodynamics of Moving Bodies That Led Him to It." In *Cambridge Companion to Einstein*, edited by M. Janssen and C. Lehner. Cambridge: Cambridge University Press.

Sartori, Leo. 1996. *Understanding Relativity: A Simplified Approach to Einstein's Theories*. Berkeley and Los Angeles: University of California Press.

Schwartz, Joseph, and Michael McGuiness. 1979. *Einstein for Beginners*. New York: Pantheon.

Stachel, John et al., eds. 1987. *The Collected Papers of Albert Einstein. Volume 1: The Early Years: 1879–1902*. Princeton, NJ: Princeton University Press.

Wertheimer, Max. 1959. *Productive Thinking*. New York: Harper.

Whitrow, Gerald J., ed. 1973. *Einstein: The Man and His Achievements*. New York: Dover.

8 At the Limits of Possibility
Thought Experiments in Quantum Gravity

Mark Shumelda

1. INTRODUCTION: WHY QUANTIZE GRAVITY?

Each of the two pillars of twentieth-century physics—quantum mechanics and general relativity—has enjoyed both tremendous theoretical development as well as convincing empirical confirmation. Perhaps it is all the more surprising then that general relativity and quantum mechanics are completely incompatible with each other. The reasons for the incompatibility are many and include the ways in which space, time, matter, and energy are treated by the two theories (Callender and Huggett 2001a). Furthermore, attempts to quantize the gravitational field using the same renormalization group techniques that have produced quantum field theories for the other three fundamental forces (strong, weak, electromagnetic) have been a failure. "Quantum gravity" describes any attempt, of which there are many, to provide some solution to this problem.

But why should we expect the gravitational field to be quantized in the first place? After all, the energy and distance scales at which interactions between the quantum and gravitational fields are expected to become nonnegligible are truly extreme (e.g., the Planck length, 10^{-35}m). It turns out that an elegant thought experiment, proposed by Kenneth Eppley and Eric Hannah in 1977, lends strong credence to the view that the gravitational field must be quantized (Eppley and Hannah 1977). The thought experiment attempts to convince us that any theory combining a classical gravitational field with quantized matter is inconsistent. This result is particularly important since we currently lack particle accelerators powerful enough, or gravity wave detectors sensitive enough, to determine empirically whether or not gravity is quantized. In a word, quantum gravity is truly a "science without data."

Although Eppley and Hannah's thought experiment has enjoyed considerable success as an argument for the necessity of the quantization of the gravitational field, it is certainly not without its critics. The purpose of this paper is to defend the thought experiment and to propose a new, more nuanced role for it in the search for a quantum theory of gravity. I proceed as follows. Section 2 describes how the thought experiment works.

In Section 3 I consider the criticisms that have been raised against the thought experiment. In light of these criticisms I argue in Section 4 that the purpose of Eppley and Hannah's thought experiment should be reconsidered: Although it cannot conclusively establish the *necessity* of quantizing the gravitational field, the thought experiment serves as a useful heuristic guide. The method in which the thought experiment functions—by reducing the space of logically possible theoretical approaches and by imposing constraints on future theories—gives us crucial insight into the methodology of thought experiments in general, especially in fields as data-starved as quantum gravity.

2. THE EXPERIMENT

2.1. Rationale

In 1977 Kenneth Eppley and Eric Hannah proposed an elegant thought experiment that aimed to establish conclusively the necessity of quantizing the gravitational field. In terms of methodology or structure the thought experiment serves as an excellent example of a "picturesque *reductio ad absurdum*" (Brown 2011, 33). The target of Eppley and Hannah's *reductio* is any theory that attempts to meld a classical description of the gravitational field with a quantum description of matter—in short, a hybrid worldview. Any such theory will include a classical description of the gravitational field: not quantized, not subject to uncertainty relations, and not allowing any superposition of gravitational states. At the same time the theory will uphold a quantum description of matter and possibly of the other three fundamental forces. Eppley and Hannah's thought experiment is specifically designed to show the absurdity of such a theory. In particular, they claim that a hybrid classical-quantum theory will violate any number of well-established physical principles: "either momentum conservation, the uncertainty principle, or relativistic causality in the form of signals traveling faster than c" (Eppley and Hannah 1977, 51). Since no such half-quantized-and-half-classical theory is tenable, the full description of the world (including the gravitational field) must therefore be quantum in nature. Evidently Eppley and Hannah's thought experiment has enjoyed considerable success within the physics and philosophy of physics community: It has for a generation been upheld as the single best argument for the necessity of quantizing the gravitational field (Mattingly 2006, 1; Wüthrich 2006, 26).

2.2. Setup

Eppley and Hannah's thought experiment proposes to measure the position of a quantum "test" particle by means of a classical gravitational wave. This simple interaction supposedly runs afoul of any number of established physical principles; hence, according to the authors it could not possibly take place. The thought experiment, they argue, shows that any semi-classical (half-quantized, half-classical) theory of gravity is inconsistent.

Here's how the thought experiment works. The proposed device consists of three parts:

1. A mass or "test particle" initially prepared with a small and well-defined momentum; by the Heisenberg uncertainty relation, its position is initially not well defined.
2. A series of harmonic oscillators (think of small masses attached to the ends of springs as an example) that can emit gravitational waves, or alternatively, create fluctuations in the gravitational field.

These oscillators produce short-wavelength, low-momentum gravitational waves which are aimed by means of shutters and collimators towards the test particle. The goal is to localize the particle by getting a wave to scatter off the particle, which leads to the critical final component of the thought experiment:

3. Another, more elaborate series of oscillators which serves as a detector array to measure the trajectory of the scattered gravitational wave.

Computing the trajectory of the scattered wave allows one to determine the location of the region where the gravitational wave interacts with the quantum particle.

The crux of Eppley and Hannah's thought experiment is precisely this interaction between a classical gravitational wave and a quantum particle. Recall that the particle is initially prepared in a state of well-defined momentum but poorly defined position. In quantum mechanical terms, this means that its initial wave function is poorly localized (it is in a superposition of eigenstates of position). We have set up the thought experiment explicitly such that the incident gravitational wave is scattered by the interaction with the particle. So what then is the nature of this quantum-classical interaction? Eppley and Hannah see two mutually exclusive possibilities: Either the interaction constitutes a "measurement" of the particle's position, which entails the *instantaneous collapse* of the particle's wave function into an eigenstate of position, or else there is no measurement of the particle's position, and hence *no collapse*. The interpretation of "measurement" here is, of course, non-trivial, and will be examined further in Section 3.2. For now we need only the minimal assumption that the gravitational wave either does or does not collapse the particle's wave function. Eppley and Hannah maintain that each alternative—both collapse and no collapse—conflicts with established physical principles; hence neither is possible. The entire set up must have been absurd from the beginning: Classical and quantum fields simply cannot interact. We examine each case in turn.

2.3. Collapse

Suppose the gravitational interaction collapses the particle's wave function. Eppley and Hannah then argue that this collapse entails a violation of either energy-momentum conservation or the Heisenberg uncertainty principle. Since the gravitational wave is a classical system, we can localize the particle as precisely as we want. The final uncertainty in the particle's position, Δx, scales with the gravitational wavelength λ. Unlike with a quantum system (a photon, for example), a classical system can simultaneously possess both arbitrarily small λ and arbitrarily small momentum. And since *both* the gravitational wave (p_x) and the particle (p_y) have arbitrarily precise initial momentum, the interaction event should not appreciably increase the uncertainty in the final momentum of the particle $(\Delta p_y \rightarrow 0)$.[1] Hence the final state of the quantum particle includes both arbitrarily precise position $(\Delta x_y \rightarrow 0)$ and arbitrarily precise momentum $(\Delta p_y \rightarrow 0)$, in clear violation of the uncertainty principle $\Delta x_y \Delta p_y \geq \hbar$.

Alternatively, if one rigorously upholds the validity of the uncertainty principle one would find a violation of conservation of momentum in the case of collapse. Assume that the momentum of both the gravitational wave (p_x) and particle (p_y) are slow enough (i.e., $p_x \rightarrow 0$ and $p_y \rightarrow 0$), and that the particle position (x_y) is determined accurately enough by the scattering event (such that $\Delta x_y \rightarrow 0$). By the uncertainty principle $\Delta x_y \Delta p_y \geq \hbar$ we will have an arbitrarily high Δp_y, which will easily include specific values of final momentum p_{x+y} that are far greater than the combined value of the two initial momenta: $p_x + p_y$. According to Eppley and Hannah, we have the possibility of $p_{x+y} > (p_x + p_y)$, in clear violation of the principle of conservation of momentum.[2]

Eppley and Hannah conclude that "if both momentum conservation and the uncertainty principle are valid, we must reject the possibility that a gravitational wave of vanishing momentum can collapse the wave packet of a quantum particle" (Eppley and Hannah 1977, 55).

2.4. No Collapse

Having found the collapse alternative untenable, Eppley and Hannah now suppose that the particle's wave function is *not* collapsed by interaction with gravity. Thus although the gravitational wave is indeed scattered by the particle's wave function, it does not constitute a position measurement of the particle. In essence, the scattering pattern of the classical gravitational wave is determined by the shape of the quantum particle's wave function—in the same way that gravity would be affected by a classical mass distribution. Of course, this arrangement flies in the face of standard quantum theory, and constitutes an "abnormal way of watching a wave function without collapsing it" (Callender and Huggett 2001b, 8).

This no-collapse hypothesis runs afoul of the prohibition against super-luminal signaling. If the wave function extends over a large spacelike inter-val, two experimenters will be able to send signals or communicate between themselves instantly. This directly violates special relativity, which forbids signals faster than the speed of light, c. The paradox here of course builds upon the famous thought experiment by Einstein, Podolsky, and Rosen (1935)—EPR—that challenged the completeness of quantum mechanics.[3] To see how the Eppley and Hannah thought experiment permits full-blown superluminal signaling, we begin by confining the quantum particle in a box so that its wave function spreads to cover the entire interior of the box. We then introduce a barrier in the middle of the box so that the particle is equally as likely to be in one half of the box (A) as the other (B). The state of the particle would be

$$\psi(x) = 1/\sqrt{2}(\psi_A(x) + \psi_B(x)) \tag{1}$$

where $\psi_A(x)$ and $\psi_B(x)$ are wave functions that are identical in shape but are located inside the left and right sides of the box, respectively.

Finally (and this is the crucial part) we split the halves of the box and give each one to a different experimenter—Alice and Bob. Now suppose that Alice looks inside her box (her half of the original box) and finds it empty; this means of course that the electron is in Bob's box. As Alice performs that measurement, the wave function of the particle instantly col-lapses to

$$\psi(x) = 1/\sqrt{2}(\psi_A(x) + \psi_B(x)) \rightarrow \psi(x) = \psi_B(x) \tag{2}$$

Of course, the alternative is that Alice performs the measurement and finds the electron in her box. In that case, the wave function collapses to

$$\psi(x) = 1/\sqrt{2}(\psi_A(x) + \psi_B(x)) \rightarrow \psi(x) = \psi_A(x) \tag{3}$$

Let's return to case (2): Alice finds her box empty. Up to this point, we have merely reproduced the results of the original EPR thought experiment: Either some kind of non-local influence causes the wave function to collapse across a spacelike distance, or else the electron was *always* in Bob's box, making quantum mechanics incomplete—since $\psi(x)$ was indeterminate between the two halves. Note that while the wave function "collapses" over a spacelike distance, the EPR setup does not actually permit superluminal signaling. If Bob now looks in his box and sees the electron, he could just as well assume that it was he who first performed the measurement; he would have no way of knowing that Alice had already collapsed the wave func-tion. In the long run, repeated measurement statistics guarantee that each experimenter will observe the electron in his or her respective box 50% of the time. The only way Alice and Bob can experimentally determine this

50–50 correlation is by comparing their results after a measurement run. Here is the crucial fact: At no point during the experimental process do Alice or Bob have access to the joint probability distribution (1).

But the problem in the Eppley and Hannah case is far more serious, since here Alice and Bob *do* in fact have access to the joint probability distribution function (1). This is because while the gravitational wave interacts with and "sees" the particle wave function, the *wave function does not collapse*. All that each experimenter has to do is to set up a gravitational source on his or her side of the experiment, enclose the electron-box with gravitational detectors, and determine the shape of the wave function by scattering gravity waves off it. The scattering depends on the form of the wave function in the box; changes in the wave function will show up as changes in the scattering pattern as registered by the detectors. This monitoring can be done on a continuous basis and will in fact enable one experimenter to communicate instantaneously with his or her counterpart.

Suppose Alice and Bob have a prior agreement whereby, at a pre-appointed time, Bob will make a choice whether or not to perform a measurement to try to detect the presence of the electron in his box. Obviously this will involve some method other than gravitational interaction—shooting a beam of photons at the box should suffice, for example. Here's the crucial point: If Bob chooses to perform a measurement, the wave function will collapse. This decision instantaneously affects the wave function, and hence the scattering source, in Alice's box: If Bob finds the electron in his box (2), Alice's scattering source completely disappears; if Bob finds his box empty (3), Alice's scattering source maximizes its intensity. Both scenarios are instantaneously revealed to Alice. On the other hand, if Bob chooses not to perform a measurement, there will be no collapse at all. Alice's gravity wave detectors will register no change in the scattering pattern.

The two experimenters agree beforehand that if Bob chooses to perform a measurement, then he'll pay for dinner tonight; otherwise, Alice pays. Assuming that Alice continuously monitors the shape of the wave function, she will know *instantly* whether or not it collapses at the appointed time.[4] Thus, Bob will be able to instantaneously signal his decision as to whether or not he is paying for dinner tonight. Surely, this runs against the well-established prohibition against superluminal signaling. Hence the original setup must be absurd:

> The conclusion of this horn of the dilemma is then the following. If one adopts the standard interpretation of quantum mechanics, and one claims that the world is divided into classical (gravitational) and quantum (matter) parts, and one models quantum-classical interactions without collapse, then one must accept the possibility of superluminal signaling. (Callender and Huggett 2001b, 8)

Callender and Huggett's reference to "the standard interpretation" of quantum mechanics is extremely important here since it highlights the fact (already hinted at in Section 2.2) that Eppley and Hannah assume that the "collapse of the wavefunction" brought about by measurement refers to some observer-independent feature of the quantum state. There are other interpretations of quantum mechanics, of course, that tie the collapse hypothesis to our epistemic access of quantum states (e.g., Bohm/DeBroglie, Everettian "relative states," etc.) The question of how well Eppley and Hannah's thought experiment fares on these kinds of interpretations will be developed further in Section 3.2.

2.5. Prognosis

Eppley and Hannah conclude that no matter how we attempt to model the hypothetical interaction between a classical gravitational wave and a quantum mass distribution, we end up running afoul of established physical principles. If the classical-quantum interaction results in the collapse of the particle's wave function, we violate either the uncertainty principle or the conservation of momentum; if the interaction does not result in collapse, then we permit superluminal signaling. Neither alternative is palatable. Hence, in true *reductio ad absurdum* fashion, Eppley and Hannah argue their thought experiment establishes the impossibility of any hybrid half-quantum, half-classical theory of gravity. In consequence, any complete physical theory, they argue, requires the gravitational field to be quantized:

> We conclude that the gravitational field cannot be a classical field without violating accepted principles of physics. We therefore conclude that this field must satisfy the principles of quantum mechanics. . . . [T]he world cannot be half classical and half quantum. (Eppley and Hannah 1977, 59)

3. WHAT ARE THE LIMITS OF POSSIBILITY?

Although Eppley and Hannah's thought experiment has enjoyed broad appeal, it is certainly not without its flaws. Over the last decade two distinct types of criticisms have been raised against the thought experiment. Callender and Huggett (2001b) maintain that Eppley and Hannah's thought experiment is not convincing because it is built on an extremely narrow interpretation of quantum mechanics. As soon as one adopts a different interpretation of the collapse hypothesis, they maintain, the experiment simply doesn't go through. At best, they conclude, Eppley and Hannah's thought experiment is conditionally sound pending the outcome of the famously hairy interpretative debates surrounding the foundations of quantum mechanics. In what follows this will be called the *problem of interpretation*. Mattingly (2006), another prominent critic, raises another succinct and serious charge: Regardless of how one cares to interpret quantum mechanics, the thought experiment fails simply because it cannot be conducted *even in principle*. I'll label this the *problem of constructibility*.

Both problems, I believe, can be overcome, though their solutions require that we reconsider the role Eppley and Hannah's thought experiment is to play in the search for quantum gravity. I argue that although Eppley and Hannah's thought experiment cannot serve as a *definitive* argument for the necessity of quantizing the gravitational field, it continues to impose strong constraints on possible models of quantum gravity. In this way Eppley and Hannah's thought experiment plays an important heuristic role.

3.1. Constructibility as Possibility

The device proposed by Eppley and Hannah to presumably establish the quantum nature of the gravitational field is, by their own account, exceedingly complex (Eppley and Hannah 1977, 67). How then are we to evaluate whether the claims made by Eppley and Hannah follow necessarily from their very outlandish setup? In other words, why should we be convinced that the thought experiment "works"?

One possible criterion for the success of any thought experiment is its constructibility. James Mattingly (2006) argues that in order for a thought experiment to succeed it must be constructible, at least in principle, given our laws of nature and the types of material we have at our disposal in our universe. Mattingly's position is certainly not new: Kathleen Wilkes (1988) also maintains that thought experiments should not violate the laws of nature. I will argue this criterion is too strong and, if adopted, would in fact eliminate much of the well-known corpus of thought experiments in the natural sciences. But before I mount my refutation of this constructibility criterion, let us see how Mattingly applies it to the example at hand.

Mattingly argues that it is not "physically possible" to construct Eppley and Hannah's device "within the bounds of the theory employed for the description of the device—in this case the semiclassical theory of gravity" (2006, 2). In particular, the detector device *cannot be constructed* because the entire experiment would be well within its own Schwarzschild radius—it would be contained inside a black hole. Thus, Mattingly explains, the Eppley and Hannah thought experiment cannot "survive its own construction" (2006, 6). Since it is not possible to construct the experiment, even in principle, Mattingly concludes, we should reject it.

The fatal flaw in the thought experiment, according to Mattingly, lies in the specific characteristics of the gravity wave detector. Recall that the detector (essentially a spherical array of harmonic oscillators, or springs) must be sensitive enough to properly detect the trajectory of gravitational waves that scatter off the test particle. A detection event consists of a spring transitioning from its ground state to an excited state. Although each individual spring is weak, the entire array must be dense enough to ensure an appreciable probability of a detection event. Herein lies the problem. Mattingly argues that according to the original numerical estimates provided by Eppley and Hannah concerning the size and mass of the detector array, the device simply cannot be constructed because it would lie well within its own Schwarzschild radius.

We know from the Schwarzschild solution to general relativity that associated with any mass m is a radius r_s, which represents a singularity.

$$r_s = 2Gm/c^2 \quad (4)$$

where G is the gravitational constant and c the speed of light. The escape velocity of light at the surface r_s is infinite. If the radius r of m is smaller than its own Schwarzschild radius (i.e., $r \leq r_s$) the object is a black hole. Eppley and Hannah estimate the radius of their detector to be 10^{15}cm. Because of the high density (and therefore high mass) of the detector array, Mattingly calculates the Schwarzschild radius r_s of the device to be on the order of 10^{19}cm. Thus the Schwarzschild radius r_s of Eppley and Hannah's proposed device exceeds the actual radius r of the device by a factor of 10,000! Assuming these calculations are correct, Eppley and Hannah's thought experiment most certainly is trapped well within (and presumably crushed by) its very own black hole. Essentially, the Schwarzschild metric of general relativity prohibits the construction of the Eppley and Hannah thought experiment, even in principle.

Mattingly seems to be expressing two different concerns here, but both can be addressed. One worry stems from the particular setup of the experiment: If the experiment is contained within its own black hole, then how, Mattingly asks, "does one communicate the results with the outside? Our experimenters, whatever they observe, are completely cut off from the rest of the universe" (2006, 6). I think Mattingly demands too much here of the situation. Certainly, if we really wanted to construct the Eppley and Hannah device it would be useless as an empirical, real-life experiment (no journal could publish its results!), but that is beside the point. The results of a thought experiment need not be "empirically accessible," even in principle; imposing this requirement reduces the entire enterprise of thought experimentation to mental "idealizations" of possible real-life experiments. While I don't propose an exhaustive definition here, it seems fair to expect the conclusion of a thought experiment to follow directly from the experiment's premises and background conditions and assumptions—rather than from an actual, reproducible empirical implementation of the setup. In this case, Eppley and Hannah's thought experiment seems viable—even if it and the associated experimenters exist for a fraction of a second before being obliterated by the gravitational stress-energy of the black hole.

Mattingly's second worry is more general and I think far more serious: Regardless of how we settle the particular "observation" question above, the experiment itself, he implies, is incompatible with the laws of physics. Again, this is because any attempt to construct the device, or anything like it, will necessarily lead to its own destruction through gravitational self-collapse. In this sense, the Schwarzschild radius serves as a sort of no-go theorem against any Eppley and Hannah–type thought experiment: "We might offer therefore, in analogy with the cosmic protection hypothesis that there are no naked singularities, the semiclassical protection hypothesis that possible inconsistencies in semiclassical gravity are hidden from observation" (Mattingly 2006, 1).

The concern here forces us to address the extent to which thought experiments need to obey the laws of nature in order to succeed. The question is certainly an important, recurring one in the literature on thought experiments, and I won't pretend to be able to settle it here. Instead I will mention two reasons Eppley and Hannah's thought experiment can succeed despite failing Mattingly's criterion of "constructibility" according to the laws of nature. The first deals with the laws of nature themselves and the fact that thought experiments can be used to discover them. Declaring the Eppley and Hannah thought experiment a failure simply because it could not be built according to classical (or even semiclassical) general relativity seems counterproductive; the stated purpose of the experiment is to demonstrate the inconsistency of a semiclassical theory of gravity and hence the need for some kind of quantum theory of gravity. This echoes James Brown's statement:

> Too often thought experiments are used to find the laws of nature themselves; they are tools for unearthing the theoretically or nomologically possible. Stipulating the laws in advance and requiring thought experiments not to violate them would simply undermine their use as powerful tools for the investigation of nature. (Brown 2011, 30)

Since we do not yet possess a complete quantum theory of gravity the laws of nature at the Planck scale remain, at least for the moment, elusive. At best one can highlight evidence (including Eppley and Hannah's thought experiment) that points to certain inconsistencies between general relativity and quantum mechanics. General relativity certainly must emerge in some appropriate energy limit from a quantum theory of gravity, but it would seem amiss to reject a thought experiment because it violates *classical* general relativity.

The second reason we should be skeptical of Mattingly's "constructibility criterion" has to do with past track record: Many of the classic, oft-quoted thought experiments in physics are not "constructible," and yet are considered highly successful. Take as a few examples Stevin's inclined plane, Newton's bucket, and Einstein's chasing a light beam. In order to establish certain properties of inclined planes, Stevin's thought experiment requires us to consider completely frictionless surfaces (Brown 2011, 3). Of course, strictly speaking, our laws of nature (electromagnetic forces in this case) require moving bodies in contact with each other to experience some form of friction—hence, a completely frictionless surface is merely an idealization, not constructible, even in principle. Similarly, Newton's attempt from his *Principia* to establish the existence of absolute space by means of water inside a rotating bucket (Brown 2011, 8) is, technically, unphysical. The thought experiment requires a universe empty of everything save the rope-bucket-water apparatus. In such a universe, without anything to be tied to, the twisted rope could not really instigate the rotation required in the bucket. Thus Newton's thought experiment, too, could not possibly be constructed.

Finally, Einstein (1949, 53) relates that one of the steps along the road to his discovery of the special theory of relativity lay in a thought experiment where he supposed that one could "catch up" to a ray of light moving at velocity c. If one could "run alongside" a light ray, much like a surfer travels alongside a water wave, Einstein reasoned, the wave of light would appear "frozen." But this result would contradict Maxwell's equations, since light is a wave, and a stationary "wave" of light cannot oscillate. Hence we have the germ of the special principle of relativity—the laws of physics, including the speed of light, must be the same in all inertial reference frames. The fact that it is biologically impossible (even in pre-relativistic classical mechanics) to travel at the speed of light is irrelevant to the success of the thought experiment. Einstein's thought experiment could not be "constructed," even in principle, and yet it remains a classic.

Returning to Eppley and Hannah's experiment, we should conclude that the fact that the proposed device cannot be constructed is not a fatal flaw *per se*. As Nicholas Rescher puts it:

> Thought experiments need not be "contemplations in thought as to how an experiment would actually work out" because they are, often as not, dealing with nonexperiments—procedures that cannot possibly be carried out at all. They are not a matter of thinking about experiments, but are, rather, experiments in thinking. (Rescher 2005, 7)

In this case the true criterion of success should be determined by the soundness of Eppley and Hannah's argument, not in any possible empirical realizability of the particular device they propose.

3.2. Problems of Interpretation

Having shown that Eppley and Hannah's thought experiment survives Mattingly's constructibility challenge, I now turn to the claim that the thought experiment is plagued by the interpretative challenges of quantum mechanics. This is the more serious challenge as it threatens the soundness of the argument proposed by Eppley and Hannah. Recall that, in terms of its *reductio* structure, the Eppley and Hannah thought experiment essentially consists of a dilemma, both alternatives of which supposedly run afoul of established physical principles. Callender and Huggett's criticism of the thought experiment attempts to show that, in fact, there is no dilemma to begin with; they claim that *both* horns of the dilemma can be diffused. This is because Eppley and Hannah's assumptions rest upon a narrow interpretation of the collapse hypothesis in quantum mechanics. As soon as this interpretation is abandoned, Callender and Huggett argue, the thought experiment no longer stands up. There is no dilemma upon which to build a *reductio* argument.

It will help to reproduce Eppley and Hannah's argument diagrammatically:

Premise A: The classical gravitational wave interacts with the quantum particle (assume for *reductio*)

Then EITHER:

Premise B: The particle wave function collapses
    Premise C: Invoke the Heisenberg uncertainty principle ($\Delta x \Delta p \geq \hbar$)
    Premise D: Invoke conservation of momentum ($p_{x+y} = (p_x + p_y)$)
        Sub-Conclusion E: B contradicts either C or D

OR:

Premise F: The particle wave function does not collapse
    Premise G: Invoke prohibition against superluminal signaling
        Sub-Conclusion H: F contradicts G

Conclusion: Both premises B and F contradict established physical principles.

Grand Conclusion: Premise A (semiclassical theory of gravity) is impossible, by *reductio ad absurdum*.

Callender and Huggett attempt to diffuse *both* of the sub-conclusions E and H, showing that there is no dilemma forcing the *reductio* conclusion. We now examine each case in turn.

3.2.1. *Premise C: Uncertainty Principle*

The first horn of the dilemma raised by Eppley and Hannah concerns the possibility that the incoming gravitational wave collapses the quantum particle's position wave function. The authors maintain that this collapse forces us to reject one of two physical principles: either the Heisenberg uncertainty principle (premise C) or the conservation of momentum (premise D).

As Callender and Huggett remind us, however (2001b, 9), the uncertainty principle admits of several distinct interpretations. The bare formalism spells out a lower bound in the uncertainty of the product of any non-commuting operator measurements (position and momentum in this case); the interpretative debate concerns the nature of this uncertainty. Eppley and Hannah understand the uncertainty as applying to the physical state of the quantum system in that "the fluctuations the quantum theory imposes on matter are inescapable" (1977, 52). In other words, non-commuting observables cannot simultaneously possess perfectly defined values, regardless of whether any measurements are made. As far as Eppley and Hannah are concerned, premise C describes the uncertainty of an observer-independent state of the physical system.

Other interpretations of the Heisenberg uncertainty relation are couched in epistemic terms. In both Bohm-de Broglie and Everettian interpretations, for example, all non-commuting observables of a quantum state are well defined and the dynamics are fully deterministic at all times (according to the Schrödinger equation) (Everett 1957, Bohm and Hiley 1993). In principle our epistemic access to these well-defined values approaches some lower-bound limit, hence the uncertainty relation reflects our in-principle "ignorance" of the full state of the system. If premise C is given this reading, Callender and Huggett argue, Eppley and Hannah's dilemma is dissipated. In "epistemic limitation" interpretations it is understood that any observable of a quantum system can be arbitrarily well defined; it is our epistemic access to the quantum state of the system that is described probabilistically. Eppley and Hannah's thought experiment establishes a conflict with quantum mechanics only on the condition that the uncertainty principle relates to the observer-independent physical state of the system. Callender and Huggett stress that premise C need not be given this reading.

3.2.2. Premise D: Momentum Conservation

A somewhat similar story can be told about premise D—the conservation of momentum. As with the uncertainty principle, the status of this conservation principle varies according to one's favorite interpretation of quantum mechanics. Eppley and Hannah take the conservation of momentum to be one of the "accepted principles of physics" (1977, 59). While many interpretations of quantum mechanics would indeed carry over this principle from classical mechanics, others explicitly break it. One notable example, as pointed out by Callender and Huggett (2001b, 10), is the Ghirardi-Rimini-Weber "spontaneous localization" approach (GRW). GRW serves as a model for understanding the mechanism of wave function "collapse," which lies at the heart of the notoriously thorny measurement problem. The formalism of quantum mechanics suggests that the act of measurement consists of an indeterministic process (as opposed to the deterministic Schrödinger evolution) whereby a superposition of multiple eigenstates of an observable "collapses" into a single eigenstate of that observable. In GRW energy is *not* conserved in collapse (which explains the indeterminism); at the same time this violation occurs on a scale small enough that it cannot be empirically detected (Ghirardi, Rimini, and Weber 1986). Regardless of the particular merits of GRW it is clear that consistent interpretations of quantum mechanics can be formulated in which energy-momentum is not conserved. Hence premise D would not seem to be required; without it, Eppley and Hannah's dilemma can be avoided.

3.2.3. Premise G: Superluminal Signaling

Recall that in the thought experiment the possibility of detecting, *without* collapsing, the wave function by means of gravity waves enables two experimenters to communicate instantaneously across spacelike separated distances. This set-up essentially amounts to breaking the Lorentz invariance of special relativity. For if each of two spacelike-separated experimenters constantly monitors her half of the experiment by means of scattered, non-collapsing gravity waves—then as soon as one experimenter collapses the wave function within her device (by some method other than a gravity wave) her fellow experimenter would instantaneously become aware of this decision. By "collapse" here, Eppley and Hannah are referring to a change in the physical state of the quantum system.

Callender and Huggett raise the same kinds of objections here as they do against premises C and D. First they point out the viability of a number of interpretations of quantum mechanics (e.g., Bohmian, Everettian) that explicitly reject Eppley and Hannah's physical understanding of "collapse" (Callender and Huggett 2001b, 9). Again, in Bohmian and Everettian interpretations, the physical state of a quantum system is always well defined: No "collapse" in Eppley and Hannah's sense occurs. If there is no collapse, there can be no genuine signaling—hence no conflict with special relativity. The Bohmian guiding function (quantum potential) that is responsible for particle dynamics is in fact explicitly non-local: The position and momentum of any one particle depends on the configuration of all other particles. Although Bohmian mechanics indeed breaks the Lorentz invariance of special relativity, we have no epistemic access to the preferred reference frame. This removes all incompatibility with the empirical predictions of special relativity. Thus a Bohmian semiclassical quantum theory of gravity is certainly logically possible, though as Callender and Huggett concede, all current work on Bohmian mechanics does in fact attempt to proceed with the project of quantizing the gravitational field.

3.3. Rejecting the Premises and Diffusing the Dilemma

According to Callender and Huggett, several key assumptions in Eppley and Hannah's thought experiment (C, D, G) are ambiguous. Depending on how these three premises are to be interpreted, the thought experiment either does or does not establish its conclusion. Eppley and Hannah consider the uncertainty principle, conservation of momentum, and prohibition against superluminal signaling as inviolable. It does not matter whether these principles are understood as structures or laws of nature—the point is that, according to Eppley and Hannah, they cannot possibly be altered. However, as Callender and Huggett demonstrate, all three of these principles can be afforded an epistemic interpretation whereby they refer to some inherent limitations in our epistemic access to the physical world. Thus while we may never be able to *observe* the violation of the physical principles Eppley and Hannah consider sacrosanct, we can construct consistent interpretations of quantum mechanics that do, in principle, break one or more of them. Callender and Huggett conclude on an agnostic note: They hesitate to endorse the experiment, but nor do they reject it outright (as Mattingly later does).

Barring any strict no-go theorem for semiclassical gravity, Callender and Huggett argue, we must wait for true experimental evidence that the gravitational field is quantized: "Empirical considerations must create the necessity, if there is any, of quantizing the gravitational field" (Callender and Huggett 2001b, 11).

4. REDUCING LOGICAL POSSIBILITY SPACE: A NEW ROLE FOR THOUGHT EXPERIMENTS

Ideally, a thought experiment aims to conclusively resolve the matter at hand. One need only point to Galileo's falling bodies thought experiment (Brown 2011, 1) as a paradigm example: Here there is little doubt that Galileo convincingly overturns Aristotelian kinematics. But this is the ideal case.

As with real-life empirical experiments, thought experiments often fail to conclusively establish their claims. Often this is because one or more premises or background assumptions are controversial. In the case of the Eppley and Hannah thought experiment, a number of premises are subject to interpretative challenges, as raised by Callender and Huggett. One might claim that these challenges undermine Eppley and Hannah's argument for a quantum theory of the gravitational field. At the same time, it must be realized that the interpretative challenges Callender and Huggett raise (such as the nature of the uncertainty principle) have yet to be settled even in the case of non-relativistic quantum mechanics. Why should we be surprised, then, that the same interpretative challenges reappear in discussions of quantum gravity? Eppley and Hannah's thought experiment should not be required, in and of itself, to provide an "interpretation-free" argument for the quantization of the gravitational field. That would be expecting too much.

If Eppley and Hannah's argument is conditionally sound (on the assumption that premises C, D, and G are inviolable), how then are we to evaluate its success? I propose that in the absence of any empirical evidence of the quantized nature of the gravitational field Eppley and Hannah's thought experiment serves a useful limiting function. Rather than showing the impossibility of *any* half-quantum and half-classical theory of gravity, the experiment demonstrates that certain kinds of assumptions about such a theory (namely, non-epistemic interpretations of premises C, D, and G) are impossible. In short, Eppley and Hannah's thought experiment limits the logical possibility space for any future theory of quantum gravity.

In the following table I represent the constraints on theory possibility imposed by Eppley and Hannah's thought experiment. We begin by considering the nature of a unified theory of gravity and matter, and note that the thought experiment places no constraints on the matter theory if gravity is assumed to be quantized from the get-go. More importantly, the thought experiment places restrictions on the nature of a unified half-and-half theory (where matter, but not the gravitational field, is assumed to be quantized).

Eppley and Hannah's original thought experiment of course seeks to eliminate entirely the upper-right-hand box, the possibility of a half-and-half theory. But as Callender and Huggett point out, the authors assume the uncertainty principle, conservation of momentum, and prohibition against superluminal signaling are all inviolable. But what if one or more of these principles is interpreted as a limit to our epistemic access? Simply put, Eppley and Hannah's thought experiment does not rule out those interpretations of quantum mechanics that already violate some of the experiment's crucial assumptions. Bohmian mechanics, which patently rejects Eppley and Hannah's reading of the uncertainty principle, is consistent with a classical treatment of gravity. Indeed, such a unified theory of classical gravity and quantized matter "may exist in the logical geography" (Callender and Huggett 2001b, 9).

The idea that a thought experiment imposes a constraint on the "space of possible theories" is tied to Kyle Stanford's (2009) and Sherri Roush's (2005) recent discussions of the scope of justifiable scientific belief. Stanford argues that justifiable scientific belief consists in the effective consideration

Table 8.1 Representation of the Restrictions on the Possibility Space for a Unified Theory of Gravity with Quantized Matter

	Pre–Thought Experiment	*Post–Thought Experiment*
Classical Gravity	No restrictions on unified theory	Unified theory requires violation of at least one of the premises C, D, or G: including Bohm-deBroglie, relative states (Everett), GRW
Quantized Gravity	No restrictions on unified theory	No restrictions on unified theory

of "the space of *alternatives* to a hypothesis we seek to evaluate and . . . their empirical consequences" (2009, 254). In particular, Stanford cautions against endorsing "catch-all" atomic hypotheses, such as, in our case, *either the gravitational field is quantized or it is not quantized.* He explains:

> We generally have no idea what empirical consequences to draw simply from the negation of a fundamental theoretical hypothesis, and therefore no way to test among the admittedly exhaustive alternatives in a space of theoretical possibilities formulated in this way. (Stanford 2009, 268)

Seen in this light, Eppley and Hannah's thought experiment need not be based on an atomic "either gravity is quantized or it is not" hypothesis. A careful consideration of the interpretation of the experiment's premises subdivides the possibility space for quantum theories of gravity in a useful manner. If we choose not to quantize the gravitational field, there are specific limited options available for constructing a unified theory. All of them require an epistemic interpretation of at least one of the principles Eppley and Hannah consider inviolable.

Interestingly enough, this role of limiting the possibility space for hypotheses can potentially breathe new life even into failed thought experiments. Thus, suppose for the sake of argument we side with Mattingly in declaring Eppley and Hannah's thought experiment a complete failure—despite the reasons I offer above for not rejecting it outright. Then, presumably, we can no longer take Eppley and Hannah's thought experiment as establishing any constraints on the nature of the fundamental quantum theory of gravity. But this conclusion would be incorrect. For if we take Mattingly's criticism to heart, then Eppley and Hannah's thought experiment fails precisely because of the gravitational collapse that is a generic feature of many solutions to the field equations of general relativity (certainly the Schwarzschild metric assumed by Mattingly). And this situation in and of itself contains a lesson to be learned: If Mattingly is right, then Eppley and Hannah's thought experiment can succeed only by assuming a classical theory of gravitation in which there is no gravitational collapse (singularity). Thus if one were to run a future thought experiment in the same vein, one would have to call upon either a very specific solution to general relativity which is singularity-free (Senovilla 1996; Misner et al. 1973, 554), or else some alternative classical theory of gravitation in which there are no singularities whatsoever.[5] This amounts to reducing the possibility space for theories of gravitation: The purpose of the revised thought experiment would be to demonstrate the incompatibility of a quantum theory of matter with a classical *singularity-free* theory of gravitation. This process demonstrates that perhaps even some flawed thought experiments can nevertheless be influential in the development of science in virtue of eliminating potential hypotheses.

Although Eppley and Hannah's thought experiment falls short of the complete "proof" that the authors seek for the quantization of the gravitational field, it nevertheless successfully imposes strong constraints on the search for a quantum theory of gravity. In particular, the thought experiment eliminates those unified theories of classical gravity and quantized matter that assume as inviolable the uncertainty principle, conservation of momentum, and the prohibition against superluminal signaling. For those who maintain a non-epistemic interpretation of these physical principles the message is clear: The gravitational field must be quantized. The idea of "limiting logical possibility space" and imposing constraints would seem to be a successful strategy in general for dealing with thought experiments in quantum gravity. In the absence of empirical evidence that normally could aid in the development and verification of approaches to quantum gravity, thought experiments indeed play a crucial role for the physicist.

ACKNOWLEDGEMENTS

I am sincerely grateful to the editors of this volume—James Brown, Méla-nie Frappier, and Letitia Meynell—as well as two readers, for extremely helpful comments and suggestions. A version of this paper was presented at the workshop "Science without Data? The Role of Thought Experiments in Empirical Investigations," held in Halifax, Nova Scotia, in June 2010. I thank the participants there for helpful comments. I am grateful to the staff at the Yukon Research Centre at Yukon College in Whitehorse, Yukon, for graciously providing space for research and writing. This work was supported by an Ontario Graduate Scholarship.

NOTES

1. $p_x \approx 0$ and $p_y \approx 0$.
2. Conservation of momentum implies, of course, that $p_{x+y} = (p_x + p_y)$.
3. The original EPR thought experiment (Einstein, Podolsky, and Rosen 1935) tried to establish a measurement scenario whereby one would be forced to conclude either that some sort of superluminal *influence* had taken place (clearly undesirable) or else that some local "hidden" variables were needed in order to complete the quantum theory.
4. And indeed to which final state it collapses, (2) or (3), though the particular case is irrelevant for the purposes of superluminal communication. The choice is whether or not to perform a measurement in the first place.
5. Both alternatives would require independent physical motivation of course, since observational evidence suggests that the cosmology of the actual universe *does* in fact contain singularities.

REFERENCES

Bohm, David, and Basil J. Hiley. 1993. *The Undivided Universe: An Ontological Interpretation of Quantum Theory.* London: Routledge & Kegan Paul.

Brown, James Robert. 2011. *The Laboratory of the Mind*. New York: Routledge.

Callender, Craig, and Nick Huggett, eds. 2001a. *Physics Meets Philosophy at the Planck Scale*. Cambridge: Cambridge University Press.

———. 2001b. Introduction to *Physics Meets Philosophy at the Planck Scale*, 1–32. Cambridge: Cambridge University Press.

Einstein, Albert. 1949. "Autobiographical Notes." In *Albert Einstein: Philosopher-Scientist*, edited by A. Schilpp, 2–95. La Salle, IL: Open Court.

Einstein, Albert, B. Podolsky, and N. Rosen. 1935. "Can Quantum-Mechanical Description of Physical Reality be Considered Complete?" *Physical Review* 47: 777–780.

Eppley, Kenneth, and Eric Hannah. 1977. "The Necessity of Quantizing the Gravitational Field." *Foundations of Physics* 7: 51–68.

Everett, Hugh. 1957. "'Relative State' Formulation of Quantum Mechanics." *Reviews of Modern Physics* 29: 454–462.

Ghirardi, G. C., A. Rimini, and T. Weber. 1986. "Unified Dynamics for Microscopic and Macroscopic Systems." *Physical Review D* 34: 470–491.

Mattingly, James. 2006. "Why Eppley and Hannah's Thought Experiment Fails." *Physical Review D* 73: 064025.

Misner, Charles, Kip Thorne, and John Wheeler. 1973. *Gravitation*. San Francisco: W. H. Freeman.

Rescher, Nicholas. 2005. *What If? Thought Experimentation in Philosophy*. New Brunswick, NJ: Transaction Publishers.

Roush, Sherri. 2005. *Tracking Truth*. Oxford: Oxford University Press.

Senovilla, Jose. 1996. "Towards Realistic Singularity-Free Cosmological Models." *Physical Review D* 53: 1799–1807.

Stanford, Kyle. 2009. "Scientific Realism, the Atomic Theory, and the Catch-All Hypothesis: Can We Test Fundamental Theories against All Serious Alternatives?" *British Journal for the Philosophy of Science* 60: 253–269.

Wilkes, Kathleen. 1988. *Real People: Philosophy of Mind without Thought Experiments*. Oxford: Oxford University Press.

Wüthrich, Christian. 2006. "Approaching the Planck Scale from a Generally Relativistic Point of View: A Philosophical Appraisal of Loop Quantum Gravity." PhD dissertation, University of Pittsburgh.

9 Craig Venter's New Life
The Realization of Some Thought Experiments in Biological Ontology

W. Ford Doolittle

J. Craig Venter's very recent (May 2010) successes in the construction of "synthetic living cells" (Gibson et al. 2010) has stimulated strong interest and fierce criticism within the disciplinary literature and the popular press (Itaya 2010; Wade 2010). The excitement has come in no small part from the fact that Venter's cellular constructs encourage us to rethink certain important elements of biological ontology. We can instructively debate whether these entities are actually *organisms*, or truly belong to *species* (and if so, ask *which* species). We can even question whether they are alive, as *life* might best be understood. Here I will consider whether Venter's creations thus fit Brown and Fehige's (2011) definition of thought experiments—*"devices of the imagination used to investigate the nature of things"*—or at least would have done before Venter took them from the imaginary into the real. In this essay I will (1) contextualize Venter's work, describing his achievement in what I hope is appropriate detail for non-biologists, (2) discuss the ethical concerns that attract most attention, but may be only peripherally relevant to thought experimentation, (3) relate Venter's constructions to some of biology's foundational concepts, and (4) explain how I see them as realized *thought experiments,* although perhaps of a special kind.

Craig Venter is one of contemporary biology's most controversial figures, an unarguably brilliant researcher and entrepreneur, and a man of no small ego (Shapin 2008). He first came to public attention in the early 1990s, when as a US National Institutes of Health researcher, he advocated the patenting of human gene data for potential commercial use. Surely his most widely noted achievement, a decade later, was completion of a draft sequence of a human genome (in large part his own). This privately funded effort by Venter's company, Celera, forced the multinational "public" Human Genome Project into an early release of data and put Venter's face and that of the director of the public endeavor on the cover of *Time*. Most notable since then might be his pioneering efforts in metagenomics, a two-year around-the-world DNA sampling expedition on his private yacht *Sorcerer II*, aimed at surveying oceanic microbiota worldwide by massive random "shotgun" sequencing of all the DNA in concentrated seawater samples. Much criticized for its incautious methodology, this feat neverthe-less has set the stage for major developments in a new field.

But trumping either, if successful, will be Venter's creation of new forms of life and his use of them in many applications from fundamental bio-physics research to the production of vaccines, pharmaceuticals, and bio-fuels. Synthetic Genomics, Venter's new venture in partnership with the 400-employee J. Craig Venter Institute (Rockville, Maryland, and San Diego, California) has as its goal developing radically new ("disruptive") technologies aimed at saving our species from itself, at considerable profit.

1. WHAT'S OLD AND WHAT'S NEW ABOUT VENTER'S "DISRUPTIVE TECHNOLOGY"

Genetic (or genomic) engineering, often entailing the production of geneti-cally modified organisms (GMOs), has been with us since the construction of the first recombinant DNA molecules in the early 1970s (Berg and Merz 2010). Probably the majority of GMOs comprise bacterial host cells bear-ing small amounts (one or a few genes' worth) of "foreign DNA", very often from another species, either on an independently replicating "plas-mid" or integrated into its chromosome, as cartooned in Figure 9.1A. Most such bacterial GMOs live in laboratory settings: It is of course genetically modified animals and plants roaming the landscape that cause most (in my view mostly misplaced) public apprehension. But even when inserted genes are expressed and significantly affect host cell phenotype, species identity of the host would not generally be considered compromised: A "new life form" would not be thought to have been created. For instance, "Roundup Ready" GMO crops, bearing chromosomal copies of genes making them resistant to a potent herbicide which can then be used to kill surrounding weeds, are still described as just varieties of the parent species, presumably because the overwhelming majority of their genes are still parental (Funke et al. 2006). (And possibly also because the notion that scientists are creat-ing and releasing "new species" would be even less acceptable, especially to those European publics who consider GMOs dangerously unnatural and those American publics who consider them blasphemous.)

Species identity questions do begin to arise when the inserted foreign genetic information approaches in amount that already borne by the host. Perhaps the previous record here is the work of Mitsuhiro Itaya and his col-leagues at Keio University (Itaya et al. 2005; Itaya 2010). In several steps they succeeded in stably integrating most or all of the 3.5 million base pairs (mbp) of a genome from a species of *Synechocystis* (a cyanobacterium or "blue-green alga") into the 4.2 mbp genome of *Bacillus subtilis*, a soil bac-terium that is a perennial favorite in laboratory genetics and quite unrelated to cyanobacteria. They called the resultant chimeric cell *Cyanobacillus*, although it appears that many of its cyanobacterial genes are not expressed.

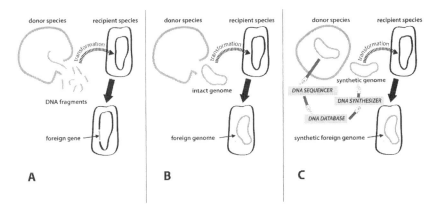

Figure 9.1   Three stages to the creation of cells with synthetic genomes. A: "Genetic engineering" or "recombinant DNA" manipulations as have been practiced since the early 1970s; B: "Genome transplantation" as described by Venter's group in 2007; C: Genome transplantation with synthetic genome, as reported by them in 2010, in the work under discussion here.

Venter's group, however, opted not merely to augment but rather to completely replace a host genome (Figure 9.1B). To make this easier biologically, the chosen donor and host were very closely related species of the same genus, *Mycoplasma*. These are cell wall–less (and often pathogenic) bacteria with very small genomes, indeed among the smallest for any bacteria capable of growth in defined media—this smallness also making the genetic manipulation easier. For example, *M. genitalium*, a human pathogen, was one of the first bacteria to have its complete genome sequenced: It carries fewer than 500 genes in 0.58 mbp of DNA. Typical bacteria like *Escherichia coli* have genomes five to twenty times larger. This does not meant that *Mycoplasmas* are "more primitive" than other bacteria or more like ancestral forms: Their genomes have clearly undergone "streamlining" as dependence on host functions increased. The two species Venter finally chose on the basis of tractability, *M. mycoides* and *M. capricolum*, are both goat pathogens, with somewhat larger but still manageably sized genomes of 1.1–1.2 mbp (1,053 and 867 genes, respectively).

In a 2007 *Science* paper, "Genome Transplantation in Bacteria: Changing One Species to Another", Venter's group claimed to have done just what that title indicates (Lartigue et al. 2007). Cells of *M. capricolum* were exposed in the presence of polyethylene glycol, a chemical agent which promotes fusion of its wall-less cells, to intact chromosomal DNA isolated by exquisitely gentle techniques from cells of *M. mycoides*. The *M. mycoides* donor was resistant to an antibiotic, tetracycline, to which the *M. capricolum* recipient was sensitive. So in principle colonies that subsequently appeared on Petri plates containing tetracycline should be descended from *M. capricolum* cells that had stably taken up at least the *M. mycoides* tetracycline resistance gene. In fact, resistant transformants had incorporated *all* the donor genes and lost *all* the recipient's, as affirmed by a variety of tests. Some recombination between donor and recipient chromosomes—producing genomic chimeras—would probably have been expected, so there is a bit of a mystery here (Itaya 2010). And how the DNA was taken up is also a (possibly related) mystery: These researchers think that two or more recipient cells fuse around a donor chromosome.

These uncertainties about the nature of the process aside, there is no reason to doubt the veracity of the result, nor the significance of this advance for synthetic biology, nor its philosophical implications. Venter has saved us from the endless sorites paradox problems posed by asking "if replacing one gene does not make a new species, what about replacing two genes . . . or three, or . . . ." As Venter sees it:

> In this process, a whole bacterial genome from one species is transformed into another bacterial species, which results in new cells that have the genotype and phenotype of the input genome. The important distinguishing feature of transplantation is that the recipient genome is entirely replaced by the donor genome. There is no recombination between the incoming and outgoing chromosomes. *The result is a clean change of one bacterial species into another.* (Lartigue et al. 2007, 632, emphasis mine)

The logical next move, which Venter has just taken and which comprises his much ballyhooed breakthrough, is to synthesize the donor DNA "from scratch" in the lab, rather than to isolate it from cells (Figure 9.1C). The difficulty and costs are not trivial. Although machines (oligonucleotide synthesizers) that string together nucleotides (familiar as A, T, C, and G) into defined sequence stretches have been around for several decades, they still could not accurately produce an entire cellular genome in one go. So a thousand stretches of about a thousand base pairs each (1 kbp, about a gene's-worth), matching the entire known genome sequence and with overlapping ends, were assembled by recombination in yeast cells into about a hundred 10 kbp molecules, and these then into about ten 100 kbp pieces, and these last into the final 1,077,947 bp genome, each step checked and the final product resequenced. The cost of this creation (I think including fifteen years of preliminary work) was about 40 million dollars. The *creature* (this word used in its original meaning of *created thing*) that resulted has been coyly dubbed "Synthia" by the ETC Group, a Canada-based NGO promoting "socially responsible development of technologies" and primarily opposed to Venter's patenting practices (ETC Group 2010, and see below). I will borrow the name, without meaning to take a position on the ethics or politics.

This would not be the first complete genome synthesized on the basis of a known natural sequence: Poliovirus was re-created in this way in 2002 (Cello et al. 2002) and the 1918 pandemic influenza virus was revived from sequences obtained from frozen victims and lab samples in 2005 (Tumpey et al. 2005), both to a chorus of concerns about safety as well as for the precedent set and potential use by terrorists. But as to the ontological implications, many would argue that viruses, because they require hosts to reproduce, are not alive. And, Venter is not wrong to boast that his *Myco-plasma* is "the first self-replicating species we've had on the planet whose parent is a computer" (Wade 2010).

2. PLAYING GOD, OWNING LIFE, AND FRANKENSTEIN MONSTERS

Two Nobelists, James D. Watson and Hamilton Smith, the latter Venter's longtime collaborator, have responded succinctly if facetiously to the inevitable accusations about "playing God". The former famously quipped, "If scientists don't play God, who will?" and the latter, even more pithily, "We don't play" (Connor 2000; Highfield 2006). Interestingly, a Dutch professor of systematic theology, Henk van den Belt, notes in his analysis of such accusations that

> liberal theologians generally deny the religious character of the 'playing God' argument—a response which fits in with the curious fact that this argument is used mainly by secular organizations. Synthetic biology, it is therefore maintained, does not offend so much the God of the Bible as a deified Nature. While syntheses of artificial life forms cause some vague uneasiness that life may lose its special meaning, most concerns turn out to be narrowly anthropocentric. As long as synthetic biology creates only new microbial life and does not directly affect human life, it will in all likelihood be considered acceptable. (van den Belt 2009, 257)

More objectionable to many might be Venter's long-established patenting practices. There is of course a venerable literature (Healey 1992) on the ethics of patenting genes and living creatures (however created). Reasons not to patent range from the enviro-aesthetic and ethical (the God issue again) to the practical—discouraging future development by too broad a reach in a field (synthetic biology) whose methods and goals are still very fluid. Venter's early efforts (in 2007) to patent many of the steps in his *Myco-plasma*-based synthetic biology platform may not have been so dangerously broad as his critics feared and many synthetic biologists think his system too clunky for general use, in any case. But other patent applications, for instance one claiming rights over a minimized *E. coli* genome, may produce a colder chill (Anonymous 2007). The academically based synthetic biology community, as represented by the not-for-profit BioBricks Foundation, seems in large part dedicated to an open-source approach to the identification of Life's fundamental building blocks and the development of new ways to put them together (see http://bbf.openwetware.org).

Then there is the issue of dangerous bugs "getting out". Molecular biologists can never address such topics without harkening in a self-congratulatory spirit back to the 1975 Asilomar Conference at which the leaders in the then very new recombinant DNA field famously agreed to what in retrospect seem to have been unnecessarily strict restrictions (Szybalski 1980) on the production and propagation of organisms carrying one or a few foreign genes (the first GMOs). The post-Venter generation of synthetic biology creations could in principle be much safer: requiring in their genetic code and yet unable to synthesize on their own a suite of amino acids unavailable outside the lab, for instance. But economical synthetic creatures expected to do serious work in the wild, such as photosynthetic biofuel producers, might not be so crippled. It may seem at first blush too incredible to imagine that some radically new life form could take hold and spread in the spaces in and between those myriads already here. But it seems equally incredible to imagine that "life, with its several powers", was originally "breathed into a few forms or into one" and has since gone on to produce "endless forms most beautiful and most wonderful" (Darwin 1859, 490). And yet biologists and most adequately educated people do believe that exactly this has happened. We should never underestimate the creative power of evolution by natural selection operating over aeons, nor the not inconsiderable time our planet is likely to remain habitable for many living things, if not necessarily us. It is *not* completely beyond imagining that in a few billion years what will be found on Earth, alone or in complex symbiotic and competitive relationships with Life as we currently know it, are the highly evolved descendants of escapees from the dark Satanic mills of Synthetic Genomics Inc., perhaps themselves celebrating their diversity and sophistication!

3. NEW QUESTIONS ABOUT THE NATURE OF LIFE

Nicholas Wade's *New York Times* article (Wade 2010) on the creation of Synthia quotes Venter as saying, "This is a philosophical advance as much as a technical advance", and venturing that his "synthetic cell" posed "new questions about the nature of life". It is these questions, more than the ethical concerns, that draw my attention to the possible relevance of this science in thought experimentology.

3.1. What Is Life?

Non-biologists often seem to think this a profoundly interesting question, one with which we in the field, especially molecular biologists, are or should be preoccupied. Indeed, generations of us have been taught that

Erwin Schrödinger's little book *What Is Life?* (1944)—in which this founding father of quantum mechanics muses about whether explaining living processes might entail the formulation of new physical laws—was foundational for *our* discipline. But many of my generation will guiltily confess that we haven't actually read the book, and Neville Symonds (1986) concluded that it actually had "little direct influence either in recruiting physicists or chemists into biology, or in affecting the direction taken by research in molecular biology".

The nature of life is not an issue, and the concept does little work for us. Few would doubt that we might someday construct a satisfyingly detailed scenario for how *E. coli*, elephants, and Elvis are the results of four billion years of evolution beginning with abiotic molecules, without having to invoke any new laws, and moreover, without ever having to decide *for any scientific purpose* what "life" is, or when we might say it first appeared (Yarus 2010). Even in a non-evolutionary context, now that we are aware of viruses with enormous (larger than some cells') genomes and quasi-autonomous metabolic potential (Van Etten et al. 2010), it would be difficult to propose a principled distinction between living and non-living. Nor, again, would anything scientific hinge upon our doing so.

So most often the need to decide "What is life?" comes up in the context of publicly touted claims that someone has just "created life in the test tube". As life scientists we may be called on to explain to reporters if and why we think such claims are justified. Here I believe I can suggest good criteria, criteria I can contextualize by recalling some earlier reports of "life created in the test tube".

The first I remember was in 1967, when Arthur Kornberg and his colleagues succeeded in producing infectious viral DNA using cell-free enzyme preparations. Apparently, in spite of Kornberg's cautions that the result not be oversold, no less a figure than then President L. B. Johnson was to announce in a speech on the day the paper appeared, "Some geniuses at Stanford University have created life in the test tube!" (Lenzer 2008). Five years later, Sol Spiegelman and his lab reported what seemed the logical next step, Darwinian evolution (Kacian et al. 1972). They also used a viral genome (but RNA this time) in the presence of appropriate replicating enzymes purified from infected cells, periodically diluting the product into a new enzyme-containing test tube. Replication could in principle go on forever in a series of such tubes, and under conditions in which mutation and natural selection occur. More rapidly replicating, often shorter RNA molecules were indeed quickly evolved, in a very life-like fashion.

Still, both these systems were completely dependent on enzymes isolated from cells (and in the first case on DNA with the "correct" viral sequence). More like real "creation", I think, is the current generation of experiments focused on RNA molecules that can serve as enzymes and, in principle, replicate themselves. Powerful *in vitro* selection systems can, again in principle, amplify such active sequences from immense libraries of randomly generated molecules. The lab of Jack Szostak at Harvard is perhaps furthest along in this effort, combining it with developing methods for encapsulating the RNAs in self-assembling synthetic vesicles capable of growth and division (Schrum et al. 2010). (Compartmentalization may be necessary for effective selection, by preventing active RNAs from altruistically squandering their efforts in replicating inactive molecules.)

I would not be surprised to see success within a decade from the team directed by Szostak, a 2009 Nobel laureate, and such a success *would* in my view comprise the "creation" of "life in the test tube". This is because no enzymes or DNA or RNA purified from real organisms—and no hereditary information derived from such molecules—(as in Venter's synthesized *Mycoplasma* genomes) will have been required. Application of *general principles* emerging from decades of advanced research on living systems of course will have been a key element, but the life of these entities will be disconnected in an informational sense from the Life we know (see below for the distinction between "life" and "Life").

One commentator, the bioethicist Arthur Caplan, considers Synthia the crucial last nail in the coffin of vitalism:

> Venter's achievement would seem to extinguish the argument that life requires a special force or power to exist. In my view, this makes it one of the most important scientific achievements in the history of mankind. (Caplan 2010, 423)

But for most biologists and most especially molecular biologists, that coffin was sealed and buried long ago, and Venter's Synthia does not represent the "creation of life in a test tube". Wade for instance quotes Jim Collins, a bioengineer at Boston University:

> My worry is that some people are going to draw the conclusion that they have created a new life form. What they have created is an organism with a synthesized natural genome. But it doesn't represent the creation of life from scratch or the creation of a new life form. (Wade, 2010)

3.2. Differentiating "life" and "Life"

Suppose we discovered on Mars an advanced civilization—or even just metabolically active and replicating microorganisms—that we could somehow safely conclude had no evolutionary connection to terrestrial living things (for instance, because they used mostly D-amino acids, different from our twenty, and employed a completely different sort of genetic code to direct their incorporation into protein.) We would surely want to say that we had found *life*, even if not "as we know it". But often when we talk about "life on Earth" we take what are the contingent properties of terrestrial organisms, all similar at the cellular level because they are related by descent, as defining features for life in general. For instance, many would not consider computer viruses alive even though they can replicate, mutate, and evolve, because they lack a clear analog to metabolism. For similar reasons, evolving self-replicating RNAs derived from random sequences but depending on researchers for a continuous supply of building blocks might be considered living by some of us, but not others. So I think it instructive to distinguish two forms of the word.

First is "life" with a small *l*, which cannot be defined non-arbitrarily and which I would submit in the end is not distinguishable in any fully principled way from non-life. One can argue for large viruses, computer viruses, even cultural memes being alive, but there is in the end no fact of the matter. Thus, life with a small *l* as I *personally* would define it has already been created many times over, sometimes deliberately. So far such life entails replication and evolution by natural selection but lacks sustained autonomous metabolism. But few think it impossible that we might some day make in the lab, or find on another planet, sustainable replication and metabolism packaged together, and unrelated to "Life" with a capital *L*.

Second is "Life" with a capital *L*. This is the name for that unique entity comprising all living and extinct organisms descendant from that one form into which, as Darwin imagined, life was "originally breathed". David Hull and Michael Ghiselin have made a good case for species, as spatio-temporally defined cohesive units, being *individuals* whose names (like *E. coli* or *Homo sapiens*) are *proper names* (Ghiselin 1974; Hull 1978). I am making the same case for a larger individual, Life (its proper name). Some members of this historical entity (loosely it is a clade) may not actually be alive, by many common definitions of "life". Certainly smaller viruses would be part of Life, but are usually thought of as lacking life. Life with a capital *L* arose only once and could not by definition ever arise again: It can only be fostered or discouraged in its continued growth. Martians, unless we had reason to believe they descended from Earthly colonists (including microbes), would not belong to Life. So one question raised by Venter's invention is whether Synthia, although surely alive by any commonly used definition of "life", is part of "Life".

3.3. Genome Transplantation and the Species Problem

I will defer that question for a while to consider whether "genome transplantations" of the sort Venter completed in 2007 really do result in "the clean change of one bacterial species into another", as he claimed. I hope to show that both questions are about how we conceive biological identity and continuity, and their coupled answers point out the real ontological interest in Venter's achievement.

The "species problem" is one of biology's most onerous, because we have two expectations of the word, and they can often be at odds. On the one hand we want to identify and name circumscribable groups of organisms of similar genotype and phenotype, recognizably separated from each other by gaps and naturally comprising a level in a hierarchical classification. On the other hand we want to formulate genetic, ecological, and evolutionary models that will of certainty generate such circumscribable groups and, preferably, apply to all organisms. Only with such universal models could we claim that our circumscribable groups are "natural", not arbitrarily defined. The trouble is that the genetic, ecological, and evolutionary processes at play are not constrained by any force or law to produce comparable circumscribable groups (Hey 2001).

One way to make this conundrum clear is to consider the limited applicability of the most popular species concept, Ernst Mayr's *Biological Species Concept*. Most of us learn it in elementary biology courses: Biological species comprise all and only those organisms that can (if suitably introduced to each other) produce fertile offspring through mating—a clear enough notion (Mayr 1975). But arguably the majority of living things do not reproduce by mating and thus cannot, by Mayr's criteria, form legitimate species (Mayr 1996). We are left with no principled way of recognizing whether clonally reproducing asexual organisms, like bacteria or surprisingly many animals and plants, are of the same or different species. And if we in desperation define asexual species simply as clusters of similar organisms, we have no non-arbitrary way to decide how similar they must be.

Periodically, biologists seek a more fundamental formulation that will at least allow each organism to belong to one and only one species, without requiring that all species be formed by the same process, or be similarly circumscribed. Recently, Kevin de Queiroz has suggested one such formulation, his *General (or Metapopulation) Lineage Concept*, which he claims underlies all accepted species definitions.

> The proposal has two components. First, it retains the element common to all contemporary concepts and definitions of species by adopting the general concept of species as separately evolving metapopulation lineages. Second, it eliminates the conflicts among rival concepts by treating this property, existence as a separately evolving metapopulation lineage, as the only necessary property of species. In other words, all of the other properties that have previously been treated as necessary properties of species, which created incompatibilities among alternative species concepts, are reinterpreted as no longer being defining properties of the species category. Instead, they are interpreted as contingent properties not only of metapopulation lineages but also of species, properties that species as metapopulation lineages may or may not acquire during the course of their existence. In other words, metapopulation lineages do not have to be phenetically distinguishable, or diagnosable, or monophyletic, or reproductively isolated, or ecologically divergent, to be species. They only have to be evolving separately from other such lineages. (de Queiroz 2005, 6604)

I think that de Queiroz is right that all contending species definitions do include this notion of metapopulation lineage, or even more basically of genealogical continuity between members of successive generations through replication or sexual reproduction. Few biologists would accept as species (polyphyetic) groups comprising individuals of different lineages, that is, individuals that did not share a common ancestor within that species. An unfortunate feature of de Queiroz's formulation, however, is that it is only by their contingent properties, as he defines them, that species can actually be *recognized* as different from each other or indeed distinguished from the varieties or subspecies that might belong to them or the genera to which they belong.

A fortunate feature of such a general formulation, though, is that it allows us to see why Venter's claim that he has effected a "clean change of one bacterial species into another" is so transgressive of the usual ontology. If there is any metapopulation lineage to be defined here, it is presumably that of reproducing cells. The recipient *M. capricolum* cells go on replicating with their replacement *M. mycoides* genome just as before, presumably—and presumably for their first generation use mostly proteins and metabolites produced under the direction of their previous *capricolum* genes. A strict application of the metapopulation concept would seem to require that we regard Synthia and her descendants as a variety of *M. capricolum*, albeit *very* extensively mutated (at each of the thousands of nucleotide positions in which the recipient's genome originally differed from the donor's).

So Venter, although he does not employ this terminology, is replacing something like de Queiroz's Metapopulation Lineage Concept with something that we might call the *Information Lineage Concept*. As well as genome transplantation in the test tube, he is seeking to effect a "concept transplantation" in the philosophy of classification. Molecular biologists naïve to the debates around species, and unconcerned or impatient with philosophical thought experiments relating to identity and persistence (like the Ship of Theseus puzzle) may not be troubled at all about this. Systematists should be, though, because what Venter's claim makes us think about is the possibility of uncoupling the inheritance of information from the processes of replication and reproduction that define organismal lineages as continuous populations of physical entities.

For Venter it would be the information that defines species, and therefore lineages (and would justify the inclusion of his re-engineered life form in Life). That identity for him is not a matter of cellular history and substance was already apparent in the 2007 "genome transplantation" paper. It is even more clearly the purport of his most recent experiment, as cartooned in Figure 9.1C. Here the information is also disembodied from its original physical carrier, the donor's DNA. If we allow Synthia and her daughters to be individuals of the species *M. mycoides*, we are endorsing the microbial equivalent of immaculate conception.

Some might object that what Venter actually holds to is neither the Metapopulation nor the Information Lineage Concept but instead a definition based on simple physical similarity or identity, divorced from history, what I will call the *Purely Material Concept*. By this measure, if Synthia or her descendant cells are physically indistinguishable from normal cells of *M. mycoides* in all material ways—in genome sequence, in internal disposition and structure and function of all gene products, and thus of necessity in all interactions with the environment—then they indeed *are M. mycoides*. Certainly in practical terms, species assignments are often based on physical examination, divorced from any direct knowledge of the history or the organism as a cellular entity or of the information encoded in its genome.

But I claim that there is more to it than this for almost any biologist, Venter included. I rest this claim on the basis of two further thought experiments. Suppose, knowing the sequence of his genome, we make an exact copy of Joe Bloggs, using as-yet-to-be-developed but not unimaginable technology, and no physical material derived from him. It is arguable whether we could call this a clone, but more to the point, would this new individual be *Joe Bloggs?* Would he be a member of *H. sapiens?* Would he be part of Life? Adherents of either the Information Lineage or Purely Material Concept should—I argue—answer "No" (or "Not for long"), "Yes", and "Yes" to these three questions. "No" (or "Not for long") to the first because once created the new man would start to accumulate experiences that physically differentiate him, ever so slightly but even down to the subcellular level, from the old. We are more than our genes. "Yes" to the second two because there would be both a *continuity of information* and as much *similarity at the physical level* as exhibited by any natural-born humans, linking this new Joe to our species and to all of Life. (Amusingly, in a review of *Darwinian Populations and Natural Selection* that appeared as I was revising this contribution, Daniel Dennett (2011) poses virtually the same question to that book's author, Peter Godfrey-Smith. As far as I can tell both philosophers would agree with "Yes" to the latter questions, although not for quite the same reasons.)

To tease apart the Information Lineage and Purely Material Concepts, we need one further modification of this thought experiment. Here the synthetic DNA used to make the new individual is randomly generated, perhaps by a stupefyingly enormous number of monkeys typing instructions into an almost unimaginable number of DNA synthesizers and by chance coming up with Joe Bloggs's sequence (having already knocked out an immense number of other creatures' genomes, including near-Bloggses and—given appropriate recoding—quite a few copies of Shakespeare's collected works). The new Joe Bloggs is physically identical to the old, but by pure chance, not through the direct or indirect transmission of information from the old. I submit that Venter, I, and most biologists (and I suspect both Dennett and Godfrey-Smith) would now answer "No" to each of my three questions. Physical indistinguishability is not enough. We would be similarly negative if Martians turned out, due to some as yet unknown principles of extreme convergence, to look just like (and even be interfertile with) us but we knew somehow with certainty that there was no evolutionary connection.

Venter's intervention is interesting because it requires systematists to get serious about what it means for any purportedly "natural" classification when gene history and population or species history are not the same (Doolittle 1999). The existence of more typical GMOs, with only a few foreign genes, or the infrequent occurrences of natural between-species lateral gene transfers have already raised the issue, of course. But I think that in general practical-minded biologists have reasoned that the majority of genes (and certainly a core of especially important genes) track population history well enough that either can be used to define species or lineages. There will be congruence between population lineages and genomic lineages as defined by the great majority of genes and worrying about what to do if they are not has seemed to many as moot and "too philosophical".

It is no longer moot, though perhaps still pretty philosophical. We cannot from now on dismiss as pure fantasy a thought experiment that begins "Well, what if *all* the genes were replaced . . ." If we stick with the Metapopulation Lineage Concept to define identity and relationship then we should probably claim that Synthia is not *M. mycoides* even though cells of this lineage are completely indistinguishable from the *M. mycoides* on deposit in culture collections. If on the other hand we accept Venter's ontology, we must rethink classification for all those cases in which genomic ancestry is mixed.

3.4. DNA, the Blueprint

Another class of "Well, what if . . ." thought experiments Venter's work can be seen to engage involves the relative importance of DNA-based and cellular, epigenetic, and environmental information in development and evolution. For the last several decades biology has seen objections from within and without the discipline to the view, common among molecular biologists of my own generation, that DNA is the "master molecule" or cellular "blueprint"—that all of development, evolution, and behavior are to be simply understood as the reading out of its sequences of As, Ts, Cs, and Gs. Eva Jablonka and Marion Lamb's *Evolution in Four Dimensions* is a very balanced presentation of a more holistic perspective (Jablonka and Lamb 2005). Often discussions of this paradigm devolve into "What if" questions that entail replacing an organism's entire genome with that of another species, to see what the lingering effects of the cellular constituents made at the direction of the replaced genome might be on the expression of its successor and the phenotype of the resulting organism. Michael Crichton's novel *Jurassic Park* and the subsequent blockbuster movie envisioned such an experiment, readers may recall (Crichton 1990). Venter has now actually performed it, on a much smaller organismal (if not financial) scale. Although Venter claims that the cells emerging from this transformation are completely normal, it would be intriguing to observe them in their first few generations.

4. THOUGHT EXPERIMENTS IN WHAT DOMAIN?

As this volume will surely show, philosophers are not in complete agreement about what thought experiments are or how easily they can be distinguished from other imaginative exercises. Certainly it is implicit in most definitions that the actual performance of the experiment is not necessary. But we do not and should not allow gratuitous performance (or performance for another reason) to deplete our supply of good examples. Many weights have been dropped from towers without damaging the paradigmatic status of Galileo's *Gedankenexperiment,* perhaps the most famous example. And actual performance can refresh our interest in underlying issues, as the flurry of learned and not-so-learned pronouncements about Synthia demonstrates.

What might more seriously disqualify Venter's work from the pantheon of thought experimentology, however, is that, aside from Jurassic Park–type questions about the strength of epigenetic inertia, the issues addressed are themselves "merely" philosophical or conceptual. It is not the physical or biological properties of genome transplants like Synthia that are at issue, but rather how we should integrate these novel entities into our systems for understanding and representing biological relationships.

Thomas Kuhn might then have seen Synthia as exemplifying one of the "easy" but "not quite right" (or complete) answers to questions about the function of thought experiments in his statement that

> the new understanding produced by thought experiments is not an understanding of *nature* but rather of the scientist's *conceptual apparatus.* On this analysis, the function of the thought experiment is to assist in the elimination of prior confusion by forcing the scientist to recognize contradictions that had been inherent in his way of thinking from the start. (Kuhn 1977, 275, emphasis in the text)

The not-quite-rightness of this analysis, in Kuhn's view, lies in the fact that it is "previously unassimilated experience" provided by Nature herself, not our intellectual realization of an inherent contradiction in our conceptual apparatus, that should bring about the "elimination of prior confusion".

> The concepts "corrected" in the aftermath of thought experiments displayed no *intrinsic* confusion. If their use raised problems for the scientist, those problems were like the ones to which the use of any experimentally based law or theory would expose him. They arose, that is, not from his mental equipment alone but from difficulties discovered

in the attempt to fit that equipment to previously unassimilated experience. (Kuhn 1977, 289, emphasis in the text)

Whether Synthia belongs to the species of the donor or the recipient is not a question about the real world, only about how we choose to describe that world. This is indeed a problem of our "mental equipment alone". So what we are informed about when we think Venter's work through is not Nature but the practice and theory of biological classification, and some of its "prior confusion". Particularly at issue is the notion of "species" as a category, illustrated in Jody Hey's trenchant observation:

> Despite many different notions of 'species', and uncertainty and disagreement over them, the word almost always gets passed back and forth with tacit understanding. This apparent consensus thrives until that awkward moment when someone asks another what he or she means by 'species', at which point the consensus and the shared thread of understanding can evaporate. It is as if on one hand we know just what 'species' means, and on the other hand, we have no idea what it means. (Hey 2001, 326)

I will leave it up to the readers of this volume, then, to decide whether—as "devices of the imagination"—Venter's newly created life forms constitute (or would have before creation) *bona fide* thought experiments (Brown and Fehige 2011). They do, I submit, "assist in the elimination of prior confusion by forcing the scientist to recognize contradictions that had been inherent in his way of thinking from the start" (Kuhn 1977, 275). But biological classification, in practice and theory, is not so much science as art, and species (especially bacterial species) as a category are philosophical inventions, not natural systems about which we can learn more through experimentation, real or thought-based (Doolittle and Zhaxybayeva 2009). It is this lesson that Venter's work really drives home.

REFERENCES

Anonymous. 2007. "Patenting the Parts" (Editorial). *Nature Biotechnology* 25: 822.

Berg, Paul, and Jane E. Merz. 2010. "Personal Reflections on the Origin and Emergence of Recombinant DNA Technology." *Genetics* 184: 9–17.

Brown, James Robert, and Yiftach Fehige. 2011. "Thought Experiments." In *The Stanford Encyclopedia of Philosophy* (Fall 2011), edited by Edward N. Zalta. http://plato.stanford.edu/archives/win2010/entries/thought-experiment (accessed August 23, 2011).

Caplan, Arthur. 2010. "The End of Vitalism." *Nature* 465: 423.

Cello, J., A. V. Paul, and E. Wimmer. 2002. "Chemical Synthesis of Poliovirus cDNA: Generation of Infectious Virus in the Absence of Natural Template." *Science* 297: 1016–1018.

Connor, Steve. 2000. "Nobel Scientist Happy to 'Play God' with DNA." *The Independent* (May 17).

Crichton, Michael. 1990. *Jurassic Park*. New York: Alfred A. Knopf.

Darwin, Charles. 1859. *On the Origin of Species by Means of Natural Selection*. London: John Murray.

Dennett, Daniel C. 2011. "Homunculi Rule: Reflections on *Darwinian Populations and Natural Selection* by Peter Godfrey-Smith." *Biology and Philosophy* 26: 475–488.

de Queiroz, Kevin. 2005. "Ernst Mayr and the Modern Concept of Species." *Proceedings of the National Academy of Sciences* (US) 102: 6600–6607.

Doolittle, W. Ford. 1999. "Phylogenetic Classification and the Universal Tree." *Science* 284: 2124–2129.

Doolittle, W. F., and O. Zhaxybayeva. 2009. "On the Origin of Prokaryotic Species." *Genome Research* 19: 744–756.

ETC Group. 2010. "Synthia is Alive . . . and Breeding: Panacea or Pandora's Box." www.etcgroup.org/en/node/5142 (accessed August 23, 2011).

Funke, T., H. Han, M. L. Healy-Fried, M. Fischer, and E. Schönbrunn. 2006. "Molecular Basis for the Herbicide Resistance of Roundup Ready Crops." *Proceedings of the National Academy of Sciences* (US) 103: 13010–13015.

Ghiselin, Michael. 1974. "A Radical Solution to the Species Problem." *Systematic Zoology* 23: 536–544.

Gibson, D. G., J. I. Glass, C. Lartigue, V. N. Noskov, R. Y. Chuang, M. A. Algire, G. A. Benders, M. G. Montague, L. Ma, M. M. Moodie, C. Merryman, S. Vashee, R. Krishnakumar, N. Assad-Garcia, C. Andrews-Pfannkoch, E. A. Denisova, L. Young, Z. Q. Qi, T. H. Segall-Shapiro, C.H. Calvey, P.P. Parmar, C.A. Hutchison III, H. O. Smith, and J.C. Venter. 2010. "Creation of a Bacterial Cell Controlled by a Chemically Synthesized Genome." *Science* 329: 52–56.

Healey, Bernadine. 1992. "On Gene Patenting." *New England Journal of Medicine* 327: 664–668.

Hey, Jody. 2001. "The Mind of the Species Problem." *Trends in Ecology and Evolution* 16: 326–329.

Highfield, Roger. 2006. "Ripped Genes." *The Daily Telegraph* (May 27). www. edge.org/3rd_culture/highfield06/highfield06_index.html (accessed August 23 2011).

Hull, D. 1978. "A Matter of Individuality." *Philosophy of Science* 45: 335–360.

Itaya, Mitsuhiro. 2010. "A Synthetic DNA Transplant." *Nature Biotechnology* 28: 687–689.

Itaya, M., K. Tsuge, M. Koizumi, and K. Fujita. 2005. "Combining Two Genomes in One Cell: Stable Cloning of the *Synechocystis* PCC6803 Genome in the *Bacillus subtilis* 168 Genome." *Proceedings of the National Academy of Sciences* (US) 102: 15971–15976.

Jablonka, Eva, and Marion Lamb. 2005. *Evolution in Four Dimensions*. Cambridge, MA: MIT Press.

Kacian, D. L., D. R. Mills, F. R. Kramer, and S. Spiegelman. 1971. "A Replicating RNA Molecule Suitable for a Detailed Analysis of Extracellular Evolution and Replication." *Proceedings of the National Academy of Sciences* (US) 68: 2843–2845.

Kuhn, Thomas S. 1977. "The function of thought experiments" in *Thinking: Readings in Cognitive Science*, P.N.Johnson-Laird and P.C. Wason, eds. Cambridge: Cambridge University Press.

Lartigue, C., J. I. Glass, N. Alperovich, R. Pieper, P. P. Parmar, C. A. Hutchison III, H. O. Smith, and J. C. Venter. 2007. "Genome Transplantation in Bacteria: Changing One Species into Another." *Science* 317: 632–638.

Lenzer, Jeanne. 2008. "Arthur Kornberg." *BMJ* 336: 50.

Mayr, E. 1975. *Evolution and the Diversity of Life*. Cambridge, MA: Harvard University Press.

———. 1996. "What Is a Species and What Is Not?" *Philosophy of Science* 63: 262–277.

Schrödinger, Erwin. 1944. *What Is Life?* Cambridge: Cambridge University Press.

Schrum, J. P., T. F. Zhu, and J. W. Szostak. 2010. "The Origins of Cellular Life." *Cold Spring Harbor Perspectives in Biology* 2 (9):a002212.

Shapin, Stephen. 2008. "I'm a Surfer." *London Review of Books* (March 20) 30 (6): 5–8.

Symonds, Neville. 1986. "What Is life?: Schrödinger's Influence on Biology." *Quarterly Reviews of Biology* 61: 221–226.

Szybalski, Waclaw. 1980. "Asilomar and Five Years." *Trends in Biochemical Sciences* 5: vi–ix.

Tumpey, T. M., C. F. Basler, P. V. Aguilar, H. Zeng, A. Solórzano, D. E. Swayne, N. J. Cox, J. M. Katz, J. K. Taubenberger, P. Palese, and A. García-Sastre. 2005. "Characterization of the Reconstructed 1918 Spanish Influenza Pandemic Virus." *Science* 310: 77–80.

van den Belt, Henk. 2009. "Playing God in Frankenstein's Footsteps: Synthetic Biology and the Meaning of Life." *Nanoethics* 3: 257–268.

Van Etten, J. L., L. C. Lane, and D. D Dunigan. 2010 "DNA Viruses: The Really Big Ones." *Annual Review of Microbiology* 64: 83–99.

Wade, Nicholas. 2010. "Researchers Say They Created a 'Synthetic Cell'." *New York Times* (May 20).

Yarus, Michael. 2010. *Life from an RNA World*. Cambridge, MA: Harvard University Press.

10 Genealogical Thought Experiments in Economics

Julian Reiss

1. INTRODUCTION

Among economic methodologists, one often hears the slogan "contemporary (mainstream/neoclassical/modern) economics is dominated by mathematical model building" (see for instance Boland 2010, 530). The reason for repeating it here is to say upfront what this paper is *not* about: mathematical modelling. Instead I am going to look at a practice that is both older and, arguably, more widely used in economics than mathematical modelling: thought experimentation. It is older in that there are good examples that go back to at least classicism in economics, a period that did not know mathematical models yet. And it is more widely used in that one can find examples in both mainstream as well as heterodox schools in economics, including those that are not particularly fond of mathematical models. To name one, Austrian economists once believed thought experimentation to be "the" method by which economics proceeds.

It is not surprising to find thought experiments widely employed in economics. Most methodologists agree with John Stuart Mill that inductive methods, be they experimental or observational, are inapplicable in economics, or applicable only with dramatically reduced reliability. Experiments are to a large extent impracticable in principle. Many areas of economics are foreclosed to experimentation altogether. When they are possible, experiments are often not very informative. Problems of internal and external validity loom large. The recent rise of so-called experimental economics and the even more recent movement promoting RCTs in development economics and elsewhere do not invalidate this basic truth: Experimentation with human subjects often, if not most of the time, creates artefacts that make the application of research findings outside experimental set-ups difficult to say the least. Observational methods such as regression analyses and structural equations modelling, in turn, tend to be sensationally underdetermined by data—and theory. What I mean by "underdetermination by theory" is that many observational methods require a great deal of causal background knowledge to identify parameters, and this is often thought to come "from theory." But in economics there is no good theory to rely on which makes these methods difficult if not impossible to use reliably.[1]

Many methodologists therefore agree with John Stuart Mill that economic science must proceed deductively from claims established by *a priori* methods. An exceptionally unambiguous statement of this idea has been made by Ludwig von Mises:

> The specific method of economics is the method of imaginary constructions. [. . .] The method of imaginary constructions is justified by its success. Praxeology [the science of action] cannot, like the natural sciences, base its teachings upon laboratory experiments and sensory perceptions of external objects. (Mises [1949] 1996, 236)

Thus, according to von Mises, thought experimentation is *the* method of economics. Indeed, one finds thought experiments in many areas of economics, in both macro and micro applications, in economic theory as much as in economic history. Let me give a few examples. Von Mises' own "evenly rotating economy" ([1949] 1996, 239), essentially the Austrian version of general equilibrium, is a fictional construct used to demonstrate the effect of entrepreneurship on the economy. It does so by positing a world in which (a) all agents' plans are fulfilled (that is, it is in equilibrium in the Austrians' sense); (b) the same market transactions are repeated again and again and no changes in market data occur; and (c) (therefore) entrepreneurship has no role to play. It enables the thought experimenter to see the role of entrepreneurship by mentally comparing the fictitious evenly rotating economy with real economies.

The method of imaginary constructions is, however, certainly not confined to Austrian economics. To methodologists George Akerlof's "market for lemons" (Akerlof 1970) is probably the most widely discussed economic *model* (see for instance Sugden 2000). What methodologists usually overlook is that the mathematical model is preceded by a piece of more informal, thought experimental reasoning in which the same result is established without the aid of mathematics and many of the idealisations mathematical modelling makes inevitable. The method of proof is closely related to that of von Mises: A hypothetical world in which no-one knows whether a car is good or bad (that is, a world of symmetric information) is compared to an equally hypothetical world in which sellers know the quality of a car but buyers don't (that is, a world of asymmetric information), and the effects of this difference on quality and quantity of sold cars is mentally contemplated.

Macroeconomics, too, is an area richly populated with thought experiments. Hume's famous monetary thought experiments have been discussed by Margaret Schabas in detail (Schabas 2008). Similar in nature are thought experiments in economic history such as Robert Fogel's well-known demonstration of the effect of the railroad on American economic growth (Fogel 1964).

All these thought experiments have in common the establishment of a causal effect—of asymmetric information on quality and quantity of used cars, of money on real variables, of the railroad on growth, and so on—by instances of Mill's method of difference where at least one of the two situations compared in order to infer the causal effect is fictitious.

In this paper I will look at a species of thought experiments that is altogether different. These thought experiments also construct imaginary scenarios but they do not purport to establish causal effects and they do not proceed by an application of Mill's method of difference. Rather, they tell a story of how a certain social institution could have originated—hence the name "genealogical" thought experiments. In so doing they establish not a causal effect but a functional role for the institution under consideration. As I will argue below, they do more than that: In showing how a desirable social role is performed by the institution, the continued existence of the institution is also justified to some extent.

The specific institution whose origins I will explore here is money. I will juxtapose two genealogical thought experiments about the origin of money: the almost universally accepted account given by Carl Menger at the end of the nineteenth century (Menger 1892) and a much more recent alternative account given by leaders of a heterodox school of economics called "property economics" (Heinsohn and Steiger 2008). I will argue that these two thought experiments are very similar with respect to the role of demonstrating the social function of an institution and the related justificatory role. Further scrutiny will show that they are also importantly different in another respect, which is related to the unifying power of their associated theoretical accounts.

2. TWO GENEALOGICAL THOUGHT EXPERIMENTS

Let us begin with Carl Menger's story (Menger 1892). His starting point is the observation that previous explanations of the nature and origin of money have been unsatisfactory. Menger thought that earlier explanations (especially those by Plato, Aristotle and the Roman jurists), according to which money was created by convention or legal act, were completely off the mark. His reason to reject the older accounts is that if there had been a legal act or a conventional decision to make a metal or other kind of stuff a universal medium of exchange, the enactment would have been retained in mankind's historical records, especially since it could only have happened in a number of places at the same time. Given that there is no evidence of such an explicit convention or legal act, Menger's question is: Could money have arisen spontaneously?

His answer is (of course), yes! This judgement is based on a fictional story that revolves around men who engage in certain economic acts arising out of pure self-interest. The story begins with men "awaking . . . to an understanding of the economic advantages . . . of . . . opportunities of exchange" (Menger 1892, 242). If farmer A has chickens and farmer B has cows, presumably, they could both gain if A gives some of his eggs to B and gets some of B's milk in return. But there is an immediate problem: People tend not to have exactly complementary needs. Thus, it is rarely the case when two parties come together to exchange goods that the first party has exactly the kind of good and the amount that the second requires and vice versa. A, for example, could not come to a successful agreement with B if B, on that day, had already been visited by C, an exchange with whom has already satisfied B's need of eggs, even though B does have other unsatisfied needs and can "pay" for their satisfaction with his excess milk.

Menger then observes that different goods have a different degree of saleability (*Absatzfähigkeit*). Goods are saleable to a greater or lesser degree depending on the ease with which they can be disposed of at a market at a *convenient time* and the *going economic price*. These two qualifications are necessary because almost everything could be sold in a market if the seller had world enough and time (that is, if he could either reduce the asking price sufficiently or wait sufficiently long). Unfortunately, Menger does not say much about what constitutes an "economic price" but we can understand it, roughly, as the price a good would achieve in a market exchange were market imperfections absent.[2]

It follows that someone who brings a highly saleable good to the market in order to exchange it for some definite good has some advantage. If the seller is not in that favourable position and brings a good with a low degree of saleability to the market, he will seek, first, to exchange his good for a more saleable good if he cannot find a trade partner for the good he ultimately seeks: "By so doing he certainly does not attain at once the final object of his trafficking, to wit, the acquisition of goods needful *to himself.* Yet he draws nearer to that object" (Menger 1892, 248).

The more people act in this way, the more agreement will emerge as to what goods have a high degree of saleability. Finally:

> And so it has come to pass, that as man became increasingly conversant with these economic advantages, mainly by an insight become traditional . . . those commodities, which . . . are most saleable, have in every market become the wares, which it is not only in the interest of every one to accept in exchange for his own less saleable goods, but which also are those he actually does readily accept. (Menger 1892, 248)

Money has therefore emerged as the good that is most useful as a "standard of exchange." Let me highlight a few points about Menger's thought experiment which, according to Gerald O'Driscoll, constitutes "a fundamental and enduring contribution to economics" (O'Driscoll 1986, 601).

First, methodological individualism plays an important role. Men are portrayed as selfish actors, pursuing nothing but their own material self-interest.

A social institution is fully explained in terms of individuals' behaviour and the constraints they face in mutually advantageous exchanges.

Second, money is an *unintended consequence* of these individuals' actions. Money has come into existence not by deliberate decision, not by convention, legal act, or fiat, but unthinkingly. In Friedrich Hayek's terms, money is a *spontaneous order*.

Third, the main function of money is to facilitate exchanges. Money is a good as any other, but one that can be exchanged for others with greater ease. The thought experiment establishes both what money *is*—a good— and what money *is for*—to facilitate exchanges.

Fourth, historical accuracy is no goal of the thought experiment whatsoever. To ask, for instance, where and when the process Menger describes has taken place would mistake the nature of the thought experiment. It establishes the *nature* and *functional origin* of money, not its historical origin.

I would like to contrast Menger's thought experiment with one that also aims to establish the origin of money, albeit from a radically different perspective. The thought experiment occurs at the heart of the theory of property economics, a heterodox economic theory developed by the German sociologist Gunnar Heinsohn and his economist colleague Otto Steiger (e.g., Heinsohn and Steiger 2008).

This thought experiment is loosely based on the legend of the founding of Rome by Romulus and Remus. Heinsohn and Steiger ask us to imagine that Romulus and Remus kill their noble stepfather Aemulius in order to found their own city. (The killing is a metaphor that stands for serfs overthrowing their feudal lords.) After dethroning Aemulius, the younger brother, Romulus, divides the land—Aemulius' estate—into equal plots and gives it to his comrades-in-arms.

With this act, the socioeconomic structure has fundamentally changed. Under feudalism, most people were unfree, with serfs dependent on a feudal lord. Serfs had duties such as the payment of fees and taxes in the form of appropriate labour. There was no private property. A serf only owned "his own belly"; everything else, including the serf's clothes, could be taken by the feudal lord without legal act. But there were benefits too: The lord had to protect his serfs from criminals or other lords and give them rations should their own product be insufficient. The killing of Aemulius overthrew this social order. People became free and the owners of an equal plot of land. But with this freedom comes responsibility: Since there is no lord to give rations in times of hardship, the free citizens have to protect themselves economically.

For this purpose, the plot of land they are allocated is crucial. Since every man is allocated an equal plot (independently of location, condition, and quality), harvests will differ between owners, for instance, because of different amounts of sun and shade, because of floods or simply because the fertility of the ground differs. Not every owner will, at the end of a harvest period, have enough to sustain himself and his family. Those in need will go to those with excess yields and ask for credit in the form of grain (or some other useful good). Those who are in the position to loan grain will do so only against security. To that effect borrowers can use their land. They make a contract with the lender specifying (a) the sum of the loan (principal), (b) the interest rate, and (c) the amount of land the borrower will have to convey to the lender in case of default. The interest rate initially plays the role of compensating the lender for his liquidity risk: Instead of loaning the grain, he could store it as reserve in case hardship befalls him.

The borrower now has grain but he cannot consume it because he has to pay it back at the end of a year with interest rate. He will therefore use it to produce. But of course, the quality of his land is still the same as last year when it did not yield sufficiently to support him and his family. He will therefore have to try harder—for instance, by innovating (such as inventing the plough and thereby making his land more productive).

Soon lenders will discover that there is no need to loan grain or other goods:

> The creditor learns fast to work with two documents. Thus, he does not lend barley another time but rather a document no. 1 (money) against charging his barley field (property), which he uses at the same time (possession), i.e., sows and harvests. This process he records in a document no. 2 (credit contract), in which the debtor, the collateral, the credit sum and the interest rate are designated. (Heinsohn and Steiger 2008: 97–98, my translation)

By this act money is created. It is a claim to a lender's property. Everyone will accept it as means of payment (as with debtors to other farmers and to buy grain or other goods, for instance) because the lender is well known to have excess yields, so money holders know they can always exchange the money for goods. The important mechanism is however the backing of the money by the creditor's *property*.

Let me make some observations about this thought experiment that parallel the ones made above.

First, in this thought experiment, money is a fundamentally *social* institution. It depends on a whole network of social arrangements such as private property, contracts, and the enforcement of the rule of law.

Second, money is a deliberate invention. It does not arise as an unintended consequence of another economic act such as the exchange of goods but rather is created on purpose in a debt contract.

Third, money is not a good but a claim to the money issuer's property.[3] Its function is not to facilitate the exchange of goods but to facilitate the creation and payment of a credit contract.

Fourth, the only characteristic this thought experiment has in common with Menger's is that there is no claim to historical accuracy. Heinsohn and Steiger intentionally have mythical figures such as Romulus and Remus (or Theseus, the mythical founder of Athens, in a different version of the story) playing central roles in their thought experiments so the reader does not misconstrue it as a report of an actual historical episode.

3. A KUHNIAN FUNCTION FOR GENEALOGICAL THOUGHT EXPERIMENTS

In the literature on thought experimentation, various functions for thought experiments have been supposed. James Robert Brown, for example, distinguishes negative or destructive, positive or constructive, and "Platonic" thought experiments (Brown 2011). As the name suggests, a negative or destructive thought experiment aims to refute a scientific theory. Lucretius, for example, has shown that space cannot be finite. If there is a purported boundary to the universe, we can toss a spear at it. If the spear flies through, it isn't a boundary after all; if the spear bounces back, then there must be something beyond the supposed edge of space, a cosmic wall that stopped the spear, a wall that is itself in space. Either way, there is no edge of the universe.

A positive or constructive thought experiment aims to establish a scientific theory. The Flemish mathematician and engineer Simon Stevin, for instance, proved the law of the equilibrium on an inclined plane using a diagram showing a rope containing evenly spaced beads draped over an inclined plane.

Platonic thought experiments combine the two virtues. They refute an old theory and establish a successor in one fell swoop. Galileo's thought experiments about falling bodies, for example, demonstrates at the same time that the Aristotelian theory according to which heavy balls fall at a greater speed than light ones is false and that Galileo's theory according to which all objects fall at the same speed must be true.

Menger's and Heinsohn/Steiger's imaginary constructs are neither negative nor positive and therefore *a fortiori* not Platonic thought experiments. Menger's, for instance, does not show that money was not created by convention or legal act. Rather, he dismisses this older theory upfront on the basis of lack of evidence. Heinsohn and Steiger similarly dismiss alternative monetary theories on grounds other than their thought experiment.

Nor do these thought experiments establish a new theory. Nothing in these thought experiments, for example, would enable us to decide which story to believe. Rather, in order to establish either of these accounts as the true theory of money, empirical evidence would have to be provided.[4]

Thomas Kuhn pointed to a different function of thought experiments (Kuhn 1964 [1977]). Since thought experiments do not produce any new empirical data, he argued, they cannot provide evidence in favour or against a scientific theory. Rather, they help us to reconceptualise empirical phenomena in a better way. Thought experiments nevertheless supply genuine scientific progress because the only way to experience empirical phenomena is through our conceptual schema, so improving our conceptual schema constitutes genuine learning.

Behind Kuhn's analysis of the function of thought experiments is a rejection of the analytic/synthetic dichotomy. According to him, concepts are always loaded with physical implications, and hence their application provides information about the world. This means in turn that there can be a nonlogical tension in a conceptual scheme when it is extended to a new situation in which its physical implications do not pan out. Showing that there is such a nonlogical tension in a conceptual scheme is just what a thought experiment can do. In the cases Kuhn discussed the tension is resolved by splitting a unified concept into several—for example, "speed" into "instantaneous velocity" and "average velocity" (Kuhn 1964 [1977]).

While I think that Kuhn comes closest to describing one important function of our genealogical thought experiments because that function is conceptual, in neither case does the thought experimental situation reveal any tension in our conceptual schema. It is not the case that "money" was previously understood in some way which, when applied to the situations described by Menger or Heinsohn and Steiger, leads to a contradiction that can be resolved by distinguishing money-1 and money-2, say.

Nevertheless, one function of these thought experiments is conceptual. If we were to follow Menger, we would regard money as a good. To use Aristotelian language, money would share the same genus as apples, grains, computers, and cleaning services. It would be differentiated from other goods by its greater degree of exchangeability and its—spontaneous rather than conventional or legal—acceptance as a standard of exchange. Following Heinsohn and Steiger, by contrast, money is a kind of entitlement and therefore shares the same genus as other rights, such as the right to vote or free speech. It differs from other rights in that it is a claim right and thus entails that another person has a duty to the right holder. In particular he has the duty to convey the specified part of his property to the bearer of money.

These conceptual differences are important for empirical tests of the respective theories.[5] For example, Menger-money may exist wherever there is regular exchange. It does not depend on property rights or any other institutions. By contrast, Heinsohn-Steiger-money presupposes these other institutions but does not depend on the presence of any goods exchanges. A society that has money in one framework might not have it in the other, and vice versa.

4. FACTS AND VALUES IN GENEALOGICAL THOUGHT EXPERIMENTS

The conceptual issue is, however, just one function of these thought experiments, and not the most striking one. Another remarkable function is that they *justify the prevalence of certain social institutions by drawing our attention to the social purpose these institutions perform.* Menger's thought experiment can be taken to vindicate the existence of money by making evident that without money people would have much greater difficulty in satisfying their needs. Money is shown to be a valuable social institution because it serves a valuable social purpose: the satisfaction of needs. Similarly, the Heinsohn-Steiger thought experiment can be taken to vindicate the existence of money by making evident that without money people would have much greater difficulty creating and satisfying debt contracts. Debt contracts, in turn, are an important social institution because they enable people to live in freedom from feudal lords (or indeed other command structures such as socialist governments).

It is important to note that this second function for genealogical thought experiments is neither purely factual or scientific nor purely normative or political. The thought experiments can be taken to point to a societal role the institution at hand—money—plays: to facilitate exchange and to facilitate the satisfaction of debt contracts, respectively. This is the factual aspect. But the respective social practices, exchange and satisfaction of debt contracts, are (taken to be) socially desirable. The exchange of goods is, in Menger's account, a good thing because it enables better satisfaction of needs which is a good thing. The satisfaction of debt contracts is a good thing because the system of institutionalised lending and repayment enables people to live in individual freedom. The institution of money inherits the desirability of these underlying social practices, which thereby contributes to justifying it.[6] This is the normative aspect.

Genealogical thought experiments are different from both those thought experiments aimed at establishing a causal effect, which are purely scientific, as well as the more purely political thought experiments one finds in Hobbes or Rawls. A given causal factor does or doesn't make a difference to an outcome of interest, and establishing either involves limited normative commitment.[7]

Hobbes' "state of nature" and Rawls' "veil of ignorance" aim to justify purely normative conclusions. Hobbes aims to justify civil government on the consideration that without it people would live in a state of "war as is of every man against every man" (*Leviathan,* Chapter 13). Rawls aims to justify his two principles of justice on the consideration that people in a certain state of knowledge (a state which, in his view, is the morally relevant state of knowledge) would choose for themselves. Neither aims to point to the societal role an existing institution plays.[8]

In contrast to both, in the genealogical thought experiments, the factual and the normative are entangled. The same piece of reasoning can be used to establish either a factual or a normative conclusion, depending on whether one focuses on the societal role actually played by the institution or on the desirability of the practice that is being facilitated by the institution.

5. THOUGHT EXPERIMENTS: INTUITIVE VERSUS SCIENTIFIC

So far I have emphasised the commonalities between the two genealogical thought experiments. But there is also an important difference. Many readers will find Menger's the more convincing story. Indeed, in it, it is very easy to see how almost inevitable money is as a social institution. Just by engaging in mutually advantageous exchanges of goods and noticing that different goods are exchangeable to a different extent, money emerges without further discretionary intervention. Observing Menger's story with the mind's eye makes one see that a society without money must be one in which there is very little economic activity.

By contrast, the Heinsohn-Steiger thought experiment seems somewhat impervious, complex, and contingent. Many social conditions have to co-occur in order for money to emerge. In turn, one can easily imagine a society without (that kind of) money. For example, one would just have to imagine a ban on using one's possessions as collateral in debt contracts.

And yet, I want to argue that the Heinsohn-Steiger thought experiment is the more scientific one. What the Heinsohn-Steiger thought experiment shows in a dramatic way is that their property economics is a genuine scientific theory—rather than an *ad hoc* pseudo-explanatory hypothesis. I take genuine scientific theories such as Newton's or Darwin's or Einstein's (or even Marx's or Freud's, if we suppress empirical doubts for the moment) not only to provide a conceptual framework within which to think about problems of interest but also a small number of explanatory hypotheses that can be used over and over again in the explanation of a wide range of phenomena. Genuine theories are *surprising* in showing that phenomena once thought to be unrelated in fact share a common origin.

And unlike neoclassicism (or Austrian economics for that matter), Heinsohn and Steiger demonstrate in a short sequence of episodes of mental imagery the interrelation of a wide array of social institutions:

- Individual freedom (independence of tribe/feudal lord): as the very basis for their social theorising; only in a society without feudal lords or other commandeering structures can private property play an important economic role and money arise.
- Private property (a *social* institution): in the role of insurance against bad luck such as an insufficient harvest; it is the analogue of the feudal lord's rations or the tribal society's mutual solidarity.
- Debt and interest: the expressions of the new social relations (relative to the feudal society) between men acting out of individual freedom.
- Money: intimately tied to property as well as debt and interest; it facilitates the creation and satisfaction of debt contracts.
- Innovation: necessary for debtors to honour their contracts; because interest rates force them to always pay back more than they borrowed, they have to be creative in their use of capital.
- Economising/efficiency: unlike in neoclassicism, not an assumption but a consequence of the economic system; debtors economise because they have to fulfil their contracts.
- The market: (at least in part) also a consequence, not a cause of the existence of money; because debtors have to fulfil their contracts, they will produce goods and sell them as profitably as possible.

Menger's theory, by contrast, shows at best that market exchange and money are related. As a consequence, many other prevalent socioeconomic practices have to be explained separately. And they are. Irving Fisher's theory of the interest rate has to do with consumption decisions and not at all with money and exchange. Property does not exist in neoclassicism. Innovation is exogenous. "Maximisation" is assumed rather than explained by the theory. And so on.

Therefore, the most striking feature of this pair of thought experiments is that one but not the other is able to establish what one might call the "theoreticity" of a theory, that is, the ability of the theory to unify and explain a fairly wide range of social practices, to show that these practices are not independent but rather share a common origin.

By demonstrating the theoreticity of the theory of property economics, the thought experiment of course does not provide any evidence that it is also true. It merely shows that if it *were* true it *would* explain a wide range of social phenomena. As I understand it, empirical work on the theory is still outstanding. Nevertheless, the importance of the thought experiment should not be underestimated. Good theory is something social science badly needs. Heinsohn and Steiger have at least shown that their account would fit the bill if it could be supported empirically.

To be sure, I am not claiming here that the standard neoclassical theories or Heinsohn and Steiger's are empirically vacuous because they make mostly conceptual and normative claims as well as claims about possible functional roles performed by social institutions. Clearly, the respective theories have different testable implications. For example, if technological innovation were indeed exogenous, as assumed by most neoclassical accounts, it would be uncorrelated with the business cycle, whereas on the Heinsohn/Steiger account it would be strongly correlated. Thus, even though it would be quite adequate to speak of two different scientific paradigms facing each other here, there are ways to empirically support one but not the other.

What I am claiming is, however, that the genealogical thought experiment is not evidence for the correctness or falsehood of some theoretical account in itself, unlike Brown's "positive" and "Platonic" thought experiments. It plays different roles, not the role of providing empirical support. That role it leaves to the more traditional types of scientific test such as observation and experimentation.

6. CONCLUSIONS

We've now come to a full circle. I began this paper with the observation that a number of inductive methods are not likely to be particularly reliable in economics because we lack the theoretical background knowledge needed to set these methods off. One role theory plays in empirical investigations is nicely illustrated by the two monetary thought experiments: its role in measurement. This is the old Popperian point that scientific investigation always begins with theory because without it we do not know what to look for. We cannot "observe *simpliciter*." If we tried to do so, we could only observe "stuff," not quantities of scientific interest. (This is, incidentally, also the main claim of Bas van Fraassen's talk at PSA 2010 in Montréal, where this paper was written.) The two monetary thought experiments demonstrate vividly that each account says something fundamentally different about what to look for when measuring "money."

The role of theory in empirical applications is of course not limited to measurement. Theory will also help to identify the causal assumptions necessary for methods such as structural equation modelling, multiple regression analysis, instrumental variables, and so on. And it will provide a framework within which to hypothesise mechanisms for causal explanation.

All this cannot be done, or not done properly, when what counts as theory in a science is in fact an impostor. And this is the main lesson to be learned from juxtaposing the two thought experiments: One shows that a theoretical account would have, if it were true, just the right characteristics to be a genuine scientific theory; the other shows that a theoretical account, if it were true, would at best be a local explanatory hypothesis with little scientific value.[9]

NOTES

1. The relevant literature on these points is too vast to even cite a small selection here. For detailed discussions, see Reiss (2008) and Reiss (Forthcoming).
2. Menger explains in a somewhat obscure footnote (1892, 245): "The price of a commodity may be denoted as *uneconomic* on two grounds: (1) in consequence of error, ignorance, caprice, and so forth; (2) in consequence of the circumstance that only a part of the supply is available to the demand, the rest for some reason or other being withheld, and the price in consequence not commensurate with the actually existing economic situation."
3. Heinsohn and Steiger argue, consequently, that paper money precedes coins. Coins in turn were used in intercity trade, when paper claims to an owner's land were impractical. See Heinsohn and Steiger (2008, Ch. 3).
4. To be sure, Heinsohn and Steiger make a beginning of providing such evidence. They argue for instance that an implication of Menger's reasoning is that money is likely to have originated independently in a number of places. By contrast, if their account is correct, it is more likely that money was created only once or very few times and under very specific historical conditions. They believe that historical facts confirm their account against Menger's. A complication in assessing this evidence is that Menger, of course, understands something quite radically different by money than Heinsohn and Steiger.
5. For an account of economic measurement, see Reiss 2001.
6. One might object that one cannot always infer "X is desirable" from "Y is desirable" and "X leads to Y" because X might also lead to Z, which is undesirable and the undesirability of Z outweighs the desirability of Y. Of course, a thought experiment is not a foolproof moral analysis. I would therefore say that the thought experiment *contributes to justifying* the existence of

an institution; that is to say, it justifies the institution insofar as it shows the institution to facilitate a desirable social practice.

7. I say "limited" here because to some extent all scientific work is value-laden: through the choice of research projects, through choice of measurement and experimental methods, through setting evidential standards—for a detailed discussion, see Reiss (Forthcoming, Interlude). The point is that establishing a causal effect doesn't require normative commitments over and above those required for all scientific work. This is different with respect to the genealogical thought experiments which in my view bring in additional normative considerations.

8. To be fair, Hobbes' and Rawls' thought experiments *could* be taken to point to the societal role actual political institutions play and if one did so, they would be parallel to Menger's and Heinsohn/Steiger's. It is not difficult to come up with relevant differences between Menger and Heinsohn/Steiger on the one hand and Hobbes and Rawls on the other—for one, neither has the state of nature ever existed nor can we put people behind the veil of ignorance; by contrast, a moneyless economy is not only conceivable but also actual. What matters for me here is that the political thought experiments aim to establish normative conclusions whereas the genealogical ones aim to establish a conclusion in which facts and values are entangled.

9. I would like to thank Letitia Meynell, Mélanie Frappier, Jim Brown, Ulrich Kühne, Johanna Thoma, John Davis, Harold Kincaid and Don Ross, participants of the 2010 Halifax Workshop on Thought Experiments, the 2010 conference of the International Network of Economic Method at the University of Alabama at Birmingham, and an EIPE seminar at Erasmus University Rotterdam held in September 2010 for invaluable comments and suggestions. Financial support of the Spanish Government (FFI2008–01580 and CONSOLIDER INGENIO CSD2009–0056) is gratefully acknowledged.

REFERENCES

Akerlof, George. 1970. "The Market for 'Lemons': Quality Uncertainty and the Market Mechanism." *Quarterly Journal of Economics* 84 (3): 488–500.

Boland, Lawrence. 2010. "Review Essay: Cartwright on 'Economics'." *Philosophy of the Social Sciences* 40 (3): 530–538.

Brown, James Robert. 2011. *The Laboratory of the Mind: Thought Experiments in the Natural Sciences.* 2nd edition. London: Routledge.

Fogel, Robert. 1964. *Railroads and American Economic Growth.* Baltimore: Johns Hopkins Press.

Heinsohn, Gunnar, and Otto Steiger. 2008. *Eigentumsökonomik.* Marburg: Metropolis.

Kuhn, Thomas S. 1964 [1977]. "A Function for Thought Experiments." In *Mélanges Alexandre Koyré, Vol. II, L'aventure de l'Esprit,* edited by René Taton and I. Bernard Cohen, 307–334. Paris: Hermann. Reprinted in Kuhn, Thomas S. 1977. The Essential Tension, 240–265. Chicago: University of Chicago Press.

Menger, Carl. 1892. "On the Origins of Money." *Economic Journal* 2 (6): 239–255.

Mises, Ludwig von. [1949] 1996. *Human Action.* 4th edition. San Francisco: Fox and Wilkes.

O'Driscoll, Gerald. 1986. "Money: Menger's Evolutionary Theory." *History of Political Economy* 18 (4): 601–661.

Reiss, Julian. 2001. "Natural Economic Quantities and Their Measurement", *Journal of Economic Methodology* 8(2): 287–311.

———. 2008. *Error in Economics*. London: Routledge.

———. Forthcoming. *The Philosophy of Economics*. New York (NY): Routledge.

Schabas, Margaret. 2008. "Hume's Monetary Thought Experiments." *Studies in History and Philosophy of Science* 39: 161–168.

Sugden, Robert. 2000. "Credible Worlds: The Status of Theoretical Models in Economics." Journal of Economic Methodology 7: 1–31.

11 Political Thought Experiments from Plato to Rawls

Nenad Miščević

1. INTRODUCTION

Political thought experiments are a relatively new topic in the literature on thought experiments, whereas thought experimenting in science, linguistics, metaphysics, epistemology, and in areas of ethics that are not (immediately) political has been an object of intense scrutiny.[1] Thought experimenting in political thought has been discussed mainly in connection with one or two authors, John Rawls mainly and to some extent Ronald Dworkin. In this paper I set the goal of attempting to somewhat systematize the approach to this activity, which involves three ambitious subgoals: first, characterize and briefly defend political thought experiments; second, point to two long and prominent traditions of thought-experimental armchair speculation in political philosophy; and third, and most briefly, connect these traditions to similar and historically related efforts in literary fiction or in the borderline areas between literature, political philosophy, and science. The price of this ambition will be extreme sketchiness and the programmatic nature of the proposals, and I apologize for it. My excuse and rationale is that one needs a general framework for thinking about this historically vast topic and even sketching properly such a framework would demand a lot of space (and time). A proposal about the starting point is needed, no matter how programmatic. Political thought experiments (which I shall in the following abridge as "political TEs", using "TE" alone for "thought experiment") are normally concerned with properties of imagined political arrangements, or more abstractly, of principles guiding and structuring them. Should property be common or privately owned? Should all be treated equally, or according to some other rule? I shall take my examples from two great works, Plato's *Republic* and Rawls's *Theory of Justice*. The latter is centered upon the TE of the original position, in which one is famously asked to imagine being behind the veil of ignorance (ignorant of one's various important actual characteristics, like gender, wealth, abilities, and particular preferences), and to judge various principles for organizing a society one is going to live in. The properties thus investigated from the armchair are moral properties in a wide sense, prominent among them justice. In this respect political TEs are a subspecies of ethical TEs, like the Trolley problem (Foot 1967) or Thomson's Violinist (Thomson 1971). On the other hand, their study belongs to political epistemology, the branch of social epistemology concerned with how people come to know (truths) about politics and political life, in particular general truths.

Let me note that the construction of the ideal state in *The Republic* has not been generally recognized as a TE. In his chapter on methodology in *The Republic,* G. Santas (2006) does not mention TE at all, and the recent excellent and authoritative book by Schofield (2006) avoids the term as well. I have managed to find a mention of it as a TE in a book for undergraduates by Martin Cohen, who describes the construction as "a carefully crafted thought experiment" and also notes that the thought-experimental character of it is "less often appreciated" (2005, 2), as he mildly puts it. A paper by Nicholas Smith (2000) does raise the issue, however. Early versions of social contract—in Hobbes, Locke, and Rousseau—have been recognized as TEs (probably thanks to Rawls), but have not been discussed as political TEs at any length.

Here is the plan. In Section 2, I propose a general account of the structure and stages of typical political TEs largely analogous to the structure of TEs in other domains. Section 3 turns to partly historical considerations, discussing the two dominant families of political TEs in the history of Western political thought. The first is the Platonic tradition of ideal states, out of which arguably derives the tradition of utopian thinking continuing in literary fiction as well as in philosophical and narrowly political writing. I shall very briefly try to show that *The Republic* is the common ancestor to the two. Then I pass to the other family of political TEs, that is, the social contract tradition. Surprisingly, it will turn out that literary negative utopias (like, for instance, *Brave New World*) usually deploy crucial philosophical ideas typical of the social contact tradition in criticism of their positive counterparts. Section 4 again combines a historical sketch and a topical-conceptual discussion for and against political TEs, arguing in their favor against the critical tradition from Aristotle to the present day.

2. WHAT DOES A POLITICAL THOUGHT EXPERIMENT LOOK LIKE?

Political TEs conform to a large extent to the pattern of TEs in other domains, like theoretical philosophy and science, with one important difference: The important political TEs are often "macro thought experiments", encompassing a lot of smaller TEs, testing the justice and other moral properties of particular political arrangements, and organizing them into a global political arrangement. (And a similar structure is often found in fictional utopias, positive and negative, in what officially counts as "literature".) This is the hypothesis that I shall try to make plausible in this section.

As I said, my main examples in this section will come from *The Republic* and *The Theory of Justice*. Let us first remind ourselves of Rawls's proposal. He is explicit about his methodology. The original position (encompassing the veil of ignorance) is in his own words a "thought experiment for the purpose of public- and self-clarification" (2001, 17). This "procedure of construction" as Samuel Freeman (2007) usefully describes it, is part and parcel of the social contract tradition. The veil of ignorance is "a natural guide to intuitions" (Rawls 1999, 139), and this instrument gets honed in the course of development of Rawlsian theory. The basic idea is "simply to make vivid to ourselves the restrictions that it seems reasonable to impose on arguments for principles of justice, and therefore on these principles themselves" (1999, 16). Finally, "conditions embodied in the description of the original position are ones that we do in fact accept. Or if we do not, then perhaps we can be persuaded to do so by philosophical reflection" (1999, 19).

For its part, Plato's *Republic* offers the rather famous imaginary scenario of the Ring of Gyges before addressing the main topic of (building) the ideal state. Its imaginary status is explicitly indicated by a speaker's (Glaucon's) appeal to interlocutors to "do the following in thought": "grant to each, the just and the unjust, license and power to do whatever he pleases" and then "observe" them (359c). Then, towards the end of Book II, Socrates invites his interlocutors to observe "in logos" the origin of a *polis,* in order "to see also the origin of justice and injustice in it" (369a). (Later, the same activity will be described as observing "in story [*mythos*]" how the *polis* is developing.) The actual construction of the "story" is guided by appeals to imagination. Socrates invites his interlocutor to imagine an arrangement, for instance the community of goods. The interlocutor does as told, and then is asked whether he thinks the arrangement is just (or useful for the parties, or even merely acceptable). The usual answer is the famous (or notorious) "Oh yes, Socrates!" or "Indeed, Socrates". Then they pass to the next arrangement to be imagined, the community of children. "Would it be just?" "Indeed it would", and so on.

If we accept that each such episode involves a small TE, a "micro-TE", as we might call it, we get the more general recipe. First, imagine each particular scenario representing some given arrangement, and judge whether it is just, convenient, and useful. Repeat the procedure as many times as needed. Of course, some arrangements will be quite encompassing, others more detailed. If the answer to the question of justice is "yes" for each arrangement, and if they fit together, the result is the perfectly just *polis,* the *kallipolis.* If all goes well, the parties to the conversation thus pass from the series of micro-TEs to the macro-TE, the resulting scenario of the *kallipolis.* Comparing Plato to Rawls, we might notice a difference: Rawls's original position is more geared to identifying general principles than particular arrangements, although one might glean some idea of suitable arrangements from the TE.

2.1. The Structure and Stages of a Political Micro-TE

Consider now the particular stages of the TE, starting with the micro-TE. Usually, at stage one, a question is asked about a particular arrangement. For example, Socrates asks whether the community of children is just, thereby prompting his interlocutor, say Adeimantos, to consider or even concretely imagine the scenario. At stage two, the question is understood, one hopes correctly, by the interlocutor. (In *The Republic*, Adeimantos understands the question correctly; he is Plato's brother, after all.) At stage three, we have a tentative conscious production, the building of the "model" of the scenario at the conscious level (for instance, Adeimantos tries to imagine the arrangement and does it to his satisfaction). Notice the exact parallel not only to the usual TEs in moral philosophy (the Trolley problem, Thomson's Violinist) but also to famous TEs in epistemology, metaphysics, and science: The basic structure of imagining plus judging is very much the same. For instance, in the case of the Ship of Theseus, the thinker reasons about a particular duo or trio of ships, and then passes to a general conclusion about the identity through time of typical material things. In the Galilean TE concerning falling bodies, one is asked to imagine two falling bodies, then to imagine them tied together and falling, and is then asked questions about their relative speeds.

One might think that it is the sheer length of the TE in *The Republic* that makes it special, and perhaps dubious. There is, however, at least one protracted TE of comparable size in philosophy of mind from Condillac. In *Treatise on the Sensations* ([1754] 1930), he asks the readers to imagine a "statue" equipped with human-like neural apparatus ("human-like robot", we would say nowadays), initially devoid of any contact with the outside world. Its senses are awakened, one by one, and the reader is asked to imagine the statue's reactions along the way.

If you think the first stages of the TE are a trivial matter, consider the cases in which things do not work so nicely. The debates around Rawls's original position illustrate well this often realized possibility. Rawls is in fact asking the readers to imagine themselves as not knowing their own important characteristics in the final arrangement: You don't know if you will be a woman or a man, dark-skinned or light-skinned, smart or stupid, and so on. But some critics demur at the outset: I don't want to imagine this, the critic replies. For instance, I don't want to abstract from my body, masculine or feminine as the case may be. They find the very requirement of such imaginary ignorance biased and offensive. Carol Pateman famously describes the result of abstraction as a state "with nothing human in it" (1988, 43), and Charles W. Mills (2007) joined her in matters of race.

The fourth stage is more demanding. It concerns the production of the answer, involving the generation of intuition as to whether the arrangement is just or unjust. This probably involves reasoning at the unconscious level. Psychologists talk about a hypothetical moral module, and

Table 11.1 Comparison of Two Thought Experiments

	The Republic	*Galileo's TE*
Stage 1	*The question* Socrates asks whether the community of children is just.	*The question* Would the body composed of a cannon ball and a musket ball fall faster or slower than either the light (musket) or the heavy (cannon) ball?
Stage 2	*Understanding the problem* Adeimantos understands the question correctly.	*Understanding the problem* Question understood.
Stage 3	*Tentative conscious production of the arrangement* Adeimantos tries to imagine the arrangement and does it to his satisfaction.	*Tentative conscious production of the arrangement* Trying to imagine the cannon and the musket ball falling (using naïve physics).
Stage 4	*Possible non-conscious elaboration of the scenario*	*Possible non-conscious elaboration of the scenario*
Stage 5	*Immediate spontaneous answer* Yes, the community of children is just in this case.	*Immediate spontaneous answer* The composite body would be falling both faster and slower than the cannon ball alone.
Stage 6	*Variation and generalization* Can it be applied in any just *polis*?	*Variation and generalization* Is there anything special in the first example? What if we tie a small cork to a heavy stone?
Stage 7	*General belief* All children in every ideally just *polis* should be common to all citizens.	*General belief* The problem generalizes to every combination of falling bodies.

philosophers like Adam Smith have talked about moral sense. So whatever the nature of moral competence in our example, Adeimantos's moral competence mechanism (module) is being asked whether the proposed arrangement is really just. The further analysis of the structure of the unconscious search is best left to psychologists. The possibility that I personally find most plausible is that there is a stage involving an immediate unconscious spontaneous answer. This answer might be the core of the final intuition—the conscious state. Maybe this is not all: There could be an unconscious appeal to memory and then theorizing by some more central, non-modular instance (say, intelligence).[2]

At the fifth stage, we finally encounter explicit intuition at the conscious level, usually geared to the particular example and having little generality ("Yes, Socrates, this is indeed a just arrangement concerning children").

If the consideration of a particular scenario is typical, the thinker will have to do some varying and generalizing (deploying both moral and rational competence) at the conscious and reflective level and, perhaps, at the unconscious one too. Sometimes this process is called intuitive induction (e.g., "What if the children were Spartan or Mycenaean rather than our own kids? Well, it's the same thing: The arrangement is valid for all"). This is our sixth stage.

Stage seven finally brings general belief at the reflective level ("All children in every ideally just *polis* should be common to all citizens"). In the Rawlsian TEs, we mostly jump directly to such general beliefs concerning principles. (When teaching Rawls, a good teacher might go through particular examples before making this jump to the general principle involved in the given scenario.)

Since this is the end of the micro-TE, let us again note the parallel and difference between this case and other theoretical TEs. Table 11.1 gives a summary of the two processes.

In the Galilean TE concerning falling bodies, one starts from a cannon ball and a musket ball, and jumps to an extremely general conclusion about the implausibility of Aristotelian kinematics. In the case of the Ship of Theseus, the thinker reasons about a particular duo or trio of ships before she passes to a general conclusion about identity through time of typical material things. However, an important difference remains: Theoretical TEs go from the world to mind, whereas to a large extent political TEs propose to go from mind to world, even if their goal is epistemic (i.e., to find objective Good, the Just, etc.). They often cry for implementation, in contrast to the purely theoretical TEs.

2.2. From Micro- to Macro-TE

We now have to consider the "procedure of construction", as Rawls calls it, passing quickly in our examples of a just political arrangement from particular micro-results (intuitions about particular arrangements concerning treatment of people with various qualities) to a global picture. To make things simpler, I will consider together the three components prominent in such a procedure: first, the aggregation of micro-TEs; second, the harmonization of the results of these micro-TEs (about which Rawls says little); and finally, the judgment of their coherence with other moral intuitions we might have. In other words, I will be describing the philosophical unification in terms of narrow reflective equilibrium. This is our stage eight.

Let me call the harmonious unification of micro-TEs "the topical narrow reflective equilibrium" and the final narrow result "the general narrow reflective equilibrium". The former, topical one is geared to the unity of narrative structure, plus the relevance and coherence between particular stages, the micro-TEs. For instance, in *The Republic* Socrates is very careful to integrate the issues of education, in which he is, as philosopher, particularly interested, with the general issue of justice in the *polis*. Small scenarios involving teaching particular skills and areas of knowledge, and arrangements involving teachers and pupils, are harmonized with general considerations of justice and functionality of a part within the whole. Indeed, stressing the functionality of the arrangements is the main strategy for harmonizing. "Are some of the micro-TEs morally relevant at all?" Klampfer asked in one of our discussions. Well, most of them are, and Plato is careful to integrate them into the picture.

We can next pass to the issue of general consistency, independent of particular topics. The search for a balanced whole at this level, for the general narrow equilibrium, is more familiar in the Rawlsian literature. "Are assumptions plausible and relevant?" is an often asked question related to the ideal of such equilibrium. Rawls proposes a methodological maxim: Argue "from widely accepted but weak premises to more specific conclusions. Each of the presumptions should be natural and plausible; some of them may seem innocuous or even trivial" (2001, 29).

Of course, a host of principled issues arises at every step. Here is a famous question from the end of the last century: Is it consistent to have representatives of families as a whole, and in particular, just indeterminate 'heads of families'? Rawls once proposed exactly this option, but his feminist critics, Jean Hampton (2007) and Suzan Okin ([1989] 1999), famously said "No": Since justice is also a concern *within* the family, family members should represent themselves; the opposite view is inequitable and infected by patriarchal bias. Notice the parallels with the discussions of narrow equilibriums in theoretical TEs. For instance, are our linguistic intuitions mutually consistent, and if not, can this be explained by some of them being "infected" by extra-linguistic social considerations and the like? Similarly, a part of the debate about Einstein's TEs in Special Relativity concerned the reliability of spontaneous intuitions, and different ways of interpreting them.

Narrow equilibrium is not sufficient. We want to have an encompassing philosophical view, informed with general knowledge of the matters. So the final stage is the wide reflective equilibrium, bringing in additional empirical information from history, psychology, and social science—or just ordinary experience. In Rawls a delicate question arises: Who would accept the original position, and who would reject it? Some actual historical traditions are friendlier to it; other are not. And this issue dovetails in his *"political liberalism"* with the stability problem: Only if the tradition is friendly will the resulting arrangement be sufficiently stable.

So much about political philosophy in this section, with apologies for sketchiness. Interestingly, one could reconstruct the standard experience of the reader of political fiction, the literary utopias (including dystopias), in roughly the same stages, but involving some literary devices, such as surprise and shock—for example, a utopian collectivist arrangement that sounds nice as presented by the propagandist character. But is it really acceptable? And the readers go through the same process of asking themselves, probing their "moral sense", and in the case of negative utopia coming up with a critical intuition: "No, this arrangement is morally disgusting". Next comes narrative topical equilibrium. Episode after episode matters: Issues, examples, reactions fall into a pattern (the Big Brother turns out not to be a brother at all, the ideology of the "beneficial" state starts showing cracks and contradictions, the hero's superiors start showing their nasty character). The components of the big collective arrangement in the story support each other and the negative judgments about most of them counterbalance the few positive instances. One hopes that personal experience and the factual knowledge of the reader join in, leading her to a wider reflective equilibrium. Of course, literary fiction often leaves questions open, since good fiction is subtle: The best contemporary science-fiction TEs, like Ursula Le Guin's (1974) *The Dispossessed: An Ambiguous Utopia,* incorporate both positive and negative utopian elements. But so do some philosophical utopias; even More's *Utopia*, which has been taken for centuries as a defense of the depicted society, prompts contemporary readers to doubts: Maybe the author is being ironical; maybe the hero, Raphael Hythloday, is an unreliable narrator, and so on. Plato himself has been reinterpreted by Leo Strauss as being sarcastic about the collectivist arrangements he seems to propose. So this presumed difference between philosophical and literary TEs turns out not to be very dramatic. We may then propose that the *fictional relatives of* The Republic *are implicit TEs or at least crucially involve thought experimenting.* We shall try very briefly to support this proposal by pointing to the common ancestry in addition to structural analogies.

3. THE TWO TE-TRADITIONS

We have characterized the main line of the conversation in Plato's *Republic* as involving a series of small TEs, to be integrated into the large whole of the scenario of the ideal city, helping the interlocutors to understand the nature of justice. Given this ethical context, there is no wonder that in *The Republic* Plato introduces a broadly ethical TE, the Ring of Gyges, before embarking upon the ambitious project of building a state in the armchair. Then the question about the nature of justice is answered by "observing in the *logos* how a city comes into being". The word *logos* has been translated as "theory", "thought", "discourse", and in other ways. In other places Plato uses the terms from the *mythos* family (e.g., 2.376d), stressing the narrative character of the construction, but perhaps also ironically connecting it to his famous philosophical "myths". This whole terminological complex merits a detailed discussion, which unfortunately we have to eschew here.

It is important to note how careful Plato is when moving to the bigger picture; for instance, he explicitly integrates his favorite topic of education with the issue of justice, preserving connectedness and coherence at every step, asking how are they (i.e. guardians) to be reared and educated? Is not this an enquiry which may be expected to throw light on the greater enquiry which is our final end—How do justice and injustice grow up in States? for we do not want either to omit what is to the point or to draw out the argument [*logos*] to an inconvenient length. Come then, and let us pass a leisure hour in story-telling [*mythologountes*], and our story [*logos*] shall be the education of our heroes. (376e)

The quotation is revealing both in its constructive intent, and in the use of both *mythos-* and *logos-*derived terms for the philosophical activity to which the interlocutor is invited. We already pointed to the method: Find or construct a system of arrangements, each of which appears just to the interlocutor, and let him conclude that the system itself is just, finding what is characteristic of the system: This is then "the just". The further goal might be motivational: implementing the system as far as possible.

Let me here note an obvious feature of *The Republic:* It is a dialogue of experts about some third persons (imaginary or future real ones), who are to be citizens of the imagined *polis*. Not only are the vast majority of them, all of the workers and most warriors at least, not going to be consulted about their political wishes; if there is a danger that they might not accept the arrangement, they should be (epistemically) manipulated with the help of a noble lie about their origin and characters (the three metals out of which humans are made). But this is in their own interest; the construction offers the best option for all.

The resulting perfectly just *polis*, the *kallipolis*, is presented as a good place to live in, the best in fact. Thomas More helped with the name: the successful macro-TE results in a utopia. It seems that the Platonic TE is the common ancestor to the philosophical and fictional utopian heritage. We should now briefly compare it to the second major tradition of political TE, the social contract.

The present day contractarianism, inspired by Rawls, sees social contract as a hypothetical construction, a straightforward TE. The student consulting the entry entitled "Original Position" in the *Stanford Encyclopedia* learns that it is "a hypothetical situation designed to uncover the most reasonable principles of justice" (Freeman 2009). She also gets informed about Rawls's reading of its history, according to which "the major advocates of social contract doctrine—Hobbes, Locke, Rousseau, and Kant—all regarded the social contract, as a hypothetical event". The formulation is suitably ambiguous (I don't know whether intentionally), and captures well the oscillations in the classical texts: Sometimes social contract is seen as the best explanatory hypothesis, propounded to explain the actual history of human social life, narrating a presumably real but undocumented event, and sometimes as being merely hypothetical, as in Chapter 17 of Spinoza's *Political Treatise*, in the sense of construction in the armchair, not pretending to concern any actual historical event. (Mélanie Frappier has correctly noted that this ambiguity is also found in scientific TEs, and that this dual status is unfortunately not well understood.) Hobbes and Locke sometimes press for the "explanatory hypothesis" version, whereas Rousseau is more clearly on the construction-in-the-armchair side. In Book I, Chapter VI of his *Social Contract* (1968) he famously describes a contract as the solution to a major intellectual task, that is, to find a form of association that would reconcile the cohesion of the community with the maximal freedom of each of its members. In the posthumously published draft of the first, later excised, methodological chapter of *The Social Contract*, he states explicitly in relation to the idea of the contract: "I am not interested in facts, but in the right and reason". Kant is even more explicit: "Properly speaking, the original contract is only the idea of this act, in terms of which alone we can think of the legitimacy of a state" (1992, 131).[3]

Here is an important feature of the social contract which can be contrasted with the Platonic-utopian tradition. The social contract rests on the agreement of the parties, and the development from Hobbes through Kant to Rawls puts increasing demands on conditions under which the agreement is made. Jeremy Waldron summarizes well the Lockean phase in stating that "as Locke puts it, 'no-one can be . . . subjected to the Political Power of another, without his own Consent'. The setting up of political institutions by force, or the setting up or altering of institutions in a way that everyone could not possibly agree to, has no effect whatever so far as the establishment of obligation or political legitimacy are concerned" (1994, 69). The contract is (imaginatively) made from the first person standpoint, and the agreement has to be fully voluntary, not from fear or blind obedience, but reflective and guided by correct information about the arrangement itself. Liberty and equality are built into the very presuppositions of the TE. This points to an invidious contrast with Plato. As we mentioned, *The Republic* is a TE from the third person point of view, in which philosophers and their friends and relatives talk about arrangements for warriors and workers. The social contract, in contrast, is a first-person TE: "Would I myself sign this contract?" is the canonical form of the question, pointing to the background of basic equality and dignity. It has far reaching consequences: the need for the noble lie in the case of the third person Platonic TE versus transparency in the case of the first-person social contract TE.

Let me end with a brief hypothesis, to be verified on some other occasion. It might seem that negative utopias are just another part of the Platonic-utopian tradition, featuring imaginary scenarios full of negative characteristics. However, the actual famous representatives—Orwell's, Huxley's, and Zamyatin's scenarios—all converge on the condemnation of the nonvoluntary, manipulation-supported character of the political arrangements they depict. Each of them can be read as the critique of utopia from the viewpoint of the basic dignity of human beings (and the attendant ideals of equality and liberty) that forbids epistemic manipulation. Negative utopias thus seem to be a kind of contrary intuition-pump, correcting the limitation of the original utopian thought experiment, from the viewpoint of ideals grounding the contract tradition. The two TE-traditions, Platonic-utopian and contractarian thus meet at a most unexpected point: in the negative-utopian criticism of the nonliberal character of the traditional positive utopia.

Once we agree to see the utopian tradition and the negative utopian reaction as part of the tradition of political thought experimenting, we notice how large and central the tradition is. Plato's work is surely central for ancient political thought, inspiring Stoic and neo-Platonic political treatises (see Vogt 2008 and O'Meara 2003 for excellent overviews and analyses). The social contract tradition in turn is of central importance for modernity. Add the positive and negative utopias, and the extent of the tradition grows beyond expectation, if not beyond belief. However, there is more. A lot of remaining great work in political philosophy is to some extent characterizable as a reaction to the TE-tradition, together with its positive utopian (and negative) outgrowths. To this reaction, and to the crucial issues it raises, we now turn.

4. POLITICAL TES—FOR AND AGAINST

As a warm up, consider the historical beginnings of the debate. "It is proper, no doubt to assume ideal conditions, but not to go beyond all bounds of possibility", famously writes Aristotle (in *Politics*, II.1265a, 18), criticizing Plato's proposal(s). His discussion is the first and paradigmatic criticism of a major political TE. The main criticism turns around the contrast of close and distant possibilities, closer to the impossible than to the reasonably possible.

Let me briefly illustrate the historical discussion. Miller indicates in this context Aristotle's subtle distinctions concerning realistic possibilities of attaining an optimal condition by pointing out that

> the role of ideals in Aristotelian statecraft, . . . may be explained in terms of two principles. The first is the principle of approximation: "While it is clearly best for any being to attain the real end, yet, if that cannot be, the nearer it is to the best the better will be its state" (*De Caelo* II.12 292b, 17–19; cf. *Generation and Corruption* II.10 336b, 25–34). (Miller 2009, 541–542)

Machiavelli went a step beyond Aristotle; in his more Machiavellian or "realist" mood he criticizes speculations about what people should do, in contrast to the study of what they really do. For him it is "more appropriate to follow up the real truth of the matter than the imagination of it" (*The Prince*, Ch. XV). Other Renaissance thinkers, more sympathetic to Plato, nevertheless did not give him full support: "Even humanists who defended Plato . . . admitted that the 'celestial polity' described in the *Republic*, while it might have some value as an ideal for saints or unfallen men, could certainly not be regarded as a blueprint for human society in its present state" (Hankins 1996, 124). The Platonic TE has been criticized ever since for its reliance upon imagination and distant possibilities.

The reader probably notes at this juncture the parallel with theoretical TEs; indeed, the debate between the friends and the foes of the armchair in political philosophy reminds one of the debates in theoretical philosophy, including philosophy of science. But there is a second point to be made, which is more speculative. Indeed, a history of TEs in political philosophy would take a book, so any generalizations at this point are clearly premature. Still, a TE enthusiast might venture an ambitious hunch: *Much of the history of political thought can be systematized from the methodological standpoint in terms of pro-TE and anti-TE attitudes, a debate for and against the use of armchairs in political thinking.* There are in Western thought two dominant political TE-traditions: the Platonic approach of *The Republic*—and the subsequent positive (and negative) utopias—and the social contract version. They fiercely debate each other and there is an impressive train of their critics, from left, center, and right. It starts from Aristotle's criticism as the first and typical negative reaction against presumably unrealistic political TEs and goes all the way to Popper, who famously saw Plato's *Republic* as a "piece of propaganda for his totalitarian state", promoting totalitarian "social engineering" (1945, 92). On the left, one has Engels's view of a communist ideal traveling "From Utopia to Science", and a tradition of pro- and anti-utopian reading of the basic texts, Marxist and/or anarchist.

Since early modern times the Platonic-utopian TE-tradition has been joined by the social contract TE-tradition, accompanied by its unfriendly tradition of criticism (starting with Hume, Burke, and Hegel on the right and Marx on the left). Let us now turn to the question of the reliability of political TEs.

In short, there are two major and conflicting methodological options concerning political TEs. The first, in favor of the armchair, claims that they are essential given the complexity of social life, and that imagining relatively distant possibilities teaches us about what is morally required, by separating in imagination the morally relevant from irrelevant aspects that cannot be so clearly separated in empirical research bogged down in actual contingent details of historically given political arrangements. The opposite view points to serious problems with TEs: Besides the general issue of the possible unreliability of one's political imagination, and the irrelevance of distant possibilities which border on the impossible, there is the problem of selection. When depicting the scenario to be imagined, one has to import various assumptions, in which one is necessarily selective. Plato notoriously imports the need for relative luxury and richness in his *polis*, and the consequent need for a strong standing army of guardians, that then becomes central for the whole TE. We mentioned Rawls not being sufficiently explicit about the status of women and the issues of "race" and the criticisms this has provoked, which together suggest that he unintentionally imported untenable assumptions about the functioning of society into his TE. Each great philosopher imports some assumptions (or forgets to import others that his critical readers find essential). Finally, since political TEs are a subspecies of ethical TEs, they might have the same weaknesses that have been explored by experimental philosophers and others: vulnerability to the contingent workings of the emotional system, cultural relativity, extreme sensibility to framework (e.g., formulation) effects, and the like.

My own preferences are for the first option: in favor of political TEs. In science the armchair plays a crucial role (controlled by other devices, from microscopes to telescopes), so why not in political philosophy? Could moral philosophy exist without TEs, my kind commentator Mélanie Frappier asked. And we both have a hunch that it could not. But what about the above worries? Well, the controlling devices are available here as well, and they enter the wide reflective equilibrium; the factual knowledge about discrimination and inequality we mentioned above should be kept in mind in social contract TEs and one can think of analogous devices for different topics.

Both kinds of problems, modal distance and the arbitrariness of selection, are to be encountered elsewhere in philosophy and even science: Think of the parallel with physics, and Galileo's conflict with the Aristotelians. Is the combination of the musket ball and a cannon ball in Galileo's TE a unitary (falling) body at all, Tamar Gendler asked. Why assume it is, if you are trying to refute Aristotle on his own ground; he would have been more inclined to deny or devaluate the unity of the composite body? The selection problem arises in most domains. Think of Jackson's black-and-white Mary TE (1982). How did Mary's color receptors develop, asked Churchland (2004); if you import the assumption that they developed somehow, you can as well import the assumption that she already knows how it feels to see red. There is an element of virtue and an element of luck here: Some assumptions turn out, with hindsight, to have been correct, or at least not misleading, while others prove catastrophic. If the present picture is on the right track and if political TEs are central for political philosophy, then we get a more unified view: Political philosophy is methodologically like other areas of philosophy and science. Schofield is right in stressing that "The picturing of alternative possibilities is . . . a fundamental human activity, and something we all of us engage in virtually all the time" (2006, 210).

5. CONCLUSION

Let us then summarize and conclude. In this paper we have offered a tentative and programmatic sketch concerning the nature and importance of political TEs. We have presented them as an important subspecies of ethical TEs, having to do with justice and justice-related qualities of political arrangements and principles governing them. We have pointed out that political TEs are often macro-TEs, encompassing a series of micro-TEs (ideally) arranged into a coherent whole. Such a series is often presented in a narrative, the strategy that has almost certainly inspired the utopian tradition closer to fictional writing. (Why narrative? Perhaps the political philosopher is aiming at a wider audience than her colleague who is only proposing a macro-TE about human mind, as Condillac for instance did, but perhaps there is a deeper, more systematic reason.) We have briefly considered the commonalities and differences between the two major political TE-traditions, taking Plato's *Republic* both as the common historical ancestor and the common topical source of inspiration of the authors of the two traditions. We have briefly stressed the commonalities between political TEs and TEs in other areas: from the nonpolitical ethical TEs to the purely theoretical ones in various other branches of philosophy, like metaphysics and epistemology, and in science, from physics to linguistics. In particular, we have presented a picture of the different stages of a typical political TE, which, particularly at the level of individual micro-TEs, resembles its purely theoretical philosophical and scientific cousins. Very often, the typical problems are analogous across domains. The unification suggested by this picture would be an important asset once it is properly developed in detail.

Next we have formulated, in a very tentative spirit, a few hypotheses about the actual history of political thought, leaving the arduous scholarly task of confirming or disconfirming them for the future. The modest hypothesis is that TEs have been central for political philosophy and theory, since the two central sources of Western political thought are the Platonic and the social contract traditions, the first being prominent in Antiquity and the Middle Ages, with interesting outgrowth in later times, and the second being prominent in modern times, from Hobbes to Rawls. We pointed to an interesting and politically significant contrast between the two TE-traditions. We also argued that political TEs organize a big swath of the history of political thought, and so suggested that, with regard to methodology, much more attention should be paid to such armchair strategies. The more ambitious hypothesis would connect the two clearly philosophical TE-traditions, the Platonic and the social contract approaches, with their positive-utopian and negative-utopian outgrowths, from More, Campanella, and Harrington to authors like Fourier and Owen all the way to clearly literary-fictional utopias, for instance the negative ones of Orwell and Zamyatin and the "ambiguous" one of Ursula Le Guin. Finally, our most ambitious hypothesis would be that, from a methodological standpoint, one of the central epistemological contrasts in the history of Western political thought (or even *the* central one, marking the whole of political epistemology) is the one existing between pro-TE and anti-TE attitudes, stances for and against the use of the armchair in political thinking. I find the modest hypothesis of the central role of TEs very plausible and the more ambitious hypothesis clearly worthy of consideration, whereas I prefer to remain agnostic, at least officially, about the third and most ambitious one.

Here is a task for the future: Since TEs are central for other areas of philosophy and for some traditions in fictional writing, once we put the big picture together, we'll get a more unified view of the whole, which could help us to integrate the methodology of political philosophy with methodology of philosophy in general, and finally contribute to a deeper understanding of fictional-literary thought experimenting.

NOTES

1. Thanks go to Mélanie Frappier, Fridi Klampfer, Nicholas Smith, Ana Smokrović, Miomir Matulović, Jim Brown, Danilo Šuster, and Tea Logar.
2. For a detailed discussion of these matters (and a fine bibliography) see the brilliant short book by Kwame Anthony Appiah (2008), *Experiments in Ethics*.
3. Some of his contemporary interpreters also propose the view, which I find correct, but will not discuss here, that his Categorical Imperative also enjoins thought experimenting (see Timmermann 2007, 45, 53, 74, 107 and Kerstein 2006, 320). That would unify the methodology of Kant's moral and political philosophy, organizing it around the TE-paradigm.

REFERENCES

Appiah, K. A. 2008. *Experiments in Ethics.* Cambridge, MA: Harvard University Press.

Churchland, Paul. 2004. "Knowing Qualia: A Reply to Jackson (with Postscript 1997)." In *There's Something about Mary*, edited by Peter Ludlow, Yujin Nagasawa, and Daniel Stoljar, 163–178. Cambridge, MA: MIT Press.

Cohen, M. 2005. *Wittgenstein's Beetle and Other Classical Thought Experiments.* Oxford: Blackwell.

Condillac, E. B. de. [1754] 1930. *Treatise on the Sensations.* London: The Favil Press.

Foot, Philippa. 1967. "The Problem of Abortion and the Doctrine of Double Effect." *Oxford Review* 5: 5–15.

Freeman, S. 2007. *Rawls.* New York: Routledge.

———. 2009. "Original Position." *The Stanford Encyclopedia of Philosophy* (Spring 2009 edition), edited by Edward N. Zalta. http://plato.stanford.edu/archives/spr2009/entries/original-position (accessed November 24, 2011).

Hampton, J. 2007. *The Intrinsic Worth of Persons. Contractarianism in Moral and Political Philosophy.* Cambridge: Cambridge University Press.

Hankins, J. 1996. "Humanism and Modern Political Thought." In *The Cambridge Companion to Renaissance Humanism*, edited by J. Kraye, 118–141. Cambridge: Cambridge University Press.

Jackson, F. 1982. "Epiphenomenal Qualia." *Philosophical Quarterly* 32: 127–136.

Kant, I. 1992. *Metaphysics of Morals.* Translated by M. Gregor. Cambridge: Cambridge University Press.

Kerstein, S. J. 2006. "Deriving the Formula of Universal Law." In *A Companion to Kant*, edited by Graham Bird, 308–321. Oxford: Blackwell Publishers.

Le Guin, U. 1974. *The Dispossessed: An Ambiguous Utopia*. New York: Harper and Row.

Miller, F. D. 2009. "Aristotle on the Ideal Constitution" (doi: 10.1002/9781444305661.ch34). In *A Companion to Aristotle*, edited by G. Anagnostopoulos. Oxford: Willey-Blackwell.

Okin, S. M. [1989] 1999. *Justice, Gender, and the Family*. New York: Basic Books.

O'Meara, D. J. 2003. *Platonopolis. Platonic Political Philosophy in Late Antiquity*. Oxford: Clarendon Press.

Pateman, C. 1988. *The Sexual Contract*. Stanford, CA: Stanford University Press.

Pateman, C., and C. W. Mills. 2007. *Contract and Domination*. Cambridge: Polity.

Pogge, T. 1989. *Realizing Rawls*. Ithaca, NY, and London: Cornell University Press.

Popper, K. 1945. *The Open Society and Its Enemies*. Volume 1: *The Spell of Plato*. London: Routledge.

Rawls, J. 1999. *A Theory of Justice*. Rev. edition. Cambridge, MA: Harvard University Press.

———. 2001. *Justice as Fairness: A Restatement*. Edited by E. Kelly. Cambridge, MA: Harvard University Press.

Rousseau, J. J. 1968. *The Social Contract*. New York: Penguin Classics.

Santas, G. 2006. "Methods of Reasoning about Justice." In *The Blackwell Guide to Plato's* Republic, edited by G. Santas, 125–145. Oxford: Willey-Blackwell.

Schofield, M. 2006. *Plato: Political Philosophy*. Oxford: Oxford University Press.

Smith, N. 2000. "Images, Education, and Paradox in Plato's *Republic*." In *Recognition, Remembrance, and Reality: New Essays on Plato's Epistemology and Metaphysics*, 126–140. Supplement to *Apeiron* 33.

Thomson, J. J. 1971. "A Defense of Abortion." *Philosophy and Public Affairs* 1: 47–66.

Timmermann, J. 2007. *Kant's Groundwork of the Metaphysics of Morals: A Commentary*. Cambridge: Cambridge University Press.

Vogt, K. M. 2008. *Law, Reason, and the Cosmic City*. Oxford: Oxford University Press.

Waldron, J. 1994. "John Locke: Social Contract versus Political Anthropology." In *The Social Contract from Hobbes to Rawls*, edited by D. Boucher and P. Kelly. New York: Routledge.

12 Thought Experiment, Definition, and Literary Fiction

Geordie McComb

Imagine that at a point deep in space a cable accelerates an elevator upwards at a constant rate. A scientist trapped inside wants to find out whether the elevator is accelerating. So he releases a ball, which falls to the floor just as it should if the elevator is indeed accelerating. Does he now know that it is accelerating? Einstein answers in the negative because, roughly, for all the scientist knows the elevator is hanging at rest near the Earth's surface and the ball falls due to gravity. Einstein took this to be good grounds for what is effectively the equivalence principle of the General Theory of Relativity (Einstein 2009, 80–83; Einstein and Infeld 1938, 230–235).

You might readily recognize this to be a thought experiment—and, like James Robert Brown, think that with a few examples like it we can identify other thought experiments, no need for a definition (2011, 1). We do well to employ this method in many cases—but not all. Is, for instance, Orwell's *1984* a thought experiment? Styron's *Sophie's Choice?* To work this out, we need some readily recognizable examples. The only uncontroversial ones are, at present, found in philosophy and physics broadly construed. So they differ in many ways from cases like *1984* and *Sophie's Choice*. To tell whether these differences preclude such cases from being thought experiments, we seem to need a principle. But we can have no such thing, for we are to get by on examples alone.

You might instead look to identify thought experiments with a sharp definition, one with ordinary necessary and sufficient conditions. But nothing adequate is easily found. Consider, for example, Ronald Laymon's definition:

> A *thought experiment* is an ordered pair $<\Phi, \vartheta>$ where Φ is a set of persons (audience and/or presenter) and ϑ is a set of statements $\{T, P_1, P_2, \ldots P_n, Q\}$ where:
>
> (1) T is a description that is not in fact true (because it is idealized) of any experiment in this world.
> (2) Members of Φ believe that $P_1, P_2, \ldots P_n$ are scientific laws or principles.
> (3) Members of Φ believe that $\exists x(Tx)$ & $P_1, P_2, \ldots P_n \rightarrow Q$. (1991, 168)

Wisely, Laymon himself implies that abstract definitions like this "tend to be neither interesting nor helpful" (1991, 168).[1]

Faced with the Scylla of employing a sharp definition like this one, and the Charybdis of relying solely on examples, I aim in this paper to introduce and motivate a non-sharp definition. It will say, in slogan form, that "thought experiment" connotes a cluster concept we apply to varying extents. After developing this definition in Section 1, I attempt to motivate it in Section 2 by indicating two of its explanatory virtues. One concerns the light it sheds—compared to the views of Edward Davenport, Catherine Elgin, and David Davies—on the relation between certain literary fictions and thought experiments. The other is that it provides for a promising account of some disagreements about what counts as a thought experiment.

1. THE DEFINITION

1.1. Groundwork

Wittgenstein begins his well-known discussion of family resemblance with the claim that we call some phenomena "language," not because they share any common features, but because they stand in certain differing relations (1958, §§65–67). To illustrate these relations, he notes that the phenomena we call "games" have nothing in common that could explain why we call them "games." They do not all involve, for instance, winning and losing, competition between players, or amusement. Rather, we call them "games," he thinks, because they stand in a network of "family resemblances," of overlapping and crisscrossing similarity relations with each other at different levels of generality.

A nominal definition of the word "game" might tell us that it connotes a certain "cluster concept"—that is, a concept we rightly apply to the objects we do, at least in part, because they stand in a certain network of family resemblances.[2] To illustrate, suppose a given definition of "game" associates it with a certain concept, one we apply to games, and only games, in virtue of two facts: First, they have common properties, such as being proceedings; and second, they stand in a particular network of family resemblances, one which involves such things as winning and losing, competition between players, and amusement. If so, we rightly apply this concept to each of the objects we do *at least in part* because they stand in that network of family resemblances. As such, by my lights, the concept would be a cluster concept.

Let us enrich this idea in two ways. First, add to the preceding suppositions that we *rightly* apply this cluster concept to Monopoly but not the CN Tower. To explain this, you might say that Monopoly, unlike the CN Tower, has a high enough ratio of relevant family resemblances, such as involving competition between players, to relevant family dissimilarities, such as being a tall narrow building. In doing so, you might rely on the principle that, if we apply a cluster concept to an object, we do so *rightly* if and only if that object has a high enough ratio of "relevant family resemblances to dissimilarities"—that is, if and only if that object stands in enough of those relations which comprise the network associated with the cluster concept, and which contribute to the object being what it is, relative to others not in this network.

Second, suppose, in addition, that we rightly apply the concept to Monopoly, Solitaire, and Russian Roulette. Suppose as well that Monopoly differs from Solitaire and Russian Roulette, with regard to the relevant family resemblances and dissimilarities, in only two ways: First, because Monopoly involves competition between players, it has one *more* family resemblance than Solitaire; and second, because it does *not* involve a high chance of suicide, it has one *less* family dissimilarity than Russian Roulette. To describe this state of affairs, you might say that we apply the concept to Monopoly to a "greater extent" than the others. You might add, by way of explanation, that a given cluster concept applies, rightly or wrongly, to one object to a "greater extent" than another if and only if it instantiates a *higher ratio* of relevant family resemblances to dissimilarities.

1.2. Definition

Given the preceding, I can now outline my definition. First and foremost, the term "thought experiment" connotes a cluster concept. As such, if we apply it to a particular object, we do so *rightly* if and only if it has a high enough ratio of relevant family resemblances to dissimilarities; and, if one object simply has *a higher such ratio* than another, then, and only then, I will say that we apply the concept to it, rightly or wrongly, to *a greater extent* than the other. To fill this definition in, let us, in Section 1.3, describe some of the relevant family resemblances and then, in Section 1.4, calibrate the ratio with examples.

1.3. Relevant Family Resemblances

When we examine a wide range of paradigm thought experiments, we find some relevant family resemblances to be particularly significant.[3] I describe them below under five headings of the form "Θ involves F"—where "Θ" stands for "each element in a *proper* subset of all possible thought experiments."[4] I will not argue for these descriptions, though I take each to be plausible in its own right. If any one seems not to be, consider it a conjecture. The first is as follows:

t_1: Θ involves a hypothetical.

Specifically, Θ has at least one part, such as a state or scenario, that we entertain either without regard to its being the case in the actual world or alongside the belief that it is not.[5]

t_2: Θ involves an imaginable.

In particular, Θ has a quasi-empirical part, one we entertain in a sensory modality, as when we visualize a case or scenario.[6]

t_3: Θ involves our own activity.

Specifically, Θ has a quasi-experimental procedure, one we follow by manipulating or reasoning about what is imagined, not just by entertaining it. We act more like an experimental physicist manipulating apparatuses and developing theoretical interpretations than an astronomer making observations.[7]

t_4: Θ involves a proper cognitive upshot.

That is, Θ has a part, such as a case or scenario, that is supposed to justify or clarify something distinctive and more general than itself, often in virtue of an intuition.[8]

t_5: Θ involves no empirical justification.

More exactly, Θ does not, or does not appear to,[9] use any new empirical data for justification.[10]

1.4. Calibration

Let us calibrate, with a series of three examples, how high the ratio of relevant family resemblances to dissimilarities is for a *right* application of the concept connoted by "thought experiment" on my definition.

1.4.1. Paradigm Case

First, consider a famous *paradigmatic* thought experiment due to Galileo. It concerns the Aristotelian thesis "that moveables[11] differing in heaviness are moved in the same medium with unequal speeds, which maintain to one another the same ratio as their weights" (Galilei 1989, 65). For instance, a stone ten times heavier than another would, given this thesis, fall through the air ten times faster. Galileo's Salviati aims to refute this thesis and establish another, as follows:[12]

> [Agree that] for every heavy falling body there is a speed determined by nature such that this cannot be increased or diminished except by using force or opposing some impediment to it. . . .
> Then if we had two moveables whose natural speeds were unequal, it is evident that were we to connect the slower to the faster, the latter

would be partly retarded by the slower, and this would be partly speeded up by the faster. . . .

But if this is so, and if it is also true that a large stone is moved with eight degrees of speed, for example, and a smaller one with four, then joining both together, their composite will be moved with a speed less than eight degrees. But the two stones joined together make a larger stone than the first one which was moved with eight degrees of speed; therefore this greater stone is moved less swiftly than the lesser one. But this is contrary to your assumption. So you see how, from the supposition that the heavier body is moved more swiftly than the less heavy, I conclude that the heavier moves less swiftly. . . .

[Moreover] . . . it is not true that the smaller stone adds weight to the larger . . . [or vice versa]. . . . [13]

From this we conclude that both great and small bodies, of the same specific gravity, are moved with like speeds.[14] (1989, 66–68)

In short, suppose you connect a small stone to a large stone, both of which fall freely with unequal speeds in the same medium. From here, together with the Aristotelian thesis, you reason to a contradiction, that the composite comprising the two stones moves *both more and less swiftly than* the large stone alone. Finally, you then move to the conclusion, not only that the Aristotelian thesis is false, but that *all* bodies with the same specific gravity fall freely with *equal speeds* in the same medium.

This thought experiment, as I understand it, stands in at least one relation in each of t_1–t_5: in t_1 (Θ involves a hypothetical) because we entertain the falling stones *without regard to* whether or not they exist in the actual world; in t_2 (Θ involves an imaginable) because we *visualize* the two stones falling together; in t_3 (Θ involves our own activity) because we *manipulate* the falling stones when we imagine connecting them, and we *reason* about them; in t_4 (Θ involves a proper cognitive upshot) because we are supposed to use the falling stones to *justify*, not just any claims, but two *more general and distinctive* ones, that the Aristotelian thesis is false and the other true; and in t_5 (Θ involves no empirical justification) because it is difficult to find in it any apparent use of new empirical data for justification.[15] Additionally, this thought experiment seems to stand in few if any relevant family dissimilarities worth mentioning. For instance, the involvement of interlocutors contributes to its being part of a dialogue, but this does not seem to be a relevant family dissimilarity worth mentioning, since its being part of a dialogue does not seem to matter very much to what it is.

We may, then, make the following initial calibration. We specify that an object instantiates a *high enough* ratio of relevant family resemblances to dissimilarities for us to *rightly* apply it *if* the ratio is *as high as* that in Galileo's paradigm case—that is, *if* it stands (i) in a relevant family relation under each of t_1–t_5, (ii) in two relations in t_3, and (iii) in few if any relevant family dissimilarities worth mentioning.

1.4.2. Clear Case

Consider, next, a *clear case* of a thought experiment due to Max Black:

> Isn't it logically possible that the universe should have contained noth-
> ing but two exactly similar spheres? We might suppose that each was
> made of chemically pure iron, had a diameter of one mile, that they had
> the same temperature, colour, and so on, and that nothing else existed.
> Then every quality and relational characteristic of the one would also
> be a property of the other. Now if what I am describing is logically
> possible, it is not impossible for two things to have all their properties
> in common. This seems to me to *refute* the Principle [of the Identity of
> Indiscernibles]. (1952, 156)

In short, we suppose two exactly similar spheres existing in an otherwise
empty universe and reason to the apparent refutation of the Principle of the
Identity of Indiscernibles.

This thought experiment, as I understand it, also stands in at least one
relation in each of t_1–t_5: in t_1 because we entertain the spheres and otherwise empty universe alongside the belief that they do not exist in the actual
world; in t_2 because we visualize what the spheres would look like were it
possible to see them; in t_3 because—even though we might not manipulate
the imagined spheres—we do reason about them; in t_4 because the spheres
are supposed to justify a specific claim about more than the spheres, that
the Principle of the Identity of Indiscernibles seems false; and in t_5 because
it is difficult to find in it any apparent use of new empirical data for justification. Also, as with the Galilean thought experiment, this one too seems
to instantiate few if any relevant family dissimilarities worth mentioning.

Now, we apply the concept connoted by my definition to a lesser extent
to this clear case than to the Galilean paradigm, for it stands in one, not
both, of the relations in t_3. This allows us to make a *further* calibration. We
specify that an object instantiates a *high enough* ratio for us to *rightly* apply
it *merely* if it stands (i) in one of the relations under each of t_1–t_5 and (ii) in
few if any relevant family dissimilarities worth mentioning.

1.4.3. Less Clear Case

Finally, consider a *less clear case* of a thought experiment due to Berkeley:

> [If] you can but conceive it possible for one extended movable sub-
> stance, or in general, for any one idea or anything like an idea, to exist
> otherwise than in a mind perceiving it, I shall readily give up the cause
> [against the existence of material substance]. . . .
> But say you, surely there is nothing easier than to imagine trees, for
> instance, in a park, or books existing in a closet, and nobody by to

perceive them. . . . But what is all this, I beseech you, more than framing in your mind certain ideas which you call *books* and *trees*, and at the same time omitting to frame the idea of anyone that may perceive them? But do not you yourself perceive or think of them all the while? This therefore is nothing to the purpose. . . . [It] does not show that you can conceive it possible, [that] the objects of your thought may exist without the mind. To make out this, it is necessary that you conceive them existing unconceived or unthought of, which is a manifest repugnancy. . . .

. . . [Therefore, it is] unnecessary to insist on any other proofs against the existence of material substance. (2004, 60–61)

In short, I may think I imagine unconceived material things like unperceived trees and books. But that is absurd, for *I* would be conceiving them all the while. Hence, there is no need to provide any other proofs against the existence of material substance. This thought experiment, as I understand it, stands in relations in t_1 and t_3–t_5—but not in t_2: in t_1 because I initially entertain, insofar as I grasp its truth condition, the thought that unperceived trees and books exist, without regard to whether or not they exist in the actual world, or any other; in t_3 because, even though I cannot manipulate *inconceivable* imaginings, I do reason about them; in t_4 because the case of unperceived trees and books is supposed, in virtue of its absurdity, to help justify a distinctive general claim, that no other proofs against the existence of material substance are required; in t_5 because it is difficult to find in it any apparent use of new empirical data for justification;[16] but *not* in t_2 because it lacks a quasi-empirical part, it plausibly being the case that I cannot entertain, even in a minimal sense, unperceived books and trees in a sensory modality. Also, as with Galileo's and Black's thought experiments, this one seems to stand in few if any relevant family dissimilarities worth mentioning.

Finally, in this less clear case we apply the concept connoted by my definition to a lesser extent than in Black's or Galileo's, for it stands in only one of the relations in t_3 and none in t_2. This allows us to make a *final* calibration, the last one I need for what follows. In full, we specify that, if we apply the concept connoted by my definition to a particular object, we do so *rightly* if and only if it has a *high enough* ratio of relevant family resemblances to dissimilarities—where it has a *high enough* ratio if it stands (i) in one relation in at least four of t_1–t_5 and (ii) in few if any relevant family dissimilarities worth mentioning.

2. TWO EXPLANATORY VIRTUES

2.1. First Explanatory Virtue

The first explanatory virtue concerns the literary fictions that are primarily at issue in the literature on thought experiment and literary fiction.[17] They may be described as being primarily classic fictional narratives, since such works are most cited in the literature. These include, for example, novels such as Jane Austen's *Mansfield Park* (Elgin 2007, 49–50), George Eliot's *Middlemarch* (Elgin 2007, 43), E. M. Forster's *Howards End* (Carroll 2002, 11–14), Aldous Huxley's *Brave New World* (Davies 2007, 33), Stanislaw Lem's *Memoirs Found in a Bathtub* (Swirski 2007, 131ff.), George Orwell's *1984* (Elgin 2007, 50; Davies 2007, 36; Davenport 1983, 283), and William Styron's *Sophie's Choice* (Swirski 2007, 72).[18]

What is the relation between these literary fictions and thought experiments?[19] Some philosophers hold that some such literary fictions *are* thought experiments, that some are "literary thought experiments." Now, I think these literary fictions are prime candidates for being thought experiments, so if any are, it is likely them. Also, I agree that some indeed are thought experiments—though not without qualification. To explain, and thereby motivate my definition, let us, first, review three arguments for the view that some such literary fictions are thought experiments, and locate which relations in t_2–t_4 each omits. Second, let us apply my definition to a case, Styron's *Sophie's Choice*, to see in what the first explanatory virtue consists.

2.1.1. Davenport's Argument

The simplest of the three arguments is Edward Davenport's. He begins with the following definition:

> Thought experiment means testing hypotheses in the mind—logically rather than physically. This may be done by making deductions from the hypothesis to see what must follow if it is true. (1983, 281)

Next, he implies that various stories[20] fall under this definition because they "dramatize certain hypotheses about society and enable us to see the logical conceptual implications of these hypotheses" (1983, 284). He then concludes, "it seems commonsense to say that such stories are thought experiments" (1983, 283–284).

Davenport's argument evidently does not account for a relation in t_2, t_3, or t_4. It might be thought that he requires one in t_2 because he thinks thought experiments dramatize hypotheses; however, it is not at all clear that this amounts to saying any more than that the hypotheses are filled in with details, not that we entertain them *in a sensory modality*. Likewise, it might be thought that he requires one in t_3 because he commits himself to the view that literary thought experiments test hypotheses in the mind. But, for all he says, such testing need involve no more than our passively observing the implications of a certain dramatized hypothesis, and what is needed is no less than *our own manipulation or reasoning* about what we imagine. Likewise, it might be thought that Davenport requires a relation in t_4, since he holds that literary thought experiments involve implications of a dramatized hypothesis. However, to stand in a relation in t_4, such implications would have to be *more general than the case under consideration*, and we should not accept this. Rather, we should think that the case comprises the dramatized hypothesis *and its implications*, that is, the literary fiction itself, given that the cognitive upshot ought to concern the *actual world*, not the fictional one.

2.1.2. Elgin's Argument

Catherine Elgin may be understood to provide a more sophisticated argument that begins with the following characterization:

> [A thought] experiment fixes certain parameters (e.g., about the relevant laws of nature and the initial conditions), provides a description of the experimental situation and exemplifies all and only the features considered relevant and teases out the consequences. In effect, it is an imaginative exercise that asks: what would happen if certain conditions obtained. (2007, 48)

Next, she gives an account of how thought experiments function. They show that the features they exemplify[21] matter in an "artificial, carefully contrived" hypothetical situation (2007, 48). Thereby, they afford "reason to suspect that . . . we would do well to consider such factors salient in related real-life situations" (2007, 48). Subsequently, she effectively claims, as follows, that works of fiction fall under this definition and have this function:

> [Literary fictions] advance understanding by exemplifying features and playing out their consequences. They constitute imaginative settings in which particular constellations of features are salient and display their significance. They thus afford reason to think that we would do well (or, in some cases, badly) to consider such features salient elsewhere. (2007, 47)

Finally, she concludes that literary fictions are "extended, elaborate thought experiments" (2007, 47–48).

Elgin evidently does not account for a relation in t_3 or t_4. It might be thought that she accounts for one in t_3 because she holds that literary thought experiments afford us reason *to think* it is to our benefit or detriment *to consider* certain features of their imaginative settings salient in related actual situations. However, for all Elgin says, such thinking or considering need not involve any *manipulation* or *reasoning* about imagined objects. Similarly, it might be thought that she accounts for one in t_4 because the imaginative setting of a literary thought experiment can *afford reason* to think it would be to our benefit or detriment to consider certain features salient *beyond its imaginary situation*. But this is to overlook that, to stand in a relation in t$_4$, the imaginary situation would have to be *supposed* to justify something *distinctive*. And, for all Elgin says, the imaginative setting may *just happen* to justify *any old thing*.

2.1.3. Davies' Argument

David Davies' argument may be divided into four steps. First, he gives "two plausible conditions on the fictionality of a narrative"; namely, the author must (i) intend that "we make-believe, rather than believe, the content of the story narrated" and (ii) have "some more general purpose in storytelling" than to relate events she believes to have occurred in the order she narrates them (2007, 31). Second, he argues that thought experiments satisfy these two conditions. That is, in short, he first claims that thought experiment narratives present a hypothetical situation in which a particular outcome of an event or process is posited and "taken to bear upon a more general question" (2007, 32). He then infers that, since "we are expected to make-believe, rather than believe" such hypothetical situations and events, thought experiments satisfy the first condition; and, since the authors of thought experiments do not think such hypothetical situations and events "actually occurred," they also satisfy the second (2007, 32). Third, upon responding to a series of objections to this argument, he claims that "the writers of many fictional narratives are similarly motivated to the authors of [thought experiments]" (2007, 33). For example, like them, "writers of utopias or dystopias such as *1984* and *Brave New World* plausibly intend that, as a result of the receiver's making-believe the content of the narrative, she will come to believe that this is how certain societies would turn out, and will therefore amend her views about the merits of alternative political or socio-economic systems" (2007, 33). Fourth, he concludes, "Perhaps[22] then, we should simply allow that some works of fiction are properly viewed as much more fully elaborated [thought experiments]" (2007, 33).

Davies evidently does not account for a relation in t$_3$ or t$_4$. It might be thought that he accounts for one in t$_3$ because he holds that the author of a literary thought experiment intends that we *make-believe* its content. After all, it might be added, our making-believe that Winston is being "cured" in the Ministry of Love in *1984* is our own activity. For all Davies says, however, making-believe might be no more than entertaining the narrative in thought like a passing show, as it were, and pretending to believe it. So it need not involve one's own manipulation of, or reasoning about, imaginary items. Likewise, it might be thought that he accounts for a relation in t$_4$ in his use of *1984* and *Brave New World* as examples. For he plausibly holds that the authors of both literary thought experiments *meant* to change their reader's views about the virtues of certain political or socio-economic systems, which are beyond the works themselves. But he does not say, as needed, that the authors intend their readers to adopt a *particular*, or *distinctive*, view as opposed to *just any of a large range of views* concerning the merits of such alternative systems.

2.1.4. Case Study

My definition, in virtue of accounting for relations in *all* of t_1–t_5, may be used, in a way unavailable on the preceding views, to shed light on the relation between the literary fictions in question and thought experiments. To explain, let us consider Styron's *Sophie's Choice*.

The title famously refers to an event briefly related at the end of the novel (1992, 525–532). Sophie and her young children, Eva and Jan, are taken to Auschwitz where they undergo "a selection." They stand before Fritz Jemand von Niemand, the SS doctor determining who goes to the gas chambers at Birkenau. He gives Sophie a choice: "You may keep one of your children. . . . The other one will have to go. Which one will you keep? . . . Choose, goddamnit, or I'll send them both over there. Quick!" (1992, 529). Sophie, tormented, in total disbelief, and at the doctor's order to send them both, thrusts Eva forward, "Take my little girl!" (1992, 529).

As central as this event is to *Sophie's Choice* it should not blind us to the novel's great complexity and variety. The novel begins in Brooklyn in 1947 with a detailed description of the editing job that Stingo, the protagonist and narrator, gives up to write a book set in his cultural origin, the American South. Throughout the novel Styron details Stingo's complex changing relationship with this culture, particularly its social norms and history of slavery. He also provides a vivid picture of Stingo's trials and tribulations with sexual norms and psychosexual issues. When Stingo begins to write his book, he meets Nathan, a charismatic and brilliant American Jew, whom, after initial dislike, he later befriends and admires. Ultimately this relationship erodes as Nathan's schizophrenic episodes, drug addiction, and violent jealousy come to light. Stingo also develops a complicated relationship with Sophie, Nathan's beautiful though deeply unstable Polish lover. She gives Stingo a rich depiction of her family life in Poland leading up to the Second World War, how she arrived at Auschwitz, and how she survived while there. The novel closes with Stingo's attempt to save Sophie, their lovemaking, and her tragic return to Nathan.

If we apply the concept picked out by my definition to *Sophie's Choice*— the novel itself, not just a part of it like the central event described above[23]— we do so *rightly* if and only if it has a high enough ratio of relevant family resemblances to dissimilarities. It has a high enough ratio if it stands (i) in a relation in at least four of t_1–t_5 and (ii) in few if any relevant family dissimilarities worth mentioning. In some circumstances, I will now argue, it has such a ratio.

Sophie's Choice arguably stands in relations in t_1 and t_5: in t_1 because we entertain fictional characters and events in it, like Sophie and her choice, without regard to their being the case in the actual world, or perhaps alongside the belief that they are not; and in t_5 because it does not appear to involve any use of new empirical data for justification. It also stands, in many circumstances, in relations in t_2 and t_3: in t_2 because—although it *qua* novel, unlike the Galilean paradigm, arguably *need not* be entertained in a sensory modality—it *normally is* so entertained, at least in part; and in t_3 because—although it *qua* novel, again unlike the Galilean paradigm, *need not* involve a procedure we follow by manipulating or reasoning about what is imagined—we *often do* follow one. For instance, we often reflect on such things as what would have happened were Stingo able to prevent Sophie's return to Nathan, manipulating this imagined possibility and reasoning about it.

It does not, however, stand in a relation in t_4. True, its narrative is plausibly supposed to justify or clarify something more general—perhaps something about how we conceive evil, religion, or the Holocaust, about the moral relation between slavery in the American South and Nazi practices, or about human psychology in deep moral dilemmas, and so on. However, given the novel's complexity and variety, the cognitive upshot could just as well be about any of these things, as opposed to a *particular,* or *distinctive,* thing. To emphasize the significance of this point, recall how distinctive the purported cognitive upshots of Berkeley's, Black's, and Galileo's cases were; not only do they contribute to their being the particular thought experiments they are, but, I claim, to their being thought experiments *simpliciter*. Moreover, *Sophie's Choice* stands in some *significant* relevant family dissimilarities in virtue of its being a classic fictional narrative. For instance, such narratives being elaborate, or multifaceted, and having various aesthetic qualities, such as being works of art, plausibly contribute significantly to their being what they are, but do not figure in t_1–t_5.

Hence, *Sophie's Choice* often stands in a relation in each of t_1–t_3 and t_5, but not t_4, as well as in some significant relevant family dissimilarities. Given the criteria provided above, then, its ratio is often approximately the same as Berkeley's less clear case, for it often has one more relation in t_3 than this case, but more relevant family dissimilarities. If so, we often rightly apply the concept connoted by my definition to *Sophie's Choice* to roughly the same extent as to Berkeley's case, and so to a lesser extent than to the Galilean paradigm or Black's clear case. This insight into the relation between *Sophie's Choice* and thought experiments, which is not available on the views discussed above, together with the potential for further light being shed on the wider class of literary fictions at issue, constitutes the first explanatory virtue of my definition, and motivation for it.

2.2. Second Explanatory Virtue

In closing, I will draw on the preceding discussion to illustrate the second explanatory virtue and source of motivation for my definition. In short, it is that the structure of my definition provides for a promising account of some disagreements about what counts as a thought experiment.

Consider the following toy example. Three parties disagree about the relation between thought experiments and literary fictions when it comes to Dumas' *The Count of Monte Cristo*. The "hardliners" think that it *is* a thought experiment, the "skeptics" that it *is not*, and the "middle-routers" that it *is to some extent*. The hardliners and skeptics, by the middle-router's lights, are both right insofar as they latched onto different sets of relevant family resemblances that account, in part, for our right application of the concept *thought experiment*. They mistakenly assume, however, that their own set comprises ordinary necessary and sufficient conditions.

Now, perhaps the hardliners also assume, roughly like Davenport, that having (i) a dramatized hypothetical situation and (ii) its various consequences are necessary and sufficient conditions on our right application of the concept *thought experiment*. Moreover, perhaps the skeptics also assume, roughly like Davies, that these conditions must also include that the case in question say something about the world. And perhaps *The Count of Monte Cristo* involves a dramatized hypothetical situation and its sundry consequences, but is supposed to entertain the reader, *not* say anything about the actual world (on which its various events are loosely based).

If so, the middle-routers can explain the hardliners' conflict with the skeptics as a mere case of verbal disagreement. That is, the hardliners call *The Count of Monte Cristo* "a thought experiment" because of their assumption about the conditions on the right application of the concept *thought experiment*; and, the skeptics' disagreement is just a matter of their using the term "thought experiment" differently, since they assume different conditions on the right application of the concept.

Of course, the correct way to proceed, by my lights, is that of the middle-routers. They, unlike the hardliners and skeptics, not only latch onto the *entire* network of family resemblances but also *avoid* the mistaken assumption that these family resemblances form a set of ordinary necessary and sufficient conditions. Their, I think, promising explanation of the hardliners' and skeptics' conflict has, to be sure, the added benefit that it does not attribute largely incorrect positions to them about the concept *thought experiment*. Insofar as this bare sketch of the middle-routers' account is promising, I take it to be a second explanatory virtue of my definition, and additional motivation for it.

ACKNOWLEDGEMENTS

Many thanks to James Robert Brown and Mélanie Frappier as well as to audiences at the 2010 Halifax Thought Experiments Workshop and the Grad Forum in Philosophy at the University of Toronto for criticisms, suggestions, and questions that had a great influence upon this paper.

NOTES

1. Accordingly, Laymon does not mean his definition of the term to capture its "ordinary scientific usage" but *inter alia* "to mark off a natural scientific practice that is of scientific importance and philosophical interest" (1991, 168).
2. I intend my use of the term "cluster concept" to be helpfully reminiscent of Searle's "Proper Names" (1958) and Kripke's *Naming and Necessity* (1980).
3. Less significant ones might concern such things as extraordinary happenings or how contents are presented.
4. Given my characterization of cluster concepts, if "Θ" were modified to stand for "every possible thought experiment" in, for instance, the first description, it would present no serious difficulty for my definition.
5. John Norton makes the related claim that thought experiments in science involve positing "hypothetical or counterfactual states of affairs" (1991, 129). Likewise, Timothy Williamson claims that at least paradigm examples in philosophy "are simply valid arguments about counterfactual possibilities" (2007, 207).
6. Brown makes the related claim that all thought experiments are "experienceable in some way or other" (2011, 17). Likewise, Norton claims that in science they have a "vivid picturesque or narrative form" (2004, 1139).
7. Brown makes the closely related claim that thought experimenters are not so much "passive observers" as "active interveners" in their imaginings (2011, 17–18). Likewise, Nancy Nersessian claims that the *practice* of thought experimenting is a "species of *simulative model-based reasoning*" (2007, 126).
8. Brown makes the related claim that "mediative thought experiment might *illustrate* some otherwise highly counterintuitive aspect" of a "specific, well-articulated theory" (2011, 35, emphasis added). Similarly, Tamar Gendler claims that the evaluation of an imagined scenario in a thought experiment is "taken to reveal something about cases beyond the scenario" (2000, 21). Likewise, Roy Sorensen claims that the person reading a thought experiment "is being invited to believe that contemplation of the [experimental] design justifies an answer to the question [the thought experiment is meant to answer] or (more rarely) justifiably raises its question" (1992, 206).
9. I add this sub-clause so as not to preclude accounts of thought experiments, like Mach's, on which new empirical data *in fact* plays a role in justification.
10. Brown makes the related claim that, in a thought experiment of Galileo's, we use "no new empirical data . . . when we move from Aristotle's to Galileo's theory of free fall" (2004, 1129). Likewise, Norton claims that thought experimental justification in physics "does not come from the reporting of new empirical data" (1991, 129). Similarly, Rachel Cooper claims we can use thought experiments to "gain new knowledge, despite the input of no new empirical data" (2005, 328).
11. Stillman Drake notes, "Galileo's 'moveable' is always to be thought of as a tangible heavy object near the earth's surface" (Galilei 1989, xli).
12. He calls it a "short and conclusive demonstration" with which "we can prove clearly" that the thesis is false "without other experiences" than one attested to in which a cannonball fell much less than twice as fast as a robinet ball half its weight (Galilei 1989, 66).
13. Salviati, in support, adduces various considerations, which, to save space, I omit here (see 1989, 67).

14. More specifically, as it is put later on, Salviati "clearly demonstrated that it is not at all true that unequally heavy bodies [of the same specific gravity], moved in the same medium, have speeds proportional to their weights, but rather have equal [speeds]" (1989, 71–72).

15. To be clear, you may read the passage quoted above without, e.g., imagining anything in a sensory modality or manipulating what you imagine, but then, by my lights, you have not carried out this particular thought experiment.

16. It might be thought that this case is a psychological experiment I perform on myself and, thus, that it does not stand in this relation. That is, my failure to conceive unperceived trees and books might be thought to be a piece of new empirical data that I use explicitly for justification; however, that I cannot conceive unconceived trees and books is meant to be justified *a priori* by the "manifest repugnancy" of anything unconceived being conceived.

17. This literature includes, among others, Davenport (1983), Sorensen (1992), Carroll (2002), Murzilli (2004), Elgin (2007), Davies (2007), and Swirski (2007).

18. Other forms of literary fiction that are cited include Sir Arthur Conan Doyle's short stories about Sherlock Holmes (Davies 2007, 35), Arthur Miller's play *The Crucible* (Elgin 2007, 51), and John Milton's epic poem *Paradise Lost* (Elgin 2007, 43). A minority of literary fictions cited in the literature that may not be classic narratives include Walker Percy's *Lost in the Cosmos* (Swirski 2007, 96), which is arguably not a classic, and William Carlos Williams' poem "Red Wheelbarrow" (Swirski 2007, 44), which is arguably not a narrative.

19. Roughly this question bears, in the literature, on the cognitive value of literary fiction. See Davenport (2007, 279–284), Carroll (2002, 3–4), Elgin (2007, 48), and Swirski (2007, 4).

20. These stories comprehend "Aesop's Fables, the parables of Jesus, the dialogues of Plato, the speeches of Thucydides' *Peloponnesian War*, Thomas More's *Utopia*, Swift's *Gulliver's Travels*, Johnson's *Raselas*, Mary Shelley's *Frankenstein*, Wells' *The Sleeper Awakes*, Orwell's *1984*, and Asimov's *Foundation Trilogy*" (Davenport 1983, 283).

21. To say that a thought experiment exemplifies features is to say that there are particular features in it that refer to features that they are instances of; the color of a paint sample, for instance, exemplifies a certain color if and only if the color of that sample refers to the color it is a sample of (Elgin 2007, 47).

22. Davies, rightly I think, also expresses some reservation about this conclusion in his section title "To what extent are TE's (like) fictional narratives" (2007, 31).

23. Sophie's choice might be, or be used in, a thought experiment, but I do not consider this here.

REFERENCES

Berkeley, George. 2004. *Principles of Human Knowledge* and *Three Dialogues between Hylas and Philonous*, edited by Roger Woolhouse. London: Penguin.

Black, Max. 1952. "The Identity of Indiscernibles." *Mind* 61: 153–164.

Brown, James Robert. 2004. "Peeking into Plato's Heaven." *Philosophy of Science* 71: 1126–1138.

———. 2011. *The Laboratory of the Mind: Thought Experiments in the Natural Sciences*. 2nd edition. New York: Routledge.

Carroll, Noël. 2002. "The Wheel of Virtue: Art, Literature, and Moral Knowledge." *Journal of Aesthetics and Art Criticism* 60: 3–27.

Cooper, Rachel. 2005. "Thought Experiments." *Metaphilosophy* 36: 328–347.

Davenport, Edward A. 1983. "Literature as Thought Experiment." *Philosophy of the Social Sciences/Philosophie des sciences sociales* 13: 279–306.

Davies, David. 2007. "Thought Experiments and Fictional Narratives." *Croatian Journal of Philosophy* 19: 29–45.

Einstein, A. 2009. *Relativity: The Special and General Theory*. Scotts Valley, CA: Kennelly Press.

Einstein, A., and L. Infeld. 1938. *The Evolution of Physics*. New York: Simon and Schuster.

Elgin, Catherine Z. 2007. "The Laboratory of the Mind." In *A Sense of the World: Essays on Fiction, Narrative, and Knowledge*, edited by John Gibson, 43–54. Oxon: Routledge.

Galilei, Galileo. 1989. *Two New Sciences: Including Centers of Gravity and Force of Percussion*. 2nd edition. Translated by Stillman Drake. Toronto: Wall & Emerson.

Gendler, Tamar Szabó. 2000. *Thought Experiment: On the Powers and Limits of Imaginary Cases*. New York: Garland Press.

Kripke, Saul. 1980. *Naming and Necessity*. Oxford: Blackwell

Laymon, Ronald. 1991. "Thought Experiments of Stevin, Mach and Gouy: Thought Experiments as Ideal Limits and as Semantic Domains." In *Thought Experiments in Science and Philosophy*, edited by Tamara Horowitz and Gerald Massey, 167–192. Lanham, MD: Rowman & Littlefield.

Murzilli, Nancy. 2004. "La Possibilisation du Monde: Littérature et Expérience de Pensée." *Critique* 682: 219–234.

Nersessian, Nancy. 2007. "Thought Experimenting as Mental Modeling: Empiricism Without Logic." *Croatian Journal of Philosophy* 20: 125–161.

Norton, John. 1991. "Thought Experiments in Einstein's Work." In *Thought Experiments in Science and Philosophy*, edited by Tamara Horowitz and Gerald Massey, 129–148. Savage, MD: Rowman and Littlefield.

———. 2004. "On Thought Experiments: Is There More to the Argument?" *Philosophy of Science* 71: 1139–1151.

Searle, John R. 1958. "Proper Names." *Mind* 67: 166–173.

Sorensen, Roy. 1992. *Thought Experiments*. Oxford: Oxford University Press.

Styron, William. 1992. *Sophie's Choice*. New York: Vintage Books.

Swirski, Peter. 2007. *Of Literature and Knowledge: Explorations in Narrative Thought Experiments, Evolution and Game Theory*. London & New York: Routledge.

Williamson, Timothy. 2007. *The Philosophy of Philosophy*. Oxford: Blackwell.

Wittgenstein, Ludwig. 1958. *Philosophical Investigations*. 3rd edition. Translated by G. E. M. Anscombe. Upper Saddle River, NJ: Blackwell & Mott.

13 Can Philosophical Thought Experiments Be "Screened"?

David Davies

1.

Can film serve as a philosophical medium in at least some of the ways that language does? Surprisingly, perhaps, philosophers of some repute have taken this question seriously. Even more surprisingly, some have argued that it should be answered affirmatively. The first notable proponent of what we may term the "film as a philosophical medium" (FPM) thesis was Stanley Cavell (1979). The cinematic medium, Cavell argued, is by its very nature philosophical, since it embodies philosophical concerns about scepticism. Other philosophers have argued, less boldly, that, while not inherently philosophical, cinema, like natural language, can be used to advance philosophical understanding. Stephen Mulhall, for example, speaks of some works of cinema as "philosophy in action". He has in mind, in particular, the *Alien* series which he presents as a philosophical exploration of "the relation of human identity to embodiment" (2002, 2). More recently, Thomas Wartenberg (2007) has argued that film is capable of "screening" philosophical thought experiments, as well as serving as a medium for other kinds of philosophical inquiry. Wartenberg also recently co-edited a special edition of *The Journal of Aesthetics and Art Criticism* on the theme "Film as Philosophy".

To assess the claim that film can serve as a philosophical medium in at least some of the ways that language does we must first ask in what ways *language* so functions. At a very general level, the answer to this question is straightforward. We use language to identify, articulate, clarify, and interrelate what are viewed as philosophical issues, to deepen our understanding of these issues, and to assess the things that others say about them. What we take to be philosophical issues, however, and what we take to be a contribution to our understanding of these issues, depends upon the philosophical tradition in which we work. More generally, how we assess the claim that film can "do philosophy" depends upon what we take to be required for an activity to count as "doing philosophy". The differences between the broadly "analytical" and "continental" philosophical traditions are as much differences in methodology as they are differences in philosophical concerns—although, to some extent, it is the difference in concerns that entails a difference in methodology. If one's concern is to clarify or refine our concepts, for example, then linguistic analysis, formalised reasoning, and thought experiments might seem to be appropriate tools. If, on the other hand, one's concern is to clarify the way in which things are given to us in experience, or to awaken us to the existential structure of human existence and to get us to ask "the question of Being", then techniques for phenomenological reduction and analysis may seem more appropriate.

Perhaps for this reason, philosophers working in the analytic and phenomenological traditions have responded very differently to the question of whether film can be a philosophical medium. Phenomenologists have generally warmed to this idea. Indeed, as we have seen, Cavell, a philosopher broadly in this tradition, has maintained that film is uniquely suited to "do philosophy" since the very medium exemplifies issues of fundamental philosophical concern.[1] In the introduction to the second edition of *The World Viewed*, for example, he argues that, in his *Days of Heaven*, Terrence Malick "discovered, or discovered how to acknowledge, a fundamental fact of film's photographic basis: that objects participate in the photographic presence of themselves; they participate in the re-creation of themselves on film; they are essential in the making of their appearances" (1979, xvi). Drawing upon this fact, Malick "found a way to transpose . . . for our meditation" central Heideggerian themes (1979, xv). According to Cavell, cinematic representation significantly resembles our naive metaphysics in the way in which it represents our relationship to the world, something of whose representational nature we have become unaware. Malick's film, in "foregrounding" and thereby making present to the viewer the nature of cinematic representation, also makes present the nature of our representation of the world, and thus can awaken us to "the question of Being". Since philosophy, for Heidegger, is a matter of "dwelling" in this question, *Days of Heaven* is itself a work of philosophy.

Other philosophers working in the phenomenological tradition have followed Cavell in seeing Malick as a paradigm example of how filmmakers can "do philosophy" in their films. Indeed, there are Heideggerian, Merleau-Pontian, and even Nietzschean readings of Malick's films, encouraged not only by his philosophical training as a phenomenologist but also by overtly philosophical musings in the disembodied voice-overs in his later films and the polysemic nature of his cinematic style.[2] In such cases, the polysemy might be thought to provide a resource for exploring philosophical themes, making possible the kind of questioning, dialogue, and commentary characteristic of some philosophical writing in the phenomenological tradition.

2.

My interest in this paper, however, is in the treatment of the FPM thesis by philosophers working in the broadly analytic tradition. Here, "doing philosophy" is taken to involve constructing arguments that support or challenge stances on particular philosophical issues, arguments that often rest upon making distinctions and clarifying concepts through various kinds of hypothetical reasoning. Such activities seem by their very nature to require the use of language, and to lend themselves ill to a realization in the essentially visual medium of cinema. Indeed, we find in the analytic tradition a more general skepticism concerning the cognitive value of the arts, and this, unsurprisingly, has proved to be a hostile environment for the idea that film not only has cognitive value but may serve as a medium for philosophising. Knowledge in general, the analytically minded sceptic reminds us, requires not merely belief but belief that is grounded either in reasons that we can furnish or in a reliable method of belief-formation. Art, on the other hand, it is claimed, moves us not by reasons but by its seductive manifolds, be they visual or verbal. The focus has for the most part been upon the predominantly narrative arts—literature, for the most part, but also film—where, so the cognitivist maintains, we can acquire certain understandings of the world in general through engaging with fictional narratives.

This claim has been subject to a number of objections, most of which find their most forthright expression in Jerome Stolnitz's paper "On the Cognitive Triviality of Art" (1992). Stolnitz raises a number of distinct challenges to cognitivist claims about literary and other narrative artworks.[3] Of most interest in the present context, however, is what Stolnitz terms the "evidence objection".[4] The most that we can get from literary artworks, it is claimed, are interesting hypotheses, which are acceptable only on the basis of independent testing. Even if there are truths, particular or general, contained in literary fictions, the fictions themselves provide us with no good reasons to accept those truths. Consider, for example, general principles that might be extracted, as "thematic meanings", from literary works. The supposed "evidence" furnished by the work for the truth of these principles is, it is claimed, flawed in three ways: (a) The work cites no actual cases, (b) it relies on a single example, and (c) it is gerrymandered to support such principles, having been carefully designed to exemplify them. While sceptics such as Stolnitz have focused on literature as a narrative art, this argument seems to transfer *mutatis mutandis* to film.[5] And it bears even more obviously on the idea that film and literature are capable of "doing philosophy". For, at least in the analytic tradition, "doing philosophy" is very much tied to the construction of arguments and the giving of reasons, and this, according to the evidence objection, is just what literary artworks don't do.

But there is a popular response to the evidence objection. Fictional narratives, it is claimed, can do serious cognitive work if they function as *thought experiments*.[6] Thought experiments (TEs), which are themselves short fictional narratives, are, it is claimed, an instrument for cognitive advance in various branches of science.[7] So why shouldn't the more extended narratives characteristic of literary and cinematic works also, at least on occasion, serve as instruments of cognitive advance? Even more germane in the present context, TEs are also a widely acknowledged philosophical resource within the analytic tradition, where fictional tales of trolley drivers and women biologically linked against their will to famous violinists are treated as contributions to answering or better understanding different kinds of philosophical questions.[8] This suggests the following way of countering the evidence objection to the FPM thesis:[9]

F1: If verbally presented fictional narratives can serve as a legitimate philosophical resource in works of philosophy, why can't they also serve in this way in works of literary fiction?

F2: And if they can do this in works of literary fiction, why shouldn't cinematically presented fictional narratives serve a similar function?

A number of authors have defended the idea that literary works can have cognitive value in virtue of presenting thought experiments.[10] But the principal proponent of such a view of cinema is Thomas Wartenberg (2007). Wartenberg (2007, 57) endorses Tamar Gendler's claim (2002, 388) that to perform a thought experiment "is to reason about an imaginary scenario with the aim of confirming or disconfirming some hypothesis or theory". Since one of his principal aims is to show that films can serve as philosophical thought experiments, he begins by identifying the kinds of roles that a thought experiment can play in philosophy. These roles include (1) providing a counterexample to a theory, as in the Gettier argument (1963) against the idea that knowledge is justified true belief; (2) establishing that something is possible, as in Descartes's "evil genius" hypothesis intended to establish that all his existing beliefs might be false; (3) establishing that something is impossible, as in Quine's imaginary scenario (1960) of the linguist trying, but failing, to find a determinate translation for *gavagai* grounded in the available linguistic evidence; and (4) contributing to the development of a philosophical theory through the imagining of an idealised scenario, as in Rawls's appeal (1971) to the "original position" in developing his theory of justice. Wartenberg then argues that films can play some of these roles. *The Matrix* (1999), for example, not only provides an illustration of Descartes's "deception" hypothesis, but also "actually deceives us, its viewers", in order to get us to consider the possibility that "computers and other devices with screens—films, video and DVD players, for example—. . . may have screened us from the world rather than allowed the world to be visible on their screens" (2007, 75). And *The Eternal Sunshine of the Spotless Mind* (2004) is offered as an example of a film that provides a counterexample to a philosophical theory—utilitarianism—and, in so doing, presents an argument against that thesis.[11]

It falls beyond the scope of this paper to assess Wartenberg's arguments for his readings of these films, or his claim that films can in other ways advance philosophical understanding. We can, however, consider arguments that call into question the general idea that films can function as philosophical TEs. Critics have challenged this version of the FPM thesis in two ways, their targets being, essentially, the two premises *F1* and *F2* in the argument for the FPM thesis sketched above:

Not-*F1*: Fictional narratives in artworks, whether literary or cinematic, differ from fictional narratives that occur in philosophical writings in that the former are not properly viewed as TEs serving a philosophical purpose. Rather, as elements in artworks, they serve a different and incompatible purpose.

Not-*F2*: Even if we grant that *literary* fictions may sometimes present thought experiments that do genuine philosophical work, *visually* presented fictional narratives cannot bear any independent philosophical weight.

I shall consider each of these challenges in turn.

3.

The first challenge, as just noted, rests on the idea that, even though it may be possible to treat a fictional narrative in an artwork as a philosophical TE, this is not to engage properly with the narrative *as an element in an artwork*. As applied to cinematic narratives, this extends a general line of argument against literary cognitivism developed by Peter Lamarque and Stein Olsen (1994) in their attack on what they term the "Propositional Theory of Literary Truth". The Propositional Theory holds that, while works of literary fiction "at the literal level" have only fictional content, at a different "thematic" level they imply or suggest general propositions about human life whose truth we must assess if we are to properly appreciate the works. It is these propositions that make literature valuable. Such "thematic statements" may occur explicitly in the literary work, but are more often implicit yet accessible to readers through interpretation. Lamarque and Olsen argue, against the Propositional Theory, that it is not part of the ordinary activity of readers or critics to assess, or inquire into the truth or falsity of, general thematic statements expressed in or by literary fictions, and that this indicates that determining such truth or falsity is not a proper part of literary appreciation. Indeed, general thematic statements in literary fictions are not properly viewed as conclusions which we are invited to accept as true on the basis of our reading of the work. Rather, they function as devices for organizing and producing aesthetically interesting structure in the story's narrative content.

Paisley Livingston (2006) presents a similar challenge to the FPM thesis. He claims that an interest in a film as a work of art and an interest in a film as philosophy are in conflict. An interest in a film as *art* is an interest in how its themes have been expressed through its style and by devices specific to the medium. This rarely requires that we bring to bear relevant philosophical background, whereas this is crucial if we view a film as philosophy. On the other hand, to take a philosophical interest in a film is to use it as an illustration, without attending to the individuality of the film.

But why think that an interest in the philosophical content of a film treats the film as merely an *illustration* of a philosophical idea. Indeed, why assume that *illustrating* a philosophical idea cannot be a genuine contribution to philosophical understanding? Wartenberg, in fact, argues (2007, Ch. 3) that some kinds of illustrations can make such a contribution. He distinguishes different roles played by pictorial illustrations. Some illustrations *merely supplement* a text without substantially enriching it; they just make the text more accessible to readers. Other illustrations, such as Tenniel's drawings accompanying Lewis Carroll's *Alice* stories, are *iconic representations* that partly determine what we are to imagine in our engagement with the narrative. The fictional world constructed by the book depends on both text and illustrations. Of interest in the present context, however, is a third class of illustrations that, while connected to texts, are equally important. Wartenberg cites illustrations in birding books, which are essential for recognising types of birds. The illustrations contain information not verbally communicable as to how the bird looks when it is flying. Thus we shouldn't conclude that, if something is an illustration, then it isn't illuminating. And it is a mistake to think that a film that "illustrates" the views of a philosopher cannot be *philosophically* illuminating. Wartenberg offers Charlie Chaplin's *Modern Times* (1936) as an example of a film that advances philosophical understanding by illustrating, in this third sense, a philosophical idea. The film, he maintains, illustrates, and thereby illuminates, Marx's view of alienated labour by giving concrete form to Marx's talk of how the worker becomes a machine in a capitalist economic system.

Murray Smith (2006) offers different reasons for thinking that the aims and purposes of cinematic narratives undermine their ability to function as philosophy. He notes that, whereas philosophical (and indeed scientific) TEs involve narratively sparse fictions, with a minimum of detail, fictional narratives in the arts, whether literary or cinematic, are lush in detail. This difference, he maintains, reflects a difference in narrative purpose. He compares a philosophical TE presented by Bernard Williams, which is intended to get us to think more clearly about the role of embodiment in the constitution of personal identity, with Carl Reiner's film *All of Me* (1984), which entertains a similar kind of hypothetical scenario in which individuals "swap" bodies. The narrative of the film is much more detailed than Williams's philosophical TE, and the details sustain what might strike one as a more nuanced philosophical exploration of the issue. Smith argues with some plausibility, however, that the tensions within the cinematic narrative are best explained not in terms of philosophical nuancing but in terms of a different primary purpose, namely, to entertain and amuse the reader. The film is primarily a vehicle of comedy, not a vehicle of philosophical thought, and the "nuances" are in fact internal inconsistencies in respect of the philosophical issues tolerated in the interests of achieving this primary purpose.

The problem, I take it, is not merely that the film has the primary purpose of entertainment, for this would seem to be compatible with its having, and having successfully, the secondary purpose of serving as a philosophical TE. Rather, the problem is that pursuing and achieving the primary purpose is incompatible with also pursuing and achieving such a secondary purpose: In tailoring the details of the narrative in light of the former purpose, we undermine its ability to serve the latter. For example, philosophical inconsistencies or vagueness, surely things to be avoided in a philosophical TE, will be not only tolerated but even welcomed to the extent that they make the film more entertaining. As we shall see below, Smith also sees an incompatibility in terms of the kind of imagining for which artistic and philosophical narratives call. Thus, to the extent that we engage with a cinematic narrative as a philosophical TE, we are thereby failing to engage with it as an artwork—we are merely putting the work's artistic vehicle to a philosophical use, as we do when we screen Kubrick's *A Clockwork Orange* (1971) to interest our students in issues of social and political philosophy relating to the treatment of social deviance.

But, however plausible Smith's analysis may be as a reading of *All of Me*, it is much less plausible when we turn to the kinds of narrative films cited by proponents of the FPM thesis. Consider Ridley Scott's *Blade Runner* (1981/1991/2007), for example, which Mulhall (2002) takes to be explicitly concerned with what it is to be a human being. It shares this philosophical preoccupation not only with the novel *Do Androids Dream of Electric Sheep?* by Philip K. Dick, whose story it adapts, but also with Hilary Putnam's paper "Robots: Machines or Artificially Created Life?" (1964). Here it seems that the philosophical issue is not merely a vehicle for the amusement or entertainment of an audience, but the driving force in the construction of the fictional narrative. Like Putnam's much sparser and dryer philosophical TE, the point of reflecting on the status of "replicants" that simulate our physical and cognitive capacities is to get us to think more clearly about our understanding of ourselves as human agents.

But what, then, is the significance of the much greater narrative detail in the artistic fiction? Drawing on a distinction made by Richard Moran (1994, 105), Smith suggests that philosophical and artistic fictions are intended to elicit different kinds of imaginings—"hypothetical" and "dramatic", respectively. To hypothetically imagine something is to entertain a counterfactual in an abstract way, whereas to dramatically imagine something is, as he puts it, to "try" on the hypothesis, to imagine inhabiting it, or to explore its implications rather than philosophically engage with it. The detail in fictional narratives is intended to promote dramatic imagining, in order to serve what are primarily non-philosophical purposes. For the purposes of philosophy, it is "hypothetical imagining" that is required.

But dramatic imagining may also serve a properly philosophical function. In the case of *Blade Runner*, for example, the greater narrative detail provides a richer analysis of our ways of interacting with other cognitive agents, which bears crucially on the philosophical issues. The central contention of Putnam's paper is that we resolve the question whether robots are conscious by making "a decision, not a discovery", but the paper in no way explores or clarifies what this involves and what import it has. Scott's film, like Dick's novel, provides much greater illumination as to what is involved in making such a decision, and, correspondingly, what is at stake in the philosophical debates about the relative status of persons and of artificial forms of life. To treat an entity as conscious is to admit it to one's moral community, to hold it responsible for its conduct, to feel both with it and for it, and these aspects of our embodied engagement with other cognitive agents are not clear in the dry presentation of Putnam's TE. In this case, dramatic imagining deepens our understanding of what the philosophical issues are, and thereby places our responses to the TE on a firmer rational foundation.[12]

In fact, the idea that the detail in literary and cinematic TEs may foster a dramatic imagining that serves a philosophical purpose resonates with Putnam's own account of these matters (1976). What we learn from reading a work like Celine's *Journey to the End of Night*, he argues, is what it would be like to "inhabit" the kind of view of human nature endorsed by the narrator of that novel. Only through such a "dramatic imagining" of this view of human nature do we realise that it is unacceptable when measured against our experientially based understanding of human action and interaction.

4.

The first objection to the sketched argument for the FPM thesis questions whether narrative artworks in general can, *qua* artworks, serve the kind of philosophical purpose served by TEs in standard philosophical works. But the FPM thesis faces a second kind of challenge, developed by Livingston, which focuses upon differences between literary and cinematic media. Livingston presents nested dilemmas for proponents of what he terms the "bold thesis", according to which films can make "creative contributions to philosophical knowledge . . . by means exclusive to the cinematic medium" (2006, 11). The overarching dilemma offers alternative ways of cashing out what it is for a means to be "exclusive" to cinema. Either we construe the representational devices that are exclusive to cinema broadly or we construe them narrowly. Broadly construed, such devices include the capacity to record what is in front of the camera. This capacity might be said to be "exclusive" to cinema since only cinema can provide moving images of past events. Livingston maintains that on this broad reading the FPM thesis is trivialised. For an audiovisual recording of a philosophy lecture will involve an exclusively cinematic resource, but, if the recording has philosophical value, this surely resides in the event recorded, not in the film.

Livingston concludes that a nontrivial version of the FPM thesis must construe the representational devices "exclusive" to the cinematic medium narrowly. On this construal, "the cinematic medium's exclusive capacities involve the possibility of providing an internally articulated, nonlinguistic, visual expression of content, as when some idea is indicated by means of the sequential juxtaposition of two or more visual displays or shots" (2006, 12). Exclusively cinematic devices will then include montage or editing, camera movement, selective focus within a shot, and correlations between sound track and moving image. But then, Livingston argues, the proponent of the FPM thesis faces the following "dilemma of paraphrase":

1. If the "exclusively cinematic insight" proposed by the proponent of the FPM thesis cannot be verbally paraphrased, we can reasonably doubt its existence.
2. If, on the other hand, it can and must be verbally paraphrased, the philosophical insight is not a purely "filmic" one, since

> linguistic mediation turns out to be constitutive of (our knowledge of) the epistemic contribution a film can make. . . . Even if specifically cinematic devices, such as montage, were essential to a film's philosophical content in the sense that this content could not have been fully articulated in another medium, the successful *philosophical* function of that device remains importantly dependent on linguistically articulated background thoughts that are mobilized in both the creation and interpretation of the film's philosophical significance. (Livingston 2006, 12–13)

More specifically, according to Livingston, "if aspects of the film's thematic and narrative design are to resonate with sufficiently sophisticated and well-articulated theses or arguments . . . an interpretative context must be established in relation to which features of the film are shown to have some worthwhile philosophical resonance" (2006, 15). He therefore rejects the "bold" thesis, while allowing that films can play lesser, but still significant, pedagogical and heuristic roles in philosophy: "Films can provide vivid and emotionally engaging illustrations of philosophical issues, and when sufficient background knowledge is in place, reflections about films can contribute to the exploration of specific theses and arguments, sometimes yielding enhanced philosophical understanding" (2006, 11).

To assess Livingston's argument, we must first examine the "exclusivity" condition that he builds into the bold thesis and uses to structure the overarching dilemma. The reference in setting up the latter to an "exclusive cinematic insight" might suggest that what is at issue here is something like the following:

Content exclusivity: An interesting version of the FPM thesis requires that there be philosophical contents articulable in film that are not articulable using other media employed for philosophising.

This, however, is surely an unreasonable requirement, since it assumes that verbal media have exclusive rights to those philosophical insights that can be attained through their means. In any case, it seems Livingston has another kind of exclusivity in mind, which we may term as follows:

Medium exclusivity: An interesting version of the FPM thesis must claim that, in at least some cases, there are philosophical insights articulated in a given film that are articulated by means that are exclusively cinematic.

It is medium exclusivity that is required to set up the overarching dilemma, which rests on the claim that a film can genuinely "do philosophy" only if it relies on resources that are *not* exclusive to cinema. An interesting version of the FPM thesis cannot be confirmed by a film that simply records a philosophy lecture. Livingston assumes that, in order to exclude such a film from the scope of the "bold thesis", we must constrain more narrowly the means taken to be exclusive to the cinematic medium. And, as we have seen, he maintains that, when we do this, a film can be seen as having philosophical resonance only through verbal mediation that injects a verbal representation of elements in the film into a verbally presented philosophical problematic.

But the presented choice between "broad" and "narrow" construals of exclusivity is a false dilemma. To rule out the "filmed lecture" kind of example, we do not need to restrict the resources of cinema to those individual elements that are unique to cinema. Rather, we need to articulate an appropriate conception of medium exclusivity for an essentially mixed art form such as film. Indeed, Livingston acknowledges the importance of the different individual media that collaborate in cinema at the end of his paper, but only does so in arguing for the value of cinema once we have rejected the FPM thesis. He does not take the mixed nature of cinema as an art form into consideration in characterising a relevant notion of medium exclusivity for the purposes of assessing that thesis.

What would such a notion of medium exclusivity look like? Consider a simple example of an enterprise in which both language and other communicative media are employed in a cognitive endeavour. When we help someone to manoeuvre a car into a parking space, we often combine verbal instructions with hand gestures. While verbal communication contributes to the overall articulated content in such cases, the content exceeds the verbal contribution. The total articulated content, we may say, exceeds the total *verbally* articulated content. More generally, suppose that $M2$ is a verbal medium that can be used to articulate content of type C, and that $M1$ is a mixed medium that incorporates $M2$ as one of its elements. Then $M1$ can be rightly viewed as a distinct medium for articulating this type of content iff for some such content C_n, an "utterance" U in $M1$ articulates C_n and it is not the case that the utterance in $M2$ contained in U articulates C_n.

Using this as a model, we can now propose the following notion of medium exclusivity applicable to the claims of the FPM theorist. For film to be capable of providing philosophical insights that are medium exclusive relative to the verbal medium employed in sound cinema, there must be some film F and some philosophically relevant content PC_a such that F articulates PC_a while it is not the case that PC_a is articulated by the verbal content of F. This requirement is clearly violated in Livingston's "recorded lecture" example. But it is not difficult to see how a film might satisfy this condition even though it contained, as an element, a recording of a philosopher presenting an argument. Consider, for example, the arguably somewhat hagiographic documentary film about Jacques Derrida produced by two of his admirers.[13] Suppose that a documentary involving the same interviews had been directed by Nick Broomfield.[14] Here, the manner in which Broomfield employs the kinds of distinctively visual cinematic resources incorporated in Livingston's "narrow" conception of medium exclusivity—other aspects of the visual image, montage, editing, selective focus, and so on—might provide a critical commentary on what is being said, so that the overall philosophically relevant content articulated by the film differs significantly from the philosophically relevant content articulated verbally.

It might seem, however, that this fails to take the sting out of the "paraphrase" argument. For, even in this case, the film surely cannot speak for itself philosophically, but requires verbal paraphrase if its "insights" are to be brought into the arena of philosophical thinking. But what role is such a paraphrase supposed to play? If it is required only in order to verbally communicate the insights gained in watching the film, this would not undermine the "bold thesis" that film can make distinctive contributions to philosophical inquiry. For operations of measuring instruments and experiments surely make distinctive contributions to scientific inquiry, but they can be brought to bear on linguistically and numerically encoded scientific hypotheses only if they are themselves linguistically and numerically encoded, something which occurs in the process of engaging in the activities of measurement and experiment.

The FPM thesis will be compromised, therefore, only if the verbal mediation necessary for bringing a film into the philosophical arena is not itself embedded in the watching of the film. This seems to be what Livingston is claiming. The problem, he maintains, is that the verbal paraphrase of cinematic content required if the latter is to do philosophical work must be an *interpretation* of what is visually presented in light of linguistically mediated philosophical background assumptions. His claim is that, even if specifically cinematic devices such as montage are essential to a film's content, the content can function philosophically only via such linguistic mediation. Only when exported into a verbally formulated philosophical "problematic" can aspects of the film's thematic and narrative content resonate with well-defined philosophical theses and arguments. Philosophical work is done not in our engagement with the film as a visually and aurally presented manifold, but only when such exportation has taken place. Livingston's objection to the FPM thesis, therefore, while intended to distinguish between verbal and cinematic fictional narratives, is in fact of a piece with the "evidence" objection to the cognitive claims of literary works— they provide at best only hypotheses whose rational credibility requires further testing independently of our engagement, as readers, with the literary text. Indeed, as I shall now suggest, the objection is also of a piece with a "deflationary" view of TEs in science, according to which the latter are at best either of merely heuristic value or must be stripped of their narrative dress to reveal the bare bones of argument underneath.

Artistic cognitivists who appeal to an analogy between fictional narratives in the arts and TEs in science and philosophy generally pay scant attention to the literature in philosophy of science and analytic metaphilosophy on the cognitive status of TEs themselves. This is ironic in that, especially in the philosophy of science, identifying TEs with fictional narratives is seen not as deproblematising the cognitive status of fictional narratives, but as problematising the status of TEs![15] Some authors—whom we may term "extreme deflationists"[16]—simply dismiss TEs as sources of scientific understanding. TEs yield no more than hypotheses that must be subjected to empirical testing before we can have any confidence in their conclusions. A more moderate deflationist view[17] holds that TEs, insofar as they have cognitive value, have it in virtue of being disguised arguments. Our trust in the general conclusion we are invited to draw from the particular fictional example in a scientific TE is, on this view, rationally grounded only to the extent that we are able to reconstruct the TE as a standard deductive or inductive argument. If the generality of the conclusion of the TE is to be legitimised, such a reconstruction must prescind from the narrative details that make TEs so attractive. On either the extreme or the moderate deflationist view, TEs considered in their customary narrative splendour teach us nothing.

If we accept this view of TEs, the prospects for defending even a general cognitivist view of fictional narratives—let alone the idea of film as a philosophical medium—by appeal to the TE analogy seem bleak indeed. For one thing, the much greater detail in artistic narratives seems cognitively unmotivated, since it is irrelevant to the cognitive import of a TE. And the plethora of details makes the task of extracting the underlying argument extremely difficult. Furthermore, this view of how TEs can have cognitive value is disastrous for any interesting FPM thesis, since we cannot evade Livingston's objection that philosophical work can be done only when a suitable verbal paraphrase of the "message" of the film is exported into a broader philosophical problematic.

Fortunately for literary and cinematic cognitivists, there is a less deflationary view of TEs in science that brings them more closely into line with our intuitive sense of what is going on in TEs in philosophy, which arguably work by mobilizing intuitions grounded in our implicit understanding of certain concepts.[18] On what we can term a "moderate inflationist" view of scientific TEs,[19] they serve a similar function. They cannot be reconstructed as explicit arguments because their power to rationally persuade draws upon cognitive resources we already possess, grounded in our experience of the world, which may not be available to us in any explicitly propositional form. According to Tamar Gendler's spelling out of this view (1998), the narrative details of the TE are crucial to its power to convince, since it is the details of the TE that mobilise our intuitions about the world as we experience it. TEs then have cognitive value because they enable us to realise certain things about the world, or (in the philosophical case) about our concepts, that we would not have been able to grasp without the detailed narrative of the TE.

This account of the cognitive value of TEs is much more promising for the defender of both literary cognitivism and the FPM thesis. For it makes the "rational assessment" of the TE, viewed as a reason for accepting a general conclusion, *internal* to the process of engaging with the TE—or, in the case of fictional narratives presented in literary or filmic fictions, internal to the reading of the novel or the watching of the film. Our sense of having learned something in reading a novel or watching a film will be justified to the extent that we have drawn upon genuine cognitive resources already possessed but not otherwise available to us. In the case of a philosophical TE, for example, the relevant philosophical background and the experientially based grasp of concepts is something that the suitably prepared reader brings to her engagement with the Trolley problem or the Chinese Room. Similarly, then, the "philosophical problematic" necessary to engage philosophically with elements in a film and, in that engagement, "do philosophy" will be something that the receiver *brings* to her encounter with the film and that enters into that encounter, not something separate from that encounter into which elements from our cinematic experience have to be imported in order for matters philosophical to be joined.

In closing, however, it is important to note a possible objection to this kind of defense of the FPM thesis. On the moderate inflationist account, the person who can be described as learning something as a result of running a TE is not in a position to provide a full justification of what she claims to have learned. This is the obverse of the claim that the TE cannot be fully reconstructed as an argument. Thus, if we are to talk of knowledge or warranted belief derived from TEs on the moderate inflationist view, it seems this must be from an externalist epistemic perspective. Where readers bring to their engagement with a TE what we regard as legitimate unarticulated cognitive resources, we can take them to be "trackers of the truth" or at least "trackers of the warranted" in their engagement with the TE. But they are in no better position to *justify* their convictions by offering reasons than other readers who reach an opposite conclusion based on what we regard as *inadequate* unarticulated cognitive resources.

The question this raises is whether such an "externalist" conception of knowledge can be adequate if film is to be a philosophical medium. For it seems central to philosophy as carried on in the analytic tradition that one be able to provide reasons for one's conclusions—having what may be right ideas is not sufficient. But if I cannot support my claim to have increased my philosophical understanding through watching a film by offering reasons in support of the purported philosophical insights, how can my engagement with the film count as a way of "doing philosophy"? Of course, this line of argument will also apply to the use of TEs in philosophy proper. And it might serve to remind us that appeals to shared intuitions play as crucial a role in analytic philosophy as appeals to valid chains of reasoning. I must leave further reflections on this to another occasion, however.

ACKNOWLEDGEMENTS

This chapter is a considerably expanded and revised version of my "Can Film be a Philosophical Medium?" which appeared as an invited keynote paper in the Summer 2008 *Postgraduate Journal of Aesthetics* 5 (2): 1–20. An even earlier version of this paper was presented at a panel on the FPM thesis at the 2007 American Society for Aesthetics meetings held in Los Angeles. I am grateful to my fellow panelists and to members of the audience for helpful and constructive comments. I am also grateful to Letitia Meynell for helpful suggestions for clarification. Finally, I would like to acknowledge the support of the Social Sciences and Humanities Research Council of Canada for a research grant that facilitated work on this paper.

NOTES

1. See Cavell (1979). Others influenced by Cavell include Mulhall (2002) and Furstenau and Macavoy (2003).
2. For a survey of the relevant literature on Malick and for papers arguing for such readings, see Davies (2008).
3. For a critical consideration of Stolnitz's objections to literary cognitivism, see Davies (2007a, Ch. 8).
4. Noël Carroll (2002) terms this the "no-evidence" objection.
5. For the evidence objection applied to the cognitive pretensions of cinema, see Russell (2000).
6. See, for example, Carroll (2002) and Elgin (2007). For a critical discussion of this kind of defence of cognitivism concerning literary fictions, see Davies (2010).
7. For a critical discussion of the literature on thought experiments in science, see Davies (2007b).

8. See, e.g., Carroll (2002).
9. For this kind of argument as applied to film, see Carroll (2006) and Wartenberg (2007).
10. See Note 6 above.
11. Bruce Russell (2000) also argues that a cinematic narrative can serve as a counterargument to a general claim. As an example, he proposes Woody Allen's *Crimes and Misdemeanors* (1989), which might be taken as countering Socrates's claim, in his discussion of the "Gyges's ring" thought experiment in *The Republic*, that acting morally can never conflict with the dictates of enlightened practical reason. In response to the objection that another film, Sam Raimi's *A Simple Plan* (1998), might be taken as confirming Socrates's thesis, Russell takes the "messages" of the two films to be consistent, the former being concerned with what is possible and the latter with what is probable. In spite of this, however, Russell is a sceptic with respect to the FPM thesis. For he also claims (1) that there is nothing essentially cinematic about these counterexamples—they could serve equally well if presented verbally, and (2) that, as the evidence objection maintains, cinematic narratives cannot establish any positive theses since they involve only a single gerrymandered non-actual example.
12. See Davies (Forthcoming).
13. *Derrida* (2002), directed by Kirby Dick and Amy Ziering Kofman.
14. Broomfield, the director of such films as *Kurt and Courtney* (1998) and *Heidi Fleiss, Hollywood Madam* (1995), is known for his ability to use the cinematic medium to present people in ways that reveal aspects that they had no intention of revealing.
15. For a much fuller critical overview of the debates about TEs in the philosophy of science that I outline in the following paragraphs, see Davies (2007b).
16. See, for example, Duhem (1954) and Hempel (1965).
17. See, for example, Norton (1996).
18. The inflationist account of TEs in science resonates with some of Carroll's remarks (2002)—see Davies (2010).
19. See, for example, Mach (1905 [1975]) and Gendler (1998).

REFERENCES

Carroll, N. 2002. "The Wheel of Virtue: Art, Literature, and Moral Knowledge." *Journal of Aesthetics and Art Criticism* 60 (1): 3–26.
———. 2006. Section Introduction to 'Art and Cognition'. In *Philosophy of Film and Motion Pictures: An Anthology*, edited by Noel Carroll and Jinhee Choi, 381–388. Oxford: Blackwell.
Cavell, S. 1979. *The World Viewed*. 2nd edition. Cambridge, MA: Harvard University Press.
Davies, D. 2007a. *Aesthetics and Literature*. London: Continuum.
———. 2007b. "Thought Experiments and Fictional Narratives." *Croatian Journal of Philosophy* 7 (19): 29–46.
———, ed. 2008. *The Thin Red Line* (from the series *Philosophers on Film*). London: Routledge.
———. 2010. "Learning through Fictional Narratives in Art and Science". In *Beyond Mimesis and Convention: Representation in Art and Science* (Boston Studies in the Philosophy of Science 262), edited by Roman Frigg and Matthew Hunter, 51–70. Dordrecht: Springer.
———. Forthcoming. *"Blade Runner,* "Electric Sheep", and the Cognitive Values of Fictional Narratives." In *Blade Runner*, edited by Amy Coplan. London: Routledge.

Duhem, P. [1906, first translated into English 1914] 1954. *The Aim and Structure of Physical Theory*. Translated by P. Weiner. Princeton, NJ: Princeton University Press.

Elgin, C. Z. 2007. "The Laboratory of the Mind." In *A Sense of the World: Essays on Fiction, Narrative, and Knowledge*, edited byWolfgang Huerner, John Gibson, and Luca Pocci, 43–54. London: Routledge.

Furstenau, M., and L. Macavoy. 2003. "Terrence Malick's Heideggerian Cinema: War and the Question of Being in *The Thin Red Line*." In *The Cinema of Terrence Malick: Poetic Visions of America*, edited by H. Patterson, 173–185. London: Wallflower Press.

Gendler, T. 1998. "Galileo and the Indispensability of Thought Experiments." *British Journal for the Philosophy of Science* 49: 397–424.

———. 2002. "Thought Experiments." In *The Encyclopedia of Cognitive Science*, 388–394. London: Routledge.

Gettier, E. 1963. "Is Knowledge Justified True Belief?" *Analysis* 23: 121–123.

Hempel, C. 1965. *Aspects of Scientific Explanation*. New York: Free Press.

Lamarque, P., and S. H. Olsen. 1994. *Truth, Fiction, and Literature*. Oxford: Clarendon Press.

Livingston, P. 2006. "Theses on Cinema as Philosophy." *Journal of Aesthetics and Art Criticism* 64: 11–18.

Mach, E. 1905 [1975]. "On Thought Experiments." Reprinted in *Knowledge and Error*, 134–147. Dordrecht: Reidel.

Moran, R. 1994. "The Expression of Feeling in Imagination." *The Philosophical Review* 103: 75–106.

Mulhall, S. 2002. *On Film*. London: Routledge.

Norton, J. 1996. "Are Thought Experiments Just What You Always Thought?" *Canadian Journal of Philosophy* 26 (3): 333–366.

Putnam, H. 1964. "Robots: Machines or Artificially Created Life?" *Journal of Philosophy* 61: 668–691.

———. 1976. "Literature, Science, and Reflection." In *Meaning and the Moral Sciences*, 83–94. London: Routledge & Kegan Paul.

Quine, W. 1960. *Word and Object*. Cambridge MA: MIT Press.

Rawls, J. 1971. *A Theory of Justice*. Cambridge MA: Belknap.

Russell, B. 2000. "The Philosophical Limits of Film." *Film and Philosophy* 6: 163–167.

Smith, M. 2006. "Film Art, Argument, and Ambiguity." *Journal of Aesthetics and Art Criticism* 64: 33–42.

Stolnitz, J. 1992. "On the Cognitive Triviality of Art." *British Journal of Aesthetics* 32 (3): 191–200.

Wartenberg, T. 2007. *Thinking on Screen: Film as Philosophy*. London: Routledge.

14 Computational Modeling
Is This the End of Thought Experiments in Science?

Sanjay Chandrasekharan, Nancy J.
Nersessian, and Vrishali Subramanian

1. INTRODUCTION

There is general agreement that thought experimenting has played an important role in the creation of modern science. Influential instances of thought experimenting include Newton's bucket, Maxwell's demon, Einstein's elevator, and Schrödinger's cat. As James Brown has argued, thought experiments can help us "learn apparently new things about nature without new empirical data"; that is, they help the scientist "get a grip on nature just by thinking" (Brown and Fehige 2011). This view leads to an obvious comparison between thought experiments and computational simulation models, which are ubiquitous in most fields of contemporary science. Indeed, the comparison has been noted, but the current framing of the discussion centers on whether computational simulations are "opaque" thought experiments or not (Di Paolo et al. 2000; Lenhard 2010).

In this paper, we focus instead on the nature of the intellectual work computational modeling allows scientists to accomplish. Based on this analysis, we argue that computational modeling is largely replacing thought experimenting, and the latter will play only a limited role in future practices of science, especially in the sciences of complex nonlinear, dynamical phenomena. We arrive at this conclusion based on three considerations:

- Thought experiments are a product of a more limited material and problem environment. The current material and problem environment is more suited to computational modeling.
- Building computational models can provide deeper insights into problems than building thought experiments.
- The central cognitive role played by thought experiments is a form of simulative model-based reasoning carried out with mental models. Computational models support this type of simulative model-based reasoning, but also allow more sophisticated simulation operations.

These points will be raised in this order in the following sections, but the central argument for them will be developed in two case studies of how computational models are built in biosciences and engineering fields, the discovery events associated with these computational models, and a discussion of the major issues raised by these cases (Section 2). Section 3 sketches the mental modeling argument for thought experiments and expands on some of the minor roles thought experiments might still fill in science practices involving complex nonlinear, dynamical phenomena.

1.1. The Need for Building Models

A signature practice of contemporary biosciences and engineering is building physical (*in vitro*) simulation models and computational (*in silico*) simulation models of phenomena of interest. However, very few accounts of this building process exist in the wide literature on modeling. An example of a built physical model is the *flow loop* (Nersessian and Patton 2009), which is an engineered artifact that simulates, and thus helps examine, different types of blood flow (laminar, oscillatory) and their influence on gene expression and other cellular-level activity in tissue-engineered blood vessels, which are built-models of human arteries. Another example is a neuronal dish model (Nersessian and Patton 2009; Nersessian and Chandrasekharan 2009), which simulates learning in a living neural network, and enables researchers to examine the neural mechanisms underlying learning—specifically, how neurons with their connections broken apart come together to form new connections and learn new behavior. Examples of computational models built to mimic biological phenomena of interest include simulation models of the plant cell wall and models of dopamine transport in Parkinson's disease. There are also "second order" computational models, such as a model built to simulate processes in the above-mentioned neuronal dish, which is a computational model of a physical model. Sometimes computational models are also built in a chain structure. The first model (say, a biophysical model) will generate virtual data of a downstream process (say, the generation of a metabolite), and these data help in the building of models of the second process, particularly in the estimation of model parameters. Building such facsimile models that mimic or approximate phenomena of interest is not a new practice. For instance, wind tunnels have helped mimic different aerodynamics for at least a hundred years (though they are now being replaced by computational versions). Recently, however, a combination of four factors has made this practice of building facsimiles more widespread, particularly in the biosciences and engineering fields:

- The complex nonlinear and dynamic nature of the problems investigated in contemporary biology (and recent science in general) *requires* building such models. This is because it is almost impossible to develop detailed conceptual models of cellular and molecular-level interactions in your head, or using pencil and paper, as these processes involve many levels of structure and can occur simultaneously or across different time scales.

- Massive amounts of data are now generated by experimental work in many areas of biology, such as high-throughput data in genetics. Computational models, particularly statistical models, are usually required to interpret these data, since the interactions between different variables are complex. Also, the technology that is used to generate the data itself is based on statistical assumptions.

- Data in biology are closely tied to their context (specific cell lines, animals, diseases, etc.), and there is no theory that helps structure all these disparate and scattered data. Building computational models helps bring together these data in a structured fashion—the models thus play a "bookkeeping" function, since they comprehensively capture data elements that are related and also try to account for how the elements are related. Because this data structure is dynamic and can be run with various inputs, the models can be thought of as "running literature reviews."

- The development and easy availability of new technology that supports modeling and rapid prototyping has made modeling more widespread.

These factors, together with the technological resource environment of contemporary science, are driving the practice of building models. Thought experiments emerged in a resource environment where the only cognitive tools available were pencil and paper and the brain, and the problems tackled were usually highly idealized to fit this resource environment. As such, the thought experiment method cannot generate and test the complex dynamic and nonlinear phenomena investigated by contemporary science. Building physical and computational models can help in understanding such phenomena. Physical models, however, do create new experimental data, and their relation to thought experiments is more complex than computational models. For clarity of analysis, in this paper we focus on the processes involved in building computational models.

2. BUILDING VERSUS INTERPRETATION

As noted above, there is an obvious point of comparison between computational modeling and thought experimenting, since both help us learn new things without generating new empirical data. However, the current state of this comparison is limited in two respects. One is that the focus of much discussion is on interpretation, rather than building. Thought experiments (TEs) can be considered to consist of two phases, roughly a "building" phase and an "interpretation" phase. When a thought experiment is presented, what we get is the final polished product, usually a narrative, which is the endpoint of a long building process (Nersessian 1992). Since the building happens inside the presenter's head, others do not have access to this process, which is one of the reasons for the focus on the interpretation phase. The interpretation phase involves relating the final results of the TE to a theory or phenomena. However, we do have access to the processes of building computational models, so the focus on the interpretation phase is not justified in the case of models. As an illustrative instance of this focus, it has been argued, based on a comparison of the interpretation phases, that models are much more opaque than TEs, and models require "systematic enquiry," that is, probing of the model's behavior (Di Paolo et al. 2000). TEs are considered to be more "lucid" than computational models (Lenhard 2010), though it is not clear what is meant by "lucid" in this context, particularly given the extensive discussions about what some TEs—such as Einstein's elevator or Schrödinger's cat—actually show.

A second issue with existing comparisons of TEs and models puts the focus on possible identity relations between thought experiments and models (Are simulations thought experiments?) and the identity relations between modeling and other methods in science (Are simulations experiments?). These questions often are addressed using feature and taxonomic analysis (necessary or sufficient conditions for something to be an experiment/theory/ TE), which is a good starting point for understanding the nature and contribution of computational modeling. However, such taxonomy exercises compare the endpoints of computational modeling and thought experimenting, and ignore the insights that could be gained by studying the model-building *process*, which can be tracked in the case of computational modeling. We hope to shift the discussion away from interpretation, taxonomies, and identity conditions to process-oriented analyses of modeling and the role models play in scientific practice. Our analysis puts the focus on the process of building models and examines how studying this process can inform us about the relationship between computational models and TEs. In the following section, we present two case studies of building computational models, based on our ethnographic studies of two leading research labs, one in systems neuroscience and the other in systems biology.

2.1. Case 1: A Dish, a Model, and the CAT

The episode of conceptual innovation summarized here occurred over a two-year period in a neural engineering laboratory and involved constructing a computational model of an *in vitro* physical model of cortical neural network activity. The model was developed to understand certain thought-to-be undesired phenomena—spontaneous "bursts"—taking place with high frequency in the *in vitro* model, but not in properly functioning *in vivo* animal brains. Importantly, as we will outline below, the computational model led to a reconceptualization of "burst" phenomena in the *in vitro* model and the development of "programmable" neurons. (See Nersessian and Chandrasekharan 2009 for a fuller discussion.)

The lab's central research problem in the period of our investigation was to develop an account of learning and plasticity in networks of cultured neurons, which were thought to more closely model learning in the brain than single neurons. To address this problem experimentally, the lab had developed a physical model-system for constructing and investigating plasticity: an *in vitro* network of cultured neurons locally referred to as "the dish." Building such an *in vitro* model-system involves extracting neurons from embryonic rats, dissociating them (breaking the connections between neurons) and plating them in a single layer on a dish with embedded electrodes known as an MEA (multi-electrode array), where the neurons regenerate connections and become a network. The researchers "talk to the dish" by stimulating the neuronal network with different electrical signals (electrophysiology) and feeding the output to "embodiments" (robotic or simulated bodies) that support closed-loop feedback (using a translator program that maps the dish signal to motor commands). The embodiments include both robotic devices and visualized "animats" that move around in simulated computational worlds.

The stated goal of the research was to understand the dynamics of learning in the neuronal network in such a way that it would lead to the development of a control structure that would allow the dish to be trained to control the embodiment systematically, using feedback. The design of the dish incorporated constraints from the current understanding of neurobiology and chemistry, as well as those relating to electrical engineering and other technologies used in the lab. To begin with, the researchers explored the problem space by stimulating the neuronal network using different electrical signals and tracking the output ("playing with the dish"). The first real experiment was initiated by researcher D4, where she tried, unsuccessfully, to replicate a plasticity result reported by another group. One of the problems she faced was bursting—a form of network-wide electrical activity spontaneously exhibited by the *in vitro* neuronal networks. Bursting created a problem in understanding plasticity, because it prevented the detection of any systematic change that arose in the network in response to the controlled stimulation. According to D4, whenever she conducted a plasticity experiment, the network produced bursts. The lab interpreted those as "*noise in the data . . . noise interference in the way . . . so it is clouding the effects of the learning that we want to induce.*"

The group hypothesized that bursting arose because of deafferentation, that is, because the neurons lacked the sensory inputs they would ordinarily get if they were in a live animal's brain. Given this view, and the engineering conception of noise as something to be eliminated, D4 began working on quieting bursts in the dish. She hypothesized that it would be possible to lower bursting by providing the network with artificial sensory input, and for this she chose electrical stimulation. Trying a range of stimulation patterns to lower the bursting activity in the networks, she achieved a breakthrough, managing to quiet bursts entirely in a neuronal network. However, in the next six months of research, D4 was unsuccessful in inducing learning in the quieted network. This was mostly because of a "drift" phenomenon: The activity pattern evoked by a stimulus did not stay constant across trials, but drifted away to another pattern. This drift prevented her from tracking the effect of a stimulus, because the network never responded in the same manner to a constant stimulus.

Early in the period when D4 was trying to quiet the network, D11 branched away from working with the *in vitro* model-system, to develop a computational model that mimicked it. As he put it, *"the advantage of [computational] modeling is that you can measure everything, every detail of the network. . . . I felt that modeling could give us some information about the problem [bursting and control] we could not solve at the time [using the* in vitro *dish model-system]."* D11 felt that to understand the phenomena of bursting he needed to be able to "see" the dish activity, make precise measurements of variables such as synaptic strength, and run more controlled experiments than could be conducted with the physical dish. This different perspective illustrates a fundamental property of building models: The construction process supports a plurality of designs and views, and also provides a multifaceted approach to the problem. There is no requirement that everyone work with a standard model structure. Each team member can start from a broad definition of the problem and build up his or her own model.

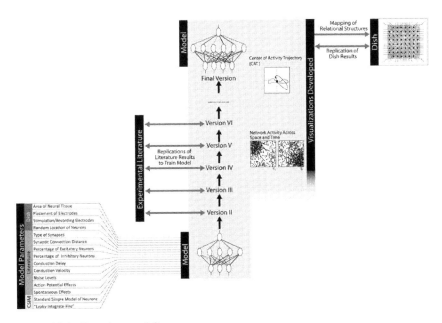

Figure 14.1   Iterative modeling processes.

Interestingly, D11 built the initial *in silico* model not using the experimental data from their dish, but drawing from intra-domain sources in neuroscience—in particular, from studies involving single neurons, brain slices, and other computationally simulated networks, using only design features of their dish. His model was tested and optimized with data from other MEA dishes first, and only after the behavior replicated the experimental results in the literature did he use their own data (see Figure 14.1). The model, as developed, was thus a second-order *in vitro* system—an *in silico* model of the activity of a *generic* dish.

Importantly, the constraints the model adapted from the lab's dish were not the group's experimental outcomes (i.e., the behavior of their dish), but had to do with the construction and structure of the dish. These included the area of the artificial neurons, the placement grid of electrodes, the number of electrodes used for recording and stimulation, and the random location of the neurons. The other parameters (constraints) of the model, such as type of synapses, synaptic connection distance, percentage of excitatory and inhibitory neurons, conduction delay, conduction velocity, noise levels, action potential effects, and spontaneous activity were based on results reported in the source literature. Further constraints came from a neuroscience modeling platform (CSIM), using a standard simple model of neurons, known as "leaky-integrate-fire." (This name derives from the way the artificial neurons respond to stimulus.)

After several months of building tentative versions of the computational simulation and probing these, D11 started to get what he called a "feel" for how the computational network behaved under different conditions. He then developed a visualization that captured the activity of the network as it ran, which figured centrally in the development of the novel concept of "center of activity trajectory" (CAT). As he stated: "*I need to—really need to look at the figure to see what is going on. So after I constructed this network—I just let it run and we visualized everything in it.*" Using the visualization, he was able to replicate successfully some of the results reported in the literature, and then results from their own dish. A major contribution of the visualization was that it enabled D11 to observe—literally see—interesting spatial patterns in the way the model responded to different stimuli. These patterns were novel and distinct from what was known about the behavior of cultured dishes.

It is important to highlight the differences between the computational model's visualization and the visual representation that was being used for the *in vitro* dish. The computational model's visualization of the network's activity showed the movement of an activity pattern across the entire network, in real time. In the visual display of the *in vitro* model-system, the individual neuronal activity was hidden. One could see activity across a channel as in Figure 14.2, but this display could only track activity at each electrode of the *in vitro* system, using graphs they had developed for this purpose (see Figure 14.2).

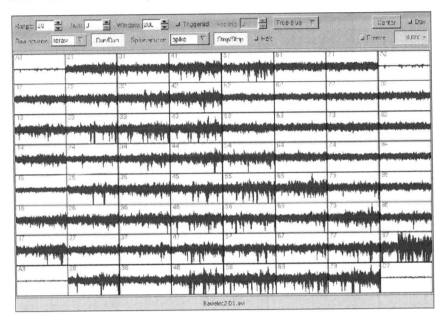

Figure 14.2   MEAscope display of bursting phenomena.

The visualization captured which electrode was activated and by how much, but it did not have a representation of the entire network itself—it could not capture *burst movement across the network*. Thus, it was not possible to see from the dish display whether there were patterns moving across the network. Such patterns, however, were revealed by the visualization of the *in silico* model. So the image of changes across discrete channels, as in Figure 14.2, was replaced by an image of changes in the activity of the whole network as in Figure 14.3, for instance, from left to center. (The diagram on the right represents the CATs for changes of activity, as we will discuss below.)

The computational model offered other advantages in exploring burst phenomena. The simulated network could be stopped at any point and started again from there. Further, it became possible to provide detailed measures of significant variables, such as synaptic strength, which were not accessible using the *in vitro* model. Finally, a large number of experiments could be run at no cost, since the computational model could be changed easily and did not require the careful, laborious, and expensive processes involved in setting up and maintaining a living dish. When coupled with the visualization that enabled tracking the activity of the network as it was happening, these features proved to be a powerful combination. They gave D11 immediate access to a range of configurations and data that the living dish could not provide, and the data could be examined and reexamined, and comparison experiments run instantly. In the process of running numerous simulations, he noticed that there were repeated *spatial* patterns in activity, as the activity propagated across the network. The spatial patterns were seen both when spontaneous bursts arose in the model network, and when the model network responded to stimuli. Basically, he found that there were "similar looking bursts" that propagated across the network, and there appeared to be a limited number of what he called "burst types." D11 began collaborating with D4 and D2, a graduate student who had been working on dish embodiments. The group then decided to investigate bursts further together, as a possibly interesting pattern, that is, *a signal*. Note the radical change in perspective here, where "burst" transforms from something akin to noise (that needs to be eliminated) to a pattern, a signal that could possibly lead to a control structure for training the network. Note also that this change arose from *the group* running many computational simulations involving different situations and parameters over time, a process leading to a group consensus on the conceptual shift. This group process was possible because of the *manifest* nature of the built model.

Further research proceeded in large part by mapping potential problem solutions from the *in silico* model to the *in vitro* model. In particular, the computational model helped them get past the problem of the drift behavior of the dish. The group came up with a range of ways to quantify the spatial properties of moving bursts, using clustering algorithms and statistical techniques, and these measures proved to be immune to the drift problem. Of particular interest to us here is the fact that they were first developed for the computational model and then equivalents (by analogy) were developed for the *in vitro* model. These included several conceptual innovations: "burst types," "spatial extent" (an estimate of the size and location of the burst in the dish), "center of activity trajectory" (CAT, a vector capturing the spatial location of the electrode along with the firing rate), and "occurrence" of burst types. These spatial measures of bursts were then shown to be better indicators of plasticity than responses to probe stimuli. So in the matter of a year, based to a significant extent on the patterns generated

network   network   center of activity trajectory (CAT)

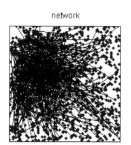 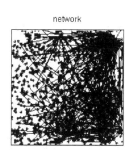 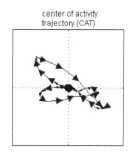

Figure 14.3 *Left:* Visual representations of changes in activity across the *in silico* network. *Center:* Time 1. *Right:* Time 2, CAT T1 to T2.

from the computational model's visualization, the group's theoretical position had shifted from bursts as noise to bursts as signals and a possible control structure.

All these measures were driven by the spatial patterns of activity noticed in the visualization of the computational model of dish activity. But of these, CAT is probably the most noteworthy, for two reasons. First, because it is a novel concept, articulated on an additional analogy with the physics notion of center of mass, which was applied to the neuronal activity pattern. Second, because it emerged entirely from the computational model, and would be almost impossible to conceptualize and properly formalize without it. Figure 14.3 (*right*) is a visualization of the CAT for a moving network burst activity in an *in silico* dish. CAT is an averaging notion, similar to the notion of a population vector, which captures how the firing rates of a group of neurons that are only broadly tuned to an action or stimulus (say an arm movement), when taken together, provide an accurate representation of the action/stimulus. However, CAT is more complex than the population vector because it tracks the *spatial* properties of activity as it *moves* through the network. For instance, if the network is firing homogenously, the CAT will be at the center of the dish, but if the network fires mainly at the left corner, then the CAT will *move* in that direction. CAT thus tracks the flow of activity (not just activity) at the population scale, and on a much quicker time scale than population vectors.

When applied to the *in vitro* network, CAT provides a novel representation of neuronal activity—a new concept. Figure 14.4 gives a side-by-side comparison of a CAT visualization that corresponds to the MEAscope representation for an *in vitro* dish. The MEAscope representation (Figure 14.4, *left*) shows activity across each recording channel over time, but the CAT (Figure 14.4, *right*) is an integrated representation of activity across the entire network.

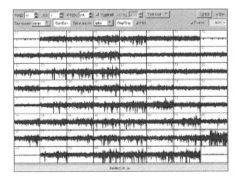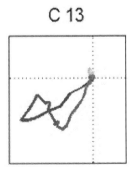

Figure 14.4 Visualization of an *in vitro* CAT (*right*) and corresponding dish burst activity (*left*).

The CAT is like a signature for a burst type in that each burst type has a corresponding range of similar-looking CATs specific to that type. Although the CAT concept arose from the visualization, the relation between the CAT concept and the visualization is not a direct mapping link. The visualization worked as a generator of many types of activity, which, when put together, led to the new CAT concept. Although our account ends here, in later work, the researchers combined CAT and techniques developed for burst quieting to develop a set of stimulation patterns (a control structure) for the dish that led to supervised learning by the living neuronal network, in effect making the *in vitro* dish neuron network programmable. Using these stimulation patterns, the living network in the dish was trained to control a computationally simulated creature and a robotic drawing arm.

2.1.1. Discussion

The most puzzling aspect of this case is that the network visualization used by D11 is largely *arbitrary*. There is no reason why a network representation should be used—he could have used one similar to their graph representation of the living dish—and even after choosing a network representation, there are many ways in which the network activity could be represented. Thus the central question raised by this case of discovery-by-building is this:

> *How could the spatial analysis of an arbitrary representation translate to the actual dish model, and provide a control structure for supervised learning?*

As D11 says: "*From the simulation, I definitely get some . . . y'know, if you run it for a year, y'know, you have this feeling for what the network you construct is doing . . . so I have a specific idea about what my simulated network is doing . . . but the problem is that I don't think it is exactly the same as in the living network . . . when our experiment worked in the living network, actually I am . . . I am surprised . . . I was surprised.*"

We believe the answer to this question lies partly in the iterative building process and partly in the nature of the visual representation. In this case, the visual representation captures the underlying artificial network's structure in an integrated fashion. The underlying network is being continually reconfigured by each experiment replication—each replication is adding complexity to the network, as it builds on the network created by the previous replication. Since the visualization captures the network structure *as a whole*, it is being fine-tuned to more closely mimic the *behavior* of the network, until the system gains sufficient complexity to *enact the behavior* of the dish. Seeing these behaviors and having the ability to stop-and-poke them, while also examining the numbers that generate them, allowed the researchers to develop the CAT concept. CAT captures activity patterns, which is an abstraction that is delinked from the (arbitrary) representation. CAT can be applied to *any* activity. It captures the model's replication of the dish activity; its ability to capture the activity of the actual dish follows from this. Note that the CAT concept cannot be directly mapped to the visualization—the visualization is a "generator" of spatial activity (behavior), which leads up to the CAT concept. This abstract concept is what transfers to the dish.

More generally, building a computational model involves developing a system that can *enact* the behavior of the phenomena under study. Each run during the building process reconfigures this enactive ability, until the model gains sufficient complexity to enact the behavior of the dish. The final runs are a *probing* of this enactive ability, the possibilities of which the modeler does not entirely understand, but has a "feel" for. The intellectual work at this stage is not interpretation of the results, but the use of different probes to generate a range of behaviors and the capture of this range of behavior within a "margin of error" framework. This range of error is then used to develop a control structure.

In contrast to this view, the standard criticism of a computational model's not being able to provide any new knowledge (because what is "fed into it" is already known) (Di Paolo et al. 2000) suggests that the building process is conceived as developing a representation that just incorporates all the existing data. The final running of the model then puts these data in a new configuration, and all the work is in interpreting how the new data configuration generates the resulting data. This criticism stems from an information "translation" approach to understanding computational modeling, which misses two important points: first, the idea that different kinds of representations provide different insights, and second, the idea that individual elements show different properties when combined into a global structure. The translation view misses the importance of the enaction of the behavior, since only the final numbers and their graphs are considered relevant. In the translation view, the transfer of the CAT concept from the visualization to the dish is mysterious, as it misses the critical thing about the visualization, which is that, even though arbitrary, it captures the enactive ability of the network as a complex *behavior*.

2.2. Case 2: Pathways, Parameters, and Engineers

In our current project, we are studying practice in two integrative systems biology labs. The research in one of the labs (Lab G) is purely modeling—building computational models of biochemical pathways to understand phenomena as varied as Parkinson's disease, plant systems for bio-fuel production, and atherosclerosis. Lab members mostly build ordinary differential equation (ODE) models, which capture how the concentration levels of different metabolites in a given biological pathway change over time.

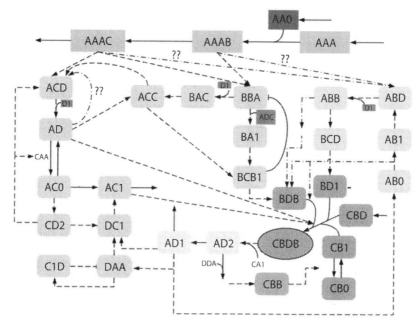

Figure 14.5 Biological pathway under construction. Names of pathway components have been replaced by alphabet aliases, with "??" indicating tentative relationships derived from the literature.

The first step in this building process is the development of a pathway diagram, which shows the main reactions involved. The pathway diagram also captures positive and negative regulation effects, where the presence of different metabolites has a positive or negative influence on different reactions (Figure 14.5). A rough diagram of the pathway is usually provided by the lab's experimental collaborators. But the modelers, who mostly come from engineering backgrounds, have to estimate the details of the pathway by themselves, particularly values of parameters related to metabolites, such as speed of the reaction (rate constant) and an index of the reaction mechanism (kinetic order), which are usually not measured by experimenters. Some of this information is available in rough form (with varying degrees of reliability) from some online databases, but most of the time these values need to be estimated, usually by testing the model using a range of numbers as parameter values.

Modelers also add some components to the pathway, usually metabolites that are known to interact with elements in the pathway provided by the experimenters. These connections are found by reading and searching biology journal articles and databases related to the problem they are modeling, and also based on results from preliminary models. Even though much of the pathway is provided by experimentalists, these kinds of additions based on literature searches are required, because the provided pathway does not identify all the components and the regulatory influences they have on the reaction.

The pathway developed by the modeler thus brings together pieces of information that are spread over a wide set of papers and databases. This pathway is usually trimmed, based on some simplifying assumptions, mostly to lower the mathematical and computational complexity involved in numerically solving the differential equations, which are developed in the next step. After the trimming, equations are generated to capture the trimmed pathway. A variable is used to represent the metabolite, while the speed of its change (rate constant) and an index of the reaction mechanism (kinetic order) are represented by parameters, which can take many values. The next step involves estimating values for these parameters, and these values are then used to initialize simulations of the models. The simulation results are then compared to actual experimental results. Usually, modelers split available experimental data: One set is used to develop the model (training data), and the other set is used to test the completed model (test data). When the data do not fit the training data, the parameters are "tuned" to get model results that fit.

Importantly, the linear work flow suggested by the above description is very deceptive—the modeling process is highly recursive. For instance, to develop the pathway diagram, preliminary models are built using the network provided by the experimenters, and these are run using tentative parameter values, and the generated model data are fit to the training data. The parameter values are then revised based on this fit. If the model data do not fit after a large number of these parameter revisions, the modeler will add some components to the network, based on elements that are known (in the literature) to be related to the pathway. *Thus the model's components—elements and values—are set by building and running the model.* These revisions are discussed with the collaborators, and if a revision is considered "reasonable" by the experimenter, it is added to the pathway. The pathway identification process is usually "bottom-up" and creates a "composite" network, made up of parameter values, and metabolites, based on experiments in different species, different cell lines, and so on.

One of the central problems the lab members face is the unavailability of rich, and dependable, data. In modeling, data are used for many purposes. One central use of data is to establish that the model captures a possible biological mechanism, and this is done by showing that the model's output matches the output from experiments (fitting data), when both are represented as graphs. Data are also used to tune parameter values during the training phase of building the model, since the fit with the experimental data from each training simulation can indicate how the parameter values need to be changed to generate model data that fit the training data. However, this latter use is dependent on the type of data available. Most of the time, the available data are "qualitative" in nature—usually how an experimental manipulation changed a metabolite level from a baseline. Mostly, this is represented by a single data point, indicating the level going up or down, and then holding steady. However, when this type of "steady-state" data fit the results of the model, this fit does not indicate an accurate model, since sparse data can be fit with a range of parameter values. Further, since the pathway is an approximation, the modeler is uncertain as to whether the lack of a unique and accurate solution is due to poor estimation of parameters, or because some elements are missing from her pathway.

To get a unique or near-unique parameter set, the data should be quantitative or time-series, where the variation of the metabolites is captured across a large number of time points (i.e., not just a few time points and then steady state). If a pathway is known (usually by bottom-up, "composite" model-building), then the time-series data provide a way of better estimating the parameters, since this type of data is "thicker," and a good fit would indicate that the model is close to an actual network. Apart from this advantage, time-series data also provide the possibility of inferring the structure of the network from the data. Extracting the network information, which is implicit in the data, is known as "top-down" modeling. It is also known as the "inverse problem."

As an example instance of modeling in this lab, consider G12, an electrical engineer by training, who is modeling atherosclerosis. She works in collaboration with a nearby lab, which has data on how oscillatory flow in blood vessels leads to atherosclerosis via a mechano-transduction process (where the style of flow of blood—laminar vs. oscillatory—leads to the expression of different genes). This in turn leads to the attraction of monocytes to locations experiencing oscillatory flow, and over time, this monocyte recruitment leads to development of plaques that are characteristic of atherosclerosis.

When she started her modeling, she had no background in atherosclerosis. She was provided a rough outline of the pathway by her collaborators, and she learned more about the pathway by reading papers. The initial papers were from the collaborating lab, but then she spread out using the reference lists of those papers. The data available were mostly steady-state data (though for some parts of the network, there was also some time-series data). Once she had read a number of papers, she started building rudimentary computer models and testing these using available data. She then added some components to the model based on connections in the literature, and some of them were considered "reasonable" by her experimental collaborators.

Estimating parameter values for her model, however, was a tough problem, since the data were sparse. To get parameter values that generated model data that fit the training data, she ran a large number of simulations and compared the results with the training data. About this process, she said:

I kind of tune the parameter and I don't know, it's not a method or, it's not algorithm, and I don't know how to explain.

Finally, she arrived at a set of values that generated data roughly matching the training data. Once this was done, she tested her model against the test data, and got a rough fit there as well. Based on this fit, she generated a number of predictions from the model, by changing the parameter values.

This case is representative of much of the modeling in this lab. For this paper, we just wish to highlight the fact that engineers with no background in biology and experimentation use a recursive building strategy to add components to a pathway given by experts and estimate the parameter values for elements in the pathway.

2.2.1. Discussion

The central question raised by this case of discovery-by-building is this:

How could building a model suggest additions to the pathway and generate values for its own variables? How could a model facilitate the prediction of its own parts?

Once again, the answer comes from the *behavior* of the model, which emerges from the complexity it has acquired during the building process. When an expected behavior does not emerge, the modeler can add "sham complexity" to the model, to see whether the desired behavior emerges. When it does, she can work backward from what she added to make a prediction about which actual component from the literature could be added to the pathway for a certain behavior to emerge. The global structure of the built-model thus sets constraints and provides pointers on how building can progress. Note that the translation approach cannot account for this result, as it assumes all information to exist before it is translated to the model. Building is thus a radically different activity from translation, because the structure and behavior of the model can specify the possible changes that could lead to a better fit with experimental data. A close analogy would be developing a scale model (called a "maquette") in architecture, which is not a translation of the blueprint, since the scale model's three-dimensional features and global structure generates behavior that the blueprint does not have, such as balance and stability.

Building computational models also help precipitate implicit knowledge, by bringing out individual elements known by an expert (say, a biologist), and inserting these elements into slots in a broader structure. The broad structure is built by the modeler, and the element to be inserted is identified by the iterative process of fitting the model data with experimental data. Not all the slots are filled in advance by the biologist, but some are proposed by the modeler, based on how the model behaves. These candidate elements are regarded as verified when they are considered "reasonable" by the biologist. The extension of the pathway thus happens through a form of consensus building and negotiation between two different practices, and it creates new knowledge by providing a larger context for individual pieces of knowledge, which themselves are tentative.

Such contextualization has been implicated in new discoveries, as in the case of Buckminsterfulerene, for which the discoverers got the Nobel Prize. The C_{60} football-shaped molecule was predicted to exist by a Japanese group many years earlier, and was also imaged by another Japanese group, but both these groups did not understand the significance of the molecule. The first group in fact considered it uninteresting. This, and other such cases of missed discoveries, have led to a distinction being made between "finding" and the "recognition of a finding," which is based on contextualizing a finding (Osawa et al. 1993; Berson 1992). The models in Lab G can be considered to serve this contextualizing function for biological elements, and can thus support significant discoveries.

2.3. Translation versus Enactment

The above two case studies show that the model-building process is very complex and not just a simple translation process. Specifically,

1. Arbitrary representations can gain sufficient complexity, to the extent that their spatial features can be used to control a system in the real world.
2. A model can predict its own parts.

To explain these features, we need to approach the model as an "enactive system" that gains sufficient complexity from building, such that it can act out the behavior of the phenomena under study. We contrast this enactive approach with a translation approach to computational modeling, which treats the building process as feeding existing information into a model (Di Paolo et al. 2000). In the latter view, any new information comes from changing the parameters in the final run and interpreting the results. In the enaction view, the building process brings together information in an integrated fashion, creating a structure that does not exist in such a form in the literature, and thereby allowing the model to replicate a range of *behaviors* under investigation, rather than replicate scattered individual results. The model supports the generation of a range of such behaviors, during building and after. Researchers can stop and study these behaviors at any point they want, while also studying the underlying mathematical structures that generate these behaviors. This means the interaction between the modeler and the final model is an "interrogation" process, not interpretation. As the model has complexity comparable to the real phenomena, the modeler is interrogating the *different possible variations of the real world* by proxy as well. That is, the computational simulation is not only a dynamical analog to the real-world system, but it also supports the generation of counterfactual scenarios not seen in the real world, and also their existence conditions (different parameter settings).

This analysis suggests that computational models are close to physical models like the flow loop, and they thus allow researchers to do even more than "get a grip on nature just by thinking." Models serve an enactive function, and while they do not generate new empirical data, they can help to radically restructure the researchers' conceptual landscape. They also restructure the way researchers approach data, supporting an interrogation mode, rather than just an interpretation mode. For all the above reasons, computational models are more sophisticated conceptual tools than thought experiments.

3. MENTAL SIMULATION: MODELING MEETS THOUGHT EXPERIMENTING

Our previous work has examined the cognitive processes that underlie the building of models and TEs. Mental simulation was proposed as the cognitive process underlying the building (and interpretation) of TEs (Nersessian 1992). In recent work, we have proposed mental simulation as the mechanism underlying the building (and interpretation) of physical models (Nersessian 2008) and computational models (Chandrasekharan 2009). Combining these two views, TEs, physical models, and computational models form a spectrum of simulative model-based reasoning. All these types of modeling generate and test counterfactual situations that are difficult to implement in the real world (see Figure 14.6).

However, TEs are built using concrete elements, while models are built using variables. This means TEs do not *naturally* support simulation of counterfactual scenarios beyond the one generated by the specific scenario and its elements, as the mental simulation process is driven by the behavior of the concrete components. A difficult and complex cognitive transformation is needed to move away from the concrete case to the abstract and generic case. Even when this happens, the generic case does not have much detail, since the elements in the generic case are abstracted from the elements of the TE, which tend to be constructed using visually salient entities. On the other hand, the abstract and generic case is what a computational modeler works with from the outset, and it is very detailed, with elements at the cellular or molecular level and each element available for manipulation. Since models are made entirely of variables, they naturally support thinking about parameter spaces, possible variations to the design commonly seen in nature, and why this variation is commonly seen, instead of many others that are possible. The contrast between the commonly seen case and other possible cases, and the detailed manipulation and analyses of the parameters associated with these cases, can lead to the identification

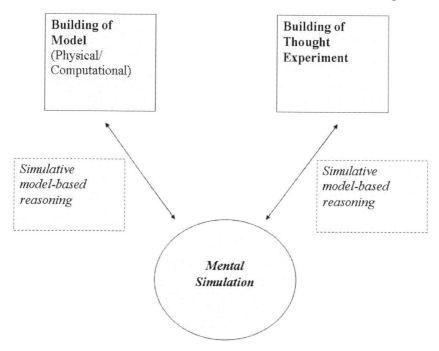

Figure 14.6 Mental simulation as the cognitive mechanism underlying building of models and thought experiments.

of broader design principles (such as thermodynamic constraints) that lead to one parameter set being commonly instantiated in nature.

Computational models, particularly ones with visualizations, go beyond TEs, as these models can generate complex behavior similar to natural phenomena, provide explanations of why these phenomena exist and not others, and also allow interrogation and "drilling down" into the behavior for details. Such models thus enable the externalization of creative thinking in science, and thereby extend the cognitive capacity for mental simulation—similar to the way telescopes have extended the perceptual capacity for seeing. (See Chandrasekharan and Nersessian 2011 for a discussion of other cognitive roles played by external representations, particularly the process of building.) And just as no scientist studies the stars with the naked eye anymore, no one would use TEs to probe the complex phenomena studied by contemporary science.

3.1. THOUGHT EXPERIMENTS TO GO MINI

This does not mean thought experiments have come to an end. As systems that generate counterfactual scenarios, thought experiments will still be used in the practice of science, but they are unlikely to have the same importance as they have had historically. They are unlikely to settle a debate. Rather, they will contribute to the design and building of computational models that provide detailed accounts of the counterfactual scenarios which TEs sought to test in the past. For instance, the scenario "Can giraffes swim?" which could only be examined using thought experiments, was recently examined in detail using a computational model, and it was shown that they could indeed swim, but poorly, and it would require holding their body in nonstandard ways (Henderson and Naish 2010).

The building of models also makes possible new thought experiments, both within the model structure (For instance, what would happen to the giraffe if I replace the digital water with digital oil?) and across model structures (Would it be possible to integrate this model of foraging with that model of mate selection?). Finally, TEs in small scale (mini-TEs) can contribute to the building of the models themselves. For instance, mini-TEs were involved in choosing the constraints (Dish, CSIM) and parameters in the first case study. In the second case study, mini-TEs were involved in the trimming of the pathway (What would be the effect of removing this component?) and judging parameters (Given what we know about the data, what could be possible values for this parameter?).

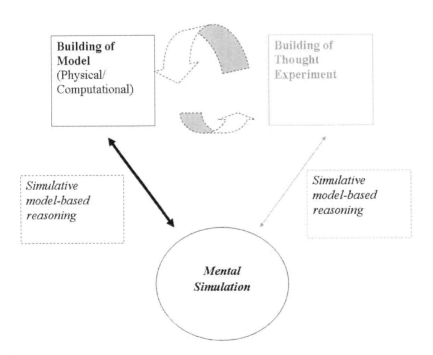

Figure 14.7   Subsumption of thought experiments within computational models in contemporary scientific practice.

In sum, there still will be a role for TEs in science, but it is likely to be a background and subsidiary role to computational modeling. We capture this role in Figure 14.7, where the two kinds of mental simulation processes still exist, but the output of the TE approach is in shadow, as it plays only a background role. Further, the two outputs interact, as TEs contribute to models, and the constructed models generate further TEs.

4. CONCLUSION

Based on the analysis of two case studies examining the building of computational models in neural engineering and integrative systems biology, we have shown that computational model building is not a direct translation of existing data. It is better understood as a constitution process, generating an enactive system that can replicate behaviors seen in the real world. The components of models interact in ways that are not readily apparent to the modeler, because the model brings together disparate data from a range of resources. However, since the model can be stopped at any point and its internal states interrogated, the modeler gains intuitions into the way behaviors are generated. This allows her to develop abstractions that transfer to actual phenomena in the world. It also allows her to make predictions about elements that are missing from what is known about the phenomena.

Models thus function as externalized probes that extend human cognition, similar to probes like telescopes and microscopes that extend human vision. Both TEs and computational models support mental simulation of counterfactual scenarios, but TEs do not naturally support the probing of all possible variations, as they are concrete scenarios, built using specific components, while models are built using variables, which naturally support examining a range of possibilities within the parameter space, and why a specific one is instantiated. TEs are a product of a previous resource environment, where the only tools available were pencil, paper, and the brain. This method addressed problems that could be idealized to fit this resource environment, but it is not suited to the many current problems that need to retain their complexity. Computational modeling thus has features that go well beyond thought experimenting, and this suggests that just as no one uses their naked eye to study stars anymore, no one would use TEs to study the complex, dynamic and nonlinear behaviors that are the focus of contemporary science. TEs still have a role to play in science, but largely within the context of computational modeling—helping design, build, and extend models.

ACKNOWLEDGEMENTS

We gratefully acknowledge the support of the National Science Foundation ROLE Grants REC0106773, DRL0411825, and REESE grant DRL0909971 in conducting this research. Our analysis has benefited from discussions with members of our research group, especially Wendy Newstetter, Lisa Osbeck, Christopher Patton, and Costas Mannouris. We thank the members of the research labs for allowing us into their work environments, letting us observe them, and granting us numerous interviews. Thanks to Joshua Aurigemma for the modeling process graphic (Figure 14.1).

REFERENCES

Berson, J. A. 1992. "Discoveries Missed, Discoveries Made: Creativity, Influence, and Fame in Chemistry." *Tetrahedron* 48: 3–17.
Brown, J. R., and Y. Fehige. 2011. "Thought Experiments." *The Stanford Encyclopedia of Philosophy* (Fall 2011 Edition), edited by E. N. Zalta. http://plato.stanford.edu/archives/fall2011/entries/thought-experiment (accessed October 15, 2011).
Chandrasekharan, S. 2009. "Building to Discover: A Common Coding Model." *Cognitive Science* 33 (6): 1059–1086.
Chandrasekharan, S., and N. J. Nersessian. 2011. "Building Cognition: The Construction of External Representations for Discovery." *Proceeding of the Cognitive Science Society* 33: 267–272.
Di Paolo, E. A., J. Noble, and S. Bullock. 2000. "Simulation Models as Opaque Thought Experiments." In *Artificial Life VII: The Seventh International Conference on the Simulation and Synthesis of Living Systems*, edited by M. A. Bedau, J. S. McCaskill, N. H. Packard, and S. Rasmussen, 497–506. Cambridge, MA: MIT Press/Bradford Books.
Henderson, D. M., and D. Naish. 2010. "Predicting the Buoyancy, Equilibrium and Potential Swimming Ability of Giraffes by Computational Analysis." *Journal of Theoretical Biology* 265: 151–159.
Lenhard, J. 2010. "When Experiments Start. Simulation Experiments within Simulation Experiments." Paper presented at the International Workshop on Thought Experiments and Computer Simulations, March 11–13, Paris.
Nersessian, N. J. 1992. "In the Theoretician's Laboratory: Thought Experimenting as Mental Modeling." *PSA: Proceedings of the Biennial Meeting of the Philosophy of Science Association* 2: 291–301.
———. 2008. *Creating Scientific Concepts*. Cambridge, MA: MIT Press.
Nersessian, N. J., and C. Patton. 2009. "Model-Based Reasoning in Interdisciplinary Engineering." In *Handbook of the Philosophy of Technology and Engineering Sciences*, edited by A. Meijers, 727–757. North Holland: Elsevier.
Nersessian, N. J., and S. Chandrashekharan. 2009. "Hybrid Analogies in Conceptual Innovation in Science." *Cognitive Systems Research Journal: Special Issue: Integrating Cognitive Abilities* 10: 178–188.
Osawa, E., H. W. Kroto, P. W. Fowler, and E. Wasserman. 1993. "The Evolution of the Football Structure for the C60 Molecule: A Retrospective [and Discussion]." *Philosophical Transactions of the Royal Society A: Mathematical, Physical and Engineering Sciences* 343: 1–8.

Index

Printed in Great Britain
by Amazon

10480015R00163